W9-DFW-328

The prevailing view among economists and policy makers is that money has no impact on production in the longer term characterised by full price and wage flexibility and rational expectations.

This book presents a revisionist view of monetary policy and monetary regimes. It presents several new mechanisms, indicating that money affects long-term production. The consequent policy implications are also discussed, including: the uses of monetary policy and monetary regimes in achieving macro-economic goals; the impact of an independent central bank; the effects of movement from floating exchange rates to fixed exchange rates in a monetary union. In addition to the theoretical and policy discussions, the book also contains a comprehensive survey of the current state of scholarship in this area. This book is both a research resource for scholars and policy makers, and a text for advanced undergraduate and graduate students in macroeconomics, labour economics, and finance.

Finn Ostrup is Associate Professor, Department of Finance, Copenhagen Business School. He also teaches at the University of Copenhagen. He has previously worked at the Danish Ministry of Economic Affairs, and as a Financial Attaché as part of the Danish Permanent Representation at the European Community.

Money and
the Natural Rate
of Unemployment

Finn Ostrup

CAMBRIDGE
UNIVERSITY PRESS

PUBLISHED BY THE PRESS SYNDICATE OF THE UNIVERSITY OF CAMBRIDGE
The Pitt Building, Trumpington Street, Cambridge CB2 1RP, United Kingdom

CAMBRIDGE UNIVERSITY PRESS
The Edinburgh Building, Cambridge, CB2 2RU, UK http://www.cup.cam.ac.uk
40 West 20th Street, New York, NY 10011–4211, USA http://www.cup.org
10 Stamford Road, Oakleigh, Melbourne 3166, Australia

First published 2000

Printed in the United Kingdom at the University Press, Cambridge

Typeset in 10pt on 12pt Times [KW]

A catalogue record for this book is available from the British Library

Library of Congress Cataloguing in Publication data
Østrup, Finn.
    Money and natural unemployment / Finn Ostrup.
        p.   cm.
    Includes bibliographical references (p.)
    ISBN 0-521-66139-0. – ISBN 0-521-66739-9 (pb)
    1. Unemployment–Effect of inflation on.   2. Monetary policy.
I. Title
HD5710.078   1999
331.13'7–dc21
                                                                    99-29143
                                                                    CIP

ISBN 0 521 66139 0 hardback
ISBN 0 521 66739 9 paperback

Contents

v

Preface

The choice of monetary regime has played an important role in economic discussion notably in connection with the discussion on a European Monetary Union. It is the aim of this book to present a new view with regard to this issue. It is argued that monetary factors play a role in the determination of long-term production also in a model context characterised by rational expectations and wage and price flexibility.

Work on the present version of the book was started in 1995. The author is very grateful to colleagues at the Copenhagen Business School and at the University of Copenhagen who have provided critical comments and suggestions to improve both the current and earlier editions of this book. I wish to thank especially Niels Henrik Børjesson for valuable comments and technical assistance. A thank also goes to Svend Ostrup who has provided technical assistance. Finally, I want to thank the Copenhagen Research Project on European Integration (CORE) and the Copenhagen Business School who have provided financial support.

Finn Ostrup

Part I
Introduction and main assumptions

1 Introduction

1.1 The aim of the book

It is a common view among economists and policy makers that money has no impact on production in the longer term characterised by full price and wage flexibility and expectations which are formed rationally. This view gained acceptance at the end of the 1960s and the beginning of the 1970s when the concept of an exogenously determined rate of natural unemployment became dominant in economics.

This book aims to present a new view in the discussion of monetary policy and monetary regimes. The book presents a number of new mechanisms, not previously discussed in the literature, which imply that money affects long-term production. This finding of a monetary impact on natural production is important from a policy perspective. The authorities lose the capability of affecting long-term production if they give up the possibility of using monetary policy, for example, by establishing an independent central bank or by joining a monetary union, or if they give up the possibility of choosing a monetary regime.

By a monetary impact on production we understand that either: (i) inflation affects production, inflation being determined through growth in the money supply and thus being controlled by the authorities; or (ii) production is affected by factors which are influenced by the monetary regime, implying that production is changed when there is a shift in the monetary regime. In some of the models which are presented throughout the book, we reach the further conclusion that long-term production can be affected by other instruments controlled through monetary policy, for example sterilised intervention, the central bank's reserve policy, and capital restrictions.

The point of departure of the analysis is essentially 'classical'. All models throughout the book are based on an economic structure with the following assumptions: (i) all economic relationships result from

3

agents' optimisation; (ii) the stochastic distributions of variables or, in the case of non-stochastic models, the actual outcomes of future values of variables are known by the agents in the economy, that is, expectations are formed rationally; (iii) the preferences of economic agents are based only on real variables; and (iv) there is perfect price and wage flexibility, implying that there are no costs associated with the adjustment of nominal variables. The third assumption (iii) means that we exclude concepts like wage illusion which would cause wage setters to place an emphasis on the nominal wage. The fourth assumption (iv) implies that we ignore costs associated with changes in prices or in the nominal wage. This last assumption has played a major role in recent New Keynesian theory.

Most analyses are based on a wage formation process which implies a relationship between the real wage and employment. This is the case when a trade union optimises preferences which include both the real wage and employment for the members of the union. A relationship between the real wage and employment arises, however, also from a number of other wage formation processes, for example when a firm sets the nominal wage but incurs costs associated with the turnover in staff, see Phelps (1994). The findings throughout the book therefore do not depend on trade union wage setting.

We refer to the production and employment levels which result from agents' optimisation as, respectively, natural production and natural employment. In the analysis of a monetary impact on long-term production we are concerned with steady-state equilibrium. Steady-state equilibrium is defined by two features: (i) there is a constant production growth rate, and (ii) financial variables lie at unchanged levels relative to nominal production in each time period.

1.2   Channels for a monetary impact on natural production

This section briefly presents the various channels, analysed throughout the book, which cause a monetary impact on natural production. In the discussion of these channels, a distinction is made between the case where the authorities' setting of monetary policy instruments is exogenous and the case where long-term production is affected by variables which are specific to the monetary regime, implying that natural production changes with a shift in the monetary regime.

In the case of an exogenous economic policy, it will be demonstrated that inflation or factors determined by the monetary regime affect natural production through the following channels:

(1) Inflation affects the real return on a domestic currency asset when there is imperfect substitution between financial assets denominated

in different currencies. The real return on domestic currency assets affects capital formation and the demand for goods which influence the combinations of the real wage and employment that can be reached by the wage setters and through this natural production. In addition, monetary policy affects natural production through capital restrictions and sterilised intervention.

(2) Inflation affects the real bank lending rate and through this the demand for goods and capital formation when banks operate in markets for lending and deposits which are characterised by imperfect competition and when one of the following three conditions is met: (i) banks incur a cost due to asymmetric information when they raise finance on an internationally integrated securities market; (ii) banks regard investment in securities and lending as imperfect substitutes, for example due to different risk characteristics; or (iii) there are economies of scope between bank deposits and bank lending. The real bank lending rate affects capital formation and the demand for goods which influence the combinations of the real wage and employment that can be reached by the wage setters and thus natural production. The authorities can further affect natural production through the reserve policy *vis-à-vis* banks. Moreover, inflation affects the banks' real profitability and thus the incentive to expand bank lending when there is imperfect competition in the market for bank deposits.

(3) Inflation influences the household saving decision and thus the demand function for goods which in turn affects natural production when securities function as a substitute for money in rendering liquidity services. Securities and money may, for example, both be used to maintain consumption in the case of unexpected income shortfalls or be used to meet unexpected expenditure needs.

In the case where the authorities' policy setting is determined endogenously from the optimisation of preferences, that is, a model framework corresponding to Kydland and Prescott (1977) and Barro and Gordon (1983a), money is able to affect natural production through the same channels as set out above. In the Kydland–Prescott and Barro–Gordon model framework this means that the authorities' preferences affect natural production, causing a change in natural production if the authorities give up attempts to use monetary policy by joining instead, for example, a monetary union or pursuing exclusively a price stability goal. Besides the channels set out above, we find that the monetary regime affects natural production through the following channels:

(4) The monetary regime affects natural production when inflation has an impact on the demand for goods and when there is centralised

wage setting, the nominal wage being set by a trade union which includes all employees in the economy.

(5) The monetary regime has an effect on natural production when fiscal policy influences the demand for goods and through this the combinations of the real wage and employment which can be reached by the wage setters. In this case, wage setting is determined not only by the monetary policy which is expected during the wage contract period, but also by the expected fiscal policy. Natural production thus comes to depend on the authorities' inclination to pursue an expansive fiscal policy. The inclination to pursue an expansive fiscal policy is determined by the extent to which it is possible through fiscal policy to reach production and inflation goals. As the authorities set fiscal policy after the nominal wage has been fixed through contracts, the impact of fiscal policy on production and inflation, and thus the authorities' inclination to pursue an expansive fiscal policy, can be found from a model with a fixed nominal wage, in the open economy a standard Mundell–Fleming model. There are further differences across monetary regimes with respect to the authorities' inclination to use fiscal policy because the extent to which fiscal policy will be used depends on whether it is possible to use the alternative policy instrument, that is, monetary policy. Due to these differences across monetary regimes with respect to the impact of fiscal policy on production and inflation, the monetary regime affects natural production.

(6) There is an impact from the monetary regime on natural production when the authorities have asymmetric preferences in the sense that they want to bring about price stability while not attempting to reduce the price level. This asymmetry with respect to preferences causes the authorities to pursue both employment and price stability goals at a positive inflation rate while they pursue only an employment goal when price stability has been brought about. This affects the real wage that is expected by the wage setters when they set the nominal wage in advance through contracts and thus affects natural production.

(7) The monetary regime affects natural production when the uncertainty regarding monetary policy is affected by inflation. Higher inflation may, for example, create stronger pressure to undertake political action and could thus cause a less predictable outcome of the political decision-making process.

(8) The authorities' preferences with respect to inflation and employment influence production in a fixed-but-adjustable exchange regime in the case where wage setters are unable to foresee a devaluation

with certainty but attach a certain probability to the event that a devaluation will take place at a given level of unemployment.

(9) The monetary regime influences the fluctuation of economic variables during the wage contract period. The fluctuation of variables has an impact on natural production when the wage setters optimise preferences which are asymmetric with respect to production.

These channels for the impact of money on natural production presented above are additional to those previously discussed in the literature. We find in the literature a discussion of four channels through which money can affect production in a model context characterised by rational expectations, full wage and price flexibility, and preferences based on real variables: (a) when money offers a nominal return, the agent's portfolio choice between money and capital is affected by inflation, implying that inflation has an impact on capital accumulation; (b) inflation tax/seigniorage constitutes a revenue source which reduces the need to resort to other tax sources (taxation of capital and labour income) that affect labour supply and saving; (c) when the use of money gives rise to efficiency gains, inflation has implications for the firm's production function and the household's consumption decision because inflation affects the size of the real money stock; and (d) unexpected one-time changes in the money supply can have lasting effects on the real economy due to hysteresis effects, for example by changing the capital stock.

1.3 Assumptions regarding the wage formation

The channels for a monetary impact on natural production presented above under (1)–(5) are based on the assumption that long-term production is determined on the basis of a wage formation process which causes a relationship between the real wage and employment. This is consistent with a wage formation where a monopoly trade union is seen as optimising preferences with respect to the real wage and employment, see, for example, Layard, Nickell and Jackman (1991). A relationship between the real wage and employment is, however, also consistent with a wage formation where an individual wage earner negotiates the wage with an employer, see, for example, Blanchard and Katz (1997), or where firms set the nominal wage but incur costs associated with the turnover of workers, see Phelps (1994). The same policy findings of a monetary impact on the natural production conclusion can also be reached if we had alternatively chosen to consider a representative agent who optimises utility with respect to consumption and leisure. In this case consumption is also determined by the real wage. The findings throughout this book are therefore consistent with a range of wage formation processes and do not depend on the assumption of a trade union (see chapter 3).

In the case of channels (1)–(5), money has an impact on natural production because inflation, or variables specific to the monetary regime, affects the wage setters' optimisation with respect to the real wage and employment. The book analyses in particular two channels through which the relationship between real wage and employment, and thus the wage setters' optimisation, can be affected by money: (i) inflation or variables affected by the monetary regime have an impact on capital formation; and (ii) inflation or variables affected by the monetary regime influences the demand for goods function which in turn has an impact on the wage setters' optimisation through the real exchange rate which influences the wage setters' real wage, a real appreciation causing an increase in the purchasing power of wages. Only the second channel (ii) is effective in a small open economy characterised by perfect financial integration, causing the real interest rate to be exogenously determined as the foreign real interest rate. The first channel (i) is present only in a closed economy or in an open economy with imperfect financial integration. In the case of the monetary regime affecting the fiscal policy stance there is a further impact on the wage setters' optimisation due to a direct impact of the tax rate on the real disposable wage.

The other channels set out above causing a monetary impact on natural production, that is, channels (6)–(9) above, are consistent with the view that wage setters optimise preferences which include the real wage and employment. They do not, however, depend on this assumption but are consistent also with wage setting where natural unemployment is determined by wage setters who aim at a fixed, exogenously given, unemployment level when they set the nominal wage in advance through contracts. This is the case when wage setters determine natural unemployment under uncertainty, the expected natural unemployment in this case being determined by the fluctuation in economic variables.

Most analyses assume nominal wage contracts. The presence of nominal wage contracts in a rational model setting may be explained by wage setters who face negotiation costs and who want to derive an optimal real wage–employment trade-off during the contract period when they are faced by unexpected shocks, see Benassy (1995b).

1.4   Microeconomic foundation

In the analyses throughout the book, production is determined through the interaction of decisions made by (i) representative firms which set the production level and determine the capital stock to maximise profit, (ii) households who determine consumption to optimise inter-temporal utility, (iii) authorities who have at their disposal monetary and/or fiscal policy, and (iv) wage setters who set the nominal wage to reach an optimal trade-off between the real wage and employment. As will be explained in chapter 3, the last assumption (iv) is not necessary as most findings apply also to the cases where an individual optimises lifetime utility with respect to leisure and consumption or where a firm sets the nominal wage but incurs costs associated with the turnover of staff in the firm.

The analysis is based on an overlapping generations model with infinitely lived households. The assumptions underlying this basic model are set out in the appendix which specifies the microeconomic foundation. The overlapping generations framework implies that fiscal policy is effective in affecting production also in the long term analysed in the steady-state equilibrium. This means that Ricardian equivalence does not hold.

1.5   The structure of the book

The book is divided into four parts. *Part I* discusses the most important general assumptions used throughout the book, notably with respect to wage formation, and thus forms an introduction to the subsequent analyses. There is furthermore a non-exhaustive survey of the literature and a brief presentation of the empirical evidence which in several areas support monetary non-neutrality in the long term.

Part II presents those mechanisms for a monetary impact which makes it possible through the choice of inflation or other monetary policy instruments directly to influence natural production. As discussed above, these mechanisms are: (i) imperfect substitution between financial assets denominated in different currencies, (ii) financial intermediation through banks which operate in deposit and lending markets characterised by imperfect competition, and (iii) households and firms derive liquidity services from securities, securities functioning as a substitute for legal tender and bank deposits. It is furthermore examined how one-time shifts in the money supply, assuming a specific economic structure, can cause permanent effects on the capital stock and thus have an effect on natural production.

Part III discusses the impact of the monetary regime on natural production. As discussed above, the following channels are examined: (i) the impact of inflation on the demand for goods in combination with a centralised wage setting, (ii) the impact of the monetary regime on the authorities' inclination to pursue an expansive fiscal policy, (iii) the impact of the authorities pursuing exclusively a price stability goal, wanting only to lower a positive price increase while not wanting to bring about an actual reduction in the price level, (iv) the impact of inflation on uncertainty with respect to economic policy, (v) uncertainty in a fixed-but-adjustable exchange rate regime with respect to the authorities' decision on a devaluation, and (vi) the impact of the monetary regime on the fluctuations in economic variables and thus on natural production when wage setters have preferences which are an asymmetric function of production.

Part IV discusses some policy implications. It is argued that the view that monetary policy and monetary regimes have an impact on long-term production levels must lead to a revision of the view that monetary policy should be used exclusively to pursue a price stability goal. The wisdom of imposing fixed rules on monetary policy is further questioned because the optimal inflation–unemployment trade-off may change over time. The microeconomic foundation of the economic analysis is specified in the appendix.

2 The literature

2.1 Introduction

While there is general agreement on the short-term effect of monetary policy, economists tend to agree that money has no effect on production and unemployment in the longer term characterised by wage and price flexibility and rational expectations.

This chapter surveys the discussion in the literature as to whether money can influence production in a model setting characterised by four features: (i) economic relationships result from the agents' optimisation, (ii) agents are able perfectly to forecast future levels of economic variables or, in the case of stochastic variables, the stochastic distributions of economic variables, (iii) agents have preferences which include only real variables, and (iv) there are no costs associated with changes in nominal variables. We speak of 'monetary neutrality' if money has no impact on production in such a model setting.

This point of departure leaves out a number of channels where a monetary impact on production would seem largely to have an effect over a shorter time horizon. We exclude, for example, adjustment costs associated with changes in prices. Menu costs associated with price changes play a major role in 'New Keynesian Economics'.[1] We also exclude informational deficiencies which may cause wage setters or other agents to over- or underestimate the real wage. This means that we do not consider the slow adjustment of expectations which form part of the early natural unemployment hypotheses, cf. Friedman (1968) and Phelps (1968). We further exclude that wage setters consider the nominal wage as an objective in itself and the costs associated with nominal wage

---

[1] See, for example, Mankiw (1985) and Akerlof and Yellen (1985). Surveys are found in Lindbeck (1998) and Mankiw and Romer (1991).

adjustments.[2] We finally leave out the more recent 'liquidity models' which are based on transaction costs associated with moving cash across markets for different financial assets.[3]

This chapter gives a non-exhaustive survey of the literature. *Section 2.2* discusses the view of monetary neutrality. *Section 2.3* surveys the channels examined in the literature which may cause inflation to have an impact on natural production in a model setting based on wage and price flexibility, rational expectations, and preferences based on real variables. *Section 2.4* examines the views in the literature concerning a possible impact of the monetary regime on natural production. *Section 2.5* reviews the empirical evidence. *Section 2.6* gives a summary and conclusion.

2.2   The view of monetary neutrality

The notion of a downward-sloping Phillips curve, making it possible to reach a lower unemployment level at the cost of higher inflation, was a main reason why economists in the 1960s and the beginning of the 1970s came out largely in favour of a floating exchange rate regime. The Phillips curve relationship between employment and inflation was seen as determined by factors individual to each country, for example, by the structure of the labour market. It was argued that each country should maintain autonomy with regard to the setting of inflation, the downward-sloping Phillips curve giving policy makers the opportunity to choose a combination of unemployment and inflation which would optimise the preferences of each individual country.[4]

---

[2]We exclude for example the impact of overlapping wage contracts where a group of wage earners are reluctant to accept a wage cut because they are uncertain to what extent such a cut will be followed by other wage earners. While symmetric adjustment costs associated with monetary variables only delay the adjustment towards a long-term equilibrium solution, asymmetric adjustment costs may cause money to be non-neutral in the long term (for a discussion, see Blanchard (1990)). Akerlof, Dickens and Perry (1996) find evidence of resistance among wage setters against nominal wage reductions, causing the adjustment process towards an equilibrium unemployment rate to be slower at low inflation, thus leading to higher average frictional unemployment at low inflation.
[3]See, for example, Fuerst (1992).
[4]See, for example, Johnson (1969a) who writes: 'The adoption of flexible exchange rates would have the great advantage of freeing governments to use their instruments of domestic policy for the pursuit of domestic objectives...a great rift exists between nations like the United Kingdom and the United States, which are anxious to maintain high levels of employment and are prepared to pay a price for it in terms of domestic inflation, and other nations, notably the West German Federal Republic, which are strongly adverse to inflation ... Flexible rates would allow each country to pursue the mixture of unemployment and price trend objectives it prefers...' (pp. 209–210).

The view of a stable Phillips curve relationship between unemployment and inflation was increasingly questioned when both inflation and unemployment rose at the end of the 1960s and the beginning of the 1970s. In economic theory, the view of the long-term downward-sloping Phillips curve was replaced by the notion of an exogenously given natural production from the beginning of the 1970s. Unemployment diverges from the natural level only over short time periods. Such deviations are caused either by firms misinterpreting general price changes as relative price changes or by incomplete information on whether shocks are permanent or transitory.[5] In addition, deviations from the natural rate may be due to the presence of nominal wage contracts which prevent flexible adjustment of the nominal wage to structural changes.[6] As information imperfections are likely to persist over only short time periods and wage contracts in most countries have a short duration, it is optimal to bring about price and exchange rate stability which reduces information and transaction costs.[7] This view became common throughout the 1970s and caused economists and policy makers to question the advantages associated with an independent monetary policy.[8]

The view of monetary neutrality held by economists implies that the effects which give money a role to play in models based on wage and price flexibility and rational expectations, and which are discussed below, are

[5]See Lucas (1972, 1978b).
[6]See Fischer (1977) and Taylor (1979, 1980). The adjustment process can be prolonged if there is no synchronisation of price and wage decisions, that is, if there is staggering. A discussion of staggering is found in Blanchard (1990).
[7]If expectations are adaptive, as suggested by Friedman (1968) and Phelps (1968), the deviation from the natural level may span over a longer time period. Phelps (1972) argues that the short-term gain from unanticipated inflation in terms of lower unemployment must be weighed against the longer-term loss in the form of permanently higher inflation.
[8]See, for example, Currie (1992) who writes: 'An important reason for the progressive abandonment of the nominal exchange rate instrument in Europe in the 1980s is the view that it is an ineffective means of obtaining adjustments in relative competitiveness except in the rather short run: nominal exchange rate changes tend to lead rather quickly to higher inflation, so that over a two-to-four year horizon gains in competitiveness are eroded through higher prices and wages' (p. 253). Bayoumi (1994) writes: 'While not uncontroversial, the existence of nominal rigidities is central to most controversies of currency unions; with fully flexible prices the costs of joining a currency union become minor, making the analysis of the issue of optimum currency areas largely pointless' (p. 3). Dornbusch and Giovannini (1990) stress that monetary policy has no real effects if there is full wage and price flexibility. Fischer (1995) writes: 'the view that there is no long-run trade-off between inflation and unemployment is widely accepted' (p. 9). Taylor (1997) writes: 'A second key macroeconomic principle is that there is no long-term trade-off between the rate of inflation and the rate of unemployment...Although controversial at one time, this does not appear to be controversial anymore; empirical and theoretical research provides strong support' (p. 233).

seen as unimportant. Fischer and Modigliani (1978) conclude: 'Overall, the nonpayment of interest on currency and the menu costs of changing prices do not generate substantial real effects at moderate rates of inflation' (p. 819). Barro and Gordon (1983b) note: 'Although people generally regard inflation as very costly, economists have not presented very convincing arguments to explain these costs' (p. 104). Rogoff (1985b) concludes: 'It is somewhat difficult, in the context of a rational expectations model, to argue that the level of the inflation rate has much direct weight in the social loss function' (p. 1174).

Based on Kydland and Prescott (1977) and on Barro and Gordon (1983a), a body of more recent economic literature sees inflation as resulting from a non-cooperative game between wage setters, who set the nominal wage in advance through contracts and who form correct expectations about the monetary policy which will be pursued during the wage contract period, and the authorities who control monetary policy. The wage setters desire a specific production–employment level while the authorities' preferences include both an inflation and a production goal. It is assumed that the wage setters' desired production level lies at a lower level than the authorities' desired production level or that the authorities for other reasons want to create inflation in excess of the wage setters' expected inflation. Positive inflation arises because the wage setters, by setting a certain wage increase in nominal wage contracts, can force the authorities to bring about a production level which corresponds to the wage setters' desired level.

An important policy conclusion from this literature is that the authorities' preferences have no impact on the production level, which lies at the level desired by the wage setters. In a model context where functional shifts are fully known by the wage setters, the use of monetary policy to increase employment is unambiguously harmful as it causes positive inflation while having no impact on production. In the case where functional shifts are known only by the authorities, a case could be made for the authorities retaining the use of discretionary monetary policy to counter such functional shifts, as monetary policy can be used to stabilise output. The most recent literature suggests, however, that both price stability and reduction in output variability can be reached through an appropriate design of the targets which are to be pursued by the monetary authorities.[9]

---

[9]Walsh (1995) suggests that the conflict between low inflation and output instability can be avoided if a contract is concluded with the central bank governor which specifies the central bank's remuneration as a linear function of inflation. A recent survey is found in Svensson (1997).

It follows from the view of monetary neutrality that the choice of monetary regime has no impact on the real economy in the longer term. Against this background, the discussion on the choice of optimal monetary regime has focused almost exclusively on two aspects: (i) to what extent the monetary regime can stabilise production around the long-term production level, and (ii) to what extent a monetary regime can help to reduce inflation. These two themes have dominated the discussion on a single European currency.[10]

2.3   The impact on natural unemployment of inflation

Making the assumptions of wage and price flexibility, rational expectations and preferences based on real variables, we find in the literature discussion of four channels through which inflation can affect the real economy. These four channels are: (i) inflation or the uncertainty surrounding inflation influence the portfolio choice between money and capital because inflation determines the opportunity cost associated with holding money; (ii) inflation reduces the size of real money holdings and thus the efficiency with which money can be utilised, in turn affecting either household utility or the firm's production function; (iii) inflation causes a redistribution of real wealth to the disbenefit of holders of money, leading to effects which may affect the real economy; and (iv) depending on the model specification, there may be a long-term impact from money on the real economy through hysteresis effects, caused by money having an impact on employment and production in the shorter term. The first three of these four channels are based on the assumption that money is non-interest bearing or carries a fixed nominal interest rate. There may further be an impact from money on the real economy because legislative provisions are based on nominal amounts, for example nominal tax brackets or depreciation clauses based on historical purchase values. Such nominal rigidities can, however, be avoided through legislative changes.

We will briefly discuss these sources of monetary non-neutrality. Hysteresis effects are taken up in chapter 7. The three channels (i)–(iii) for a monetary impact on the real economy, have been incorporated into standard neoclassical growth models. It follows that inflation affects the level of capital and production relative to labour.[11] In more recent litera-

---

[10]See, for example, Bayoumi (1994) and Tavlas (1993). A fixed natural unemployment rate is used to justify a fixed exchange rate regime, see, for example, Buiter (1995) and Eichengreen (1993).
[11]See, for example, Levhari and Patinkin (1968), Stockman (1981), and Tobin (1965).

ture, these channels have been modelled in endogenous growth models in which money has the effect of influencing the output growth rate.[12]

2.3.1   *The impact of inflation on the agent's portfolio decision*

The impact of the inflation rate

Tobin (1995) suggests that an increase in the money supply lowers capital accumulation and thus economic growth because money is a substitute for capital in saving, an increase in real money balances causing a reduction in the saving which takes place through real capital. This basic insight is further developed in the monetary growth literature. In the neoclassical monetary growth model first set out by Tobin (1965), a rise in inflation causes a reduction in the real money stock which the private sector is willing to hold. Assuming a fixed savings rate of the private sector's disposable income, it is demonstrated by Tobin that a smaller real money supply increases the share of private saving which is placed in capital, thus causing a positive relationship between inflation and capital intensity. This increase in capital intensity results from two effects. The first effect arises because higher inflation causes an income transfer to the government in the form of seigniorage/inflation tax (see below), this effect working to reduce saving. A second effect arises because higher inflation makes money less attractive relative to real capital as a saving outlet, inducing agents to increase capital accumulation.[13]

The same basic mechanism is found in Mundell (1963) where higher inflation lowers the real money stock by increasing the nominal interest rate which is the opportunity cost of holding money. The lower real money stock increases saving through a real wealth effect.

The finding that inflation, determined by the growth rate in the money supply, has an effect on saving because money functions as a substitute for real capital in the private sector's saving, is questioned by Sidrauski (1967). The point of departure is taken in a representative household which optimises utility over an infinite time horizon. A representative agent derives utility from the consumption of goods and from services rendered by the real money supply (see below). Sidrauski (1967) finds real money to be neutral with respect to capital accumulation. A representa-

---

[12]See van der Ploeg and Alogoskoufis (1994).

[13]The early neoclassical monetary growth models assume that money issued by the government is the only savings outlet for the private sector besides real capital. In the case, examined by Turnovsky (1978, 1987b), where the government finances expenditure also through bond issues, it follows that government bonds also have the effect of decreasing capital intensity.

tive agent is willing to transfer consumption from the current to a subsequent time period insofar as the return which is received on saving is
higher than or equal to the rate of time preference. The return received by
the representative household through capital accumulation equals the
marginal productivity of capital and is thus determined by the capital
intensity. As neither the marginal productivity of capital nor the rate of
time preference is determined by monetary factors, money is neutral.[14]

A number of studies modify this conclusion of monetary neutrality
reached by Sidrauski (1967). Drazen (1981) demonstrates that higher
inflation decreases capital intensity in an overlapping generations
model. The reasoning is that inflation involves an income transfer
between generations, constituting a tax on the money transfers from
the old to the young generation. Fischer (1979) shows that an increase
in the money supply growth rate causes higher capital intensity in the
Sidrauski model in the adjustment period leading up to a new steady-
state equilibrium.[15] Marty (1969) demonstrates an impact of money on
savings when money enters as an input in the firm's production. Finally,
real money may affect saving when the household utility function
includes not only consumption and real money, but also leisure, provided
that the consumption of physical goods and leisure do not enter as separable items in the utility function.[16]

The impact of inflation uncertainty

Money may affect the representative agent's portfolio choice
between money and real capital not only by affecting the real return on
money, determined by the inflation rate, but also through fluctuation in
inflation. Empirical investigations, see, for example, Edey (1994), find a
positive relationship between the level of inflation and fluctuation in the
inflation rate. The increased inflation variability at a higher inflation
indicates that there is a rise also in the uncertainty which surrounds
inflation. This is confirmed by surveys of inflation forecasts which
show an increase in forecast errors when there is higher inflation.[17]

---

[14]This finding is demonstrated in the appendix where inflation has no impact on private
saving.
[15]This is expanded by Cohen (1985).
[16]See Brock (1974). Benassy (1995a) shows that there is monetary neutrality when real
money and leisure enter as separable arguments in the utility function. The same conclusion
follows from the non-stochastic version of the model examined by Turnovsky (1993).
Models which include both consumption, leisure, and real money services in the household
utility function, are examined by, for example, Dutkowsky and Dunsky (1996).
[17]See, for example, Evans (1991) and Ungar and Zilberfarb (1993).

A number of explanations have been advanced to account for a positive correlation between the inflation rate and inflation variability. Holland (1993, 1995) demonstrates that there is a rise in the variation of inflation forecasts at higher inflation when agents include the lagged inflation rate in their forecasts due to learning about a regime shift. Devereux (1989) explains the relationship between the inflation rate and inflation variability with the degree of indexation in the economy. At a high inflation rate, indexation is more widespread. This means that real shocks to a larger extent are translated into price fluctuations at high inflation, while at a low inflation rate where indexation is less widespread to a larger extent they cause changes in employment. According to Cukierman and Meltzer (1986), increased inflation variability at higher inflation may arise because larger fluctuations in economic relationships increase the effectiveness of monetary policy due to the resulting uncertainty. This induces the authorities to pursue a more expansive monetary policy which in turn increases inflation.

Ball (1992) suggests that the rise in inflation variability at a high inflation is caused by the policy process. If inflation is viewed as a problem, economic policy is to a larger extent directed towards the reduction of inflation when inflation is high and the pursuit of such an anti-inflationary policy increases uncertainty.[18] Evans and Wachtel (1993) find evidence that the increase in inflation uncertainty at high inflation rates is due to uncertainty regarding shifts in the monetary regime.

2.3.2   The impact of inflation on economic efficiency

The nominal return on legal tender, that is, notes and coins, equals zero. This means that lower inflation decreases the opportunity cost associated with the use of notes and coins. This increases the overall efficiency with which financial assets are used for payments and for saving. The economic literature points to a number of efficiency gains which result from an increase in real money holdings.

One effect arises because a rise in real money holdings, caused by lower inflation, makes it possible to save resources associated with financial transactions.[19] Thus, an increase in real money holdings implies a reduction in the costs associated with changing between money and other financial assets. An increase in real money holdings further makes it

---

[18]The same explanation is found in Bruno (1995).
[19]General discussions of the utility derived from money are found in Brunner (1971), Friedman (1969), and Johnson (1972).

possible to save resources associated with the synchronisation of expenditure and revenue.[20] Johnson (1972) argues that lower inflation, causing an increase in real money balances, makes it possible to save costs associated with financial management. Gillman (1993) points out that lower inflation saves resources in the financial sector because the agents in the economy use legal tender instead of credit-based purchases which involve a larger use of real resources.[21]

An additional saving of resources arises because a reduction in inflation makes it more attractive for firms to hold money as an insurance against unexpected events. The alternative for the firm would be to hold stocks and lower inflation could thus entail a reduction in stocks.[22]

Inflation may further affect the efficiency with which information can be processed. High inflation may increase the need for information activities, causing an economic cost due to reduced transparency and thus a less efficient allocation of resources and possibly lower production.[23] Moreover, the monetary regime can affect the efficiency with which agents can obtain information about the economy. Kimborough (1984) and Lächler (1985) argue that it is easier for agents to observe signals through changes in the exchange rate than through changes in the money supply. This means that economic adjustment is facilitated in a floating exchange rate regime.

Further utility gains from real money holdings may arise because the holding of money enables agents to make use of unexpected offers of purchases which are considered advantageous. If agents hold interest-bearing financial assets they will have to incur a transaction cost before being able to make use of advantageous offers. In addition, a rise in real money holdings may increase frictional unemployment because wage earners are able to finance longer job search periods.[24] Finally, it increases utility that agents, when there is lower inflation, incur lower costs with respect to deferring purchases of goods, as it becomes more attractive to hold money.

A number of empirical investigations show a positive relationship between inflation and the variability of relative prices. This supports

---

[20]See Friedman (1969) and Moroney (1972).
[21]Ireland (1994) similarly argues that higher inflation causes a larger use of private money and thus of resources. The same point is made by Lucas (1986).
[22]See, for example, Johnson (1972) who argues that an increase in real money holdings makes it possible to save capital.
[23]As a special effect, Fischer and Modigliani (1978) emphasise that inflation may cause agents to misinterpret company accounts which are based on nominal principles.
[24]See Phelps (1972).

the view that inflation increases the need for search activities.[25] Cukierman (1982) explains the relationship between inflation and relative price variability with producers who are unwilling to change production due to the costs associated with production changes. Production is only changed if a shift in the relative demand for the good in question can be observed through a change in the relative price. As higher inflation causes larger fluctuations in inflation, it is more difficult for producers to ascertain whether a price increase represents a change in the relative price or in the general price level. This makes producers more unwilling to change output at high inflation, causing producers to make more use of price changes and thus explaining the increased variability in relative prices.

In the case where several currencies are used, the creation of a monetary union entails the saving of transaction costs. A larger currency area increases the utility of money, a point stressed by McKinnon (1963). Seen from the perspective of having more assets for savings, a monetary union must, however, be seen as negative as it reduces the number of currencies and thus provides less scope for risk reduction through diversification.[26]

The efficient use of money which is affected by inflation and thus by the monetary regime, has been modelled in different ways. In one approach real money enters the representative household utility function, thus having a direct impact on utility.[27] A second way to model the services rendered by real money is to include real money balances in the production function, treating real money as an input alongside with capital and labour.[28] A third approach specifies through a 'transaction cost function' the costs incurred on search activities, in particular shopping time.[29]

Finally, a number of models, following Clower (1967), are based on a cash-in-advance motive for holding money which causes expenditure to

---

[25]See, for example, Andersen (1989), Drazen and Hamermesh (1986), Domberger (1987), and Edey (1994).

[26]See Neumeyer (1998).

[27]This approach is first used by Johnson (1968) and Levhari and Patinkin (1968). Among other models which incorporate real money in the utility function, may be mentioned Rankin (1994), Sidrauski (1967), and Turnovsky (1987b). A discussion is found in Dornbusch and Giovannini (1990).

[28]See Levhari and Patinkin (1968) and Johnson (1969b). Gylfason and Herbertsson (1996) examine an endogenous growth model where real money enters as a production factor. In this model context, a higher inflation has the effect of lowering the economy's growth rate.

[29]See amongst others Correia and Teles (1996). Chari, Christiano, and Kehoe (1996) specify the services rendered by real money both through a utility function including money and through transaction cost functions which specify shopping time and the resources spent in the financial sector on money creation.

be constrained by prefixed money holdings.[30] In a model setting where all future purchases can be foreseen with certainty, the cash-in-advance constraint does not in itself cause real effects. Inflation acts, however, as a tax on consumption when cash is held in advance of consumption and may thus reduce the work incentive, causing a reduction in production.[31] In addition, real effects will arise from inflation if there is uncertainty regarding future purchases as the demand for real money balances is affected by this uncertainty.[32]

2.3.3 Distributional effects arising from inflation

Inflation as a source of government revenue

Inflation and the resource transfer associated with the issue of new money imply a transfer of resources from holders of money to the government which issues money. Inflation thus constitutes a source of taxation. The literature suggests three reasons why the authorities may find it optimal to raise resources through inflation tax/seigniorage rather than using other sources: (i) the use of inflation tax makes it possible to reduce the use of other costly tax instruments, notably the tax on labour income which distorts the choice between work and leisure;[33] (ii) inflation tax/seigniorage may be easier to collect than other taxes;[34] and (iii) inflation tax/seigniorage is efficient in taxing also underground activities.[35]

Several economists attach considerable weight to the use of inflation tax/seigniorage.[36] Other economists have argued either that the revenue from inflation tax is low or that inflation tax is an undesirable source of

---

[30] The cash-in-advance motive corresponds to the finance motive set out by Keynes (1936). It is introduced in the recent literature by Helpman (1981) and Lucas (1982). A recent survey is found in Giovannini and Turtelboom (1994).

[31] See Cooley and Hansen (1989).

[32] See Svensson (1985).

[33] See Phelps (1972). This argument is further stressed by Lucas (1986) who suggests that inflation shall be determined with the aim of stabilising the marginal tax rate on labour income. Jensen (1994) shows that the natural unemployment is lowered by the reduction in the marginal tax rate on labour income which is made possible through seigniorage/inflation tax. Palokangas (1997) argues that inflation, by making it possible to hold a lower tax rate on labour and capital income, acts as an incentive for firms to place production in a country, diminishing the incentive of moving production abroad.

[34] See Phelps (1972).

[35] See Giavazzi (1989).

[36] Dornbusch (1989) underlines the efficiency of inflation tax/seigniorage, making it possible to avoid a distorting tax on labour income, Van der Ploeg (1991) argues: 'To assess the case for an independent common central bank such as the EuroFed, one should tradeoff the welfare gains associated with enhanced monetary discipline and lower inflation against the welfare losses associated with a suboptimal resource mix' (p. 36).

revenue.[37] Drazen (1989) stresses the difficulties with respect to maintaining a large revenue from inflation tax due to reserve requirements on banks as high reserve requirements may be difficult to maintain due to the resulting distortion of competition among financial institutions in an integrated financial market. Drazen (1989) further stresses that high reserve requirements cause a low return on saving, leading to a reduction in saving and thus in capital accumulation and growth. Ireland (1994) argues that the importance of government money in payments will decline over time as the cost of using bank-based payment systems will be lowered due to economies of scale when an increasing number of transactions takes place through the bank-based systems. Neumann (1991) sees inflation tax as socially undesirable as the burden falls primarily on the low-income households with few possibilities for investing in financial assets other than money.

Other distributional effects arising from inflation
It was discussed above that inflation constitutes a revenue source for the government because real wealth is transferred from the holders of money to the government. One may point to other distributional effects of inflation.

McKinnon (1973) suggests that high inflation increases the cost associated with capital accumulation, as money is held prior to investments. On the basis of a cash-in-advance model and assuming a representative agent who maximises welfare over an infinite horizon, Stockman (1981) shows that higher inflation, by imposing an additional cost on capital accumulation, causes lower capital accumulation and thus a reduction in capital intensity.

Inflation tax/seigniorage may further affect relative prices in the economy. Lucas (1986) makes a distinction between goods which are bought with cash and goods which are financed through credit. A rise in inflation increases the relative cost of buying cash-financed goods, in turn increasing the price on these goods relative to credit-financed goods.

Duca (1987) suggests that unanticipated inflation may cause a socially inefficient distortion between 'classical' and 'non-classical' sectors in the economy. Nominal wages are adjusted more flexibly to changes in demand in classical relative to non-classical sectors of the economy.

---

[37]See, for example, Friedman and Schwartz (1986) who find inflation tax/seigniorage unimportant as it constitutes only a small proportion of government revenue. This view is also taken by Bean (1992).

Unanticipated inflation thus causes a transfer of resources from 'non-classical' to 'classical' sectors.

2.4   The impact on natural unemployment of monetary regimes

While it is the general view that the monetary regime has no impact on natural unemployment (see section 2.2), the literature discusses some channels which could cause the choice of monetary regime to affect natural unemployment.

Several writers suggest that inflation variability affects the natural unemployment level. This opens up the possibility that there is an impact from the monetary regime on natural unemployment insofar as the monetary regime has an impact on inflation variability (see chapter 14). Analysing the wage setting of a monopoly union, Sørensen (1992) concludes that inflation variability influences the mean level of unemployment. Rankin (1998) analyses a model in which a positive correlation arises between production and the price level due to nominal wage contracts. This positive correlation affects households' decision making on saving and consumption and thus also the labour supply in a model where leisure enters the household's utility function.

It is argued by several economists that a shift in monetary regime may change the political incentive for implementing labour market reform. In particular, a stronger political incentive to increase labour market flexibility may arise when there is a shift from a flexible to a fixed exchange rate.[38] This can affect natural unemployment insofar as the labour market reform affects the wage setters' desired natural unemployment rate, for example by making it less attractive to undertake job search and thus causing a reduction in frictional unemployment.

2.5   The empirical evidence

The empirical evidence confirms that monetary policy has an effect over the shorter term.[39] A number of investigations also support, however, a role for monetary variables or the monetary regime in the long term. We will give a brief survey of these investigations. Our discussion will cover investigations which indicate that monetary variables impact on the real economy through the following channels: (i) the impact of monetary policy instruments, notably monetary aggregates and interest rates, on

---

[38]See Hayek (1978), Sibert and Sutherland (1997), and Wihlborg (1994).
[39]An overview of this evidence is presented in Friedman (1995).

production, (ii) the impact of inflation on output growth or unemployment, (iii) the impact of inflation on the real interest rate, on capital accumulation, and on the real stock return, (iv) the impact of the nominal exchange rate on the real exchange rate, (v) the impact of the monetary regime on the variability of real variables, (vi) estimates concerning the inflation tax/seigniorage, and (vii) investigations which analyse efficiency losses due to inflation.

2.5.1   The impact of monetary policy on production

The relationship between money and production

Examining the 1867–1960 period, Friedman and Schwartz (1963) show that a positive relationship exists in the USA between the broad nominal money aggregate (M2) and production. This finding has been confirmed in subsequent studies, for example, Backus and Kehoe (1992), Huh (1993), and Jefferson (1997), although the correlation between money and production seems to have been weakened in the post-war period.

The positive relationship between monetary aggregates and production indicates that monetary policy is powerful in affecting production. This proposition has, however, met with two objections. Firstly, it is possible that the causation runs from production to money, money being determined endogenously by production. It is secondly possible that changes both in the money stock and in production are caused by the same underlying phenomena. Studies have in particular pointed to oil price changes as a common cause of changes in both the money stock and production.

The view of money being determined endogenously by banks formed part of the 'Keynesian' criticism of monetarists in the 1960s. Gurley and Shaw (1960) outlined a mechanism through which banks can accommodate the private sector's demand for money through interest rate changes which affect the public's demand for different monetary assets, thus providing the public with the liquidity which is needed for transactions. The same mechanism is found in the Radcliffe Report (Committee on the Working of the Monetary System, 1959) which stresses banks' ability to create new monetary instruments to meet the demand for liquidity. Endogenous money creation is also analysed in King and Plosser (1984). A more recent contribution is Coleman (1996) who analyses three different mechanisms for making purchases: (i) by using fiat money, (ii) through a draft on interest-bearing deposits, and (iii) through credit.

The view of endogenous money creation has led to research on the causation between money and output based on Granger tests and on vector auto regression (VAR) techniques. Christiano and Ljungqvist (1988) conclude from US evidence that money Granger-causes production while Huh (1993) fails to find conclusive evidence about the causation between money and production. In an analysis of five OECD countries, Sims (1992) finds the impact of money on output to diverge across countries. In a study of the USA from 1869 to 1975 using an ARIMA model, Fisher and Seater (1993) find no evidence of monetary neutrality. A similar study for Canada also fails to reject monetary neutrality.[40] Leeper (1997) concludes on the basis of the empirical investigations that increases in M1 and M2 precede production rises, implying that causation runs from money to output. Most of the output variation is, however, due to non-monetary factors, and one cannot exclude the possibility that money has no impact on output. Analysing data which reach back more than a century, Serletis and Krause (1996) find support for monetary neutrality in estimations which include ten industrialised countries. Davis and Tanner (1997) show that changes in M2 have caused changes in real GDP since 1873 with the exception of the 1952–82 period where the Federal Reserve targeted the interest rate.

In an analysis of seven countries (Canada, France, Germany, Italy, Japan, the UK and the USA), Weber (1994) finds that the data mostly support the hypothesis of long-run neutrality while it is easy to find evidence against monetary super-neutrality. Examining data with observations covering a hundred years for ten industrialised countries, Serletis and Koustas (1998) reach the same conclusion in support of monetary neutrality. Monetary super-neutrality can only be tested for Italy where Serletis and Koustas (1998) find the data supportive of monetary super-neutrality.

A number of studies have demonstrated that the predictive power of money is diminished when market-related interest rates are included in vector auto regressions alongside with monetary aggregates.[41] Interest rates dominate money as a forecaster of output. As these interest rates are determined in the financial markets and could be unrelated to monetary policy, this weakens the monetary non-neutrality hypothesis.

If money is determined endogenously by banks through a process which involves changes in the relationship between different monetary aggregates, one might expect to find evidence of such changes. Coleman (1996) fails to find support for such a model for the money creation process, concluding that changes in the currency/deposit ratio are too small to be consistent with endogenous money creation. Similar conclu-

---

[40]See Haug and Lucas (1997).
[41]This was first demonstrated by Sims (1992). The same finding is reached in Huh (1993).

sions are reached by Jefferson (1997) who interprets a stable relationship between inside and outside money as evidence against the money creation process described by Gurley and Shaw (1960).

Analysing the impact on real variables of two monetary aggregates (M1 and M2) and of the three-month treasury bill rate in cointegration analyses, Boschen and Mills (1994) in an analysis of a US data series for the 1950–90 period largely fail to find evidence which supports monetary non-neutrality. The best predictive power is found for M2 but this impact may be explained by a correlation between changes in M2 and changes in total factor productivity, implying that monetary shocks have coincided with real shocks.

The tests of causation between money and production are based on changes in the money supply preceding changes in production. A systematic positive correlation between money and production arises, however, if the monetary authorities are more inclined to tighten monetary policy at high production levels.

The impact of interest rate instruments on production

Bernanke and Blinder (1992) argue that the monetary authorities have used the short-term interest rate as their policy instrument. The impact of monetary policy on production should therefore be tested by studying the impact of the short-term interest rate on production. Bernanke and Blinder (1992) find evidence of such an impact of the federal funds rate on production. Using Granger tests and VAR models which include also monetary aggregates (M1 and M2) and market-related interest rates (the three-month treasury bill rate and the ten-year treasury bond rate), they further find that the federal funds rate dominates these other financial variables as a forecaster of nine macroeconomic variables, that is, industrial production, capacity utilisation, employment, the unemployment rate, housing starts, personal income, retail sales, consumption, and durable-goods orders (with the sole exception that the ten-year bond rate has a stronger forecasting power with respect to housing starts).

Dornbusch, Favero, and Giavazzi (1998a, 1998b) estimate the reaction function for the authorities' setting of the short-term interest rate to distinguish between the effects of anticipated and unanticipated monetary policy. It is demonstrated that expected changes in the short-term interest rate give rise to permanent output changes which are statistically significant for five countries (Germany, France, Italy, the UK, and Sweden). No output effect can be found for Spain. Examining Canada, a similar finding is reached by Cushman and Zha (1997) who demonstrate that interest rate changes, which can be predicted from a reaction function, have persistent output effects. Cochrane (1998) shows both unexpected and expected changes in the federal funds rate to have an effect on production, although the impact from unexpected policy is most important.

The short-term interest rate controlled by the monetary authorities may affect production both through 'the money channel' – having an impact on the real economy through the condition for money market equilibrium – and through the 'credit channel' – influencing the real economy through access to credit. Bernanke and Blinder (1992) argue that the impact of the federal funds rate on the real economy should be seen as evidence of the 'credit view'.[42] Bernanke, Gertler, and Watson (1997) find that the federal funds rate influences the real economy through an effect on other interest rates.

A number of investigations show that the authorities have set the interest rate in response to developments in unemployment and inflation.[43] As one may expect the private sector to have knowledge of this reaction function, this can be seen as confirmation that expected monetary policy has an impact on the real economy (Cochrane, 1998). Bernanke, Gertler, and Watson (1997) and Friedman (1997) support the view of monetary non-neutrality.[44]

Monetary tightenings and cyclical downturns

Romer and Romer (1989, 1990) analyse six episodes after World War II where US monetary authorities changed monetary policy in deliberate attempts to reduce output in order to lower inflation.[45] It is demonstrated that these episodes of monetary tightenings are followed by cyclical downturns. Episodes of monetary tightening are determined on the basis of the minutes from meetings in the Federal Open Market Committee.

[42]The opposite view is found in Romer and Romer (1990).
[43]See Bernanke and Blinder (1992) and Dornbusch, Favero, and Giavazzi (1998a, 1998b). Clarida, Gali, and Gertler (1997) find the USA, Japan, and Germany to have set the interest rate on the basis of inflation and unemployment since 1979 while France, Italy, and the UK have been influenced also by the German monetary policy.
[44]Bernanke, Gertler, and Watson (1997) write: 'despite ongoing debates about precisely how the policy innovation should be identified, the estimated responses of key macroeconomics variables to a policy shock are reasonably similar across a variety of studies and suggest that monetary policy shocks can have significant and persistent real effects' (p. 95).
[45]Monetary tightenings are found to have taken place in October 1947, September 1955, December 1968, April 1974, August 1978, and October 1979. Romer and Romer (1994) point to December 1991 as an additional episode of monetary tightening.

The Romer and Romer (1989, 1990) approach has been criticised on different accounts.[46] It has been found that the monetary tightenings have coincided with oil price increases, making it difficult to ascertain whether the cyclical downturns have been caused by monetary policy or by the oil price increases. The monetary tightenings may have been undertaken due to fear of the inflationary pressure which may arise from the oil price increases. Second, it is uncertain how the economy would have developed without the monetary tightenings. Shapiro (1994) argues that the episodes of monetary tightenings can be found from a monetary reaction function. The 'narrative approach' used by Romer and Romer (1989, 1990) is thus still open to the criticism that the monetary tightenings are a reaction to developments in the real economy. In support of Romer and Romer (1989, 1990), Bernanke, Gertler, and Watson (1997) reject oil price increases as the prime explanation behind cyclical downturns.

Bernanke (1983) shows that the collapse of the financial system in the USA was a main cause behind the Great Depression in the beginning of the 1930s. Further evidence is presented in Bordo, Choudhri, and Schwartz (1995).

2.5.2   Inflation and output

The relationship between inflation and economic growth has been studied in a number of empirical investigations. Until recent years, the studies mostly indicated a negative relationship between inflation and economic growth. Examining inflation and economic growth over the 1961–88 period, Fischer (1993) finds a rise in inflation of 10 percentage points to cause a reduction in average annual GDP growth of 0.4 percentage points. Similar results are derived by Barro (1995) and by de Gregorio (1993). Examining 24 OECD countries over the 1960–91 period, Andrés, Doménech, and Molinas (1996) find output growth to be negatively correlated with inflation and positively correlated with money supply growth. If the money supply growth is deleted as an explanatory variable, inflation becomes insignificant. Gylfason and Herbertsson (1996) find for most countries a negative relationship between economic growth and inflation over the 1960–93 period.

---

[46]A criticism is found in Hoover and Perez (1994a, 1994b). A response is given in Romer and Romer (1994). Hoover and Perez (1994b) stress that monetary policy may have had some impact on the real economy but it is uncertain whether the influence is as important as stressed by Romer and Romer (1989, 1990).

Some recent investigations indicate that the relationship between output and inflation is asymmetrical. An increase in inflation at a low inflation rate increases output while higher inflation lowers output at inflation rates above a certain level. Examining 87 countries over the 1970–90 period, Sarel (1996) finds that inflation rates above approximately 8 per cent are correlated with lower output while a rise in inflation at rates below 8 per cent has a positive impact on output. A similar conclusion is derived by Bullard and Keating (1995) who study 58 countries in the post-war period. Of these 58 countries, 16 countries experienced a permanent inflation shock. For 11 of these countries, the estimated long-run response of output to higher inflation was not statistically different from zero. Four of the countries, all with low inflation rates (Austria, Finland, Germany, the UK), experienced a positive increase in output as a result of higher inflation. One country with high inflation (Argentina), experienced a permanent negative output change from a permanent inflation increase. No evidence is found of inflation causing a change in the growth rate of the economy.

Bullard and Keating (1995) emphasise that studies of the relationship between inflation and output/output growth may exaggerate the harmful effects which arise from inflation. This is because both high inflation and low output/low output growth may be caused by overall bad management of the economy. In chapter 10 we will point to a further reason why studies may overestimate the harmful effects of inflation. In a model setting where natural unemployment is endogenously determined, policy makers react to high unemployment with an expansive monetary policy to increase production. Assuming that wage setters take the policy setting of policy makers into account in wage setting, we find that inflation is higher at low production.

Several studies indicate that the relationship between inflation and output growth depends on both the time period chosen and the inclusion of a few countries with either high growth or high inflation. Bruno and Easterley (1998) find no evidence of a relationship between inflation and output growth when developing countries with an inflation above 40 per cent are excluded from the study while the pooling of observations over several years weakens the correlation.[47]

King and Watson (1994) examine the relationship between unemployment and inflation for the US post-war period. Evidence is found of a negative relationship between inflation and unemployment, an increase in

---

[47]Similar conclusions are reached by Clark (1997).

inflation of 1 per cent leading to a reduction of 1.3 per cent in unemployment. Testing the seven largest OECD countries, Weber (1994) likewise finds a negative long-run relationship between unemployment and inflation but cannot reject the hypothesis of a vertical long-term Phillips curve.

Several studies support the view that inflation uncertainty affects the real economy. Evans and Wachtel (1993) find evidence that uncertainty about the monetary regime increases unemployment. Huizinga (1993) concludes that uncertainty concerning inflation is correlated with uncertainty about real variables, that is, the real wage, real output prices, and profit rates. The uncertainty about real variables in turn has a negative impact on investments. Davis and Kanago (1996) find that an increase in uncertainty regarding inflation, measured by the variance in inflation forecasts found in surveys on inflation, causes a reduction in output while not affecting long-term real output growth.

2.5.3   *The impact of inflation on the real interest rate and capital accumulation*

Most empirical investigations indicate a negative relationship between the real interest rate and inflation. Summers (1983) finds a negative correlation between inflation and the real interest rate. Mishkin (1992) concludes that a rise in inflation of 1 percentage point raises the nominal interest rate by 0.7 percentage points. Examining the 1959–89 period and using spectral band techniques, Thoma (1994) likewise finds a negative relationship between the real interest rate and inflation. The same conclusion is reached on the basis of UK bonds over the 1983–95 period by Evans (1998). Deriving inflation expectations on the basis of the price difference between index bonds and fixed interest rate bonds in Israel, a negative relationship between the real interest rate and inflation is demonstrated by Kandel, Ofer, and Sarig (1996). Weber (1994) finds a significant negative relationship between the real interest rate and inflation for Germany, the USA, and the UK. In Canada, France, Italy, and Japan, inflation has a modest impact on the real interest rate.

Evans and Lewis (1995) find evidence of structural shifts in the determination of inflation in the USA over the 1958–90 period. Against this background, they cannot reject the hypothesis that inflation leads to a one-to-one change in the nominal interest rate. Investigating the three-month interest rate in the US over the 1952–92 period, Cowder and Hoffman (1996) find evidence of a one-to-one relationship between inflation and the tax-adjusted interest rate.

Several empirical investigations show a negative relationship between inflation and the real stock return. This finding was first reached by Fama

(1981) and has been confirmed by subsequent studies.[48] Thorbecke (1997) shows changes in the federal funds rate to have a strong effect on the real stock return. Changes in the interest rate are found to have a stronger effect on stock prices for small companies than for large companies, supporting the view that monetary policy affects the real economy by influencing companies' borrowing constraints.

A macroeconomic explanation of the relationship between inflation and the real stock return can be based on the agent's portfolio choice between capital and money, that is, the explanation suggested by Mundell (1963) and Tobin (1965). Fama (1981) argues that the relationship may result from an expectation of low economic growth, when there is a high inflation, depressing the real stock return. This view is rejected by Balduzzi (1995) who finds evidence of a direct impact from inflation on the real stock return. Santoni and Moehring (1994) argue that the inclusion of goods with a long life time in the price index may explain the relationship. When there is a rise in the real interest rate, demand for durable goods is reduced, causing a reduction in the prices of durable goods and thus a lowering of general inflation.

Most empirical studies fail to support a positive relationship between inflation and capital accumulation as predicted by the Mundell–Tobin models (Fischer, 1988). Fama and Gibbons (1982) conclude on the basis of an investigation covering the 1953–77 period that a positive relationship exists between private non-residential investment and the real yield on financial assets, implying that a low real interest rate has not given rise to an increase in investments as might have been expected. Fama and Gibbons (1982) explain this result by the real yield on financial assets being forced up to attract saving when there are good investment possibilities. Bruno (1995) shows that capital accumulation, estimated for 16 countries over the 1961–91 period, is positively affected by the real return on capital and by the growth rate in output while being negatively affected by inflation. Bruno (1995) explains the negative impact of inflation with uncertainty regarding macroeconomic variables.

2.5.4   The determination of the real exchange rate

While empirical investigations throughout the 1970s in general reported findings in favour of purchasing power parity (PPP), implying that the real exchange rate is determined independently of the nominal exchange

---

[48]See, for example, Patelis (1997) and Thorbecke (1997).

rate, analyses throughout the 1980s were not supportive of PPP. Recent research shows that the real exchange rate is mean reverting over long time periods, indicating that PPP holds in the very long run.[49] On the basis of empirical investigations, Rogoff (1996) concludes that the speed of convergence to PPP is extremely slow, deviations appearing to dampen out at a rate of roughly 15 per cent per year.

Lothian and Taylor (1997) argue that standard tests of mean reversion have poor characteristics over shorter time periods. Tests for mean reversion are only reliable over very long time periods, possibly 100 years. Abuaf and Jorion (1990) find the real exchange rate to follow an autoregressive process with a root smaller than one, implying that the real exchange rate is mean reverting. The adjustment towards equilibrium takes place over a long time period.[50]

2.5.5   The variability of real variables under monetary regimes

The empirical evidence indicates that real exchange rate volatility is affected by the monetary regime. On the basis of evidence from the 1970s, Stockman (1983) shows the real exchange rate to exhibit larger fluctuations under a floating exchange rate regime relative to a fixed exchange rate regime. The same conclusion is derived by subsequent studies, see, for example, Artis and Taylor (1988), Baxter and Stockman (1989), and Mussa (1986). Alogoskoufis and Smith (1991) find evidence of larger persistence in wage formation under a floating than under a fixed exchange rate regime. Examining 18 OECD countries and covering the 1960–91 period, Caporale, Kalyvitis, and Pittis (1994) find larger persistence for industrial production, real exchange rates, real interest rates, and unemployment rates under a floating exchange rate regime.[51] Based on data reaching back more than a hundred years in an analysis of Canada, France, Japan, and the UK, Hasan and Wallace (1996) find larger fluctuations in the real exchange rate under a floating exchange rate regime. A number of investigations, see, for example, Artis

---

[49]See Evans and Lothian (1993), Hasan and Wallace (1996), Huizinga (1987), Jorion and Sweeney (1996), Mark (1995), and Kuo and Mikkola (1997). A survey is found in Rogoff (1996).
[50]Krugman (1995) writes: 'in international even more than domestic economics, the evidence for some kind of nominal rigidity is overwhelming...International macroeconomics must face up to much stronger evidence, the nearly perfect correlation between nominal and real exchange rates in industrial countries since 1980...I personally think that the effort to explain away the apparent real effects of nominal shocks is silly, even if one restricts oneself to domestic evidence' (p. 523).
[51]Similar findings are reported in Caporale and Pittis (1995).

and Taylor (1994), demonstrate a reduction in real exchange rate volatility for countries which have joined the European Exchange Rate Mechanism (ERM), indicating that the ERM has exercised a stabilising effect on the real exchange rate. The reduction in real exchange rate volatility has not been matched by an increase in interest rate volatility.

There is no evidence that increased variability in the real exchange rate under a flexible exchange rate system is caused by a change in the fluctuation of other real macroeconomic variables. Baxter and Stockman (1989) find no evidence of a change in the fluctuation of real macroeconomic variables which may determine the real exchange rate when there is a shift of monetary regime. Flood and Rose (1993) investigate a possible relationship between exchange rate volatility and a number of fundamental economic variables but fail to uncover any systematic impact. Edison and Pauls (1992) are unable to find economic time series which can explain the real exchange rate.

2.5.6   Estimates of inflation tax/seigniorage

A number of empirical studies give fairly low estimates of inflation tax/ seigniorage. Gros (1989) reaches the conclusion that seigniorage in the EC countries in 1987 made up between approximately 3 per cent (in Greece) and −1 per cent of GDP (in Denmark).[52] Inflation tax/seigniorage is most important for the Mediterranean countries, which have a relatively large monetary base and higher levels of inflation. Drazen (1989) emphasises the importance of inflation tax in Italy, Portugal, and Spain. The large monetary bases in the Mediterranean countries are largely due to high reserve requirements for banks. Cohen and Wyplosz (1989) conclude that inflation tax over the 1979–87 period has brought in on average between 0.6 per cent and 1.1 per cent of GDP for Germany, France, the UK, Belgium, Holland, and Denmark, while for Italy, Spain, and Ireland it has brought in respectively 3.9 per cent, 3.5 per cent, and 2.1 per cent of GDP. Bruno (1991) investigates the level of inflation tax under the assumption that money holdings are adjusted to the optimal inflation rate, reaching revenue estimates which are higher than in previous estimations. Buiter (1995) gives estimates for inflation tax and seigniorage in the EU countries which, with the exceptions of Greece and Portugal, vary between 0 and 1 per cent of GDP over the

---

[52]In Denmark, banks have traditionally had a negative liquidity position *vis-à-vis* the central bank, at times causing a negative monetary base.

1990–95 period for inflation tax and between −0.5 per cent and 1.5 per cent for seigniorage.

Diba and Martin (1995) and Roubini and Sachs (1989) examine whether differences with respect to inflation result from an optimal trade-off between inflation and the marginal tax rate on labour income. Negative findings are reached.[53]

2.5.7   *Efficiency losses from inflation*

Although many models assume money in either the household's utility function or as a factor in the production function, several studies question the importance of the effects which arise from a more efficient utilisation of money. Edey (1994) concludes that a more efficient utilisation of money in the USA will lead to a saving of 0.3 per cent of GDP when inflation is reduced from 10 per cent to 0 per cent.

In a widely quoted study, the EC Commission estimates the total saving of costs associated with transactions between EC countries at 1 per cent of GDP for small economies and approximately 0.4 point of GDP for large economies (EC Commission, 1990b). This estimate is, however, clearly overrated as it would imply that one out of three or four bank employees would be occupied with transactions involving exclusively changes between EU currencies.

2.6   Summary and conclusion

This chapter has surveyed the views in the literature concerning the neutrality of monetary variables. It has been demonstrated that the view of long-term monetary neutrality is shared by a large number of economists. The literature advances four channels through which inflation may affect the real economy in a model characterised by rational expectations, preferences based on real variables, and no costs associated with wage and price changes: (i) inflation has an impact on capital accumulation as inflation affects the portfolio choice between capital and money with a fixed nominal return, (ii) inflation determines real money holdings which in turn affects the productive efficiency of the economy and the utility of households, (iii) inflation implies a redistribution of real wealth from holders to issuers of money, especially in the form of inflation tax/ seigniorage, and (iv) depending on the economic structure, one-time

---

[53]Dornbusch (1989) likewise questions whether inflation tax plays a role for the determination of inflation.

changes in the money supply may lead to long-term changes in the capital stock. We find in the literature a discussion of several channels which could cause the monetary regime to have an impact on natural unemployment, for example by affecting the incentive to undertake labour market reform.

The chapter has further discussed the empirical evidence regarding long-term monetary neutrality. A number of investigations, notably the effect of interest rate changes on the real economy and the impact of inflation on the real interest rate and on the real stock return, largely support monetary non-neutrality in the long term. The evidence concerning the impact of monetary aggregates on output and a possible relationship between inflation and production is mixed. The real exchange rate adjusts towards purchasing power parity only over long periods, suggesting that there is an impact from nominal exchange rate changes on the real exchange rate over prolonged time periods.

3 The wage formation process

3.1 Introduction

Most analyses throughout the book are based on the assumption of a wage setting or labour supply function which implies a relationship between the real wage and employment. A positive relationship between the real wage and employment can arise from one of the following possibilities: (i) the nominal wage is set by a trade union which optimises preferences with respect to employment and the real wage, (ii) the nominal wage is set by an individual wage earner who is in a short-term monopoly position with respect to setting the nominal wage, for example, due to specialised skills, (iii) a representative household determines the labour supply to optimise lifetime utility with respect to consumption and leisure, and (iv) the nominal wage is set by firms which incur costs associated with turnover in staff. The production and unemployment levels which follow from wage setters' and firms' optimisation, are termed respectively natural production and natural unemployment.

This chapter analyses the main assumptions that are made with respect to wage formation throughout the book. It is demonstrated that all of the four above-mentioned wage formation processes cause a relationship between the real wage and employment. To simplify, we have chosen to base subsequent analyses throughout the book on a wage setting where the nominal wage is set by a trade union which includes all employees in an industrial sector comprising a large number of firms and which optimises preferences involving the real wage and employment. It follows, however, from the discussion in this chapter that the findings throughout the book regarding the impact of money on production do not depend on such an assumption of a trade union. The book suggests a variety of channels which cause inflation or variables specific to the monetary regime to affect the structural relationship between the real wage and employment and thus natural production. This means that there is a monetary impact on production in all cases where the wage

36

setting process is such as to create a relationship between the real wage and employment.

We use throughout the book a specific preference function for the wage setters, based on positive but declining marginal utilities from higher employment and higher real wage. It is demonstrated that the findings which are derived on the basis of this specific function, apply to all preference functions where the wage setters obtain positive utility from higher real wage and higher employment and where preferences are optimised at an employment level which is lower than full employment.

Section 3.2 briefly presents the main assumptions about wage formation/labour supply which are used throughout the book. *Section 3.3* analyses a benchmark model based on trade union wage formation. *Section 3.4* examines wage setting by an individual employee who is in a short-term monopoly position with respect to wage setting. *Section 3.5* discusses a representative household which optimises utility over an infinite time horizon with respect to consumption and leisure. *Section 3.6* examines a wage formation where the wage is set by the firm but where the wage relative to the wage in other firms affects workers' inclination to shift to other jobs. *Section 3.7* demonstrates that the findings derived from the specific preference function used throughout the book for a trade union apply to all preference functions where the wage setters reach their optimum at an employment level lower than full employment and where positive utility is derived from higher employment and higher real wage. *Section 3.8* discusses further model modifications. *Section 3.9* gives a summary and conclusion.

3.2   Basic assumptions

3.2.1   The relationship between the real wage and employment

In most analyses throughout the book, the basic conclusion of a monetary impact on natural employment is derived on the basis of a positive relationship between the real wage and employment. The book suggests a number of channels through which monetary factors can affect this relationship.

A distinction can be made between four kinds of wage formation processes which cause a relationship between the real wage and employment: (i) the wage is determined by a monopoly trade union which optimises preferences that include the real wage and employment, (ii) the wage is set by a single worker who is in a monopoly position *vis-à-vis* the firm, (iii) consumption and leisure are determined by a representative household which optimises lifetime utility, and (iv) the wage is set by a firm which faces an increase in costs associated with the turnover of staff when the nominal wage is lowered relative to other firms. With the exception of the individual who optimises lifetime utility with respect to consumption and leisure, it is common to these approaches that unemployment is involuntary.[1]

The wage setting of a trade union is analysed in a number of models, first developed by Layard and Nickell (1986).[2] Most of these models assume that the trade union includes all employees in the firm or in the economy and is thus able to set the nominal wage while the firm determines employment. It follows that natural unemployment is determined by the trade union's preferences. Three hypotheses are generally used to characterise the trade union's wage setting. In some models the trade union is seen as optimising the utilities of all union members ('the utilitarian union objective function'). In other models, the nominal wage is determined by a median employee who weighs the utilities of the real income derived under respectively employment and unemployment with the probabilities of being employed and unemployed. Finally, trade union behaviour is explained by the diverging interests of heterogeneous groups. According to the insider–outsider hypothesis, the employed wage earners have a disproportionate influence on wage setting while the unemployed members of the union are less active in the decision-making process. Other analyses take as their point of departure a conflict between union members and union leadership, the latter having a particular interest in the enlargement of the union. There is little empirical evidence on the objectives of the trade union.[3]

A relationship between the real wage and unemployment further results from models which analyse the bargaining between a single firm and a single wage earner.[4] Due to the wage earner's specialised skills, the firm exercises some degree of monopsony power while the employee has some degree of monopoly power. The employee demands a real wage above the reservation wage, that is, the wage which causes the employee to be indifferent with respect to being employed or unemployed. A lower unemployment induces the employee to demand a higher wage, causing a

---

[1]This is different to the hypothesis of the 'expectations-augmented Phillips curve' which views natural unemployment as being determined by workers' search for jobs, see Lucas (1972, 1978b).
[2]Surveys of the theory are found in Booth (1995), Dixon (1995), Layard, Nickell, and Jackman (1991), and Wren-Lewis (1995). Specific discussions of the trade union's preference function are found in Farber (1986) and in Oswald (1985).
[3]See Booth (1995) who concludes on a basis of a survey of the literature: 'we have little systematic evidence as to what trade union objectives are' (p. 87).
[4]See Blanchard and Katz (1997).

negative relationship between unemployment and the real wage. Firing costs become important in determining the relationship between the real wage and unemployment in the wage earners' 'labour supply function'.[5]

In addition to these approaches, a relationship between the real wage and employment arises when a representative household optimises lifetime utility with respect to consumption and leisure.

A positive relationship between the real wage and employment finally arises in models where the productivity of labour depends on the relative wage paid by the firm to the single wage earner. Phelps (1994) and Hoon and Phelps (1992, 1997) examine models in which the wage earners' decision to quit depends on unemployment and on the wage offered by the firm relative to the wage offered by other firms.

The endogenous determination of natural unemployment through optimisation which implies a relationship between the real wage and employment, means that natural production is determined by a variety of factors, for example, the income tax, labour market regulation, labour market institutions, and the real exchange rate. Shifts in these exogenous factors may explain why natural production changes. Phelps (1994) discusses that natural production is affected by supply shocks, changes in asset holdings, real interest rate changes, social transfers, taxes, customs, the rate of time preference, government transfers, government debt, and population growth. Gordon (1995, 1996, 1997) stresses the impact on natural production of shifts in the production function, taxes, and changes in the trade union's negotiating position. Dixon (1995) and Wren-Lewis (1995) analyse how natural production is affected by changes in the real exchange rate and in taxes.

The hypothesis of a positive relationship between the real wage and employment is supported by the empirical evidence which fails to show a counter cyclic development in the real wage.[6] The rise in unemployment experienced by the OECD countries since 1973 further seems to support the view of involuntary unemployment. Possible explanations behind the

[5]See Manzini and Snower (1996) who find that higher firing costs block entry and thus create a bilateral monopoly in the wage setting. A discussion of firing costs is also found in Blanchard and Katz (1997).
[6]MacDonald (1995) concludes that it is difficult to find a general cyclic pattern: 'There is a large empirical literature investigating the cyclic behaviour of real wages. The conclusion of this literature is that real wages are acyclic. This literature fails to find a strong and consistent procyclic or counter cyclic pattern to real wages. Some studies find a mild procyclic pattern, some studies an acyclic pattern and other studies a mild counter cyclic pattern. A reasonable description of these results is that real wages are roughly acyclic' (p. 114). The same conclusion is found in Abraham and Haltiwanger (1995).

higher unemployment could be, for example, a rise in the real interest rate and/or higher taxation.[7]

3.2.2   Other assumptions

The time horizon of the optimisation

While the time horizon of individual wage setters is determined by their rate of time preference, the time horizon in a trade union is influenced by the decision-making process in the trade union. One may conceive of a trade union leadership which discounts the future at a low rate because it faces the risk of being replaced. The trade union's time horizon is further affected by the turnover of members in the union, the trade union optimising the interests only of its current members. The risk of the firm going bankrupt further affects the time horizon of the wage setting which relates to an individual firm, a higher bankruptcy risk working to shorten the time horizon of the trade union. In all analyses throughout this book it is assumed, to simplify, that the time perspective of optimisation corresponds to the wage contract period.

The time perspective of optimisation is important for the determination of natural unemployment because a longer time horizon means that changes in the capital stock increasingly become endogenised in the model, implying that the wage setters take account of the impact which the wage setting has on the capital stock. This is important because it can be demonstrated, assuming Cobb–Douglas production technology, that the wage setters will aim at full employment in the case where (i) the wage setters are able to affect the firm's capital adjustment, and (ii) there is full adjustment of capital during the wage setters' time horizon. To simplify, we assume that the time horizon of the union, corresponding to the wage contract period, is so short that capital is exogenous to the wage setters, the investment decision being taken prior to wage setting. This assumption can be justified by a long planning period with respect to investments.[8]

---

[7]Rowthorn (1995) emphasises the lack of capital accumulation as a main factor behind the rise in unemployment. Phelps and Zoega (1998) argue that the rise in the real interest rate has been the main cause behind the rise in unemployment. Daveri and Tabellini (1997) find evidence in European OECD countries of the tax burden being important in explaining the rise in unemployment. Madsen (1998) examines the ability of three 'structuralist' theories for the wage formation to explain the rise in unemployment in OECD countries over the 1960–93 period. The real interest rate, the taxation of labour income, and the real oil price appear to offer the best explanations. It is, however, the general conclusion that all models give less than satisfactory empirical results.

[8]One could alternatively have assumed that capital is less than fully adjusted during the wage contract period, due to costs associated with capital adjustment.

Wage contracts

Most analyses throughout the book are based on nominal wage contracts. The assumption of nominal wage contracts in models based on rational behaviour has been criticised.[9] According to Benassy (1995b), nominal wage contracts can, however, be explained as rational behaviour when there are negotiation costs associated with changes in the nominal wage and when the wage setters desire an optimal trade-off between the real wage and employment. Nominal wage contracts reduce the deviation from the optimal trade-off between the real wage and employment when the economy is subjected to shocks during the wage contract period.

The institutional level of trade union wage setting

In a trade union wage setting, wage negotiations can take place at three different levels: (i) centralised wage negotiations where the trade union comprises all employees in the total economy, (ii) industry-wide wage negotiations where the trade union covers all employees in a single industrial sector which includes a large number of firms, and (iii) firm-specific wage negotiations where the trade union includes all employees in a single firm. Throughout the following discussion, we refer to the last two kinds of wage formation as decentralised wage setting while we refer to the first kind of wage formation as centralised wage setting.

The distinction between centralised and decentralised wage setting is important because the wage setters evaluate the impact which a given change in the nominal wage has on the variables which affect the wage setters' preferences. In the case of a centralised trade union, the wage setters control the nominal wage in the economy as a whole. The impact of a nominal wage change on other variables can thus be found on the basis of the macroeconomic model. In a wage formation where the wage setters do not control the aggregate wage level in the economy, that is, a trade union which covers employees in an industrial sector or a single firm, the price level in the economy is unaffected by the change in nominal wage while the impact on employment can be found from the reaction of a single firm to a change in the nominal wage.

---

[9]Lucas (1981) criticises the assumption of nominal wage contracts made by Fischer (1977) and Taylor (1979, 1980) because there is no obvious interest on the part of wage earners to conclude such contracts. Rankin (1994) remarks: 'While it is very desirable to explain rigid prices themselves, many major research programs on this topic during the past fifteen years (into implicit contracts, efficiency wages, imperfect competition, menu costs, to name a few) have so far failed to produce a non-Walrasian paradigm which has been widely accepted as having all the features we would reasonably seek in a basis for macroeconomics' (p. 4).

The distinction between wage setting which covers an industrial sector and wage setting which covers a single firm is important because it determines to what extent the firm is able to affect the wage setting through its decisions on capital and employment.

In the case where wage negotiations take place at the level of the industrial sector, a single firm is unable to affect the nominal wage. The nominal wage is thus exogenous to the firm when the firm undertakes its optimisation with respect to capital and employment. In the case where the wage is negotiated between the firm and a trade union covering all the employees in the firm, the question arises to what extent the firm through its decisions on employment and capital is able to affect the trade union's wage setting. With respect to the firm's employment decision, one may find it plausible that the firm is able to adjust employment instantaneously, implying that the firm sets employment on the basis of the prefixed nominal wage. With respect to capital formation, one may think of two possibilities. If the firm is able to adjust its capital stock during the wage contract period, the nominal wage can be treated as exogenous to the firm when it optimises the capital stock, the capital being set on the basis of a prefixed nominal wage. In the case where decisions about capital formation are made prior to wage setting, the firm will take the effect of the capital formation on wage setting into account when capital is adjusted. Wage setting is thus endogenous to the firm when capital is adjusted.

Most analyses throughout the book are based on the assumption that wage setting takes place at the level of the industrial sector. This means that the wage can be treated as exogenous when the firm undertakes its optimisation with respect to capital and employment.[10]

Expectations formation

In the case of wage contracts, the variables which enter the wage setters' preference function are the values of the endogenous variables, that is, production and the real wage, which are expected to be realised during the wage contract period. Depending on the information available to the wage setters and the costs associated with processing this information, one may perceive different kinds of expectations formation. The analyses throughout the book assume that wage setters are able to foresee perfectly the levels of the variables which are relevant for the wage setters'

---

[10]No change in basic conclusions would result if it had alternatively been assumed that the firm can influence wage setting through its capital decision. The question is briefly considered in section A.2 in the appendix.

optimisation or, in the case of stochastic variables, the stochastic distributions of these variables. This means that the wage setters form correct expectations concerning the production and real wage levels over the time horizon for wage setting, implying that correct expectations are formed concerning (a) future changes in economic policy, (b) future shifts in functional relationships, and (c) the economic structure.

3.3   Trade union wage setting

This section examines a basic model which determines natural production within a trade union wage setting. The point of departure is taken as a situation where (i) wage setting takes place at the level of the industrial sector, implying that the nominal wage is unaffected by the single firm's optimisation, and (ii) decisions on investments are taken in advance, implying that nominal wage setting has no impact on capital during the wage contract period. It is further assumed that the demand for goods is unaffected by monetary variables.

3.3.1   Model specification

The wage setters' optimisation
Consider a decentralised wage formation where the nominal wage is set at the level of an industrial sector, the assumptions regarding the wage formation can be expressed as

$$\max_{w}\left\{ U_t^u \left| \left(\frac{\partial p}{\partial w}\right) = 0, \quad \left(\frac{\partial q}{\partial w}\right) = 0, \quad \left(\frac{\partial k}{\partial w}\right) = 0 \right. \right\}, \tag{3.1}$$

where U^u is the wage setters' utility (a higher positive net value denoting an increase in utility), p the producer price (logarithmic value), w the nominal wage (logarithmic value), q the consumer price (logarithmic value), and k the capital stock (logarithmic value).

Relation (3.1) shows that changes in the nominal wage in decentralised wage setting have no impact on the macroeconomic variables which enter the wage setters' preferences, that is, the producer and consumer price levels (cf. below). It is further assumed that wage setters have no influence on capital stock. This may be explained by inflexibility with respect to investment, for example due to a long planning period.

The trade union optimises preferences which include employment relative to full employment and the real wage. Preferences are specified as

$$U_t^u = -f^u \left(\frac{L_t}{L_t''}\right)^{-\gamma} - \left(\frac{W_t}{Q_t}\right)^{-\theta}, \; f^u > 0, \; \gamma > 0, \; \theta > 0, \; L_t'' \equiv 1,$$

$$(3.2)$$

where L is employment, L'' full employment, W the nominal wage, and Q the consumer price.

The preferences specified by (3.2) express that the wage setters derive positive utility from an increase in the real wage and an increase in employment/production. The weight attached to employment relative to the real wage is expressed by f^u.

The preference function shown by (3.2) implies that the marginal utilities derived by the wage setters from higher employment and the higher real wage are positive and declining. From (3.2) follows

$$\frac{\partial U^u}{\partial L} = f^u \gamma L_t^{-\gamma-1} > 0,$$

$$\frac{\partial^2 U^u}{\partial L^2} = -f^u \gamma (\gamma + 1) L_t^{-\gamma-2} < 0,$$

$$\frac{\partial U^u}{\partial (W/Q)} = \theta \left(\frac{W_t}{Q_t}\right)^{-\theta-1} > 0,$$

$$\frac{\partial^2 U^u}{\partial (W/Q)^2} = -(\theta + 1)\theta \left(\frac{W_t}{Q_t}\right)^{-\theta-2} < 0. \qquad (3.3)$$

The preference function specified by (3.2) is concave if the following condition is met

$$\frac{\partial^2 U^u}{\partial L^2} = -\gamma(\gamma + 1) f^u L_t^{-\gamma-2}$$

$$- \theta(\theta + 1)\left(\frac{W_t}{Q_t}\right)^{\theta-2} \left(\frac{\partial(W/Q)}{\partial Y}\right)\left(\frac{\partial Y}{\partial L}\right)$$

$$+ \theta \left(\frac{W_t}{Q_t}\right)^{-\theta-1} \left(\frac{\partial^2(W/Q)}{\partial Y^2}\right)\left(\frac{\partial Y}{\partial L}\right) < 0, \qquad (3.4)$$

where Y is the non-logarithmic value of production.

It follows that the first term on the right-hand side of (3.4) is negative. The second term is positive as $(\partial Y/\partial L) > 0$ and $\partial(W/Q)/\partial Y < 0$ for the economic models examined in the following. It depends on the economic model whether $\partial^2(W/Q)/\partial Y^2$, and thus the last term on the right-hand side of (3.4), is negative. This means that it cannot be determined unambiguously whether the condition given by (3.4) is met. Throughout the book, for all analyses, we simply assume that the condition of concavity is met.

The firm's profit optimisation

We consider a representative firm which maximises the firm-owners' consumption possibilities over an infinite time horizon. This gives the following specification of the firm's profit maximisation at a given time

$$\max_{K,L}\left\{\left(\frac{v_T}{P_T}\right)\bigg|\frac{\partial P}{\partial Y}=0,\ \frac{\partial W}{\partial Y}=0,\ \frac{\partial r}{\partial Y}=0\right\}, \tag{3.5}$$

$$T = t, t+1, \ldots,$$

$$\frac{v_T}{P_T} = Y_T - L_T\frac{W_T}{P_T} - K_T(1 + r_{T-1}), \tag{3.6}$$

$$Y_T = (K_T)^a(L_T)^{1-a}, \quad 0 < a < 1, \tag{3.7}$$

$$\log(1 + r_T) = \log(1 + i_T) - (p_{T+1} - p_T), \tag{3.8}$$

where v is profit, i the nominal interest rate, and r the real interest rate. K shows the non-logarithmic value of the capital stock. a is the elasticity of production with respect to capital.

Relation (3.5) specifies that the firm in each period maximises real profit with respect to employment and capital. The optimisation takes place under the following assumptions: (i) the firm is unable to affect the producer price, that is, there is perfect competition in the goods markets; (ii) the firm is unable to affect the nominal wage which is determined at the level of the industrial sector; and (iii) the firm is unable to affect the nominal interest rate, that is, there is a perfect financial market. (3.6) gives the definition of the real profit, the capital stock depreciating fully in the course of the time period. (3.7) expresses Cobb–Douglas production technology with a homogeneous production function of degree 1. (3.8) gives the definition of the real interest rate.

Optimising (3.6) with respect to employment, and using (3.5) and (3.7)–(3.8), gives the conditions for the firm's optimisation as

$$y_t - k_t = \log(1 + r_{t-1}) - \log(a), \tag{3.9}$$

$$y_t - l_t = w_t - p_t - \log(1 - a). \tag{3.10}$$

Relation (3.9) gives the optimum condition with respect to capital, (3.10) with respect to employment.

Goods market equilibrium

A small economy A is considered, with all variables relating to economy A unless otherwise specified. The rest of the world is represented by a large economy B. To simplify, we do not take into account the import demand from country B. The economic structure can be presented as

$$y_t = z(p_t^B + x_t - p_t) + d_t, \quad z > 0, \tag{3.11}$$

$$\Omega_s = \Omega_s(r, g, \tau), \quad \Omega_s \equiv \log\left(\frac{D}{Y}\right), \quad g_t = \bar{g}_t, \quad \tau_t = \bar{\tau}_t,$$

$$\frac{\partial \Omega_s}{\partial r} \equiv \Omega_{sr} < 0, \quad \frac{\partial \Omega_s}{\partial g} \equiv \Omega_{sg} > 0, \quad \frac{\partial \Omega_s}{\partial \tau} \equiv \Omega_{st} < 0, \tag{3.12}$$

$$q_t \equiv p_t + \varphi(p_t^B + x_t - p_t), \quad 0 < \varphi < 1, \tag{3.13}$$

$$p_t^B = \bar{p}_t^B, \tag{3.14}$$

where d and D represent domestic demand (respectively logarithmic and non-logarithmic values), g government purchases of goods and services relative to production, x the nominal exchange rate (number of country A's currency units per currency unit of the foreign country B) (logarithmic value), and τ the tax rate on labour income. Ω_s shows domestic demand relative to domestic production in the steady state (logarithmic value). Variables without time indications show steady state levels.

Relation (3.11) expresses goods market equilibrium, the demand for goods being a function of the real exchange rate and total domestic demand. The derivation is found in the appendix. (3.12) shows total domestic demand relative to production as a function of the real interest rate and fiscal policy. As we are interested in the long-term determination of production, the demand for goods relative to production refers to a steady-state equilibrium, a steady-state equilibrium being characterised by a constant production growth rate and constant levels of financial variables relative to nominal production (see section A.6 in the appendix for a discussion). (3.12) is derived in the appendix on the basis of an overlapping generations model and corresponds to (A.47). (3.13) gives the consumer price. Relation (3.14) expresses that country A is a small economy, all variables relating to the large economy B (the rest of the world) being exogenously given. In the further analysis, we do not make any specific assumptions regarding the determination of the real interest rate, treating it as exogenously given.

3.3.2   Determination of natural production

The wage setters determine the nominal wage through optimising the preference function given by (3.2). As all variables relate to steady-state equilibrium, time indications are deleted. Combining (3.1)–(3.2) and (3.7)–(3.14) gives the condition for the wage setters' optimum under decentralised wage formation

$$
y^{DW} - y'' = \left(\frac{\theta}{\gamma}\right)\left(\frac{\varphi}{z}\right)\Omega_s(r, g, \tau) - \left(\frac{1}{\gamma}\right)\epsilon^{DW} - \left(\frac{a}{1-a}\right)\left(1 + \frac{\theta}{\gamma}\right)\log(1 + r)
$$

$$
+ \left(\frac{\theta}{\gamma}\right)\log(1 - \tau) + \left(\frac{\theta}{\gamma}\right)\log(1 - a) + \left(\frac{a}{1-a}\right)\left(1 + \frac{\theta}{\gamma}\right)\log(a),
$$

$$
\epsilon^{DW} = \log\left(\frac{\theta a}{f^u \gamma}\right), \tag{3.15}
$$

where y^{DW} is natural production under decentralised wage formation at the level of the industrial sector (logarithmic value), and ϵ^{DW} reflects the wage setters' preferences with respect to employment and the real wage and the trade-off faced by the wage setters between employment and the real wage.

There is only unemployment when the right-hand side of (3.15) is negative. From (3.15) it follows that the natural production is determined by the following factors:

(1) *The wage setters' preferences for employment relative to the real wage and the trade-off between the real wage and employment faced by the wage setters, represented by the term ϵ^{DW}*. A stronger preference for employment relative to the real wage, that is, a higher value of f^u, and a larger increase in the utility derived from a given rise in employment, represented by a higher value of γ, causes natural production to rise. Conversely, a larger increase in the utility derived from a given increase in the real wage, represented by θ, means that the wage setters set natural production at a lower level to reach a higher real wage. The wage setters' trade-off between employment and the real wage, that is, the change in the real wage which can be reached for a given change in employment, is given by $-a$ under a decentralised wage setting, cf. (3.7) and (3.10). This trade-off enters the term ϵ^{DW}. A larger numerical value of the sacrifice ratio between the real wage and employment implies that the wage setters can reach a bigger increase in the real wage for a given decrease in production. This induces wage setters to opt for a higher real wage, causing natural employment and production to fall.

(2) *The real interest rate r.* The real interest rate influences natural production through an impact on the demand for goods function and through a direct impact on capital accumulation. A shift in the demand for goods function leads to a real appreciation and thus a higher real wage, driving a wedge between the consumer and producer price. This improves the combinations of the real wage and employment which can be reached by the wage setters, causing the wage setters to aim at higher production. A rise in capital stock likewise improves the wage setters' possibility of reaching a high real wage at a given employment level.

(3) *Government purchases of goods and services relative to production g.* A rise in government purchases of goods and services increases the demand for goods, causing a real appreciation which improves the combinations of the real wage and employment that can be reached by the wage setters.

(4) *The tax rate on labour income τ.* A lower tax rate on labour income affects the demand for goods and thus increases natural production through a real appreciation. A further positive effect arises from a lower tax rate because it directly improves the wage setters' possibility of reaching a high real wage at a given employment level.

The analysis above concerns a small economy. The same factors affect natural production when several large countries are considered. In a model with n large economies, the $n-1$ real exchange rates and the real interest rate bring about equilibrium in the goods markets for the n large countries. The natural production levels in the large economies are determined by the same factors as in the small economy, that is, by the variables which enter (i) the wage setters' preferences, (ii) the production functions, and (iii) the relations for goods market equilibrium.

3.3.3   Policy implications

An important finding from the analysis above is that fiscal policy instruments, that is, government purchases of goods and services relative to production g and the tax rate on labour income $τ$, have an impact on natural production. Both the two fiscal policy instruments have an impact on natural production through the demand for goods which affects natural production because the real exchange rate drives a wedge between the consumer price and the producer price, that is, a terms-of-trade effect. In addition, the tax rate has a direct effect on natural production.

Relation (3.15) gives no direct support to the proposition that natural production is affected by variables which are influenced by monetary policy, for example, the inflation rate, or by factors which depend on the monetary regime, for example, parameters which enter the money demand function. As the model is formulated, it is consistent with monetary neutrality. Changes in the money supply cause similar changes in the price level without affecting natural production. The model opens, however, the possibility of a monetary impact on natural production insofar as monetary policy instruments or factors specific to a monetary regime influence the factors which determine natural production. This could be either domestic demand relative to production, the real interest rate, or the fiscal policy stance. Throughout the following chapters we will examine several channels which could create such a monetary impact on natural production, working either through the demand for goods, the real interest rate, and/or the fiscal policy stance.

In the case of perfect financial integration, the real interest rate is exogenously determined through the international capital market (see section A.10 in the appendix). The impact of domestic monetary factors on the real interest rate in an open economy therefore pre-supposes imperfect integration of financial markets.[11] In a closed economy the real interest rate is determined by equilibrium in the goods market while there is no impact from the real exchange rate on natural production.

Although monetary factors have no direct impact on natural production, the monetary regime may have an indirect influence through changes in the economic structure. Thus, one may perceive that a monetary union increases the integration of goods markets due to the removal of exchange rate uncertainty. A deeper integration of goods markets appears in the model as an increase in real exchange rate elasticity with respect to goods from the foreign union country, that is, an increase in z. It results from (3.15) that it depends on the economic structure whether a rise in z reduces or increases natural production. In the case where the economy runs a trade balance deficit, that is, $\Omega_s < 0$, it follows from (3.15) that a rise in z reduces natural production.[12] This reduction in production arises because a larger value of z causes a lower real wage rate at each given level of production. It further follows from (3.15) that an increase in goods market integration, that is, a higher value of z, dampens the impact on production of fiscal policy g.

---

[11]An analysis of imperfect integration of securities markets is found in chapter 4, while chapter 5 considers imperfect integration of bank markets.
[12]Danthine and Hunt (1994) find that goods market integration has a positive impact on natural production.

3.4   Individual monopoly wage setting

We next turn to the case where a single wage earner negotiates the wage with an employer. It was claimed in section 3.3.1 that a labour supply function characterised by a relationship between the real wage and employment can be derived when an individual wage earner negotiates with the employer. In this section we will present a hypothesis which explains such a relationship. The analysis assumes that the wage earner is in a short-term monopoly position to determine the real wage, for example due to specialised skills, but has to weigh an increase in the real wage against the risk of subsequently being fired during the wage contract period. It is further assumed that the risk of being fired depends on the employee's wage relative to the general wage level in the economy and on the unemployment rate.

3.4.1   Model specification

The wage earner's preference function
    The behaviour of a representative wage earner i is considered. The wage earner negotiates a nominal wage contract with a duration of one time period, maximising over an infinite time horizon the discounted utility of the real income. Wage earner i's optimisation at time t is expressed as follows

$$\max_{w^i}\left\{E_t(U_t^{i,e}) = \sum_{T=t}^{\infty} \beta^{T-t}E\left[u\left(\frac{W_T^i}{Q_T}\right)\right]\right\}, \ 0 < \beta < 1,$$

$$T = t, t+1, \ldots, \tag{3.16}$$

$$E_t(U_T^{i,e}) = \pi u\left(\frac{W_T^i}{Q_T}\right) + \beta\pi E_t(U_{T+1}^{i,e}) + \beta(1-\pi)E_t(U_{T+1}^{i,u}),$$

$$0 < \pi < 1, \tag{3.17}$$

$$E_t(U_T^{i,u}) = \nu u\left(\frac{W_T^i}{Q_T}\right) + \beta\nu E_t(U_{T+1}^{i,e}) + \beta(1-\nu)\Theta E_t(U_{T+1}^{i,u}),$$

$$0 < \nu < 1, \ 0 < \Theta < 1, \tag{3.18}$$

$$u\left(\frac{W_T^i}{Q_T}\right) = \log\left(\frac{W_T^i}{Q_T}\right), \ \frac{W_T^i}{Q_T} \geq 1, \ u' \equiv \frac{\partial u^i}{\partial(W^i/Q)} > 0, \tag{3.19}$$

$$\frac{W_T^i}{Q_T} = \frac{W_{T+1}^i}{Q_{T+1}} \equiv \frac{W^i}{Q}, \tag{3.20}$$

where $U^{i,e}$ is the utility over an infinite time horizon for a representative wage earner i who is in employment at the beginning of the time period, $U^{i,u}$ is the utility over an infinite time horizon for a representative wage earner who is unemployed at the beginning of the time period, W^i the nominal wage for the representative wage earner i, $u(\cdot)$ the period utility, π the probability for an employed wage earner of staying in employment in a given time period, v the probability that an unemployed wage earner finds employment in the course of the time period, Θ the likelihood that the wage earner remains in the labour force after having been unemployed in one time period, and β the time discounting factor. $E_t(\cdot)$ shows the expectation concerning a variable at the beginning of time t.

Relation (3.16) gives the utility expected by wage earner i over an infinite time horizon. The utility from real income in each time period is discounted at the subjective time discounting factor β. The wage earner sets the nominal wage to optimise preferences. We assume that the utility which is derived from the real earnings in unemployment, is zero. The wage earner's asset holdings are neglected.

Relation (3.17) shows that the expected utility for a wage earner in employment at the beginning of the time period corresponds to (i) the utility from the real wage in time period t, weighed with the probability of the wage earner being in employment π, (ii) the discounted value of the expected utility for the wage earner at the beginning of the subsequent time period when the wage earner is in employment, weighed with the probability that the wage earner is in employment at the beginning of the next time period π, and (iii) the discounted value of the expected utility for the wage earner at the beginning of the subsequent time period when the wage earner is unemployed, weighed with the probability that the wage earner is unemployed at the beginning of the next time period $1 - \pi$. We consider an equilibrium in which the probability of being in employment π lies at a constant level.

Relation (3.18) shows that the expected utility for an unemployed wage earner corresponds to (i) the utility from the real wage in time period t weighed with the probability that the unemployed wage earner finds employment v, (ii) the discounted value of the expected utility for the wage earner at the beginning of the subsequent time period when the wage earner is in employment, weighed with the probability that the wage earner is in employment at the beginning of the next time period v, and (iii) the discounted value of the expected utility for the wage earner at the beginning of the subsequent time period when the wage earner is unemployed, weighed with the probability that the wage earner is unemployed at the beginning of the next time period $1 - v$ and with the probability that the wage earner remains in the labour force, expressed by Θ.

We assume that a wage earner with a certain probability, expressed by $1 - \Theta$, leaves the labour force after having been unemployed during one time period.

Relation (3.19) shows the utility derived by employee i from the real wage in each time period, represented by the logarithmic utility function. The wage earner derives a positive but declining marginal utility from a higher real wage. We finally assume by (3.20) that the real wage lies at a constant level in each time period, implying that the labour productivity of employed wage earners is constant. (3.20) is consistent with equilibrium.

Explaining the firing risk

We next discuss how the wage earner's risk of being fired is determined. The following relationship is assumed

$$\pi_t = i(y_t - y'', w_t^i - w_t), \ \ y_t \leq y'' \equiv 0,$$

$$\pi_y \equiv \frac{\partial \pi}{\partial (y - y'')} > 0, \ \ \pi_w \equiv \frac{\partial \pi}{\partial (w^i - w)} < 0, \tag{3.21}$$

where y'' is the production which corresponds to full employment.

Relation (3.21) expresses that the probability of maintaining present employment during the wage contract period depends on (i) production in the economy, and (ii) the nominal wage set by the wage earner relative to the general wage level in the economy. The probability of maintaining the current job is a positive function of production, that is, there is a smaller risk of being fired when there is higher production, while a higher wage for wage earner j relative to the general wage level in the economy, that is, a higher value of W^i/W, increases the risk of being fired.

We will next discuss the rationale behind the hypothesis of firing risk shown by (3.21). As one justification, we can take the point of departure in the contacts which a firm makes to other wage earners in the course of the wage contract period. One may assume that wage earner i is fired if the firm during the wage contract period encounters another wage earner z whose nominal wage demand relative to marginal productivity is smaller than for wage earner i. Wage earner i is thus fired if the following condition is met

$$\left(\frac{W_t^i}{P_t}\right) \bigg/ \left(\frac{\partial Y}{\partial L}\right)^i > \left(\frac{W_t^z}{P_t}\right) \bigg/ \left(\frac{\partial Y}{\partial L}\right)^z, \tag{3.22}$$

where $\partial Y/\partial L$ expresses the marginal labour productivity, and P the producer price.

Assuming that all wage earners except wage earner i receive the average wage, that is, W, and normalising the marginal productivity for employee i to unity, (3.22) can be rewritten as

$$\left(\frac{\partial Y}{\partial L}\right)^z > \frac{W_t}{W_t^i}. \qquad (3.23)$$

Relation (3.23) shows that the wage earner is fired if the firm during the wage contract period encounters another wage earner whose marginal productivity relative to wage demand is higher than that of the wage earner in employment.

It follows immediately from (3.23) that a higher nominal wage relative to other wage earners increases the risk of being fired, explaining the positive relationship between firing risk and relative wage assumed by (3.21).

From (3.23) it further follows that the risk for wage earner i of being fired depends on two factors: (i) how labour productivities are distributed among wage earners, and (ii) the process through which the firm encounters wage earners who are willing to take on employment in the firm. With respect to the second factor, that is, the extent of contacts between a firm and other wage earners, one may conceive of the firm having contacts with a larger number of employees when production lies at a low level. The rationale is that a firm receives more applications for vacant jobs and is thus more likely to find wage earners with high labour productivity relative to the wage demand under high unemployment than when unemployment is low. This can explain the negative relationship between firing risk and production specified in (3.21). The relationship between firing risk and production is, however, not unambiguous. One may alternatively conceive of a firm having a larger choice of possible candidates for a job when there is low unemployment because a low unemployment makes wage earners more inclined to take the risk involved in a job shift.

The explanation of the firing risk set out above takes as the point of departure the firm evaluating possible candidates for a job on the basis of contacts. An alternative explanation could be based on the costs incurred by a firm when there is a change of employee. It may be assumed that the firm incurs one-time costs when there is a change of employee, for example, costs associated with the training of the new wage earner. The firm only considers firing an employee if a lower wage for another employee makes it worthwhile to incur such one-time costs. One may further perceive that the firm has imperfect information regarding the productivity of the new employee; the productivity of newly employed wage earners following a stochastic distribution. In this case, a high nominal wage for wage earner i relative to the other wage earners increases the likelihood that the firm can benefit from firing wage earner i and incur the one-time cost associated with employing a new wage earner. This means that the firing risk becomes a function of the nominal wage relative to other wage earners as specified in (3.21). The larger choice among wage earners in the case of large unemployment can be seen as reducing the variation in the stochastic distribution for the productivity of a new wage earner, thus increasing the firing risk. This explains the positive relationship between production and firing risk assumed in (3.21).

The macroeconomic structure
Turning to the macroeconomic level, the wage for wage earner i corresponds to the average wage level in the economy, that is

$$W_t^i = W_t. \tag{3.24}$$

A small open economy is considered. The macroeconomic structure is given as (3.7) and (3.9)–(3.14). We only consider an equilibrium where production in each time period lies at the same level, that is, $y_t = y_{t-1}$.

3.4.2   Determination of natural production

Time indications are deleted as variables lie at the same level in each period. The wage earner in employment optimises lifetime utility by setting the nominal wage in time period t. Optimising the lifetime utility given by (3.17) with respect to the nominal wage in period t, and using (3.20) and (3.24), gives the condition for the wage earner's optimum as

$$\left(\frac{\pi}{\pi_w}\right)\left(\frac{W}{Q}\right)u'\left(\frac{W}{Q}\right) + u\left(\frac{W}{Q}\right) + \beta[E(U^{i,e}) - E(U^{i,u})] = 0. \tag{3.25}$$

Combining (3.17)–(3.18) and (3.20) gives lifetime utility for an unemployed wage earner as a function of lifetime utility for an employed wage earner as

$$E(U^{i,u}) = \left(\frac{v}{N_1}\right)u\left(\frac{W}{Q}\right) + \left(\frac{\beta v}{N_1}\right)E(U^{i,e}), \quad N_1 \equiv 1 - \beta\Theta(1 - v) > 0. \tag{3.26}$$

Combining (3.17), (3.20), and (3.26) gives the expected lifetime utility for an employed wage earner as function of the utility of the real wage as

$$E(U^{i,e}) = u\left(\frac{W}{Q}\right)\left(\frac{N_1\pi + \beta(1 - \pi)}{(1 - \beta\pi)N_1 - \beta^2 v(1 - \pi)}\right). \tag{3.27}$$

Combining (3.19) with (3.25)–(3.27) gives the following condition for natural production, that is, the production level at which the representative wage earner optimises preferences:

$$w - q = -\left(\frac{\pi}{\pi_w}\right)\left(\frac{1}{N_2}\right) - \log(1 - \tau), \quad N_2 \equiv 1 + \left(\frac{\beta\Phi}{N_1}\right),$$

$$\Phi \equiv \frac{\pi(N_1 - \beta v)^2 + \beta v(N_1 - \beta v)}{-\pi\beta(N_1 - \beta v) + N_1 - \beta^2 v} = \Phi(\pi). \tag{3.28}$$

Relation (3.28) specifies the real wage in equilibrium, that is, the real wage which corresponds to natural production. As the term Φ is a function of the firing risk π which in turn is determined by production, cf. (3.21), it follows from (3.28) that the wage formation causes a relationship between the real wage and production. This corresponds to trade union wage setting. It results from (3.28) that the impact of production on Φ cannot be determined without knowledge of the parameter values. This means that it cannot be determined unambiguously whether a rise in production causes a higher or lower real wage.

Further combining (3.7) and (3.9)–(3.14) with (3.28) shows the impact of exogenous variables on natural production as

$$d(y^{IW} - y'') = \left(\frac{1}{N_3}\right)\left(\frac{\varphi}{z}\right)d\Omega_s - \left(\frac{1}{N_3}\right)\left(\frac{a}{1 - a}\right)d\log(1 + r)$$

$$+ \left(\frac{1}{N_3}\right)d\log(1 - \tau),$$

$$N_3 \equiv -\left(\frac{\pi_w\pi_y}{N_2}\right) + \left(\frac{\pi\pi_{wy}}{N_2}\right) + \left(\frac{\beta}{N_1}\right)\left(\frac{\Phi_\pi\pi_y\pi_w\pi}{(N_2)^2}\right), \tag{3.29}$$

where y^{IW} denotes natural production under individual wage setting.

Natural production is determined by the factors which determine the demand for goods, that is, domestic demand relative to production Ω_s, the real interest rate r, and the tax rate on labour income τ. The sign of the term Φ_π depends on the economic structure. It thus depends on the economic structure whether a change in the exogenous variables increases or decreases natural production.

3.4.3 Policy implications

Basically the same conclusions with respect to natural production result from (3.29) as when a trade union sets the nominal wage. Thus, factors which affect the demand function for goods, for example, fiscal policy, have an impact on natural production. Monetary variables have no impact on natural production. Again, the model opens up the possibility that monetary variables can have an impact on natural production if monetary factors affect either the demand function for goods, the real interest rate, or the fiscal policy stance. A monetary impact on these factors is analysed in the following chapters.

The time discounting factor has an impact on natural production by affecting the discounted value of future income streams. A similar effect can be found in models based on trade union wage setting if the optimisation reaches beyond the wage contract period.

Comparing the above analysis of a single wage earner's wage setting with the trade union's wage setting, analysed in section 3.3, it follows that no unambiguous conclusion can be reached as to whether natural production lies at a higher or lower level when a single wage earner negotiates the wage compared with trade union wage setting. When the nominal wage is set by the trade union, natural production depends on the union's preferences with respect to employment and the real wage, while in the case of an individual wage setting, natural production is determined by the single wage earner's preferences with respect to the real wage and the risk of being fired during the wage contract period. No comparison can be made between these preferences. The analysis thus fails to support the view that it is possible to reach lower unemployment by implementing labour market reforms which weaken the power of trade unions.

3.5   Optimisation of consumption and leisure

Natural employment is also affected by the real wage and employment when an individual optimises preferences with respect to leisure and consumption. The real wage determines the agent's consumption possibilities. This means that findings of a monetary impact on production which are due to an impact of monetary factors on the relationship between the real wage and employment, extends also to the case of an individual who optimises consumption and leisure. Thus, it would not affect the conclusions derived throughout the following chapters if we, as an alternative point of departure, had chosen to consider an individual who optimises utility with respect to consumption and leisure over an infinite time horizon.[13]

There are, however, differences between, on one side, the wage setting undertaken by a trade union and, on the other side, the wage formation

---

[13]Such an approach would correspond to Rankin (1998).

which follows from a single individual's optimisation. First, the impact of the exogenous factors which affect the real wage, is ambiguous when a representative agent maximises lifetime utility with respect to leisure and consumption. In this latter case, a change in the relationship between the real wage and production affects the labour supply through both a substitution effect and a real income effect. An improvement in the possibility of reaching a higher real wage due to changes in exogenous factors thus works to increase labour supply through the substitution effect and to depress labour supply through the real income effect. Second, a trade union can endogenise the impact of wage setting on capital accumulation in the firm while an individual is unable to affect capital accumulation.[14] A centralised trade union can include also the effects of changes in macroeconomics variables. Finally, the time horizon is different in the different kinds of wage setting. While one may expect an individual agent to optimise lifetime utility, the time perspective of the trade union is determined by factors which are specific to trade union wage setting, most importantly by the decision-making procedure in the trade union and by the turnover of staff in the firm (see above).

We have chosen in the following analyses to ignore the view of a representative agent who optimises lifetime utility with respect to consumption and leisure. In general, wage earners are unable to affect the number of working hours. Moreover, there is little empirical foundation for the view that agents optimise with respect to consumption and leisure.[15]

3.6   The firm's wage setting

In this section, we examine the relationship between the real wage and employment when a firm sets the nominal wage. The analysis is based on Phelps (1994) and Hoon and Phelps (1992, 1997) who take as the point of departure a situation where firms want to reduce the number of wage earners quitting the firm, as an increase in staff turnover affects the costs incurred on training. Firms bid up wages when there is low unemployment and thus a high turnover rate of staff, causing at the macroeconomic level an increase in unemployment which in turn dampens the wage earners' willingness to quit the firm. This process continues until

---

[14]This would not affect the findings throughout the book which are based on the assumption that wage setters are unable to affect capital adjustment due to inflexibility with respect to investment planning, see section 3.2.2 above.
[15]See, for example, Heckman (1993).

a balance between the real wage and unemployment is reached. Similar conclusions result if it is assumed that firms want to reduce 'shirking' by paying a higher real wage.

3.6.1   Model specification

We assume that the nominal wage is set by a representative firm which optimises profit. The firm produces with Cobb–Douglas production technology. The firm incurs a cost associated with the turnover of staff, due to costs associated with training. This gives the following specification of the firm's profit

$$\max_{L^j, K^j, W^j} \left\{ \left(\frac{\upsilon_T^j}{P_T} \right)(1 + r_T)^{-(T-t)} \,|\, \frac{\partial P}{\partial Y^j} = 0, \; \frac{\partial r}{\partial Y^j} = 0 \right\}, \quad T = t, t+1, \dots$$

(3.30)

$$\frac{\upsilon_T^j}{P_T} = Y_T^j - L_T^j \frac{W_T^j}{P_T} - K_T^j(1 + r_{T-1}) - C\left(\frac{W_T^j}{W_T}, \frac{L_T}{L_T''} \right),$$

$$C_W \equiv \frac{\partial C}{\partial (W^j/W)} < 0, \; C_L \equiv \frac{\partial C}{\partial (L/L'')} > 0,$$

(3.31)

$$C = \left(\frac{W_T^j}{W_T} \right)^{-c_1} \left(\frac{L_T}{L_T''} \right)^{c_2}, \; c_1 > 0, \; c_2 > 0,$$

(3.32)

where C shows the real cost to a firm from the turnover of staff. υ^j, Y^j, L^j, K^j, and W^j are respectively profit, production, employment, capital, and nominal wage in the representative firm j while Y, L, K, and W show production, employment, capital, and nominal wage levels at the macroeconomic level.

It is specified by (3.30) that the firm sets employment, capital, and the nominal wage to optimise profit. The firm is unable to control variables at the macroeconomic level (not written). (3.31) shows the firm's profit in a given time period. Profit deflated by the price level is given as production with the deduction of the real wage cost, the real cost of capital, and a term C which reflects the cost related to the turnover of staff, for example, caused by costs associated with training. This cost is a positive function of staff turnover which depends on (i) the wage paid to the employees in the firm relative to the wage paid in other firms, shown by W^j/W, and (ii) the unemployment rate L/L''. Staff turnover is negatively affected by a higher relative wage in the firm and positively affected by lower unemployment. It is assumed by (3.31) that capital fully depreciates in the course of the time period. To simplify, (3.32) gives a specification of the cost associated with the turnover of staff.

We further assume that the firm produces with Cobb–Douglas production technology, shown by (3.7). Combining (3.7) with (3.30)–(3.32) gives the following optimum conditions

$$y_t^j - k_t^j = \log(1 + r_{t-1}) - \log(a), \tag{3.33}$$

$$y_t^j - l_t^j = w_t^j - p_t - \log(1 - a), \tag{3.34}$$

$$\log(c_1) - c_1(w_t^j - w_t) + c_2(l_t - l_t'') = l_t^j + (w_t^j - p_t), \tag{3.35}$$

where y^j, k^j, l^j, and w^j show the logarithmic values of respectively Y^j, K^j, L^j, and W^j.

Relations (3.33)–(3.35) show the relationship between the nominal wage, capital, and employment which characterises the firm's profit optimisation.

3.6.2 *Determination of natural production*

Production, capital stock, employment, and the nominal wage in the representative firm corresponds to the macroeconomic levels, that is

$$y_t^j = y_t, \quad k_t^j = k_t, \quad l_t^j = l_t, \quad w_t^j = w_t. \tag{3.36}$$

Combining (3.36) with (3.34) and assuming a fixed labour supply which is normalised at one, that is, $L'' = 1$, we reach the following relationship between the real wage and employment

$$w_t - p_t = (c_2 - 1)l_t + \log(c_1). \tag{3.37}$$

Relation (3.37) specifies a relationship between the real wage and employment. In contrast to the relationship derived in previous sections, the real wage is expressed by the producer price, not the consumer price. Furthermore, it depends on the size of the parameter c_2 whether the relationship is positive or negative.

Relation (3.37) can be combined with (3.32)–(3.34) and (3.36) to give the equilibrium employment as a function of the real interest rate

$$y_t^{FW} = -\left(\frac{1}{N_4}\right)\log(1 + r_{t-1}) + \left(\frac{1}{N_4}\right)\log(a)$$

$$+ \left(\frac{1}{N_4}\right)\left(\frac{1-a}{a}\right)\left(\frac{1}{c_2}\right)[\log(1-a) - \log(c_1)],$$

$$N_4 \equiv \left(\frac{1-a}{a}\right)\left(1 - \frac{1}{c_2}\right), \tag{3.38}$$

where y^{FW} shows natural production when the firm sets the wage.

Relation (3.38) shows production as a function of the real interest rate. It depends on the size of the parameter c_2 whether production is increased or lowered by a higher real interest rate.

3.6.3   Policy implications

Relation (3.38) shows a relationship between the real interest rate and production in the case where the firm sets the nominal wage and the firm incurs costs associated with the turnover of staff. In the case of perfect financial integration, the real interest rate in a single country is determined exogenously, implying that the authorities are unable to affect natural production. If, however, the authorities can control the real interest rate, in the case of imperfect integration in securities markets (cf. chapter 4) or monopolistic competition in bank markets (cf. chapter 5), the mechanism described above gives a channel through which demand policies can affect natural production. Monetary factors have an impact on natural production insofar as they influence the real interest rate.

As employment is related to the real wage expressed by the producer price, not the real wage expressed by the consumer price, the model does not allow for an impact from real exchange rate changes on the natural production, that is, the channel which was described in sections 3.3–3.4 above.

3.7   A general preference function

We use the specification of the trade union's preferences given by (3.2) in analyses throughout the book. It is demonstrated in this section that the findings of a monetary impact on natural production do not depend on this specific formulation of the preference function but apply to all preference functions that are optimised at a level below full employment and which are characterised by wage setters who derive positive utility from a higher real wage and higher employment.

The analysis takes as its point of departure two assumptions: (i) there is a functional relationship between the real wage, production, and an exogenously given variable Δ which implies that a higher real wage follows from lower production and from a higher value of Δ, and (ii) wage setters optimise a preference function which includes the real wage and production and which is characterised by positive marginal utilities with respect to production and the real wage. Based on these two assumptions, we will demonstrate the following proposition: If the wage setters' preferences are optimised at a production level which lies below the full employment level, the exogenous variable Δ changes the wage setters' optimal production, a higher value of Δ causing an increase in the wage setters' optimal production.

This finding is important because we derive throughout the book a number of channels through which monetary variables affect the functional relationship between the real wage and production. The analysis shows that monetary variables in these cases have an impact on natural production, provided the wage setters optimise preferences which include production and the real wage but without making any specific assumptions regarding the preference function except that it is optimised at a production level lower than the full employment level and is characterised by positive marginal utilities from higher employment and a higher real wage.

Basic assumptions

We assume that a relationship exists between the real wage, production, and an exogenous variable Δ. This functional relationship is specified as

$$\frac{W}{Q} = F(Y, \Delta),$$

$$F_Y \equiv \frac{\partial(W/Q)}{\partial Y} < 0, \quad F_\Delta \equiv \frac{\partial(W/Q)}{\partial \Delta} > 0,$$

$$F_{YY} \equiv \frac{\partial^2(W/Q)}{\partial Y^2}, \quad F_{Y\Delta} \equiv \frac{\partial^2(W/Q)}{\partial Y \partial \Delta}. \tag{3.39}$$

It is assumed by (3.39) that the real wage is affected (i) negatively by a change in production, that is, $F_Y < 0$, and (ii) positively by a change in Δ, that is, $F_\Delta > 0$. The function is twice differentiable. It is shown below that a negative relationship between the real wage and production, that is, $F_Y < 0$, is necessary to ensure that the wage setters' preference function is optimised at a level which is lower than the full employment level.

We further assume that wage setters optimise a preference function which involves positive marginal utilities from both production and the real wage, that is

$$U^u = U^u\left(Y, \frac{W}{Q}\right),$$

$$U_Y^u \equiv \frac{\partial U^u}{\partial Y} > 0, \ \ U_W^u \equiv \frac{\partial U^u}{\partial(W/Q)} > 0, \ \ U_{YY}^u \equiv \frac{\partial^2 U^u}{\partial Y^2}, \ \ U_{WW}^u \equiv \frac{\partial^2 U^u}{\partial(W/Q)^2}.$$

(3.40)

Relation (3.40) specifies the general preference function which the wage setters optimise when setting the nominal wage. The marginal utilities with respect to both production and the real wage are positive. No assumptions are made as to whether the marginal utilities are declining. Throughout the analysis we refer to the production level at which the wage setters optimise the preference function given by (3.40) as natural production, denoted as Y'.

We finally assume that the wage setters optimise the preference function given by (3.40) at a production level which is lower than full employment production. This means that the following two properties, derived from the optimisation of (3.40), characterise natural production

$$Z \equiv U_Y^u + U_W^u F_Y = 0, \tag{3.41}$$

$$\frac{\partial Z}{\partial Y} = U_{YY}^u + U_{WW}^u F_Y^2 + U_W^u F_{YY} < 0. \tag{3.42}$$

As $U_Y^u > 0$ and $U_W^u > 0$, the condition given by (3.31) is met only if $F_Y < 0$. This implies that natural production lower than the full employment level exists only if there is a negative relationship between the real wage and production. A non-negative relationship between the real wage and production induces the wage setters to set the nominal wage so that full employment is always brought about.

The following proposition is demonstrated:

If the three assumptions specified by (3.39)–(3.42) are met, that is, (i) there is a functional relationship between the real wage, production, and an exogenous variable Δ as specified in (3.39), (ii) the wage setters optimise a preference function which implies that positive utility is derived from a higher real wage and production, that is, the wage setters' optimisation is characterised by (3.40), and (iii) the wage setters reach their optimum at a production level lower than full employment, that is, the wage setters' optimum is characterised by relations (3.41)–(3.42), it follows that

$$\frac{\partial Y'}{\partial \Delta} > 0. \tag{3.43}$$

Relation (3.43) specifies that natural production is increased when there is an increase in the exogenous variable which has a positive impact on the relationship between the real wage and production.

Proof: The proposition can be demonstrated as follows. It follows from (3.41) that the impact of the exogenous variable Δ on natural production can be expressed as

$$\frac{\partial Y'}{\partial \Delta} = -\left(\frac{\partial Z}{\partial \Delta}\right) \Big/ \left(\frac{\partial Z}{\partial Y}\right). \tag{3.44}$$

We want to determine the signs of $\partial Z/\partial \Delta$ and $\partial Z/\partial Y$. From (3.42) it follows that $\partial Z/\partial Y < 0$. Multiplying both sides of (3.42) with F_Δ/F_Y, and using $F_\Delta > 0$ and $F_Y < 0$, gives

$$\frac{\partial Z}{\partial \Delta} = \left(\frac{\partial Z}{\partial Y}\right)\left(\frac{F_\Delta}{F_Y}\right) > 0. \tag{3.45}$$

Relation (3.45) shows that $\partial Z/\partial \Delta$ is positive because it follows from (3.42) that $\partial Z/\partial Y < 0$ while it follows from (3.39) that $F_\Delta > 0$ and $F_Y < 0$.

Using from (3.45) that $\partial Z/\partial \Delta > 0$, it follows from (3.44) that $\partial Y'/\partial \Delta > 0$, that is, Δ has a positive impact on natural production.

Conclusion

We have demonstrated that exogenous variables which affect the relationship between the real wage and production, causing an increase in the real wage at a given production level, have a positive impact on natural production, when the wage setters optimise a preference function that includes production and the real wage and when this preference function is optimised at a level which lies below full employment.

In subsequent chapters we will suggest a variety of channels through which monetary factors affect the relationship between the real wage and production specified by (3.39). In these cases, it follows from this analysis that monetary factors have an impact on natural production in all cases of preference functions where positive utility is derived from higher production and a higher real wage and where the wage setters' optimal production lies below the full employment level. The findings derived in the subsequent analyses therefore do not depend on the specification of the wage setters' preference function.

The analysis has further demonstrated that the wage setters' preferences are optimised only at an employment level lower than full employment if the wage setters expect that there is a negative relationship between the real wage and employment. If the relationship between the real wage and employment is non-negative, the wage setters can reach both a higher employment and a higher real wage by increasing the nominal wage. They will thus increase the nominal wage until full employment is reached.

3.8   Model modifications

Based on the models specified in sections 3.3 and 3.4, it was demonstrated that natural production is affected by the factors which enter the demand function for goods, either through a terms-of-trade effect or because the demand for goods may affect the real interest rate which in turn has an impact on natural production through capital accumulation. This finding is important because we derive throughout the book a number of channels through which monetary factors can have an impact on the demand for goods, in these cases monetary factors thus also being able to influence natural production.

Besides the terms-of-trade effect and the impact of the demand for goods on the real interest rate and thus on capital accumulation, one may think of further channels through which the demand function for goods can have an impact on the relationship between the real wage and employment and thus on natural production, for example when there is imperfect competition in goods markets. The demand for goods may also have an impact on firm's profit maximisation,[16] and thus on the relationship between the real wage and employment, when a firm faces bankruptcy costs, a higher real interest rate increasing the bankruptcy risk.[17] Phelps (1994) discusses that the real interest rate, by determining the income derived from financial assets, affects the workers' inclination to quit a firm. In the Phelps model, the real interest rate thus affects the functional relationship between unemployment and the real wage which is consistent with the firm's profit maximisation. Phelps (1994) also stresses that a change in the real interest rate affects the discounted value of investment which firms undertake in order to maintain customer loyalty.

---

[16]A discussion is found in Lindbeck and Snower (1994) and in Lindbeck (1998).
[17]See Greenwald and Stiglitz (1993).

The model used in the previous sections does not incorporate technical progress. In the literature on endogenous growth, based on the assumption of a fixed natural unemployment, it is analysed that the demand for goods affects the output growth rate.[18] The analyses throughout the following chapters suggest a number of channels through which monetary factors can affect the demand function for goods. In the case where output growth is determined by the demand for goods corresponding to Romer (1986) and there is fixed natural unemployment, we would reach the conclusion that monetary factors, while being unable to affect natural unemployment, have an impact on output growth.

3.9   Summary and conclusion

The determination of natural production has been analysed, assuming that a relationship between the real wage and employment results from the wage formation process. A distinction has been made between different kinds of wage formation/labour supply which cause a relationship between the real wage and employment: (i) the nominal wage is set by a trade union which optimises preferences with respect to the real wage and employment, (ii) the nominal wage is set through negotiations between a single firm and a single wage earner who is in a monopoly position due to specialised skills but has to weigh a higher real wage against a rise in the risk of being fired during the wage contract period, (iii) an agent optimises lifetime utility with respect to consumption and leisure, and (iv) the nominal wage is set by a firm which wants to avoid the costs associated with a high turnover in staff. In these cases of wage formation, it was shown that factors which enter as elements in the demand function for goods, the production function, and – for the first three wage formation processes – the wage setters' preferences have an impact on natural production. It is important that natural production is affected by basically the same factors under these four kinds of wage formation because this means that findings regarding the effectiveness of economic policy, which are obtained on the basis of one kind of wage formation, apply also to the other wage formation processes.

The analyses throughout the book are based on a specific preference function for a trade union. We have demonstrated that factors which affect the relationship between the real wage and production, have an impact on natural production in the case of all preference functions with the following characteristics: (i) positive marginal utilities which are

---

[18]See, for example, Romer (1986) and Barro (1990).

derived from higher employment and a higher real wage, and (ii) preference function which is optimised at an employment level that is lower
than full employment. This conclusion is important because it means that
the findings throughout the book of a monetary impact on natural production, derived on the basis of a specific preference function, apply to all
preference functions where positive marginal utilities result from higher
employment and a higher real wage and which are optimised at a level
lower than full employment. It has further been demonstrated that wage
setters only optimise their preferences at a lower employment level than
full employment when they face a negative relationship between the real
wage and employment.

The book suggests a number of channels through which monetary
factors can affect the demand for goods. In this chapter, we have examined two channels through which the demand for goods can have an
impact on the relationship between the real wage and employment and
thus on natural production: (i) shifts in the demand for goods affect the
terms-of-trade which in turn has an impact on the real wage by driving a
wedge between the consumer and producer prices, and (ii) shifts in the
demand for goods affect the real interest rate which in turn influences
capital accumulation. We briefly considered other channels through
which the demand for goods can affect the relationship between the
real wage and employment. Thus, shifts in demand affect the firm's
price–production decision when there is imperfect competition in goods
markets. In addition, the real interest rate may affect bankruptcy costs
and workers' inclination to quit a firm. In the case where the wage formation process causes natural unemployment to be at an exogenously
given level, monetary factors which affect the demand for goods, have an
impact on the output growth rate in the case of endogenous growth.

Part II
The impact of monetary policy and inflation

4 Imperfect integration of securities markets

4.1 Introduction

This chapter demonstrates a monetary impact on production in a model based on wage and price flexibility and rational expectations when there is imperfect integration of markets for securities denominated in different currencies. The wage setters set the nominal wage to reach an optimal trade-off between the real wage and production. The model analyses an equilibrium in which production increases at a constant rate and holdings of financial assets lie at constant levels relative to nominal production.

The analysis shows that monetary policy, working through inflation, sterilised intervention, and/or capital restrictions, has an impact on natural unemployment. This means that money is non-neutral. Monetary non-neutrality arises because inflation, sterilised intervention, and capital restrictions affect the portfolio composition of securities denominated in domestic and foreign currencies. This in turn determines the return on domestic securities relative to foreign securities and thus the real interest rate. The real interest rate influences natural production through two channels: (i) through an impact on the demand for goods and thus on the real exchange rate which affects the wage setters' trade-off between the real wage and employment, driving a wedge between the consumer price and the producer price, and (ii) through capital accumulation, a lower real interest rate causing an increase in the capital stock and thus in the real wage, inducing wage setters to opt for higher production. Inflation has an impact on the portfolio composition of securities because inflation affects government issues of securities and thus the net supply of securities denominated in the domestic currency. The analysis thus supports the view that monetary autonomy is valuable as a means of affecting production in the longer term where no nominal rigidities exist.

The finding that money affects natural unemployment in a model characterised by price and wage flexibility and rational expectations and by imperfect substitution between securities denominated in different currencies is new. The implications of imperfect integration of securities markets have been discussed comprehensively in the literature, see, for example, Eichengreen, Tobin, and Wyplosz (1995), Garber and Taylor (1995), Grilli and Milesi-Ferretti (1995), Kenen (1995), and Obstfeld (1995). A recent survey is found in Dooley (1996). It is the general view that the benefits associated with imperfect financial integration, notably more efficient capital allocation and the possibility of consumption smoothing, should be weighed against the disadvantages, in particular possible erosion of the tax base and an increase in uncertainty arising from speculative capital flows. It is further argued that capital restrictions may cause monetary policy to be effective in the short term, while there is neutrality in the long term.[1] Razin and Yuen (1995) find that the short-term Phillips curve is affected by capital restrictions, implying that the adjustment path of the economy is influenced by capital controls.

Throughout the analysis we refer to a fixed interest rate security denominated in the domestic currency as a domestic security while we refer to a fixed interest rate security denominated in the foreign currency as a foreign security.

Section 4.2 discusses possible theoretical justifications behind imperfect integration of international securities markets. *Section 4.3* presents the basic model. *Section 4.4* derives natural production. *Section 4.5* discusses policy implications. *Section 4.6* gives a summary and conclusion.

4.2   Explanations of imperfect financial integration

Theoretical explanations

Besides formal capital restrictions, six main explanations are commonly offered as to why there is imperfect substitution between securities with otherwise similar characteristics which are denominated in different currencies: (i) a preference among investors for a specific currency composition in order to reduce the uncertainty which is related to

---

[1]Grilli and Milesi-Ferretti (1995) write: 'capital controls may allow a country to pursue an independent monetary policy for a given period of time' (p. 518). Dooley (1996) emphasises the efficiency of capital controls in driving a wedge between domestic and foreign interest rates but stresses that capital restrictions are ineffective when there is full wage and price flexibility: 'changes in the domestic money stock with perfect capital mobility and flexible exchange rates generate proportional changes in all nominal prices so that the stabilization role for monetary policy disappears, along with the associated arguments for capital controls' (p. 649).

unexpected changes either in the consumer price or the investor's income, (ii) imperfect information concerning foreign investment and/or borrowing possibilities, (iii) transaction costs, (iv) discriminatory taxation, (v) fear on the part of investors that the authorities will impose capital restrictions or discriminatory taxation, and (vi) country-specific differences in the credit worthiness of borrowers in different countries.[2]

The first reason constitutes the rationale behind the International Capital Asset Pricing Model (ICAPM) which explains the interest rate differential between domestic and foreign assets as determined by (i) the relative supplies of financial assets, (ii) the correlation between the return on financial assets and the consumer price in the home country, (iii) the standard deviation of the return on financial assets, and (iv) the correlation between the return on financial assets.[3] Imperfect substitution between domestic and foreign securities has further been explained by the correlation between the investor's expected future non-saving income and the expected return on domestic assets which is different from the correlation between the investor's expected future non-saving income and the expected return on foreign assets.[4]

Much empirical evidence supports imperfect substitution between financial assets denominated in different currencies. Thus, empirical evi-

---

[2]Besides the ICAPM, Adler and Dumas (1983) emphasise limited information, discriminatory taxation, and capital restrictions as reasons behind imperfect integration of securities markets. Branson and Henderson (1985) base imperfect substitution between domestic and foreign securities on the ICAPM. Fukao and Hanazaki (1986) stress exchange rate uncertainty, capital restrictions, and discriminatory taxation. Gros (1989) suggests that imperfect substitution among domestic and foreign securities may be due to differences with respect to the institutional characteristics of national securities markets and to different payments systems. Oxelheim (1990) points to transaction costs and exchange rate risk as explanations of imperfect substitution among otherwise identical securities denominated in different currencies. The authorities may affect transaction costs, for example, through capital restrictions. Obstfeld (1995) emphasises the fear of investors that the authorities may reintroduce capital restrictions or discriminatory taxation. Dumas (1994) explains a 'home equity preference' with sovereign risk. Obstfeld (1995) concludes in a survey article: 'the available data on international portfolio positions suggest that many industrial countries are not diversified nearly to the extent that standard models of global portfolio choice would predict. The reasons could range from transaction costs. . .to internationally asymmetric information. . .differential tax treatment of domestic and foreign investors. . .to irrational expectations concerning the relative returns on domestic and foreign investments' (p. 231–232). Bayoumi and Gagnon (1996) demonstrate that the real after-tax cost of borrowing is reduced by inflation when investors are taxed on the basis of the residence principle.
[3]For a discussion, see Adler and Dumas (1983). Lucas (1982) suggests that a systematic difference between the forward exchange rate and the subsequently realised exchange rate can be explained through a non-zero correlation between the expected future marginal utility of consumption and the subsequently realised exchange rate.
[4]See Bottazi, Pesenti, and van Wincoop (1996), and Baxter and Jerkmann (1997).

dence shows that investors predominantly place in assets denominated in the home currency.[5] Moreover, a large number of studies fail to find evidence that interest rate differentials correspond to expected exchange rate adjustments, whether this is measured on the basis of rational expectations or through survey data.[6] Several studies suggest that indicators which could reflect the risk associated with placing in a currency, especially exchange rate variation, have an effect on the excess return received by an investor when placing in a foreign currency, indicating that interest rate differentials between assets in different currencies may be explained by risk.[7]

It further supports the hypothesis of imperfect financial integration that the real exchange rate in the short term closely follows the nominal exchange rate, while real exchange rate volatility is determined by the monetary regime (see sections 2.5.4 and 2.5.5). If domestic and foreign securities were perfect substitutes, one would expect the real exchange rate to bring about equilibrium in the goods market, and in this case the real exchange rate would be unaffected by the monetary regime. If, however, there is imperfect substitution among domestic and foreign securities, the real exchange rate would, under a floating exchange rate regime, be determined by the demand and supply of securities, offering a possible explanation for differences with respect to real exchange rate formation across monetary regimes.

A number of studies focus specifically on the relative supplies of domestic and foreign securities as a possible explanation of interest rate differentials. If the relative supply of securities can affect interest rate differentials, sterilised intervention is effective in influencing the exchange rate. The evidence from most investigations throughout the 1980s is mixed.[8] Some recent investigations support, however, the hypothesis of risk premia being explained by relative asset supplies. Dominguez and Frankel (1993a, 1993b) examine the effectiveness of intervention over the 1984–88 period using daily intervention data from the US Federal Reserve Bank and the German Bundesbank. Investors' expectations are found from survey data, and it is assumed that the share placed in the

---

[5]See, for example, Cooper and Kaplanis (1994), French and Poterba (1991), and Tesar and Werner (1992).
[6]For surveys, see for example Dumas (1994), MacDonald and Taylor (1992), and de Vries (1994). With respect to survey data, see, for example, Chinn and Frankel (1994).
[7]See, for example, Diebold and Pauly (1988).
[8]See, for example, Rogoff (1984), Fukao and Hanazaki (1986), and Golub (1989). Studies by Boughton (1984) and Fukao (1987) provide some support for the hypothesis of interest rate differentials being affected by the relative supplies of securities.

foreign currency varies with fluctuations in the exchange rate. Support is found for the hypothesis that sterilised intervention is effective. Sterilised intervention affects the exchange rate not only through an announcement effect, but also by changing the investors' portfolios. Analysing US interventions in DM and yen over the 1985–90 period, Baillie and Osterberg (1997) fail to uncover evidence of sterilised intervention being effective. Baillie and Osterberg point, however, to the relatively small amounts used in the interventions as a possible explanation why it is difficult to find evidence of effectiveness.

Other investigations by Faruqee (1995) and MacDonald (1995) suggest that exchange rates in the long run are determined by real interest rate differentials between two countries. This supports the portfolio model. Examining six currencies over the 1976–90 period, Ott (1996) shows exchange rates to be determined by variables which affect the current account, notably relative prices. Obstfeld and Rogoff (1995) and de Gregorio, Giovannini, and Wolf (1994) demonstrate a significant correlation between a sustained current account deficit and a depreciation of the real exchange rate. This indicates imperfect financial integration.

On the basis of more recent research, Taylor (1995) concludes in a survey article: 'Although the empirical evidence is still somewhat mixed, policy makers and researchers may be reaching a new consensus that intervention is effective' (p. 62).

While much of the empirical evidence is consistent with imperfect integration of international financial markets, the investigations largely fail to support any of the specific hypotheses which have been suggested to explain such non-integration.

The empirical evidence thus fails to support the ICAPM model.[9] The empirical evidence is also unsupportive of the hypothesis which explains imperfect integration of financial markets by differences in the correlation between, on the one side, investor's non-saving income and, on the other side, returns on financial assets denominated in different currencies. Thus, the consideration to reach a negative correlation between the income from non-saving sources and the return on saving favours international portfolio diversification while the empirical evidence shows a strong home currency bias.[10]

---

[9]See, for example, Thomas and Wickens (1989), Giovannini (1990b), and Lewis (1990). Empirical investigations also fail to support the Lucas (1982) hypothesis that imperfect substitution between domestic and foreign financial assets is due to a correlation between the future exchange rate and the marginal utility of consumption. See, for example, Hansen and Hodrick (1983) and Mark (1985a).

[10]See Baxter and Jerkmann (1997).

It is probably difficult to base an explanation of sizable interest rate differentials exclusively on transaction costs. Most studies show transaction costs to be small. If transaction costs are important in limiting foreign placements, one may further expect lower portfolio turnover rates on foreign portfolios than domestic portfolios. Tesar and Werner (1995) find evidence of the opposite, that is, a higher turnover on foreign portfolios.

Differences with respect to information may possibly explain non-integration of stock markets. It is, however, difficult to explain the non-integration of markets for government securities by differences regarding available information as the information required for investment in the market for government securities, essentially macroeconomic data, is available to all investors.[11] Yet, there are large and persistent differences in the return on government securities denominated in different currencies.

Finally, it seems difficult to explain the non-integration of markets for financial assets denominated in different currencies by systematic differences in credit worthiness among borrowers resident in different countries. Borrowers are not restricted to borrow in their home currency but are able to borrow also in foreign currencies.

4.3   Model specification

Below we will present a macroeconomic model based on imperfect substitution between securities denominated in different currencies. Both households and firms undertake financial transactions in domestic and foreign securities. The households' foreign financial transactions are based on a standard ICAPM model. Firms exploit differences in the return between domestic and foreign securities to optimise profit. The firms' foreign financial transactions are restricted by risk aversion. The modelling of foreign financial transactions in firms on the basis of risk aversion is non-conventional. It lends, however, realism to the model in a world with large-scale financial transactions undertaken by financial institutions and financial departments in commercial enterprises. The analysis considers a steady-state equilibrium characterised by constant production. In the short term, we allow for fluctuations in the exchange rate caused by disturbances in the demand for goods.

---

[11]Brennan and Cao (1997) find evidence of differences between US and foreign investors with respect to the expectations formation.

The firm's optimisation

Two economies are analysed, a small home country A and a large economy B. All variables relate to country A unless otherwise stated. We consider a representative firm which optimises profits using Cobb–Douglas production technology, allowing for the possibility that the firm can undertake financial transactions which exploit differences in the expected return between financial assets and liabilities denominated in different currencies. The firm's profit maximisation at a given time t is specified as follows

$$\max_{K_T^j, L_T^j, S_T^j, F_T^j} E_t \left\{ -\exp\left\{ -\left(\frac{v_T^j}{P_T}\right) \right\} \mid \frac{\partial P}{\partial Y^j} = 0, \frac{\partial r^\ell}{\partial Y^j} = 0, \frac{\partial W}{\partial Y^j} = 0, \frac{\partial X}{\partial Y^j} = 0 \right\},$$

$$v_T^j = P_T Y_T^j + (1 + i_{T-1}^B) X_T F_{T-1}^j - (1 + i_{T-1}) S_{T-1}^j - W_T L_T^j,$$

$$S_{T-1}^j = P_{T-1} K_T^j + X_{T-1} F_{T-1}^j, \quad \ell = A, B, \quad T = t, t+1, \dots, \tag{4.1}$$

$$Y_T^j = (K_T^j)^a (L_t^j)^{1-a}, \quad 0 < a < 1, \quad L_t < L'' \equiv 1, \tag{4.2}$$

$$\log(1 + r_{T-1}) \equiv \log(1 + i_{T-1}) - (p_T - p_{T-1}),$$

$$\log(1 + r_{T-1}^B) \equiv \log(1 + i_{T-1}^B) - (p_T^B - p_{T-1}^B), \tag{4.3}$$

$$r_T^B = r_{T-1}^B \equiv r^B = \bar{r}^B, \quad v_{p,T}^B = v_{p,T-1}^B \equiv v_p^B = \bar{v}_p^B, \quad v_{p,T}^B \equiv \frac{P_T^B - P_{T-1}^B}{P_{T-1}^B}, \tag{4.4}$$

where v^j is the cash flow of the representative firm j, K^j the capital stock of firm j, L^j employment of firm j, S^j net issues of fixed interest rate financial assets (securities) issued by firm j in the domestic currency, F^j the firm's net holding of fixed interest rate financial assets denominated in the foreign currency, P and p the producer price (non-logarithmic and logarithmic values), Y^j production of firm j, r the real interest rate, W the nominal wage, X the nominal exchange rate (number of domestic currency units per foreign currency unit), L'' full employment (normalised at one), i the nominal interest rate, and v_p^B the foreign price increase. a is the output elasticity of capital in the production function. $E_t(\cdot)$ shows the expected value of a variable.

In relation (4.1) the firm optimises preferences which include the real value of the cash flow in each time period. The preference function reflects that the firm is risk averse. The assumption of risk aversion on the part of the firm can be explained in several ways, for example by the consideration to avoid bankruptcy which involves costs for the management and staff of the firm. The firm is unable to affect the producer price, corresponding to perfect competition in the goods market. The firm is furthermore unable to influence the real interest rate and the nominal wage. As cash flows are separable in time, we can consider optimisation of cash flows in each time period separately. The firm undertakes financial transactions in the home and foreign currencies. The net holding of securities denominated in the foreign currency, expressed in the home currency, is given as XF^j. The firm's net issue of securities denominated in the domestic currency is S^j. The cash flow in a given time period T corresponds to the sum of (i) the nominal value of production $P_T Y_T$ and (ii) the net holding of foreign securities in the previous period with the addition of interest rate income expressed in the home currency, shown by $(1 + i_{T-1})X_T F^j_{T-1}$, with the deduction of (iii) net issues of securities in the previous period with the addition of interest income, shown by $(1 + i_{T-1})S^j_{T-1}$, and with the deduction of (iv) total labour costs $W_T L^j_T$.

Relation (4.1) further shows that total finance raised in the domestic currency in a given period $T - 1$, shown as S^j_{T-1}, corresponds to the sum of (i) the expenditure on capital investment, determined in period $T - 1$ as the capital stock in the subsequent time period K^j_T bought at the price level of period $T - 1$, and (ii) the firm's net holding of foreign securities, shown as $X_{T-1}F^j_{T-1}$. Capital depreciates fully in the course of one time period. All financial transactions take place in fixed interest rate securities.

Relation (4.2) is the Cobb–Douglas production function with constant returns to scale. (4.3) gives the definitions of domestic and foreign real interest rates. (4.4) expresses the assumption of a small home country, foreign variables being exogenously given. In addition, the foreign real interest rate and foreign inflation lie at the same level in each time period.

We assume that there are short-term fluctuations in the real exchange rate while other variables relevant to the firm's optimisation are known. The short-term fluctuation in the real exchange rate is specified as

$$e_T \sim N(\mu_e, \sigma_e^2), \quad e_T \equiv \log(\cancel{E}_T), \quad \cancel{E}_T \equiv \frac{X_T P_T^B}{P_T}, \tag{4.5}$$

where $\cancel{E}$ and e represent the real exchange rate (non-logarithmic and logarithmic values respectively).

Relation (4.5) shows the logarithm of the real exchange rate to be normally distributed with mean μ_e and variance σ_e^2. It follows from the authorities' setting of monetary policy (see below) that the price level in each period is pre-fixed and known. This means that fluctuations in the real exchange rate correspond to fluctuations in the nominal exchange rate. It is explained below that the real exchange rate in the short term brings about equilibrium in the goods market at a pre-fixed production level (see below), justifying the assumption made by (4.5) regarding the stochastic distribution of the real exchange rate.

Combining (4.1) and (4.3)–(4.5) gives the expected real cash flow in a given time period as

$$E_{T-1}\left(\frac{v_T^j}{P_T}\right) = Y_T^j - (1 + r_{T-1})K_T^j - \left(\frac{W_T}{P_T}\right)L_T^j$$

$$+ \left(\frac{F_{T-1}^j}{P_{T-1}^B}\right)\mathcal{Æ}_{T-1}\left[\left(\frac{E_{T-1}(\mathcal{Æ}_T)}{\mathcal{Æ}_{T-1}}\right)(1 + r_{T-1}^B) - (1 + r_{T-1})\right]$$

$$- \left(\frac{1}{2}\right)\left(\frac{F_{T-1}^j}{P_{T-1}^B}\right)^2 (1 + r_{T-1}^B)^2\sigma^2, \tag{4.6}$$

where σ^2 shows the variance of the non-logarithmic value of the real exchange rate.

The last two terms on the right-hand side of (4.6) reflect the impact of foreign transactions on the firm's expected real cash flow. σ^2 is the variance of $\mathcal{Æ}$, that is, the non-logarithmic value of the real exchange rate.[12] Optimising (4.6) and using (4.1)–(4.2), gives the conditions for the firm's optimum with respect to capital and labour

$$(1 - a)\left(\frac{Y_T^j}{L_T^j}\right) = \left(\frac{W_T}{P_T}\right), \tag{4.7}$$

$$\left(\frac{K_T^j}{Y_T^j}\right) = \frac{a}{1 + r_{T-1}}. \tag{4.8}$$

Relation (4.7) specifies the condition for the firm's profit maximisation with respect to labour, (4.8) with respect to capital. It follows from (4.8) that capital formation is unaffected by the possibility of foreign transactions.

---

[12]It can be found from the logarithmic value of the real exchange rate as $\sigma^2 = \exp\{2\mu_e + \sigma_e^2\}\exp\{\sigma_e^2 - 1\}$.

Optimising (4.6) with respect to foreign assets, and using (4.4), gives the optimum condition for the firm's net holding of foreign securities

$$\left(\frac{F_{T-1}^j}{P_{T-1}^B}\right) = \left[\left(\frac{E_{T-1}(\cancel{E}_T)}{\cancel{E}_{T-1}}\right)(1 + r_{T-1}^B) - (1 + r_{T-1})\right]\left(\frac{1}{1 + r_{T-1}^B}\right)\left(\frac{1}{\sigma^2}\right)\cancel{E}_{t-1}.$$

(4.9)

Relation (4.9) shows that the firm's net placement in a foreign currency depends on the expected increase in domestic purchasing power which can be reached by placing in a foreign currency asset, expressed by the term $[E_{T-1}(\cancel{E}_T)/\cancel{E}_{T-1}](1 + r_{T-1}^B)$ with the deduction of the increase in domestic purchasing power which can be reached by placing in a domestic currency asset, shown by $1 + r_{T-1}$. The firm becomes a net borrower in the foreign currency, causing F^j/P^B to become negative, when the expected increase in purchasing power, which can be reached from placing in a domestic security, exceeds the increase in purchasing power which can be reached from placing in a foreign currency asset, implying that the right-hand side of (4.9) becomes negative. Net foreign borrowing and net foreign placement are reduced when fluctuations in the exchange rate increase, that is, when there is an increase in σ^2.

Combining (4.1) and (4.8) with (4.9) and making the assumption that the firm is constrained in its foreign transactions by capital restrictions (or other costs related to foreign transactions) and by production, gives the firm's net issue of domestic securities at a given time $T - 1$ as

$$\left(\frac{S_{T-1}^j}{P_{T-1}}\right) = \xi_1 Y_{T-1}\left[\left(\frac{E_{T-1}(\cancel{E}_T)}{\cancel{E}_{T-1}}\right) - \left(\frac{1 + r_{T-1}}{1 + r_{T-1}^B}\right)\right]\left(\frac{1}{\sigma^2}\right)(\cancel{E}_{T-1})^2$$

$$+ Y_T^j\left(\frac{a}{1 + r_{T-1}}\right), \quad 0 \le \xi_1 \le 1, \quad (4.10)$$

where ξ_1 is the effect of capital restrictions on the firm's net borrowing in a foreign currency.

Relation (4.10) shows the firm to increase the net issue of domestic securities when the firm wants to increase its net holdings of foreign securities and when there is a rise in capital investment. The firm's foreign transactions are affected by the factor ξ_1. Full capital mobility means that the firm can realise all desired foreign transactions, implying that $\xi_1 = 1$. The firm is restricted to financing investment through issues of domestic securities when $\xi_1 = 0$. This corresponds to a ban on foreign transactions. It is further assumed from (4.10) that the firm's foreign transactions are affected by production. This can be explained by, for example, credit constraints which are affected by production.[13]

Steady-state equilibrium

The analysis is concerned with steady-state equilibrium. In the absence of technical progress, steady-state equilibrium is defined as a situation in which production lies at the same level in each time period. This gives

$$
\begin{aligned}
y_T = y_{T-1} &\equiv y, \quad E(e_T) = E(e_{T-1}) \equiv e = \mu_e, \\
r_T = r_{T-1} &\equiv r, \quad T = t, t+1, \ldots,
\end{aligned}
\qquad (4.11)
$$

where variables without time indications show levels in the steady state. Relation (4.11) gives the definition of steady-state equilibrium. Constant production implies that the conditions for long-term solvency must be met, implying that financial assets and liabilities lie at unchanged levels relative to nominal income in each time period for all groups of agents (households, firms, the central bank, and the government). In addition, other real variables, for example, the mean level of the real exchange rate and the real interest rate, lie at constant levels in each time period.

The household's optimisation

We consider a representative household which plans consumption over an infinite time horizon and which faces a declining probability of staying in the labour market (see section A.3 in the appendix). There is perfect information about macroeconomic variables relevant for the optimisation except the exchange rate. The household's optimisation at the beginning of time period t is characterised as

$$
\left\{ \left(C_{A,T}^h \right)^*, \left(C_{B,T}^h \right)^*, S_T^h, F_T^h, \left(M_T^h \right)^* \right\}
$$

$$
= \arg\max E_t \left\{ \sum_{T=t} \beta^{T-t} \left[U_c^h(C_{A,T}^h, C_{B,T}^h) + \log(M_T^h/P) \right] \right\},
$$

$$
U_c^h(C_{A,T}^h, C_{B,T}^h) = \left\{ (1 - \varphi)^{\frac{1}{\eta}} (C_{A,T}^h)^{\frac{\eta-1}{\eta}} + \varphi^{\frac{1}{\eta}} (C_{B,T}^h)^{\frac{\eta-1}{\eta}} \right\}^\delta,
$$

$$
0 < \beta < 1, \quad \eta > 1, \quad 0 < \delta \le 1,)
$$

$$
T = t, t+1, \ldots, \quad h = 1, 2, \ldots, \qquad (4.12)
$$

---

[13]This assumption simplifies the further presentation but does not affect the basic conclusions derived throughout the rest of the chapter.

$$\Gamma_T^h\left(\frac{L_T}{L''}\right)W_T(1-\tau_T)+(1+i_{T-1})S_{T-1}^h+(1+i_{T-1}^B)X_T F_{T-1}^h$$

$$+\,M_{T-1}^h+\Gamma_T^h\Theta_T P_T$$

$$=P_T C_{A,T}^h+P_T^B X_T C_{B,T}^h+S_T^h+X_T F_T^h+M_T^h,$$

$$\Theta_T=\xi_1 Y_{T-1}\left(\frac{F_{T-1}^j}{P_{T-1}^B}\right)\text{\AE}_{T-1}\left[\left(\frac{\text{\AE}_T}{\text{\AE}_{T-1}}\right)(1+r_{T-1}^B)-(1+r_{T-1})\right],$$

$$\Gamma_T^h=\Gamma_0\Gamma^{(T-t)+(h-1)},\quad \tau_T=\tau_{T-1}\equiv\tau,\quad \sum_h\Gamma_T^h=1,\qquad (4.13)$$

where $(C_A^h)^*$ is planned consumption of the home country good by a representative household h, $(C_B^h)^*$ the household's planned consumption of foreign country goods, S^h the household's net holding of domestic securities, F^h the household's net placement in foreign securities, $(M^h)^*$ the household's planned money holdings, U_c^h the household's utility from the consumption of goods, Γ^h the likelihood of finding employment, τ the tax rate on labour income, and Θ the dividend payments from firm j (paid as lump-sum transfers).

We assume that households at the beginning of each time period plan the consumption of domestic and foreign goods C_A^h and C_B^h, and holdings of domestic securities S^h, foreign securities F^h, and money M^h to optimise utility over an infinite time horizon. The household's optimisation is specified by (4.12)–(4.13). The optimisation corresponds to section A.3 in the appendix. Due to fluctuations in the exchange rate, the household's actual consumption of the two goods and money holdings may diverge from planned levels while the planned levels of holdings of domestic and foreign securities correspond to the levels which are subsequently realised. This is explained below.

Optimising (4.12) with respect to the consumption of the two goods and domestic securities and using (4.13) gives the following optimum conditions in steady-state equilibrium characterised by constant real exchange rates and constant real interest rates, cf. (4.11)

$$E_t\left(\frac{\left(C_{T+1}^h\right)^*}{\left(C_T^h\right)^*}\right)=\beta^\Upsilon(1+r)^\Upsilon,\quad \Upsilon\equiv\frac{\eta}{1+(\eta-1)(1-\delta)},\quad 0<\Upsilon<1,$$

$$C_T^h\equiv C_{A,T}^h+\text{\AE}_T C_{B,T}^h,\quad T=t,t+1,\ldots,\qquad (4.14)$$

$$\left(C_{B,T}^h\right)^*=[E_t(\text{\AE}_T)]^{-\eta}\left(\frac{\varphi}{1-\varphi}\right)\left(C_{A,T}^h\right)^*,\qquad (4.15)$$

$$u'\left[(C^h_{A,T})^*\right] = \beta(1+r^B)E_t\left\{u'\left[(C^h_{A,T+1})^*\right]\left(\frac{\mathcal{E}_{T+1}}{\mathcal{E}_T}\right)\right\}, \tag{4.16}$$

$$\left(\frac{M^h_T}{P_T}\right)^* = \left(\frac{1}{\delta}\right)\left[(C^h_T)^*\right]^{\frac{1}{\gamma}}\left\{(1-\varphi)+\varphi[E_t(\mathcal{E}_T)]^{1-\eta}\right\}^{1-\frac{\delta}{\eta}}\left(\frac{\eta}{\eta-1}\right)\left(\frac{1+i_T}{i_T}\right), \tag{4.17}$$

where C^h is the household's total consumption of domestic and foreign goods.

Relation (4.14) shows the planned growth of consumption over the household's lifetime (assuming a constant expected real exchange rate). (4.15) gives the composition of consumption of domestic and foreign goods. (4.16) shows the optimum condition for foreign securities holdings. (4.17) shows the optimum condition for money holdings.

Combining (4.13)–(4.15) with (4.7) and the condition for the firm's optimum with respect to foreign transactions, shown by (4.10), gives the household's planned consumption relative to income in the steady state

$$\left(\frac{C^h_T}{Y_T}\right)^* = \left(\frac{V^h_{T-1}}{P_{T-1}Y_{T-1}}\right)N_1(1+r)(1+\Phi\rho) - \left(\frac{M_{T-1}}{P_{T-1}Y_{T-1}}\right)N_2$$

$$+ (1-a)[(1-\tau)+E(\Theta)]\Gamma^h_T N_1\left(\frac{1}{1-\Gamma(1+r)^{-1}(1+\Phi\rho)^{-1}}\right),$$

$$N_1 = 1 - \beta^\Upsilon(1+r)^{\Upsilon-1}(1+\Phi\rho)^{-1} > 0,$$

$$N_2 = \beta^\Upsilon(1+r)^\Upsilon(1+\Phi\rho)^{-1} - \left(\frac{1}{1+v_p}\right)\left(\frac{N_1}{1-N_1(1+v_p)}\right) > 0,$$

$$V^h_T \equiv S^h_T + X_T F^h_T, \quad X_T F^h_T \equiv \Phi V^h_T, \quad E(\Theta) = \xi_1\rho^2\left(\frac{1}{\sigma^2}\right)\mathcal{E}^2, \tag{4.18}$$

$$\log(1+\rho_T) \equiv \log(1+r_T) - \log(1+r^B_T) - (e_{T+1}-e_T), \tag{4.19}$$

where V^h is the household's net financial wealth, Φ the share of foreign securities in the household's net financial wealth, and ρ expresses the real return on domestic securities relative to foreign securities.

Relation (4.18) shows the household's planned consumption as a function of real financial wealth and the levels of production, real interest rate, and the expected real exchange rate in the steady state. (4.19) gives the definition of ρ which represents the real return on a domestic security relative to the real return on a foreign security. In the following discussion, we refer to ρ as the relative return on the domestic security.

Combining (4.16) with the definition of the relative return on domestic securities shown by (4.19) and with the assumption that only the real exchange rate is stochastic, gives the following relationship between the relative return on domestic and foreign securities and the correlation between consumption and the real exchange rate at a given time t in the steady state

$$E_t\{\rho_t\} = \Im_t, \quad \Im_t \equiv \left\{ \frac{COV\left\{ u'(C_{A,t+1}^h), \left(\frac{\cancel{E}_{t+1}}{\cancel{E}_t}\right)\right\}}{E_t\left\{\frac{\cancel{E}_{t+1}}{\cancel{E}_t}\right\} E_t\left\{ u'(C_{A,t+1}^h)\right\}} \right\}. \tag{4.20}$$

Relation (4.20) specifies that the expected real return on domestic securities relative to the real return on foreign securities in the optimum is determined by (i) the correlation between the marginal utility derived from the household's consumption of domestic goods and the real exchange rate, (ii) the expected rise in the real exchange rate, and (iii) the expected marginal utility derived from the consumption of the home country good. The household determines its net holding of foreign securities in such a way that the condition specified by (4.20) is met.

The coefficient $\Im$ is affected by the share of financial wealth which a household places in foreign securities, expressed by Φ. The relationship can be explained as follows. Using the utility function shown by (4.12) and using the optimum conditions specified by (4.15) and (4.16), the marginal utility derived from the consumption of the home country good can be found as a function of the household's total consumption C_T^h as: $u'(C_{A,t+1}^h) = \delta(C_t^h)^{\frac{-\delta - \eta(\delta-1)}{\eta}}\left\{1 + \left(\frac{\varphi}{1-\varphi}\right)(\cancel{E}_T)^{1-\eta}\right\}^{\frac{\delta}{\eta}}(1 - \varphi)^{\frac{\delta}{\eta}}\left(\frac{\eta-1}{\eta}\right)$. In the absence of foreign assets/liabilities, it follows that a rise in $\cancel{E}$, that is, a real depreciation which makes foreign goods more expensive relative to domestic goods, leads to an increase in the consumption of the domestic good, causing a reduction in the marginal utility derived from the consumption of domestic goods and thus a negative correlation between the marginal utility derived from the consumption of domestic goods and changes in the real exchange rate. It follows from (4.13) that an increase in holdings of foreign securities implies that the household experiences a rise in total consumption C^h when there is a real depreciation which causes the value of foreign securities to rise. This leads to a reduction in the marginal utility derived from the consumption of domestic goods if $\eta < [\delta/(1 - \delta)]$. Assuming this condition is met, a rise in foreign securities holdings Φ thus leads to a reduction in the marginal utility derived from the consumption of the home country good. It thus follows that there is a negative relationship between on the one side, the share of a household's portfolio which is placed in foreign securities Φ and, on the other side, the correlation between the real exchange rate and consumption. The relationship can be expressed as follows

$$\Im_t = \Im(\Phi_t), \quad \frac{\partial \Im}{\partial \Phi} < 0. \tag{4.21}$$

Relation (4.21) expresses that the household, by increasing the share of foreign securities in its portfolio, experiences a decrease in the correlation between the marginal utility of consumption and fluctuations in the real exchange rate. This means that $\Im$ is negatively affected by a rise in the household's portfolio share of foreign securities Φ.

The precise relationship shown by (4.21) depends on to what extent households take account of the foreign positions which are incurred by firms. In the case of full transparency, the household fully offsets the foreign positions incurred by firms, implying that the firms' foreign transactions have no impact on holdings of foreign assets in a country. A number of reasons make it, however, implausible to perceive such a complete neutralisation of the firms' foreign transactions. Most importantly, firms are interested in hiding their true foreign currency positions in order not to reveal information to competitors.[14] In the following discussion, it is assumed that households' net holdings of foreign securities, shown by (4.21), are additional to the firms' foreign transactions, implying that the firms' foreign transactions have an impact on net holdings of foreign securities in a country.

Combining (4.20)–(4.21), it follows that the household's demand for foreign securities depends on the relative return between domestic and foreign securities ρ. In addition, we assume the household's demand for foreign securities to be determined by capital restrictions expressed by ξ_2. This gives

$$X_t F_t^h = \Phi_t V_t^h, \quad \Phi_t = \Phi(\rho_t, \xi_2),$$

$$\Phi_\rho \equiv \frac{\partial \Phi}{\partial \log(1 + \rho)} < 0, \quad \Phi_{\xi_2} \equiv \frac{\partial \Phi}{\partial \xi_2} > 0, \tag{4.22}$$

where ξ_2 represents the impact of capital restrictions on the household's placement in foreign securities.

Relation (4.22) shows the household's net placement in foreign securities to be negatively affected by a rise in the relative real return on domestic securities. The demand for foreign securities is further deter-

---

[14] A discussion is found in Adler and Dumas (1983).

mined by obstacles to free capital mobility, shown by ξ_2. ξ_2 could reflect for example limits on the share of foreign securities in portfolios which can be held by investors. An increase in ξ_2 implies that the household's possibility of foreign transactions is improved.

It follows from the analysis above that households, in the absence of foreign securities, experience a negative correlation between the marginal utility derived from the consumption of the domestic good and the real exchange rate. Using this, it follows from (4.20) that $\Im$, and thus also ρ, are negative when $\Phi = 0$. As relation (4.22) shows a negative relationship between the relative return on domestic securities ρ and the households' net holding of foreign assets Φ, it follows that there is net borrowing in the foreign currency when $\rho > 0$, that is, when the return on domestic securities is higher than the foreign return while the households' net holdings of foreign securities may be both positive and negative when $\rho < 0$. This relationship implies a home currency preference. Households only find it advantageous to have positive net holdings of foreign securities when there is a certain interest rate differential in favour of foreign securities.

Combining (4.18) and (4.22) it follows that the household's demand for domestic securities can be represented as

$$S_t^h = (1 - \Phi_t)V_t^h, \quad \Phi_t = \Phi(\rho_t, \xi_2), \quad \Phi_\rho < 0, \quad \Phi_{\xi_2} > 0. \quad (4.23)$$

Relation (4.23) shows the household's demand for domestic securities to be positively affected by (i) a rise in the household's total securities holdings V^h, (ii) a rise in the real return on domestic securities relative to foreign securities ρ, and (iii) by a tightening of capital restrictions which affect the possibility of foreign placements, shown by ξ_2.

The government

The government determines in each time period taxes on labour income and government purchases of goods and services. The government's financial balance is given as follows

$$S_t^g = (1 + i_{t-1})S_{t-1}^g + g_t P_t Y_t - \tau(1 - a)P_t Y_t - \sum_h (M_t^h - M_{t-1}^h),$$

$$g_t = \overline{g}_t, \quad g_t = g_{t-1} \equiv g, \quad \tau_t = \overline{\tau}_t, \quad \tau_t = \tau_{t-1} \equiv \tau, \quad (4.24)$$

where S^g are securities issued by the government, and g represents government purchases of goods and services relative to production.

Relation (4.24) specifies that the stock of government securities corresponds to the sum of (i) the stock of government securities in the previous period with the addition of interest payments, and (ii) government purchases of goods and services, with the deduction of (iii) tax revenue from households imposed on labour income, shown by $\tau(1 - a)PY$, and (iv) the increase in the money supply.

It is assumed from (4.24) that the government issues securities only in the domestic currency. This is supported by the empirical evidence. Several explanations can be offered for this assumption. Thus, the consideration not to reveal the authorities' expectations concerning future exchange rate movements makes it advantageous to conduct transactions in a single currency. Furthermore, there may be pressure from the financial community to maintain an efficient market in the home currency.

Monetary policy

The monetary authorities dispose of two instruments: (i) they set the money supply, and (ii) they determine sales of domestic securities against purchases of foreign securities (sterilised intervention). The supply of money is set to bring about a constant price increase in each time period. The monetary regime is characterised as follows

$$v_{p,t} = \bar{v}_{p,t}, \quad v_{p,t} = v_{p,t-1} \equiv v_p, \quad v_{p,t} \equiv \frac{P_t - P_{t-1}}{P_{t-1}}, \tag{4.25}$$

$$S_t^m = (1 + i_{t-1})S_{t-1}^m + \lambda_t P_t Y_t, \quad \lambda_t = \bar{\lambda}_t, \quad \lambda_t = \lambda_{t-1} \equiv \lambda, \tag{4.26}$$

where S^m is the net supply of domestic securities by the monetary authorities in return for foreign securities, that is, as a result of sterilised intervention, and v_p is the rate of price increase. λ represents the scale of sterilised intervention.

Relation (4.25) gives the assumption of a constant price increase in each time period. (4.26) specifies sterilised intervention. If $\lambda > 0$, the central bank undertakes net purchases of foreign securities against sales of domestic securities while $\lambda < 0$ implies central bank purchases of domestic securities against sales of foreign securities.

Goods market equilibrium

The demand for domestic goods is determined by the real exchange rate and by total domestic demand, composed of total consumption, investment, and government purchases of goods and services. The goods market equilibrium at a given time t is specified as

$$y_t = ze_t + d_t^* + \chi_t, \quad \chi_t \sim N(0, \sigma_\chi^2), \quad z > 0,$$
$$y_t = \bar{y}_t = y, \quad d_t^* = \log[C_t^* + I_t + G_t], \tag{4.27}$$

$$\left(\frac{C}{Y}\right)^{*} \equiv \sum_{h}\left(\frac{C^{h}}{Y}\right)^{*} = N_{1}\left(\frac{V}{PY}\right)(1+r)(1+\Phi\rho) - N_{2}\left(\frac{M}{PY}\right)$$

$$+ (1-a)[(1-\tau) + E(\Theta)]N_{1}\left(\frac{1}{1-\Gamma(1+r)^{-1}(1+\Phi\rho)^{-1}}\right),$$

$$N_{1} = 1 - \beta^{\Upsilon}(1+r)^{\Upsilon-1}(1+\Phi\rho)^{-1},$$

$$N_{2} = \beta^{\Upsilon}(1+r)^{\Upsilon}(1+\Phi\rho)^{-1} - \left(\frac{1}{1+v_{p}}\right)\left(\frac{N_{1}}{1-N_{1}(1+v_{p})}\right),$$

$$\left(\frac{V}{PY}\right) \equiv \sum_{h}\left(\frac{V^{h}}{PY}\right), \left(\frac{M}{PY}\right) \equiv \sum_{h}\left(\frac{M^{h}}{PY}\right)^{*}, \tag{4.28}$$

$$\left(\frac{I}{Y}\right) = \left(\frac{a}{1+r}\right), \tag{4.29}$$

where d^{*} is planned domestic demand (logarithmic value), χ a demand shock, C total consumption, V households' total non-monetary financial holdings, M planned holdings of money for all households, and I investment. Variables without time indications show steady-state levels.

Relation (4.27) specifies goods market equilibrium. The demand for domestic goods depends on the real exchange rate, total domestic demand, and foreign production. This corresponds to section A.7 in the appendix. We assume that domestic demand in each time period corresponds to the level which would follow from households' and firms' optimisation, shown as d^{*} (logarithmic value), with the addition of a stochastic disturbance χ (demand shock). The demand shock is normally distributed with mean zero and variance σ_{χ}^{2}. We further assume that production in each time period is pre-fixed by firms at the steady-state level, corresponding to the level which would follow from firms' and households' optimisation. This assumption can be justified by the presence of adjustment costs related to production changes. In each time period, equilibrium in the goods market is thus brought about through changes in the real exchange rate. This means that the logarithm of the real exchange rate is normally distributed with mean corresponding to the steady-state level of the real exchange rate, represented by e, and variance σ_{e}^{2} which corresponds to $(1/z)^{2}\sigma_{\chi}^{2}$. This specification of goods market equilibrium provides the rationale for the assumption made by (4.5) of the real exchange rate being log-normally distributed.

We assume that the fluctuation in demand is financed through unplanned changes in money holdings. This means that demand fluctuations do not spill over into the securities market, explaining the assumption made throughout the preceding discussion of the real interest rate being known beforehand. This assumption can be explained by costs associated with changes in households' and firms' portfolios. Thus, it requires time to prepare securities issues, and households may react slowly to changes in the real interest rate.

Relation (4.28) shows planned consumption in the economy as a whole, determined as the sum of planned consumption for individual households in the steady state. Relation (4.29) specifies total investment in the economy in the steady state. As capital depreciates fully in one time period, investment corresponds to the capital stock in the subsequent time period which is derived from (4.8).

Equilibrium in the securities market

The non-monetary net financial wealth of households V is given as

$$V_t \equiv S_t^p + S_t^g + S_t^m + X_t F_t^p, \quad S_t^p \equiv \sum_j S_t^j, \qquad (4.30)$$

where F^p is the net foreign position of domestic households. The net foreign position is defined as net claims of domestic households on foreign residents in return for the exchange of goods between the two economies.

Relation (4.30) shows the net stock of securities held by households to equal the sum of (i) the net issue of domestic securities by domestic firms S^p, (ii) the net issue of securities by the domestic government S^g, (iii) the net supply of domestic securities from the monetary authorities as a result of sterilised intervention S^m, and (iv) the net foreign position XF^p. We assume that claims between households in the two countries are settled in the foreign currency. A positive net foreign position ($F^p > 0$) thus reflects that domestic households hold securities issued by foreign agents. A negative net foreign position ($F^p < 0$) signifies that households issue foreign securities which are transferred to foreign agents in return for goods and interest payments on foreign debt. The total amount of securities issued by domestic firms equals the sum of securities issued by individual firms.

Next turning to the net foreign position of domestic households and firms, it is given as

$$X_t F_t^p = (1 + i_{t-1}^B)\left(\frac{X_t}{X_{t-1}}\right) F_{t-1}^p + P_t Y_t - P_t D_t. \qquad (4.31)$$

Relation (4.31) shows that the stock of net claims held by households on agents in the foreign country equals the net foreign assets held by domestic households in the previous period increased with interest payments and with the addition of net foreign assets received by households in payment from foreigners due to the net export of goods. (4.31) is based on the assumption that domestic firms receive payments in assets that are denominated in foreign currency. The net surplus on the balance-of-payments current account is valued in the domestic price level.

Equilibrium in the securities market implies that total issues of domestic securities by firms and the government equals the demand for domestic securities. Securities market equilibrium can thus be specified as

$$\sum_h S_t^h = S_t^p + S_t^g + S_t^m. \tag{4.32}$$

Relation (4.32) shows the demand for domestic securities from households to equal the supply of domestic securities from firms, from the government, and from the monetary authorities through sterilised intervention.

Wage formation

The nominal wage is determined by wage setters who optimise preferences that include employment and the real wage, that is,

$$\max_w E_t \left\{ U_t^u \mid \left(\frac{\partial P}{\partial W} \right) = 0, \ \left(\frac{\partial Q}{\partial W} \right) = 0, \ \left(\frac{\partial K}{\partial W} \right) = 0 \right\}, \tag{4.33}$$

$$U_t^u = -f^u \left(\frac{L_t}{L''} \right)^{-\gamma} - \left(\frac{W_t(1-\tau)}{Q_t} \right)^{-\theta}, \quad f^u > 0, \quad l'' \equiv 0, \tag{4.34}$$

$$q_t \equiv p_t + \varphi e_t, \quad 0 < \varphi < 1, \tag{4.35}$$

where U^u shows the wage setters' utility (a higher positive net value reflecting an increase in utility), and Q and q the consumer price (respectively non-logarithmic and logarithmic values). l and l'' show the logarithmic values of respectively employment L and full employment L''.

Relation (4.33) reflects decentralised wage formation, implying that the nominal wage is set by wage setters who are unable to affect macroeconomic variables. We further assume that capital in the wage contract period is determined prior to wage setting, for example, due to a long planning period for investment. (4.34) specifies the wage setters' preferences which involve positive but declining marginal utilities from higher production and a higher disposable real wage. (4.35) is the definition of the consumer price.

Assuming that the real exchange rate follows a log-normal distribution while other variables are non-stochastic, cf. (4.5), and using the definition of the consumer price given by (4.35), it follows from (4.34) that the wage setters' expected utility during the wage contract period is given as

$$E_t(U_t^u) = -f^u \left(\frac{L_t}{L''}\right)^{-\gamma} - \exp\left\{-\theta[w_t - E_t(q_t)] + \left(\frac{1}{2}\right)\theta^2 \varphi^2 \sigma_e^2\right\}.$$

$$(4.36)$$

Relation (4.36) shows the expected utility which is optimised by the wage setters in each time period.

4.4 Determination of natural production

To maintain a constant growth rate in production in steady-state equilibrium, levels of securities and net financial positions must lie at unchanged levels relative to production. Combining (4.10), (4.17), (4.24), (4.26), (4.29), and (4.31), and using (4.28), this gives

$$\left(\frac{S^p}{PY}\right) = \left(\frac{a}{1+r}\right) - \xi_1 \rho \left(\frac{1}{1+r^B}\right)\left(\frac{1}{\sigma^2}\right) \mathcal{E}^2, \tag{4.37}$$

$$\left(\frac{S^g}{PY}\right) = -\left(\frac{1}{r}\right)\left[g - \tau(1-a) - \left(\frac{M}{PY}\right)\left(\frac{v_p}{1+v_p}\right)\right], \quad r < 0, \tag{4.38}$$

$$\left(\frac{S^m}{PY}\right) = -\left(\frac{1}{r}\right)\lambda, \tag{4.39}$$

$$\left(\frac{XF^p}{PY}\right) = -\left(\frac{1}{r^B}\right)\left(1 - \frac{D}{Y}\right), \quad r^B < 0, \tag{4.40}$$

$$\left(\frac{M}{PY}\right) = L(i, \vartheta, e), \vartheta \equiv \frac{C}{y},$$

$$L_i \equiv \left(\frac{\partial L}{\partial \log(1+i)}\right) < 0, \quad L_\vartheta \equiv \left(\frac{\partial L}{\partial \vartheta}\right) > 0, \quad L_e \equiv \left(\frac{\partial L}{\partial e}\right) < 0.$$

$$(4.41)$$

It is assumed from (4.38) and (4.40) that domestic and foreign real interest rates are negative. In the absence of technical progress and thus zero production growth, only negative real interest rates are compatible with non-zero government budgetary net deficits, non-zero balances on the balance-of-payments current account, and sterilised intervention which implies permanent purchases/sales of domestic securities.

Relation (4.41) is derived from the household's money demand shown by (4.17). It follows from (4.17) that the household's demand for money increases more than proportionate with household consumption, implying that a rise in consumption relative to production increases money demand at the macroeconomic level. In addition, it follows from (4.17) that money demand is negatively affected by a rise in the real exchange rate and by a higher nominal interest rate.

To simplify the discussion further, we assume that the monetary authorities' sterilised intervention does not change the sign of the households' net foreign position and has the same sign as the trade deficit. This gives

$$|\lambda| < g - \tau(1-a) - \left(\frac{M}{PY}\right)\left(\frac{v_p}{1+v_p}\right). \tag{4.42}$$

The condition imposed by (4.42) implies that sterilised intervention does not exceed the net financing requirement by the government, shown by $g - \tau(1-a) - (M/PY)[v_p/(1+v_p)]$.

It cannot be determined from (4.28), without knowledge of the economic structure, how changes in the real interest rate, in the relative return on domestic securities, in inflation, and in capital restrictions affect total consumption relative to production in the steady state. Throughout the following discussion, we assume the following functional relationship

$$\vartheta \equiv \left(\frac{C}{Y}\right) = \vartheta\{\tau, r, e, \rho, v_p, \xi_1, \xi_2, \sigma^2\},$$

$$\vartheta_\tau \equiv \left(\frac{\partial \vartheta}{\partial \tau}\right) < 0, \quad \vartheta_r \equiv \left(\frac{\partial \vartheta}{\partial \log(1+r)}\right) < 0, \quad \vartheta_e \equiv \left(\frac{\partial \vartheta}{\partial e}\right) > 0,$$

$$\vartheta_\rho \equiv \left(\frac{\partial \vartheta}{\partial \log(1+\rho)}\right) < 0, \quad \vartheta_{v_p} \equiv \left(\frac{\partial \vartheta}{\partial \log(1+v_p)}\right) < 0,$$

$$\vartheta_{\xi_1} \equiv \left(\frac{\partial \vartheta}{\partial \xi_2}\right) > 0, \quad \vartheta_{\xi_2} \equiv \left(\frac{\partial \vartheta}{\partial \xi_2}\right) < 0, \quad \vartheta_{\sigma^2} \equiv \left(\frac{\partial \vartheta}{\partial \sigma^2}\right) < 0. \tag{4.43}$$

From relation (4.43) it is assumed that consumption relative to production increases as a result of (i) a lower tax rate on labour income τ, (ii) a lower real interest rate r, (iii) a lower real return on domestic securities relative to foreign securities ρ, (iv) lower inflation v_p, and (v) a tightening of capital restrictions on the households' foreign transactions ξ_2. An increase in the domestic real interest rate and in the relative return on domestic securities improves the households' investment possibilities, leading to a rise in saving. The same effect is present when capital restrictions on households' foreign transactions, shown by ξ_2, are liberalised. There is further an increase in consumption relative to production when firms increase their earnings from foreign arbitrage, implying that consumption relative to production is positively affected by the real exchange rate e, and by a liberalisation of firms' foreign arbitrage, shown by a rise in ξ_1, and negatively affected by the fluctuation in the real exchange rate σ_e^2.

Combining the condition for securities market equilibrium shown by (4.32) with (4.8), (4.10), (4.23), and (4.30), gives the condition for equilibrium in the securities market in a given time period t as

$$
\Psi_t = - \Phi(\rho_t, \xi_2)\left(\frac{a}{1+r_t}\right)\left(\frac{E_t(Y_{t+1})}{Y_t}\right) + \rho_t\xi_1\Phi(\rho_t, \xi_2)\left(\frac{\text{Æ}_t}{\sigma^2}\right)E_t(\text{Æ}_{t+1})
$$

$$
- \Phi(\rho_t, \xi_2)\left(\frac{S_t^g}{P_tY_t}\right) - \Phi(\rho_t, \xi_2)\lambda
$$

$$
+ \left(\frac{F_t^p}{P_t^B}\right)\left(\frac{1}{Y_t}\right)[1 - \Phi(\rho_t, \xi_2)]\text{Æ}_t = 0, \tag{4.44}
$$

where Ψ represents the real net demand for domestic securities relative to production.

Relation (4.44) shows that the net demand for domestic securities at a given time t is determined by (i) capital investment, (ii) the firms' foreign transactions, (iii) the government's net issue of securities, (iv) the net issue of securities from the monetary authorities as a result of sterilised intervention, and (v) the households' net claims on foreigners, acquired through the exchange of goods and services with foreigners. It follows from (4.44) that it depends on the sign of Φ, that is, whether households are net borrowers or net investors in foreign securities, how these factors affect the net securities demand.

It follows from the analysis above that a positive net holding of foreign securities among households, that is, $\Phi > 0$, is only compatible with a real return on domestic securities which is lower than the real return on foreign securities, that is, $\rho < 0$. In the case where $\Phi > 0$ and $\rho < 0$, it follows from (4.44) that the net demand for domestic securities is negatively affected by a rise in investment, shown by $[a/(1 + r)]E_t(Y_{t+1})$. As a result of firms' investments and the resulting increase in the amount of securities issued by firms, households increase their net financial wealth but only part of this, that is, the share $1 - \Phi$, is placed in domestic securities, leading to a negative impact of investment on the households' net demand for domestic securities. The second term on the right side of (4.44) reflects the firms' foreign arbitrage transactions. When $\rho < 0$, that is, the expected real return associated with placing in foreign securities is higher than the domestic real return, firms increase the issue of domestic securities to finance not only capital investment but also positive holdings of foreign securities. The third term on the right side of (4.44) shows the effects of the government financing requirement. When the government runs a budgetary deficit (implying $S^g > 0$), there is an increase in the households' financial wealth due to the government securities which are issued to finance the budgetary deficit. Only part of this increase in financial wealth gives rise to an increased demand for domestic securities, causing a reduction in the net demand for domestic securities corresponding to ΦS^g. The same effect arises from sterilised intervention, represented by the fourth term on the right side of (4.44). The last term on the right side of (4.44) finally shows that a rise in the households' total financial wealth caused by an increase in net claims on foreigners raises the net demand for domestic securities. As households receive foreign securities as payment for the export of goods to foreigners, they will convert the share $1 - \Phi$ of these claims on foreigners shown by (F^p/P^B) into domestic securities.

Combining (4.30) and (4.32) with (4.37)–(4.40) gives the specification of securities market equilibrium in the steady state

$$\Psi_s = -\left(\frac{a}{1+r}\right) + \xi_1\rho\left(\frac{1}{\sigma^2}\right)\!\mathcal{E}^2$$
$$+ \left(\frac{1}{r}\right)\!\left[g - \tau(1-a) - L(i,e,\vartheta)\left(\frac{v_p}{1+v_p}\right)\right] + \left(\frac{1}{r}\right)\!\lambda$$
$$- \left(\frac{1}{r^B}\right)\!\left[1 - \left(\frac{a}{1+r}\right) - g - \vartheta\right]\!\left[\frac{1 - \Phi(\rho,\xi_2)}{\Phi(\rho,\xi_2)}\right] = 0, \qquad (4.45)$$

where Ψ_s represents net demand for domestic securities relative to production in steadystate equilibrium.

Relation (4.45) shows the net demand for domestic securities to depend on: (i) the firms' financing requirement for investment, expressed by $a/(1+r)$, (ii) the firms' foreign currency transactions, specified by $\xi_1\rho(1/\sigma^2)\mathcal{E}^2$, (iii) the government's net financing requirement, shown by $g - \tau(1-a) - (M/PY)[v_p/(1+v_p)]$, (iv) sterilised intervention,

shown by λ, and (v) the balance-of-payments current account, shown by
$1 - (a/1 + r) - g - \vartheta$.

It results from (4.45) that the variables which are endogenously
determined, have the following impact on the net demand for domestic
securities

$$\Psi_{sr} \equiv \frac{\partial \Psi_s}{\partial \log(1+r)} = \left(\frac{a}{1+r}\right) - \left(\frac{1}{r^B}\right)\left[\frac{1-\Phi(\rho,\xi_2)}{\Phi(\rho,\xi_2)}\right]\left[\left(\frac{a}{1+r}\right) - \vartheta_r\right]$$

$$- \left(\frac{1+r}{r^2}\right)\left[g - \tau(1-a) - L(i,e,\vartheta)\left(\frac{v_p}{1+v_p}\right) + \lambda\right]$$

$$+ \left(\frac{1}{r}\right)\left(\frac{v_p}{1+v_p}\right)(L_i + L_\vartheta \vartheta_r),$$

$$\Psi_{s\rho} \equiv \frac{\partial \Psi_s}{\partial \log(1+\rho)} = \xi_1\left(\frac{1}{1+r^B}\right)\left(\frac{1}{\sigma^2}\right)\!Æ^2 + \left(\frac{1}{r^B}\right)\vartheta_\rho\left[\frac{1-\Phi(\rho,\xi_2)}{\Phi(\rho,\xi_2)}\right]$$

$$+ \Phi_\rho\left(\frac{1}{r^B}\right)\left(\frac{1}{\Phi(\rho,\xi_2)}\right)^2\left[1 - \left(\frac{a}{1+r}\right) - g - \vartheta\right],$$

$$\Psi_{se} \equiv \frac{\partial \Psi_s}{\partial e} = 2\xi_1\rho\left(\frac{1}{\sigma^2}\right)\!Æ^2 - \left(\frac{1}{r}\right)[L_e + L_\vartheta \vartheta_e]\left(\frac{v_p}{1+v_p}\right)$$

$$+ \vartheta_e\left(\frac{1}{r^B}\right)\left[\frac{1-\Phi(\rho,\xi_2)}{\Phi(\rho,\xi_2)}\right]. \tag{4.46}$$

It follows from (4.46) that it depends on the economic structure how
endogenous variables affect the net demand for domestic securities.
Thus, a rise in the real interest rate has a positive effect on the net
demand for domestic securities by depressing investment and by reducing
domestic demand, leading to a rise in the net financial wealth of domestic
households which raises net demand. A rise in the real interest rate has
the further effect of decreasing the discounted value of government debt,
this effect causing a reduction in household financial wealth and thus a
lowering of the net demand for domestic securities. The government's
financial constraint is further affected by the real interest because real
interest determines households' real money holdings and thus the extent
to which it is possible for the government to use monetary financing
instead of securities issues to finance the budgetary deficit.

It further follows from (4.45) that the variables which are exogenously determined, have the following impact on the net demand for
securities

$$\Psi_{s\lambda} \equiv \frac{\partial \Psi_s}{\partial \lambda} = \left(\frac{1}{r}\right),$$

$$\Psi_{sg} \equiv \frac{\partial \Psi_s}{\partial g} = \left(\frac{1}{r}\right) + \left(\frac{1}{r^B}\right)\left[\frac{1 - \Phi(\rho, \xi_2)}{\Phi(\rho, \xi_2)}\right],$$

$$\Psi_{s\tau} \equiv \frac{\partial \Psi_s}{\partial \tau} = -\left(\frac{1}{r}\right)(1 - a) + \left(\frac{1}{r^B}\right)\vartheta_\tau\left[\frac{1 - \Phi(\rho, \xi_2)}{\Phi(\rho, \xi_2)}\right],$$

$$\Psi_{sv_p} \equiv \frac{\partial \Psi_s}{\partial \log(1 + v_p)} = -\left(\frac{1}{r}\right)\left[L_i + \left(\frac{M}{PY}\right)\left(\frac{1}{1 + v_p}\right)\right],$$

$$\Psi_{s\sigma} \equiv \frac{\partial \Psi_s}{\partial \sigma^2} = -\xi_1 \rho \mathcal{E}^2 \left(\frac{1}{\sigma^2}\right)^2,$$

$$\Psi_{s\xi_1} \equiv \frac{\partial \Psi_s}{\partial \xi_1} = \rho\left(\frac{1}{\sigma^2}\right)\mathcal{E}^2 + \left(\frac{1}{r^B}\right)\vartheta_{\xi_1}\left[\frac{1 - \Phi(\rho, \xi_2)}{\Phi(\rho, \xi_2)}\right],$$

$$\Psi_{s\xi_2} \equiv \frac{\partial \Psi_s}{\partial \xi_2} = \left(\frac{1}{r^B}\right)\vartheta_{\xi_2}\left[\frac{1 - \Phi(\rho, \xi_2)}{\Phi(\rho, \xi_2)}\right]$$
$$- \left(\frac{1}{r^B}\right)\left[1 - \left(\frac{a}{1 + r}\right) - g - \vartheta\right]\left[\frac{\Phi_{\xi_2}}{\Phi(\rho, \xi_2)}\right],$$

$$\Psi_{sr^B} \equiv \frac{\partial \Psi_s}{\partial \log(1 + r^B)} = \left(\frac{1 + r^B}{(r^B)^2}\right)\left[1 - \left(\frac{a}{1 + r}\right) - g - \vartheta\right]\left(\frac{1 - \Phi(\rho, \xi_2)}{\Phi(\rho, \xi_2)}\right).$$

$$(4.47)$$

Relation (4.47) shows how the net demand for domestic securities is affected by the exogenously determined variables. The impacts depend on the economic structure.

Optimising (4.36) and using (4.2), (4.5), and (4.7)–(4.8) gives the following levels of production, real exchange rate, and real interest rate which are consistent with the wage setters' optimum

$$y = -\left(\frac{\theta}{\gamma}\right)\varphi e - \left(1 + \frac{\theta}{\gamma}\right)\left(\frac{a}{1 - a}\right)\log(1 + r) + \left(\frac{\theta}{\gamma}\right)\log(1 - \tau)$$
$$- \left(\frac{\theta}{\gamma}\right)\left(\frac{1}{2}\right)\theta\varphi^2\sigma_x^2 + \left(1 + \frac{\theta}{\gamma}\right)\left(\frac{a}{1 - a}\right)\log(a) + \left(\frac{\theta}{\gamma}\right)\log(1 - a).$$
$$- \left(\frac{1}{\gamma}\right)\epsilon, \quad \epsilon \equiv \log\left(\frac{\theta a}{f^u \gamma}\right).$$

$$(4.48)$$

The natural production in steady-state equilibrium can be found by combining the condition for labour and goods market equilibrium, given by (4.27), (4.29), (4.43), and (4.48), with the condition for securities market equilibrium, shown by (4.45). Exogenous variables affect natural production as follows

$$dy = J_\epsilon d\epsilon + J_\sigma d\sigma_e^2 + J_g dg + J_\tau d\tau + J_\lambda d\lambda + J_{v_p} dv_p + J_{\xi_1} d\xi_1 + J_{\xi_2} d\xi_2$$

$$+ J_{r_B} dr^B,$$

$$J_\epsilon \equiv \left(\frac{\partial y}{\partial \epsilon}\right) = -\left(\frac{1}{\gamma}\right) < 0,$$

$$J_\sigma \equiv \left(\frac{\partial y}{\partial \sigma_e^2}\right) = -\left(\frac{1}{2}\right)\left(\frac{\theta}{\gamma}\right)\theta\varphi^2 + \vartheta_\sigma\left(\frac{N_5}{N_3}\right) - \left(\frac{\Psi_{s\sigma}}{\Psi_{sr} + \Psi_{s\rho}}\right)\left(\frac{\partial\sigma^2}{\partial\sigma_e^2}\right)\left(\frac{N_4}{N_3}\right),$$

$$\left(\frac{\partial\sigma^2}{\partial\sigma_e^2}\right) > 0,$$

$$J_g \equiv \left(\frac{\partial y}{\partial g}\right) = \left(\frac{N_5}{N_3}\right) - \left(\frac{\Psi_{sg}}{\Psi_{sr} + \Psi_{s\rho}}\right)\left(\frac{N_4}{N_3}\right),$$

$$J_\tau \equiv \left(\frac{\partial y}{\partial \tau}\right) = -\left(\frac{\theta}{\gamma}\right)\left(\frac{1}{1-\tau}\right) + \vartheta_\tau\left(\frac{N_5}{N_3}\right) - \left(\frac{\Psi_{s\tau}}{\Psi_{sr} + \Psi_{s\rho}}\right)\left(\frac{N_4}{N_3}\right),$$

$$J_\lambda \equiv \left(\frac{\partial y}{\partial \lambda}\right) = -\left(\frac{\Psi_{s\lambda}}{\Psi_{sr} + \Psi_{s\rho}}\right)\left(\frac{N_4}{N_3}\right),$$

$$J_{v_p} \equiv \left(\frac{\partial J}{\partial v_p}\right) = \vartheta_{v_p}\left(\frac{N_5}{N_3}\right)\left(\frac{1}{1+v_p}\right) - \left(\frac{\Psi_{sv_p}}{\Psi_{sr} + \Psi_{s\rho}}\right)\left(\frac{N_4}{N_3}\right)\left(\frac{1}{1+v_p}\right),$$

$$J_{\xi_1} \equiv \left(\frac{\partial y}{\partial \xi_1}\right) = \vartheta_{\xi_1}\left(\frac{N_5}{N_3}\right) - \left(\frac{\Psi_{s\xi_1}}{\Psi_{sr} + \Psi_{s\rho}}\right)\left(\frac{N_4}{N_3}\right),$$

$$J_{\xi_2} \equiv \left(\frac{\partial y}{\partial \xi_2}\right) = \vartheta_{\xi_2}\left(\frac{N_5}{N_3}\right) - \left(\frac{\Psi_{s\xi_2}}{\Psi_{sr} + \Psi_{s\rho}}\right)\left(\frac{N_4}{N_3}\right),$$

$$J_{r^B} \equiv \left(\frac{\partial y}{\partial r^B}\right) = -\vartheta_\rho\left(\frac{N_5}{N_3}\right)\left(\frac{1}{1+r^B}\right) - \left(\frac{\Psi_{sr^B} - \Psi_{s\rho}}{\Psi_{sr} + \Psi_{s\rho}}\right)\left(\frac{N_4}{N_3}\right)\left(\frac{1}{1+r^B}\right),$$

$$N_3 \equiv \frac{D}{Y} + \vartheta_e\left(\frac{1}{z}\right) + \left(\frac{\Psi_{se}}{\Psi_{sr} + \Psi_{s\rho}}\right)\left(\frac{1}{z}\right)\left[\frac{a}{1+r} - \vartheta_r - \vartheta_\rho\right],$$

$$N_4 \equiv -\left(\frac{\varphi}{z}\right)\left(\frac{\theta}{\gamma}\right)\left[\frac{a}{1+r} - \vartheta_r - \vartheta_\rho\right] - \left[\frac{D}{Y} + \vartheta_e\left(\frac{1}{z}\right)\right]\left(\frac{a}{1-a}\right)\left(1+\frac{\theta}{\gamma}\right),$$

$$N_5 \equiv \left(\frac{\varphi}{z}\right)\left(\frac{\theta}{\gamma}\right) - \left(\frac{\Psi_{se}}{\Psi_{sr} + \Psi_{s\rho}}\right)\left(\frac{1}{z}\right)\left(\frac{a}{1-a}\right)\left(1+\frac{\theta}{\gamma}\right), \tag{4.49}$$

Relation (4.49) shows the impact of exogenous variables on natural production. Natural production is affected positively by a change in the wage setters' preferences where greater weight is attached to employment relative to the real wage corresponding to a reduction in ϵ. The signs of the impacts of the other exogenous variables depend on the economic structure. Especially, the signs of N_3 and N_5 cannot be determined unambiguously.

4.5   Policy implications

Effectiveness of economic policy

It follows from (4.49) that the authorities dispose of three channels through which natural production can be affected: (i) fiscal policy instruments g and τ, (ii) net sales of domestic securities in return for foreign securities, that is, sterilised intervention λ, and (iii) changes in the growth rate of the money supply v_p. In addition, the authorities can affect natural production through the choice of monetary regime which determines the fluctuation in the real exchange rate, shown by σ_e^2, and through restrictions on firms' and households' foreign transactions, shown by ξ_1 and ξ_2. Assuming that there are costs associated with the use of economic policy instruments, overall policy effectiveness is increased when the authorities have a larger number of instruments at their disposal. This means that overall policy effectiveness is increased when securities markets are imperfectly integrated relative to a perfect integration of securities markets where only fiscal policy can be used to affect natural production (cf. the model analysed in section 3.3). This also means that a monetary union which causes an integration of securities markets, entails a reduction in economic policy effectiveness.

Sterilised intervention and inflation influence natural production by affecting the equilibrium in the securities market, having an impact on the real return on domestic securities relative to foreign securities and thus on the domestic real interest rate. Sterilised intervention affects the net demand for domestic securities through net purchases of domestic securities against sales of foreign securities, thus replacing domestic securities with foreign securities in the households' portfolios. Inflation has an impact on the government's net issue of domestic securities by affecting the extent to which the government has to rely on securities for financing budgetary deficits. The change in real interest rate brought about by sterilised intervention and changes in inflation influences natural production through two channels: (i) through an impact on the demand for goods which changes the real exchange rate, that is, a terms-of-trade effect, and (ii) through an impact on capital formation. An increase in the demand for goods caused by a lower real interest rate leads to a real appreciation that improves the trade-off faced by wage setters between the real wage and inflation. A higher capital intensity brought about by a lower real interest rate increases the real wage, in turn inducing wage setters to increase natural production. The impact of inflation on the currency composition of domestic portfolios is additional to the channels of monetary non-neutrality which are discussed in the literature and which were surveyed in section 2.3, that is, (i) the impact of inflation on the investor's portfolio choice between money and capital, (ii) inflation tax/seigniorage, and (iii) the impact of inflation on the efficiency of money.

It follows from (4.49) that fiscal policy instruments affect natural production (i) through an impact on the demand for goods which changes the real exchange rate, (ii) by changing the supply of securities, and, in the case of the tax rate, (iii) through a direct effect on the combinations of disposable real wage and employment which can be reached by the wage setters. The first effect (i) is also present under perfect integration of securities markets. These effects work in different directions. Thus, on the one side, a more expansive fiscal policy causes an increase in the demand for goods which leads to a real appreciation, improving the combinations of the real wage and production that can be reached by the wage setters. A more expansive fiscal policy makes it at the same time necessary to increase the supply of securities to finance the rise in the budgetary deficit. This may cause a rise in the real interest rate, in turn depressing capital formation and thus having a negative impact on the combinations of the real wage and employment that can be reached by the wage setters.

The authorities can further affect natural production through the choice of monetary regime which affects the short-term variation in the real exchange rate, i.e., σ_e^2. By choosing a monetary regime which leaves more room for exchange rate stabilisation, the government can determine σ_e^2. The fluctuation in the exchange rate has an impact on natural production through two channels: (i) by reducing the expected level of the real wage and thus inducing wage setters to opt for a lower production level, and (ii) by affecting the foreign arbitrage of firms and through this the net demand for securities. With respect to the first effect, a rise in the exchange rate variation σ_e^2 lowers the wage setters' expected utility and thus reduces the utility which can be reached by the wage setters. With respect to the latter effect, a rise in the fluctuation in the real exchange rate reduces the amount of foreign transactions undertaken by firms. This leads to a reduction in the net demand for domestic securities when the real return on domestic securities is higher than the real return on foreign securities, that is, when $\rho > 0$, while it increases the net demand for domestic securities when the real return on domestic securities lies below the real return on foreign securities, i.e., when $\rho < 0$.

Obstacles to capital mobility, in the form of formal restrictions or non-formal obstacles, are reflected by ξ_1 and ξ_2. As explained above, an increase in these parameters reflects a liberalisation of capital restrictions. It follows from (4.49) that natural production is affected by such obstacles to capital mobility. Capital restrictions can thus be used to affect natural production.

Uncertainty about the impact of policy instruments

It follows from the analysis that the impact of policy instruments on natural production depends on the economic structure. If policy makers lack precise knowledge of the economic structure, this may cause uncertainty regarding the effect of policy instruments and thus hamper policy effectiveness.

To facilitate the analysis, we make the following assumptions: (1) we assume that $N_3 > 0$ and $N_5 > 0$, (2) we assume that the impact of the real exchange rate on the demand for goods has a negligible impact on the demand for money, implying that the term $L_e + L_\vartheta \vartheta_e$ does not affect the impact of the real exchange rate on the net demand for domestic securities, expressed by Ψ_{se}, and (3) we assume that a rise in inflation reduces the need for government borrowing through securities, implying that $L_i + (M/PY)[1/(1 + v_p)] > 0$. We finally assume that the conditions expressed by (4.42)–(4.43) are met. To simplify the presentation, we comment on a case where the government runs a budgetary deficit, that is, $g - \tau(1 - a) - (M/PY)[v_p/(1 + v_p)] > 0$.

It follows from the analysis above that a real return on domestic securities which is higher than the real return on foreign securities, implying $\rho > 0$, is incompatible with households having positive net holdings of foreign securities, that is, $\Phi > 0$. We can therefore in our analysis of the impact of policy instruments on natural production distinguish between three situations:

(1) The real return on domestic securities is higher than the real return on foreign securities, that is, $\rho > 0$, and households are net borrowers in foreign currency, that is, $\Phi < 0$: It results from (4.46) that the signs of Ψ_{sr} and $\Psi_{s\rho}$ depend on the economic structure while Ψ_{se} is positive. In the case where $\Psi_{sr} + \Psi_{s\rho} > 0$, it follows from (4.47) that natural production is positively affected by (i) a reduction of domestic securities as a result of sterilised intervention, shown by a lower value of λ, (ii) a reduction in the fluctuations of the exchange rate, expressed by a reduction in σ^2, and (iii) a liberalisation of capital restrictions on firms' foreign transactions ξ_1. Even in the case where $\Psi_{sr} + \Psi_{s\rho} > 0$, it follows from (4.47) that it depends on the economic structure how natural production is affected

by fiscal policy instruments g and τ, a liberalisation of the restrictions on households' foreign transactions ξ_2, and by a rise in inflation v_p.

(2) The real return on domestic securities is lower than the real return on foreign securities, that is, $\rho < 0$, and households are net borrowers in foreign currency, that is, $\Phi < 0$. In this situation, firms borrow in the domestic currency to purchase foreign securities. It thus follows from (4.45) that the balance of the balance-of-payments current account must be negative to ensure equilibrium in the securities market, that is, $1 - (a/1 + r) - g - \vartheta < 0$. The signs of Ψ_{sr}, $\Psi_{s\rho}$, and Ψ_{se} depend on the economic structure. In the case where $\Psi_{sr} + \Psi_{s\rho} > 0$, it follows that there is a positive impact on net securities demand and thus on natural production when there are net purchases of domestic securities as a result of sterilised intervention, shown as a reduction in λ. It follows from (4.47) that it depends on the economic structure how the demand for net securities and thus natural production are affected by sterilised intervention λ, fiscal policy instruments g and τ, a liberalisation of capital restrictions on firms' and households' foreign transactions ξ_1 and ξ_2, inflation v_p, and changes in fluctuations of the exchange rate σ^2.

(3) The real return on domestic securities is lower than the real return on foreign securities, that is, $\rho < 0$, and households are net investors in foreign currency, that is, $\Phi > 0$. Firms borrow in the domestic currency to purchase foreign securities. It follows from (4.45) that the balance on the balance-of-payments current account must be positive, that is, $1 - (a/1 + r) - g - \vartheta > 0$. It follows from (4.46) that $\Psi_{sr} > 0$ and $\Psi_{s\rho} > 0$ while the sign of Ψ_{se} depends on the economic structure. As $\Psi_{sr} + \Psi_{s\rho} > 0$, it follows that there is a positive impact on the net securities demand when (i) the monetary authorities as a result of sterilised intervention increase net purchases of domestic securities against net sales of foreign securities, implying that λ is reduced, (ii) there is a reduction of government purchases of goods and services, shown by a reduction in g, (iii) there is an increase in taxation τ, (iv) there is an increase in inflation v_p, (v) there is a rise in fluctuations of the exchange rate, expressed by an increase in σ^2, (vi) there is a tightening of capital restrictions on firms' foreign transactions, implying that ξ_1 is decreased, and (vii) there is a liberalisation of capital restrictions on households' foreign transactions ξ_2. For most of these variables, it depends on the economic structure how natural production is affected. It can only be established unambiguously that natural production is increased by net purchases of domestic securities as a result of sterilised intervention.

The impact of financial integration on policy effectiveness
It follows from (4.49) that obstacles to free capital mobility have an impact on economic policy effectiveness. Capital restrictions affect Ψ_{sr}, $\Psi_{s\rho}$, Ψ_{se}, Ψ_{sg}, and $\Psi_{s\tau}$ and thus the impact of inflation, sterilised intervention, and fiscal policy instruments on the real interest rate and on natural production.

As discussed above, inflation and sterilised intervention affect natural production because they change the currency composition of portfolios and thus the real return on domestic securities relative to foreign securities. This presupposes some degree of financial integration where foreign and domestic securities represent alternative possibilities of placement. Under autarchy, the real interest rate is determined exclusively by real factors, bringing about goods market equilibrium at the natural production level which is determined by the wage setters' preferences and by the production function. Sterilised intervention under autarchy has no impact on the real interest rate, and there is no possibility of affecting the real interest rate through the impact of inflation on the net demand for securities. [15] If, however, there is perfect financial integration, the real interest rate is determined as the foreign real interest rate. Seen from the perspective of maximising monetary policy effectiveness, there is thus an 'optimal' degree of financial integration at which the impact of the domestic inflation rate on the real interest rate, and thus on natural production, is maximised.

The impact of capital restrictions on the effectiveness of monetary policy instruments can be seen from $J_{s\lambda}$ in (4.49). It follows from (4.47) that a liberalisation of firms' possibility of foreign transactions, expressed by a rise in ξ_1, leads to a rise in $\Psi_{s\rho}$. This decreases $J_{s\lambda}$, leading to a reduction in monetary policy effectiveness. It depends, however, on the economic structure how a liberalisation of the households' foreign transactions, shown by a rise in ξ_2, affects the net demand for securities and thus Ψ_{sr} and $\Psi_{s\rho}$. We thus reach the conclusion that it depends on the nature of the capital restrictions to what extent a capital liberalisation leads to a reduction in the effectiveness of monetary policy.

It has been argued in the literature that an optimum currency area is characterised by a high degree of financial integration, cf. Ingram (1973). It has further been argued that policy makers face a trade-off between

---

[15]This can be seen from (4.44) where no capital movements imply $\Phi = 0$ and $F^p = 0$. It follows that the real interest rate is determined to bring about goods market equilibrium, i.e. $D = Y$.

capital mobility and monetary autonomy.[16] The findings which result from the analysis above, are more ambiguous. Financial integration is in fact a precondition for monetary policy instruments to be effective. A country can increase the impact of monetary policy instruments by liberalising certain capital restrictions.

4.6   Summary and conclusion

The analysis shows economic policy effectiveness to be increased when securities markets are imperfectly integrated relative to the case where there is perfect substitution between domestic and foreign securities. It follows from the analysis that monetary policy is able to affect natural production both through changes in the inflation rate and through sterilised intervention. A change in inflation and in net purchases of domestic securities through sterilised intervention influence the net demand for domestic securities and thus the real interest rate. The change in the real interest rate influences natural production by changing the combinations of the real wage and production which can be reached by the wage setters through a terms-of-trade effect and by affecting capital accumulation. The effectiveness of monetary policy means that the authorities, by joining a monetary union characterised by perfect integration of securities markets, lose instruments for influencing natural production. In addition, the authorities can affect natural production through capital restrictions which affect the degree of financial integration.

A number of other findings result from the analysis. The liberalisation of capital restrictions can increase monetary policy effectiveness and some integration of financial markets is a precondition for monetary policy instruments to be effective. It depends on the economic structure whether a rise in inflation increases or reduces the real interest rate. It likewise depends on the economic structure whether fiscal policy increases or depresses natural production.

---

[16]See, for example, Eichengreen, Tobin, and Wyplosz (1995), Padoa-Schioppa (1983, 1985), and Obstfeld (1995).

5 Monopolistic competition in bank markets

5.1 Introduction

This chapter examines the impact of monetary variables on natural production in a model setting based on rational expectations and full price and wage flexibility when the wage setting implies a relationship between the real wage and employment, for example, in the case of a monopoly trade union which sets the wage, and when part of financial intermediation takes place through banks. The markets for bank deposits and bank lending are characterised by imperfect competition. The banks have access to investing and borrowing in a market for external finance. It is assumed that this market, termed the securities market, is internationally integrated, the interest rate being determined through uncovered interest rate parity. The chapter demonstrates that inflation and the central bank's reserve policy have an impact on production if one of the following three conditions is met: (i) the bank faces a cost when raising external finance through the internationally integrated securities market, (ii) the bank has preferences with respect to the choice between placing in securities or increasing bank lending, or (iii) there are economies of scope between deposit taking and bank lending. Natural production is furthermore affected by currency restrictions and restrictions on lending.

The basic working of the model can be explained as follows. Legal tender and bank deposits are substitutes in the investor's portfolio. As legal tender gives no nominal return, it follows that inflation affects the investor's portfolio choice between placing in bank deposits or in legal tender, implying that real bank deposits are affected by inflation. Bank deposits affect bank lending when the bank pays a risk premium on its borrowing through the securities market or when the bank has preferences with respect to the portfolio choice between bank lending and securities. A relationship between bank deposits and bank lending may

102

also arise due to economies of scope. Bank lending affects capital accumulation and the demand for goods when borrowers face constraints in raising funds through the securities market. An increase in bank lending leads to a larger capital stock which improves the wage setters' possibilities of reaching a high real wage and high employment, thus raising natural production. The impact of bank lending on the demand for goods further affects natural unemployment through a terms-of-trade effect, a rise in the demand for goods causing a real appreciation which improves the combinations of the real wage and employment that can be reached by the wage setters.

It is a new finding that monetary policy is effective in a model which incorporates monopolistic competition in bank markets and which otherwise builds on full wage and price flexibility and rational expectations. Previous analyses which study the effectiveness of monetary policy in a model based on the 'credit view', see, for example, Bernanke and Blinder (1988), assume nominal wage or price rigidity. Kashyap and Stein (1994) argue that nominal wage or price rigidities are required for there to be a real effect from monetary policy in models based on the 'credit view'.

Kashyap and Stein (1994) point out that costs for the bank associated with raising external finance can create a link between bank deposits and bank lending when the bank has access to investing and borrowing in a market for external finance. This basic insight is expanded in the present model which suggests further channels through which real bank deposits can affect real bank lending.

Section 5.2 discusses the literature. *Section 5.3* gives the model specification. *Section 5.4* examines the determination of natural production. *Section 5.5* discusses policy implications. *Section 5.6* briefly analyses other channels which can establish a link between bank deposits and bank lending. *Section 5.7* gives a summary and conclusion.

5.2 The literature

Kashyap and Stein (1994) emphasise that three conditions must be met for there to be real effects from monetary policy in a model which incorporates bank lending: (i) borrowers must not be able to raise funds by issuing securities on similar terms as borrowing through banks, (ii) the monetary authorities must be able to affect bank lending, and (iii) the economy must be characterised by inflexible price or wage adjustments.

The first of these conditions implies that borrowing through banks and borrowing through the securities market are imperfect substitutes seen from the viewpoint of the borrower. This condition can be explained by the cost for lenders associated with obtaining information regarding borrowers. This assumption is at the heart of models based on the 'credit view'. The information asymmetries between borrowers and lenders were first examined by Stiglitz and Weiss (1981, 1983) and have subsequently been discussed in a considerable literature.[1] Banks may obtain information at a lower cost than the agents in the securities markets as banks can obtain information directly from the borrowers or because of economies of scale associated with the gathering and use of information. According to Bernanke and Gertler (1995), a lower bank lending rate has a positive impact on the demand for goods for two reasons: (i) by increasing the present value of investments, and (ii) by increasing the firm's possibility of self-financing due to the increase in profit after the deduction of interest expenditure. Diamond (1984) explains the existence of banks with asymmetric information. The 'credit view' was first incorporated into a macroeconomic model by Bernanke and Blinder (1988) who take the point of departure in an IS-LM-model framework. It is supported in a number of empirical investigations.[2]

The second condition set out by Kashyap and Stein (1994) implies that there must be some kind of relationship between bank deposits and bank lending as the monetary authorities, through their control of bank reserves, are able to affect bank deposits. Kashyap and Stein (1994) demonstrate that bank deposits affect bank lending when the bank is charged a risk premium when raising external funds through the securities market and when the size of this premium depends on the bank's lending. This is also stressed by Bernanke and Gertler (1995). The analysis below incorporates this feature which is present only when bank lending is larger than bank deposits. We extend, however, the analysis by suggesting further mechanisms which can create a link between bank deposits and bank lending when bank lending is equal to or smaller than bank deposits. A number of models, for example, Bernanke and Blinder (1988) and Stiglitz and Weiss (1992), assume equality between bank deposits and bank lending.

Kashyap and Stein (1994) note that price and wage rigidities are a prerequisite for there to be real effects from monetary policy in any

---

[1]See, for example, Stiglitz and Weiss (1992) and Greenwald and Stiglitz (1993). A substantial literature describes the bank's behaviour in markets for deposits and lending characterised by monopolistic competition, see, for example, Baltensperger (1980) and Santomero (1984).
[2]A survey regarding investments is found in Hubbard (1998).

model.[3] The model examined below goes beyond this assumption since full price and wage flexibility are assumed.

The model analysed in this chapter is further based on the assumption that banks are in a monopoly position with respect to deposit taking. This can be explained by, for example, public regulation and information asymmetries which restricts competition in the market for deposits.

The analysis below shows that the monetary authorities can affect production by regulating the bank's lending policies. This point is emphasised in some of the literature on optimum currency areas. Branson (1990) stresses that banks, due to asymmetric information, are in a monopoly position with respect to granting loans in a local area. This may give the national central banks a key position with respect to exercising pressure on commercial banks, offering the national central banks the possibility to affect real activity also when exchange rates have been fixed. Von Hagen and Fratianni (1993) emphasise that commercial banks may experience difficulties in obtaining reserves in a monetary union, possibly inducing commercial banks to restrain their lending. Based on the credit view, Dornbusch, Favero, and Giavazzi (1998a, 1998b) present evidence of a differential impact of monetary policy in the European countries.

5.3   Model specification

Economic structure

Firms maximise profit with respect to employment and capital using Cobb–Douglas production technology. This gives the following optimum conditions for the firm's production

$$y_t = ak_t + (1 - a)l_t, \quad 0 < a < 1, \tag{5.1}$$

$$y_t - l_t + \log(1 - a) = w_t - p_t, \tag{5.2}$$

$$y_t - k_t + \log(a) = 1 + v_{t-1}$$
$$\log(1 + v_t) \equiv \log(1 + \zeta_t) - (p_{t+1} - p_t), \quad v_t \geq r_t, \tag{5.3}$$

where y is production (logarithmic value), k the capital stock (logarithmic value), l employment (logarithmic value), w the nominal wage (logarith-

---

[3]Kashyap and Stein (1994) write: 'There must be some form of imperfect price adjustment that prevents any monetary policy shock from being neutral. If prices adjust frictionless, a change in nominal reserves will be met with an equiproportionate change in prices, and both bank and corporate balance sheets will remain unaltered in real terms. In this case, there can be no real effects of monetary policy through either the lending channel or the conventional money demand' (p. 226).

mic value), p the producer price (logarithmic value), v the real bank lending rate, ζ the nominal bank lending rate, and r the real interest rate on securities.

Relation (5.1) shows the firm's production function, the firm using Cobb–Douglas production technology. (5.2) and (5.3) give the conditions for the firm's maximisation of profit with respect to employment and capital. Capital depreciates fully in the course of one time period. To simplify, we have assumed that all firms are credit constrained, the firm's real financing cost thus corresponding to the real bank lending rate. The bank lending rate is higher than the interest rate on securities.

We examine a small economy A which is in steady-state equilibrium. Steady-state equilibrium is characterised by (i) a constant growth rate of production, and (ii) financial variables which lie at unchanged levels relative to nominal production in each time period. The point of departure is taken in the overlapping generations model analysed in the appendix. The rest of the world is represented by a large economy B. The goods market equilibrium is specified as follows (all variables refer to the small economy A unless otherwise indicated)

$$y_t = ze_t + d_t, \quad e_t \equiv p_t^B + x_t - p_t, \quad z > 0, \tag{5.4}$$

$$\frac{D}{Y} = g + \left(\frac{a}{1+v}\right)[1 + N_1(1+r)]\left(\frac{1}{N_3}\right) - \tau(1-a)\left(\frac{N_1 N_2}{N_3}\right) - \left(\frac{1+r}{r}\right)\left(\frac{N_1}{N_3}\right)$$

$$N_1 = 1 - (1+r)^{\Upsilon-1}\beta^\Upsilon > 0$$

$$N_2 = \left(\frac{1}{1 - \Gamma(1+r)^{-1}}\right) + \left(\frac{1+r}{r}\right)$$

$$N_3 = 1 - N_1\left(\frac{1+r}{r}\right) > 0, \quad 0 < \beta < 1, \quad 0 < \Upsilon < 1, \quad r < 0,$$

$$y_t = y_{t-1} \equiv y, \quad g_t = g_{t-1} \equiv g, \quad \tau_t = \tau_{t-1} \equiv \tau, \tag{5.5}$$

$$\log(1 + i_t) = \log(1 + i_t^B) + (x_{t+1} - x_t),$$
$$\log(1 + r_t) \equiv \log(1 + i_t) + (p_{t+1} - p_t), \tag{5.6}$$

$$p_t^B = \bar{p}_t^B, \quad i_t^B = \bar{i}_t^B, \tag{5.7}$$

where e is the real exchange rate (logarithmic value), x the nominal exchange rate (number of home country currency units per currency unit of the foreign country) (logarithmic value), D and d represent domestic demand (non-logarithmic and logarithmic values), g the government's purchases of goods and services relative to production, τ the tax rate on labour income, i the nominal interest rate on securities, β the time discount factor, and Γ shows the development over time of a worker's probability of finding employment. (D/Y) shows domestic demand relative to production in steady-state equilibrium.

Relation (5.4) represents goods market equilibrium. The demand for goods depends on the real exchange rate, and real domestic demand. This function is derived in the appendix. To simplify, we do not consider the exogenously given foreign production.

Relation (5.5) shows domestic demand, specified as the sum of consumption, investment, and government purchases of goods and services, in steady-state equilibrium. (5.5) is derived from an overlapping generations model with a gradual retirement from the labour market. It corresponds to (A.45) in the appendix. In the specification of (5.5) it is assumed, to simplify, that there are no wealth effects on consumption from government money and from bank deposits, inflation tax/seigniorage and bank profits being transferred to the households through lump-sum transfers and dividend payments. In the framework of the overlapping generations model, it follows from (5.5) that fiscal policy, working both through government purchases of goods and services and taxes on labour income, has an impact on the economy also in steady-state equilibrium. The bank deposit rate has no impact on consumption (see section A.9), and the only impact of banks on the real economy thus arises from the impact of the banks' lending rate on investment.

Relation (5.6) shows the uncovered interest rate parity which applies only to the securities market. (5.7) reflects that the home country is a small economy.

To simplify, we rewrite the relationship for domestic demand relative to production specified by (5.5) as follows

$$\Omega_s = \Omega_s(r, v, g, \tau),$$

$$\Omega_{sr} \equiv \frac{\partial \Omega_s}{\partial r} < 0, \quad \Omega_{sv} \equiv \frac{\partial \Omega_s}{\partial v} < 0, \quad \Omega_{sg} \equiv \frac{\partial \Omega_s}{\partial g} > 0, \quad \Omega_{s\tau} \equiv \frac{\partial \Omega_s}{\partial \tau} < 0,$$

$$(5.8)$$

where Ω_s represents domestic demand relative to production in steady-state equilibrium (logarithmic value).

Relation (5.8) shows domestic demand relative to production as a positive function of (i) a lower real bank lending rate v, (ii) higher government purchases of goods and services g, and (iii) a lower tax rate on labour income τ. We further assume that domestic demand relative to production is increased by a lower real interest rate on securities r.

The wage setters determine the nominal wage to optimise preferences which include the real wage and employment. The wage setters' optimisation is characterised as follows

$$l_t - l'' = \left(\frac{\theta}{\gamma}\right)(w_t - q_t) + \left(\frac{\theta}{\gamma}\right)\log(1 - \tau) - \left(\frac{1}{\gamma}\right)\epsilon,$$

$$\epsilon \equiv \log\left(\frac{\theta a}{\gamma f^u}\right), \quad l'' \equiv 0, \quad \gamma > 0, \quad \theta > 0, \tag{5.9}$$

$$q_t \equiv p_t + \varphi e_t, \quad 0 < \varphi < 1, \tag{5.10}$$

where q is the consumer price (logarithmic value), l'' full employment (logarithmic value), and ϵ reflects changes in the wage setters' preferences with respect to the real wage and employment.

Relation (5.9) shows the combinations of production and real wage levels which are consistent with the wage setters' optimisation. Decentralised wage setting is assumed, implying that the wage setters are unable to affect macroeconomic variables. (5.9) is derived under the assumption that wage setters are unable to affect capital accumulation, investment decisions being taken in advance of wage setting. (5.10) is the definition of the consumer price.

Combining (5.1)–(5.10) gives natural production in the steady-state as follows

$$y^{DW} = -\left(1 + \frac{\theta}{\gamma}\right)\left(\frac{a}{1 - a}\right)\log(1 + v) + \left(\frac{\varphi}{z}\right)\left(\frac{\theta}{\gamma}\right)\Omega_s - \left(\frac{1}{\gamma}\right)\epsilon$$

$$+ \left(\frac{\theta}{\gamma}\right)\log(1 - \tau) + \left(\frac{1 + \theta}{\gamma}\right)\left(\frac{a}{1 - a}\right)\log(a) + \left(\frac{\theta}{\gamma}\right)\log(1 - a). \tag{5.11}$$

It follows from (5.11) that the real bank lending rate affects natural production through two channels: (i) by affecting capital accumulation, an increase in the capital stock causes an increase in the real wage which induces wage setters to opt for higher production, and (ii) through a terms-of-trade effect, implying that a rise in the demand for goods causes a real appreciation which increases the real wage and thus leads to higher production.

Markets for bank lending and deposits

The demand functions for bank lending, bank deposits, and legal tender are given as follows

$$h_t - y_t = \log(a) - \log(1 + v_t), \tag{5.12}$$

$$b_t = b_1 y_t - b_2 \log\left(\frac{r_t - \varpi_t}{1 + r_t}\right) - b_3 \log\left(\frac{i_t}{1 + i_t}\right) + \mu_t,$$

$$b_1 > 1, \quad b_2 > 1, \quad b_3 > 1, \tag{5.13}$$

$$\log(1 + \varpi_t) \equiv \log(1 + \rho_t) - (p_{t+1} - p_t), \quad r_t \geq \varpi_t,$$

$$\mu_t = \mu_{t+1} \equiv \mu,$$

$$\ell = \ell_1 y_t + \ell_2 \log(1 + \varpi_t) - \ell_2 \log(1 + r_t) - \ell_3 \log\left(\frac{i_t}{1 + i_t}\right),$$

$$\ell_i > 0, \quad i = 1, 2, 3, \tag{5.14}$$

where h is real bank credit (nominal bank credit deflated with the producer price) (logarithmic value), b real bank deposits (nominal value of bank deposits deflated with the producer price) (logarithmic value), ϖ the real interest rate on bank deposits, ρ the nominal interest rate on bank deposits, μ a shift in the demand for bank deposits, and ℓ the real demand for legal tender from non-financial domestic agents (nominal value of legal tender deflated with the producer price) (logarithmic value).

Relation (5.12) expresses that the real demand for bank lending equals investment, specified in (5.3) as $Y_t(a/1 + v_{t-1})$. Relations (5.13)–(5.14) specify demand for real bank deposits and legal tender. A derivation is found in section A.9 of the appendix.[4] (5.13) shows the real demand for bank deposits to be negatively affected by the interest rate differential between securities and bank deposits and by the nominal interest rate on securities and positively affected by the nominal interest rate on bank deposits and by production. μ reflects exogenous shifts in the demand for bank deposits. It follows from section A.9 that the demand elasticity of bank deposits with respect to production, with respect to the interest rate differential between securities and bank deposits, and with respect to the nominal interest rate are larger than one, that is, $b_1 > 1$, $b_2 > 1$, and $b_3 > 1$. (5.14) gives the demand for legal tender. The demand depends on the utility of liquidity services, reflected by the production and price levels, and on the opportunity cost of legal tender, expressed by the interest rate on securities and the interest rate on bank deposits. Legal tender carries no interest.

The model specified above includes three assets held by non-financial domestic agents: (i) securities traded in an internationally integrated market, (ii) bank deposits which can be used for payments and which carry

---

[4]To simplify, consumption has been replaced with production relative to the derivation in the appendix. This is valid as the analysis considers a steady-state equilibrium in which consumption is constant relative to production.

an interest rate determined by the banks' profit maximisation, and (iii) financial assets, termed legal tender, which can be used for payments and which carry a nominally fixed interest rate, assumed to be zero. The exact delineation of these financial assets depends on institutional characteristics which may differ among countries and banks. One may conceive of certain bank deposits, for example, standardised euro-deposits, the return on which is determined through perfect competition and which would therefore be characterised as securities in the classification above. One may also conceive of certain bank deposits on which banks offer a fixed nominal interest due to, for example, a ban on interest payments or a ceiling on the interest rate. Such bank deposits would be categorised as legal tender in the categorisation above.

The bank's profit maximisation

We consider a representative bank which operates in lending and deposit markets characterised by imperfect competition. The representative bank does not expect to gain market shares from other banks when changing bank lending and bank deposit rates. Two explanations may justify this assumption: (i) borrowers of bank loans and depositors of bank deposits face transaction costs when changing to another bank, and (ii) the representative bank expects other banks to set the same interest rates and thus react in the same way as the bank itself.

The representative bank sets deposit and lending rates to maximise expected profit. The bank's profit optimisation is characterised as follows

$$\max_{\zeta,\rho}\left\{v_t^b \mid \frac{\partial y}{\partial \zeta^b} = 0, \ \frac{\partial p}{\partial \zeta^b} = 0, \ \frac{\partial x}{\partial \rho^b} = 0\right\}, \tag{5.15}$$

$$\frac{v_t^b}{P_t} =$$

$$\begin{cases} \zeta_t^b H_t^b - [\rho_t^b + \eta_t(1 + v_p)]B_t^b - (H_t^b - B_t^b)[i_t + \kappa_t(1 + v_p)], & \forall H_t^b > B_t^b, \\ \zeta_t^b H_t^b - [\rho_t^b + \eta_t(1 + v_p)]B_t^b, & \forall H_t^b = B_t^b, \\ \zeta_t^b H_t^b - [\rho_t + \eta_t(1 + v_p)]B_t^b + (B_t^b - H_t^b)[i_t - \Phi_t(1 + v_p)], & \forall H_t^b < B_t^b, \end{cases} \tag{5.16}$$

$$\kappa_t = \kappa_1(h_t^b - y_t) + \xi_t, \quad \forall H_t^b > B_t^b, \quad \kappa_1 > 0, \quad \xi_{t+1} = \xi_t \equiv \xi, \quad \xi > 0, \tag{5.17}$$

$$\Phi_t = \Phi_1(b_t^b - h_t^b) + \Delta_t, \quad \forall H_t < B_t, \quad \Phi_1 > 0, \quad \Delta_{t+1} = \Delta_t \equiv \Delta, \quad \Delta > 0, \tag{5.18}$$

where v^b is bank profit, η reflects a cost to a bank of receiving deposits, and H and B are the non-logarithmic values of respectively real bank lending and real bank deposits. The cost for a bank of raising funds through the securities market is expressed by $i + \kappa(1 + v_p)$, where κ reflects a premium in real terms above the interest rate in the securities market and where ξ expresses shifts in this relationship. The return to a bank of investing in the securities market is expressed by $i - \Phi(1 + v_p)$ where Φ expresses a lower (real) return, for example, due to liquidity risk. Δ expresses shifts in the return for banks of investing in the securities market. Variables which relate to the single representative bank, are denoted with b.

Relation (5.15) specifies that banks set lending and deposit rates to maximise expected profit. Banks form correct expectations concerning macroeconomic and other variables. The representative bank is small, implying that it is unable to affect macroeconomic variables.

Relation (5.16) gives the definition of bank profits. Three cases are distinguished: (i) bank lending is larger than bank deposits ($H^b > B^b$), (ii) bank lending equals bank deposits ($H^b = B^b$), and (iii) bank lending is smaller than bank deposits ($H^b < B^b$). Bank lending exceeds deposits when banks can finance the lending at a lower marginal cost by raising finance through the securities market than through deposits. Bank deposits equal bank lending when the marginal cost of raising funds through deposits is lower than the marginal cost of raising funds through the securities market and higher than the marginal return of investing in the securities market. Finally, bank deposits exceed bank lending when the marginal return from investing in securities exceeds the marginal return which can be obtained from bank lending.

It is assumed from (5.16) that a cost, shown by η, is associated with receiving bank deposits. This cost may reflect: (i) the resource cost associated with receiving deposits, for example, expenditure on staff and computer costs; and (ii) a cost associated with holding a low-interest liquidity reserve or with being able to raise funds at short notice through the securities market or the central bank. The first kind of cost depends on the production structure in the bank. The second kind of cost depends on a variety of factors, for example, the solvency of the bank, the information concerning the bank among other financial agents, the efficiency of inter-bank markets, the variation in the public's liquidity needs, and the reserve policy pursued by the central bank.

Relation (5.17) expresses the cost at which a bank can raise finance through the securities market. The bank is charged a premium above the risk-free rate, expressed by κ. It is assumed that this premium depends on real bank lending relative to production, that is, $h^b - y$. It is thus assumed, corresponding to Kashyap and Stein (1994) and Bernanke and Gertler (1995), that the risk premium depends on the volume of real bank lending. ξ reflects exogenously determined changes, for example, a shift in the credit assessment of the bank caused by improved access to information among agents operating in the securities market.

Relation (5.18) shows that the bank's return from investing in the securities market corresponds to the risk-free interest rate with the deduction of a term Φ. Φ may reflect the larger liquidity risk which the bank runs by investing in securities and thus depends on the share of bank deposits on balance, expressed by $b^h - h^h$. Securities have on average a longer maturity than bank lending as many bank loan contracts include provisions which make it possible to foreclose on loans at short notice. This means that the bank faces a larger liquidity risk when investing in securities rather than increasing bank lending. One may conceive of other characteristics in addition to the difference in liquidity risk which would cause the risk to vary between bank lending and investment in securities. For example, the bank may have better access to information regarding the borrower in the case of bank lending than when investing in a security.

As banks are uniform, it follows that the bank lending and deposit rates at the macroeconomic level correspond to the bank lending and deposit rates set by the individual bank, that is

$$h_t^b = h_t, \quad b_t^b = b_t, \quad v^b = v, \quad \varpi^b = \varpi. \tag{5.19}$$

Relation (5.19) specifies the connection between microeconomic and macroeconomic levels.

Monetary regime
The authorities control inflation v_p and thus the opportunity cost of holding legal tender. Inflation is set at the same level in each time period. This gives

$$v_{p,t} = \bar{v}_{p,t}, \quad v_{p,t} = v_{p,t-1} \equiv v_p, \quad v_{p,t} \equiv \frac{P_t - P_{t-1}}{P_{t-1}}, \tag{5.20}$$

where v_p is the price increase.

The authorities can further control the cost for banks of receiving deposits, for example, through reserve requirements. This gives

$$\eta_t = \bar{\eta}_t, \quad \eta_t = \eta_{t-1} \equiv \eta. \tag{5.21}$$

The variable η reflects the authorities' reserve policy. It is further assumed by (5.21) that the authorities maintain an unchanged reserve policy in each time period.

5.4 Determination of natural production

Bank lending larger than bank deposits $(H > B)$

The model relates to a steady-state equilibrium. As there is no technical progress, the output growth rate is 0, and time indications can be deleted. The representative bank optimises profit with respect to bank lending and bank deposits. Optimising (5.16) with respect to real bank lending h^b and real bank deposits b^b, and using (5.3), (5.12)–(5.13), (5.15), (5.17), and (5.19)–(5.21) gives the first-order conditions as

$$v - \left(\frac{1}{\varepsilon_h}\right) = r + \kappa + \kappa_1\left(\frac{H - B}{H}\right), \quad \varepsilon_h \equiv \frac{\partial h}{\partial v}, \quad (5.22)$$

$$\varpi + \left(\frac{1}{\varepsilon_d}\right) + \eta = r + \kappa, \quad \varepsilon_d \equiv \frac{\partial b}{\partial \varpi}, \quad (5.23)$$

where ε_h and ε_d express the price elasticities of respectively bank lending and bank deposits.

Relation (5.22) expresses that the marginal revenue from bank lending, shown by $v - (1/\varepsilon_h)$, equals the marginal cost of raising funds through the securities market, given by $r + \kappa + \kappa_1[(H - B)/H]$. (5.23) shows that the bank optimises the earnings from deposits when the marginal cost of attracting deposits, given by $\varpi + (1/\varepsilon_d) + \eta$, equals the cost of raising external funds, shown by $r + \kappa$. The first-order conditions are shown at the macroeconomic level. With the specification of bank lending and bank deposits given by (5.12)–(5.13), it follows that $(1/\varepsilon_h) = 1 + v$ while $(1/\varepsilon_d) = (r - \varpi)/b_2$.

The second-order conditions for the bank's optimum impose the following conditions on levels of bank lending and bank deposits for the bank's optimisation of profit

$$\left(1 - \frac{1}{b_2}\right) > 0, \quad \left(1 - \frac{1}{b_2}\right)\left(\frac{r - \varpi}{b_2}\right)\left(1 + \frac{H}{B}\right) - \kappa_1 > 0. \quad (5.24)$$

Throughout the following discussion, we assume that the second-order conditions shown by (5.24) are met. It follows directly from the assumption in (5.13) of the demand for bank deposits being interest elastic, i.e., $b_2 > 1$, that $1 - (1/b_2) > 0$.

Combining (5.11)–(5.13), (5.17), and (5.19)–(5.21), and assuming the conditions shown by (5.24) are met, gives the impact of exogenous variables on natural production when bank lending is larger than bank deposits

$$d(y)^{CS} = J_1^{CS} d\epsilon + J_2^{CS} dr + J_3^{CS} dg + J_4^{CS} d\tau + J_5^{CS} dv_p + J_6^{CS} d\eta + J_7^{CS} d\mu$$
$$+ J_8^{CS} d\xi + J_9^{CS} d\Delta,$$

$$J_1^{CS} \equiv \left(\frac{\partial y^{CS}}{\partial \epsilon} \right) = -\left(\frac{N_5}{N_5 + N_4(1 - N_6)} \right)\left(\frac{1}{\gamma} \right) < 0,$$

$$J_2^{CS} \equiv \left(\frac{\partial y^{CS}}{\partial r} \right) = \left(\frac{N_5}{N_5 + N_4(1 - N_6)} \right)\left(\frac{\varphi}{z} \right)\left(\frac{\theta}{\gamma} \right)\Omega_{sr}$$

$$+ \left(\frac{N_4}{N_5 + N_4(1 - N_6)} \right)\left(1 - \frac{1}{b_2} \right)\left(\frac{r - \varpi}{b_2} \right)\left[\left(\frac{1}{1+r} \right)\left(b_2 \frac{b_3}{i} \right) \right.$$

$$\left. - \left(\frac{1}{\kappa_1} \right)\left(\frac{H}{B} \right) \right],$$

$$J_3^{CS} \equiv \left(\frac{\partial y^{CS}}{\partial g} \right) = \left(\frac{N_5}{N_5 + N_4(1 - N_6)} \right)\left(\frac{\varphi}{z} \right)\left(\frac{\theta}{\gamma} \right)\Omega_{sg} > 0,$$

$$J_4^{CS} \equiv \left(\frac{\partial y^{CS}}{\partial \tau} \right) = \left(\frac{N_5}{N_5 + N_4(1 - N_6)} \right)\left(\frac{\varphi}{z} \right)\left(\frac{\theta}{\gamma} \right)\Omega_{s\tau}$$

$$- \left(\frac{N_5}{N_5 + N_4(1 - N_6)} \right)\left(\frac{\theta}{\gamma} \right)\left(\frac{1}{1 - \tau} \right) < 0,$$

$$J_5^{CS} \equiv \left(\frac{\partial y^{CS}}{\partial v_p} \right)$$

$$= \left(\frac{-N_4}{N_5 + N_4(1 - N_6)} \right)\left(1 - \frac{1}{b_2} \right)\left(\frac{r - \varpi}{b_2} \right)\left(\frac{b_3}{i} \right)\left(\frac{1}{1 + v_p} \right) < 0,$$

$$J_6^{CS} \equiv \left(\frac{\partial y^{CS}}{\partial \eta} \right) = \left(\frac{-N_4}{N_5 + N_4(1 - N_6)} \right) < 0,$$

$$J_7^{CS} \equiv \left(\frac{\partial y^{CS}}{\partial \mu} \right) = \left(\frac{N_4}{N_5 + N_4(1 - N_6)} \right)\left(1 - \frac{1}{b_2} \right)\left(\frac{r - \varpi}{b_2} \right) > 0,$$

$$J_8^{CS} \equiv \left(\frac{\partial y^{CS}}{\partial \xi} \right)$$

$$= \left(\frac{N_4}{N_5 + N_4(1 - N_6)} \right)\left[1 - \left(1 - \frac{1}{b_2} \right)\left(\frac{r - \varpi}{b_2} \right)\left(\frac{1}{\kappa_1} \right)\left(\frac{H}{B} \right) \right],$$

$$J_8^{CS} \equiv \left(\frac{\partial y^{CS}}{\partial \Delta} \right) = 0,$$

$$N_4 \equiv \left(1 + \frac{\theta}{\gamma} \right) \left(\frac{a}{1-a} \right) - \left(\frac{\varphi}{z} \right) \left(\frac{\theta}{\gamma} \right) (1 + v) \Omega_{sv} > 0,$$

$$N_5 \equiv \left(1 - \frac{1}{b_2} \right) \left(\frac{r - \varpi}{b_2} \right) \left(1 + \frac{H}{B} \right) - \kappa_1 > 0,$$

$$N_6 \equiv \left(1 - \frac{1}{b_2} \right) \left(\frac{r - \varpi}{b_2} \right) \left(b_1 + \frac{H}{B} \right) - \kappa_1 > 0, \tag{5.25}$$

where CS denotes the case where bank lending is larger than bank deposits ('credit surplus').

It follows from (5.25) that natural production is increased if (i) the wage setters place a larger weight on the real wage relative to employment, that is, ϵ decreases, (ii) there is an increase in government purchases of goods and services relative to production g, (iii) there is a reduction in the tax rate on labour income τ, (iv) there is lower inflation v_p, (v) there is a reduction in the costs associated with deposits η, and (vi) there is a change in preferences causing an increase in the demand for bank deposits μ. It depends on the economic structure how a change in the costs associated with attracting external funds through the securities market ξ affects natural production.

Monetary variables, that is, inflation v_p, the cost associated with deposits η, and shifts in the demand for bank deposits μ influence natural production through the real bank lending rate. This is also the case with respect to exogenous shifts in the banks' risk premium related to non-deposit external finance ξ. The impact on natural production takes place through two channels: (i) through a terms-of-trade effect, a lower real bank lending rate causing a rise in the demand for goods and thus a real appreciation which induces wage setters to increase employment; and (ii) through capital stock, a lower real bank lending rate increasing the capital stock and thus the real wage, a higher real wage inducing wage setters to aim at a higher production.

The reason why monetary variables affect natural production is the cost incurred by the bank when it raises non-deposit external funds to finance bank lending which is a function of bank deposits. This can be seen from (5.22). There is a monetary impact on bank lending if variables affected by monetary factors appear in the Euler condition for the bank's optimisation of bank lending, that is, (5.22). It follows that real bank deposits enter the right side of (5.22), affecting the bank's marginal funding cost, because $\kappa_1 \neq 0$. The rise in the marginal cost associated with raising external non-deposit funds when lending is increased, induces the bank also to increase the funding through deposits, causing the bank to raise the interest rate on bank deposits. The cost of receiving deposits thus affects the total marginal funding cost and through this the real bank lending rate. This finding corresponds to Kashyap and Stein (1994).

Inflation v_p affects real bank deposits through an impact on the nominal interest rate on securities, a higher nominal interest rate on securities reducing demand for bank deposits. The impact of inflation increases when the interest rate elasticity of bank deposits with respect to the bank deposit rate increases, that is, there is an increase in b_3.

Government purchases of goods and services g affect natural production only through the terms-of-trade effect while the tax rate on labour income τ influences natural production both through a terms-of-trade effect and through a direct impact on the wage setters' weighting between disposable real income and employment.

The real interest rate in the securities market r influences natural production both through a terms-of-trade effect and by affecting the real bank lending rate. It depends on the economic structure how a higher real interest rate on the securities market influences natural production. There is a direct influence on the demand for goods through the impact of the securities rate on household saving, a higher rate causing an increase in saving and thereby a reduction in the demand for goods. A higher rate on securities further depresses capital accumulation and thus natural production by increasing the cost to banks of raising external finance through the securities market. An opposite effect arises because a higher real securities rate increases the demand for bank deposits, thus working to increase bank lending and through this capital accumulation and natural production.

Bank lending equals bank deposits ($H = B$)
Combining (5.3), (5.12)–(5.13), (5.15)–(5.16), and (5.19)–(5.21), the optimum condition for the bank's optimisation of profit when bank lending equals bank deposits, is found as

$$v - \left(\frac{1}{\varepsilon_h}\right) = \varpi + \eta + \left(\frac{1}{\varepsilon_d}\right). \tag{5.26}$$

Relation (5.26) shows the bank to optimise profit when the marginal revenue from bank lending, shown by $v - (1/\varepsilon_h)$, equals the marginal cost of attracting deposits, shown by $\varpi + \eta + (1/\varepsilon_d)$. The second-order condition for the bank's optimum is given as

$$\left(1 - \frac{1}{b_2}\right) > 0. \tag{5.27}$$

The second-order condition for profit maximisation is met when $b_2 > 1$, that is, the demand for bank deposits is elastic with respect to the bank deposit rate. This condition is met by (5.13).

Bank lending equals bank deposits when there is equality between the bank's marginal funding cost and the bank's marginal revenue, shown by (5.26), at a level at which the marginal funding cost/marginal revenue lies between (i) the real interest rate on the securities market with the addition of the risk premium which is charged on the bank in the securities market κ, and (ii) the real interest rate on the securities market with the deduction of the cost to the bank of investing in securities rather than increasing bank lending Φ. This means that bank lending equals bank deposits when the following condition is met

$$r + \kappa \geq v - \left(\frac{1}{\varepsilon_h}\right) \geq r - \Phi. \tag{5.28}$$

When (5.28) is fulfilled at levels of bank lending/deposits for which also (5.26)–(5.27) are met, bank lending equals bank deposits. Relation (5.28) together with (5.26)–(5.27) thus specify a range of bank lending/deposit levels for which bank lending equals bank deposits. This insight is important. Due to the presence of risk premia when borrowing in the securities market and/or costs associated with investing in the securities market, there is a range of production values for which bank deposits equal bank lending. For this range of production levels monetary policy, through its impact on bank deposits, has a direct impact on real bank lending and thus on natural production.

Combining (5.11), (5.19)–(5.21), and (5.26)–(5.27) gives natural production when bank lending is equal to bank deposits as

$$d(y)^{CE} = J_1^{CE} d\epsilon + J_2^{CE} dr + J_3^{CE} dg + J_4^{CE} d\tau + J_5^{CE} dv_p$$

$$+ J_6^{CE} d\eta + J_7^{CE} d\mu + J_8^{CE} d\xi + J_9^{CE} d\Delta,$$

$$J_1^{CE} \equiv \left(\frac{\partial y^{CE}}{\partial \epsilon}\right) = -\left(\frac{1}{1 + N_4(1 - b_1)}\right)\left(\frac{1}{\gamma}\right),$$

$$J_2^{CS} \equiv \left(\frac{\partial y^{CE}}{\partial r}\right) = \left(\frac{N_4}{1 + N_4(1 - b_1)}\right)\left(\frac{\varphi}{z}\right)\left(\frac{\theta}{\gamma}\right)\Omega_{sr} + \left(\frac{N_4}{1 + N_4(1 - b_1)}\right)$$

$$\times \left[\left(\frac{b_2}{1 + r}\right) - \left(\frac{b_2}{r - \varpi}\right) - \left(\frac{1}{1 + r}\right)\left(\frac{b_3}{i}\right) + \left(\frac{1}{b_2 N_4 N_7}\right)\right],$$

$$J_3^{CE} \equiv \left(\frac{\partial y^{CE}}{\partial g}\right) = \left(\frac{1}{1 + N_4(1 - b_1)}\right)\left(\frac{\varphi}{z}\right)\left(\frac{\theta}{\gamma}\right)\Omega_{sg},$$

$$J_4^{CE} \equiv \left(\frac{\partial y^{CE}}{\partial \tau}\right) = \left(\frac{1}{1 + N_4(1 - b_1)}\right)\left(\frac{\varphi}{z}\right)\left(\frac{\theta}{\gamma}\right)\Omega_{s\tau}$$

$$- \left(\frac{1}{1 + N_4(1 - b_1)}\right)\left(\frac{\theta}{\gamma}\right)\left(\frac{1}{1 - \tau}\right),$$

$$J_5^{CE} \equiv \left(\frac{\partial y^{CE}}{\partial v_p}\right) = \left(\frac{-N_4}{1 + N_4(1 - b_1)}\right)\left(\frac{b_3}{i}\right)\left(\frac{1}{1 + v_p}\right),$$

$$J_6^{CE} \equiv \left(\frac{\partial y^{CE}}{\partial \eta}\right) = \left(\frac{1}{1 + N_4(1 - b_1)}\right)\left(\frac{1}{N_\tau}\right),$$

$$J_7^{CE} \equiv \left(\frac{\partial y^{CE}}{\partial \mu}\right) = \left(\frac{N_4}{1 + N_4(1 - b_1)}\right),$$

$$J_8^{CE} \equiv \left(\frac{\partial y^{CE}}{\partial \xi}\right) = 0,$$

$$J_9^{CE} \equiv \left(\frac{\partial y^{CE}}{\partial \Delta}\right) = 0,$$

$$N_4 \equiv \left(\frac{\theta}{\gamma} + 1\right)\left(\frac{a}{1 - a}\right) - \left(\frac{\varphi}{z}\right)\left(\frac{\theta}{\gamma}\right)(1 + v)\Omega_{sv} > 0,$$

$$N_7 \equiv \left(1 - \frac{1}{b_2}\right)\left(\frac{r - \varpi}{b_2}\right) > 0, \tag{5.29}$$

where CE denotes the case where bank lending equals bank deposits.

It follows from (5.29) that it depends on the sign of the term $1 + N_4(1 - b_1)$ and thus on the economic structure how exogenous variables affect natural production. From (5.13) it follows that $b_1 > 1$. Assuming $1 > N_4(1 - b_1)$, it follows that natural production is positively affected by (i) a shift in the wage setters' preferences towards more weight being given to employment (a lower value of ϵ), (ii) an increase in government purchases of goods and services g, (iii) a reduction in the tax rate on labour income τ, (iv) lower inflation v_p, (v) a decrease in the exogenously determined cost for banks of receiving deposits, shown by a lower value of η, and (vi) an increase in the non-financial sector's demand for deposits μ. Similar to the case where bank lending is larger than bank deposits (see above), the sign for the impact of the real interest rate on securities cannot be determined unambiguously.

There is a monetary impact on real bank lending, and thus on natural production, even though the bank's marginal cost of borrowing through the securities market is unaffected by the size of bank lending (see above) and even though the bank's cost of investing in securities rather than increasing bank lending is unaffected by the size of bank deposits (see below).

Bank lending smaller than bank deposits $(H < B)$

Optimising (5.16) with respect to bank lending h^b and bank deposits b^b, and using (5.3), (5.12)–(5.13), (5.15), and (5.18)–(5.21), gives the conditions for optimum as

$$v - \left(\frac{1}{\varepsilon_h}\right) = r - \Phi - \Phi_1\left(\frac{B - H}{H}\right), \tag{5.30}$$

$$r - \Phi - \Phi_1\left(\frac{B - H}{B}\right) = \varpi + \eta + \left(\frac{1}{\varepsilon_d}\right). \tag{5.31}$$

The condition shown by (5.30) specifies that the marginal revenue from bank lending equals the marginal revenue from placing in securities. (5.31) expresses that the marginal revenue from placing in securities equals the marginal cost of attracting more deposits. The second-order optimum condition for the bank's profit maximisation is given by (5.27), implying that $b_2 > 1$.

Combining (5.11), (5.19)–(5.21), (5.27), and (5.30)–(5.31) gives the impact of the exogenous variables on the natural production as

$$d(y)^{DS} = J_1^{DS} d\epsilon + J_2^{DS} dr + J_3^{DS} dg + J_4^{DS} d\tau + J_5^{DS} dv_p$$

$$+ J_6^{DS} d\eta + J_7^{DS} d\mu + J_8^{DS} d\xi + J_9^{DS} d\Delta,$$

$$J_1^{DS} \equiv \left(\frac{\partial y^{DS}}{\partial \epsilon}\right) = -\left(\frac{N_8}{N_8 + N_4(1 + b_1 N_8)}\right)\left(\frac{1}{\gamma}\right) < 0,$$

$$J_2^{DS} \equiv \left(\frac{\partial y^{DS}}{\partial r}\right) = \left(\frac{N_8}{N_8 + N_4(1 + b_1 N_8)}\right)\left(\frac{\varphi}{z}\right)\left(\frac{\theta}{\gamma}\right)\Omega_{sr} + \left(\frac{N_8}{N_8 + N_4(1 + b_1 N_9)}\right)$$

$$\times \left(1 - \frac{1}{b_2}\right)\left(\frac{r - \varpi}{b_2}\right)\left[\left(\frac{1}{1+r}\right)\left(b_2 - \frac{b_3}{i}\right) - \left(\frac{1}{\kappa_1}\right)\left(\frac{H}{B}\right)\right],$$

$$J_3^{DS} \equiv \left(\frac{\partial y^{DS}}{\partial g}\right) = \left(\frac{N_8}{N_8 + N_4(1 + b_1 N_8)}\right)\left(\frac{\varphi}{z}\right)\left(\frac{\theta}{\gamma}\right)\Omega_{sg} > 0,$$

$$J_4^{DS} \equiv \left(\frac{\partial y^{DS}}{\partial \tau}\right) = \left(\frac{N_8}{N_8 + N_4(1 + b_1 N_8)}\right)\left(\frac{\varphi}{z}\right)\left(\frac{\theta}{\gamma}\right)\Omega_{s\tau}$$

$$- \left(\frac{N_8}{N_8 + N_4(1 + b_1 N_8)}\right)\left(\frac{\theta}{\gamma}\right)\left(\frac{1}{1 - \tau}\right) < 0,$$

$$J_5^{DS} \equiv \left(\frac{\partial y^{DS}}{\partial v_p}\right) = \left(\frac{-N_4}{N_8 + N_4(1 + b_1 N_8)}\right)\left(1 - \frac{1}{b_2}\right)\left(\frac{r - \varpi}{b_2}\right)\left(\frac{b_3}{i}\right)\left(\frac{1}{1 + v_p}\right) < 0,$$

$$J_6^{DS} \equiv \left(\frac{\partial y^{DS}}{\partial \eta}\right) = \left(\frac{-N_4}{N_8 + N_4(1 + b_1 N_8)}\right) < 0,$$

$$J_7^{DS} \equiv \left(\frac{\partial y^{DS}}{\partial \mu}\right) = \left(\frac{N_4}{N_8 + N_4(1 + b_1 N_8)}\right)\left(1 - \frac{1}{b_2}\right)\left(\frac{r - \varpi}{b_2}\right) > 0,$$

$$J_8^{DS} \equiv \left(\frac{\partial y^{DS}}{\partial \xi}\right) = 0,$$

$$J_9^{DS} \equiv \left(\frac{\partial y^{DS}}{\partial \Delta}\right) = \left(\frac{N_4}{N_8 + N_4(1 + b_1 N_8)}\right)\left[\left(1 - \frac{1}{b_2}\right)\left(\frac{r - \varpi}{b_2}\right) + \Phi_1\left(\frac{H}{B} - \frac{B}{H}\right)\right],$$

$$N_4 \equiv \left(1 + \frac{\theta}{\gamma}\right)\left(\frac{a}{1-a}\right) - \left(\frac{\varphi}{z}\right)\left(\frac{\theta}{\gamma}\right)(1 + v)\Omega_{sv} > 0,$$

$$N_8 \equiv \left(1 - \frac{1}{b_2}\right)\left(\frac{r - \varpi}{b_2}\right)\left(1 + \frac{B}{H}\right)\Phi_1 > 0, \tag{5.32}$$

where DS denotes the case where bank deposits are larger than bank lending ('deposit surplus').

Relation (5.32) shows natural production to be positively affected by (i) a shift in the wage setters' preferences towards more weight being given to employment (a lower value of ϵ), (ii) an increase in government purchases of goods and services g, (iii) a reduction in the tax rate on labour income τ, (iv) a reduction in inflation v_p, (v) a decrease in the exogenously determined cost for banks of receiving deposits, reflected by a lower value of η, and (vi) an increase in the non-financial sector's demand for deposits μ. It depends on the economic structure how a change in the cost associated with placing in securities relative to bank lending, is reflected by a lower value of Δ.

The monetary impact on natural production arises because the cost to the bank of investing in securities relative to bank lending depends on the size of deposits. This can be seen from (5.30). Monetary factors affect real bank lending, and thus natural production, because deposits appear in the bank's optimum condition for real bank lending, shown by (5.30). If $\Phi_1 = 0$, deposits do not affect bank lending.

5.5 Policy implications

Effectiveness of monetary policy

It follows from (5.25), (5.29), and (5.32) that monetary policy affects natural production through two channels: (i) through inflation v_p, and (ii) because the authorities can influence the cost to commercial banks of receiving bank deposits η. Inflation determines the opportunity cost to the public of holding legal tender, a rise in inflation inducing the public to hold either bank deposits or securities. The authorities can thus affect bank deposits through inflation, in turn influencing bank lending and thus the demand for goods. The monetary authorities can further affect the cost associated with receiving deposits either by increasing the cost for commercial banks of holding reserves in the central bank or by imposing reserve requirements on bank deposits.

It results that lower inflation increases bank deposits, inducing banks to increase real lending and thus causing higher natural production. The model can thus be seen as a justification for the authorities pursuing a price stability goal. This argument for low inflation is additional to the traditional reasons for low inflation offered in the literature, most importantly the consideration to increase the efficiency of payments transactions and reducing information costs, cf. the discussion in chapter 2.

It has been assumed in the model above that the whole of capital formation is financed through bank loans. It is more realistic to perceive that at least part of firms can finance investments through the securities market, although possibly at a cost. In this case the authorities are able to affect natural production by measures which change the firms' incentives for raising funds through respectively the securities market and the bank market. Such measures may include restrictions on lending, for example, a quantitative regulation of lending rates or of total credit, or changes in tax rules with respect to company finance. While inflation and reserve policy affect only the financial institutions which receive deposits, credit restrictions influence natural production, when financial intermediation takes place through financial institutions that are funded exclusively through the securities market.

Currency restrictions may affect natural production through various channels. Through currency restrictions, the authorities can increase the cost to a firm of raising finance through foreign sources. This corresponds to a change in the demand for bank lending, implying that the demand for bank credit increases at each given level of total domestic demand relative to production. The authorities may further through currency restrictions make it more difficult for banks to raise external finance through securities. This shows up in the model as an increase in ξ.

The finding of monetary policy and of currency and credit restrictions being effective in affecting natural production is important when seen from the viewpoint of choosing the optimal monetary regime. The authorities may incur a loss in the form of higher unemployment in the long term, characterised by full wage and price flexibility, if monetary autonomy is abandoned by joining a monetary union. This is important as the monetary regime is traditionally considered as having no impact on natural unemployment.

The possibility of using credit restrictions also gives the national authorities the capability of affecting natural production when a monetary union is formed, that is, the point stressed by Branson (1990). Against this background one may question whether it is advisable, as in the Maastricht Treaty, to place competence with respect to all monetary policy instruments with a common central bank.

The possibility of affecting natural production through several policy instruments is important when determining optimal inflation. The authorities may find it advantageous to set inflation higher when the possibility of affecting natural production through reserve policy or through credit and currency restrictions is reduced.

It also follows from the model that a country is still subjected to shocks originating in the financial sector after having joined a monetary union. This means that one of the perceived advantages associated with a monetary union, viz. to avoid monetary shocks, cannot be realised.

Effectiveness of fiscal policy

A further policy implication arising from the model is the impact of monetary factors on fiscal policy effectiveness. It follows from (5.25), (5.29), and (5.32) that a narrowing of the difference between the real bank deposit rate and the real interest rate on securities reduces the impact which a given change in government purchases of goods and services and a given change in the tax rate on labour income have on natural production. The interest rate differential between securities and bank deposits is affected by inflation, a higher inflation causing a lower differential and thus reducing the effectiveness of fiscal policy. Policy makers may thus be faced with a policy dilemma. Lower inflation will work to increase natural production but decreases at the same time the effectiveness of fiscal policy.

The impact of monetary regimes on the inter-country transfer of funds

It follows from the model that natural production depends on the cost for a bank associated with raising external finance through non-deposit sources. An improvement in the bank's possibility of raising external funds from non-deposit sources corresponds to a lower value of ξ. It follows from (5.25) that a change in ξ affects natural production.

One may point to several effects which may change a bank's capability of raising finance through non-deposit sources in a monetary union relative to a monetary regime with exchange rate flexibility. Thus, the absence of exchange rate risk in a monetary union reduces the risk associated with inter-country transfers.[5] It also facilitates the possibility of a bank raising finance through non-deposit sources that a monetary union may increase the efficiency of securities markets. Moreover, a monetary union may induce banks to operate in several countries. Banks have a stronger incentive to enter a foreign market in a monetary union because they no longer have to consider balancing assets and liabilities in individual currencies to avoid exchange rate risk, thus lowering entry barriers. A bank which operates in several countries can channel funds from a country with a savings surplus to a country with a savings deficit more efficiently than when the funds are transferred through the securities market. Due to asymmetric information, an extra premium is added to the funding cost when funds pass through external markets.

We may, however, also point to effects which make it more difficult for banks to raise finance through inter-bank and securities markets in a monetary union. There is likely to be more uncertainty regarding the role played by a common central bank as a lender of last resort when this role is exercised by a common central bank covering several econo-

---

[5]This corresponds to Eichengreen (1990) who argues: 'Establishing permanently fixed exchange rates...will fundamentally alter the balance-of-payments adjustment process. US evidence suggests that, in the absence of devaluation risk and exchange controls, capital should flow more freely among Member States to finance payments imbalances' (p. 164).

mies than when it is exercised by a national central bank. This is because a national central bank is likely to go further in its efforts to rescue banks hit by crises than a common central bank. A common central bank may be constrained in its rescue operations by political considerations, as the rescue of a bank in one member state harms the interest of banks in other member states. It is furthermore likely that a common central bank is less preoccupied with bank failures which have effects in only a smaller part of the area covered by the monetary union.

Moreover, a possible synchronisation of business cycles in a monetary union increases the difficulties with which banks can raise finance through external sources. The risk associated with lending to a bank depends on production in the country where the bank has its major operations. If the business cycle in one country is different from other countries, lenders in other countries have an incentive to spread the risk by lending to banks in that particular country.

Insofar as bank earnings are reduced in a monetary union with a price stability goal (see chapter 8), it becomes finally more difficult for banks to raise finance from non-deposit external sources due to the lowering of the bank's credit rating.

In conclusion, it is uncertain to what extent the recycling of funds is facilitated in a monetary union, making it easier for banks to raise finance through non-deposit external sources and thus affecting natural production. It is therefore difficult to argue that the problems associated with balance-of-payments disequilibria disappear in a monetary union.[6] The above discussion of inter-country financing operations leads to the same conclusion as Kenen (1969) who argues that a common financial system is an important characteristic of an optimum currency area since it facilitates the transfer of funds from rich areas to other regions.[7]

---

[6]Hayek (1978) points out: 'With the disappearance of distinct territorial currencies there would of course also disappear the so-called 'balance-of-payments' believed to cause intense difficulties to present-day monetary policy. There would, necessarily, be continuous redistributions of the relative and absolute quantities of currency in different regions as some grow relatively richer and relatively poorer. But this would create no more difficulties than the same process causes today within any large country. People who grew richer will have more money and those who grew poorer would have less. That would be all' (p. 21). In the House of Lords (1989), one of the arguments in favour of a monetary union is that governments will no longer be preoccupied with balance-of-payments problems, being able to concentrate on other economic problems.

[7]Based on this consideration, Branson (1990) questions whether the EU constitutes an optimum currency area. According to Branson (1990), there is no mechanism for the smooth transfer of funds between the countries of the European Union due to the lack of a common financial system.

5.6 Other channels for an impact of bank deposits on bank lending

It follows from the discussion above that monetary policy has an impact on natural production if bank deposits affect real bank lending. In the case where bank lending is different from bank deposits, this presupposes that deposits or other variables affected by monetary policy appear in the bank's optimum condition for real lending. This is the case in (5.22) where B enters because the cost of raising non-deposit external finance depends on the amount of external finance required by the bank, which in turn is affected by the size of deposits. In (5.30) the cost of investing in securities depends on the size of securities holdings relative to bank lending which also depends on bank deposits. We will discuss below two additional channels through which bank deposits can affect bank lending, that is, an impact from bank deposits on the cost of external funding and economies of scope between bank deposits and bank lending.

5.6.1 Bank deposits affecting the cost of external funding

The cost for banks of raising external funds through the securities market may be affected not only by the amount of credit, as specified by (5.17), but also by lending relative to deposits. In this case, (5.19) would be replaced by

$$\kappa_t = \kappa_1(h_t^b - y_t) + \kappa_2(h_t^b - b_t^b) + \xi_t. \tag{5.33}$$

Relation (5.33) shows the cost to the bank of raising non-deposit external finance when affected by the amount of credit relative to the amount of deposits, that is, by the share of a bank's funds which is raised through deposits. This gives a further channel through which bank deposits can affect bank lending.

We may point at several reasons why the bank's non-deposit external funding cost is affected by bank deposits relative to bank lending. First, external finance may be legally subordinate capital to deposits, implying that the security behind external non-deposit finance is reduced when a bank increases the share of bank deposits on balance. A larger share of bank deposits in the bank's balance thus increases the cost to a bank of raising non-deposit external funds. A second effect arises due to the authorities' handling of bank crises. If a bank is financed mostly through deposits, the bank is more likely to be supported by the authorities in the case of a crisis, thus decreasing the risk of the bank defaulting on the loans raised through external non-deposit funds. It follows that no unambiguous conclusion can be drawn regarding the impact of a larger share of deposits on the bank balance.

5.6.2   *Economies of scope between deposit taking and lending*

Bank deposits can affect bank lending if lending and deposits enter the bank's production function as non-separable inputs. For simplicity considering only the case where bank lending is larger than bank deposits, we can write the representative bank's real profit as

$$
\frac{v_t^b}{P_t} = \varsigma_t^b H_t^b - \left[\rho_t^b + \eta_t(1 + v_p)\right]B_t^b - (H_t^b - B_t^b)[i_t + \kappa_t(1 + v_p)]
$$

$$
- F(H_t^b, B_t^b),
$$

$$
F_H \equiv \frac{\partial F}{\partial H^b} > 0, \quad F_B \equiv \frac{\partial F}{\partial B^b} > 0,
$$

$$
F_{HH} \equiv \frac{\partial^2 F}{\partial (H^b)^2} < 0, \quad F_{BB} \equiv \frac{\partial^2 F}{\partial (B^b)^2} < 0,
$$

$$
F_{HB} \equiv \frac{\partial^2 F}{\partial H^b \partial B^B} > 0, \quad \forall H_t^b > B_t^b, \tag{5.34}
$$

where $F(\cdot)$ denotes the bank's cost function in real terms.

Relation (5.34) shows the bank's profit when the bank's operating cost depends on real bank lending and on real bank deposits. It is assumed that the marginal productivities of bank lending and deposits are positive but declining. Economies of scope with respect to deposit taking and lending in the bank's production function may arise because a bank, through deposit taking, receives information about a customer, thereby reducing the risk associated with bank lending. The integration of lending and deposit taking in banking indicates that such economies of scope are important.

Optimising (5.34) with respect to bank lending and bank deposits, and assuming, to simplify, that the cost for the bank of raising funds in the securities market is unaffected by the bank's lending, that is

$$
\kappa_t = \bar{\kappa}_t, \tag{5.35}
$$

gives the following optimum condition with respect to bank lending

$$
v_t + \left(\frac{1}{h_1 \Omega_v}\right) = i_t + \kappa_t + F_H. \tag{5.36}
$$

Relation (5.36) shows that the bank increases lending to the point where the marginal revenue from bank lending corresponds to the marginal cost, shown as the funding cost with the addition of the production cost to the bank of increased lending. It follows from (5.36) that a larger volume of real bank deposits, by increasing the marginal productivity of bank lending in the bank's production function and thus decreasing the marginal cost to the bank of increasing lending, has a positive impact on bank lending. It follows that monetary policy can affect bank lending and thus natural production by influencing the size of real bank deposits.

5.7 Summary and conclusion

The chapter has examined a model based on full price and wage flexibility and rational expectations, assuming that financial intermediation takes place through banks. Markets for bank deposits and bank lending are characterised by imperfect competition while the bank has access to investing and borrowing through a market for external funds which is internationally integrated (the securities market). The bank has to pay a premium when raising external funds through this market due to asymmetric information. The bank likewise incurs a cost when investing in the securities market relative to increased bank lending due to different risk characteristics of bank lending and securities. The wage formation is characterised by a positive relationship between the real wage and employment and is thus affected by the capital stock and by real exchange rate changes caused by shifts in the demand for goods.

The analysis demonstrates that natural production is affected by monetary variables through a number of channels. The authorities can affect natural production through monetary policy instruments which influence the size of bank deposits, that is, inflation and reserve policy, and through credit and currency restrictions. Inflation further affects the effectiveness of fiscal policy. The establishment of a monetary union affects the banks' capability of raising finance through non-deposit external funds. No unambiguous answer can, however, be given as to whether the locking of exchange rates makes it more or less difficult to transfer funds between the countries in the monetary union relative to a monetary regime characterised by exchange rate flexibility.

6 Utility from securities holdings

6.1 Introduction

This chapter examines the macroeconomic implications of substitution between money and financial assets which offer a positive return and which can be sold in a market at a short notice and at low transaction costs. Throughout the following discussion, we refer to this last category of financial assets broadly as securities. Two main reasons may be suggested why securities function as a substitute for money. First, securities can substitute for money in the case of unexpected payment needs, as securities can be sold at short notice and with low transaction costs. Second, holdings of securities enhance the possibility of using credit-based payments systems. Throughout the following discussion, we refer broadly to these uses as the liquidity services from securities. The view that both money and securities offer liquidity services is argued by Tobin (1961, 1969).

This chapter analyses a model which views both money and securities as offering utility. It is a well-known feature from many macroeconomic models that real money offers utility by reducing the time spent on financial transactions. Because both money and securities can be used to meet unexpected expenses and cover unexpected income shortfalls, and because payments can be made on the basis of securities, we treat securities as offering utility. Securities affect the amount of time spent on financial transactions.

The point of departure is a model based on full wage and price flexibility and rational expectations. The wage setters set the nominal wage to reach an optimal trade-off between the real wage and employment. The analysis demonstrates that inflation affects the wage setters' optimal trade-off between the real wage and employment and thus natural production. The substitution between money and securities in the provision of payment services therefore constitutes a mechanism which creates monetary non-neutrality in a model based on wage and price flexibility and rational expectations. This can be explained as follows. When securities offer services which can also be provided through money, the demand for securities and thus saving will be affected by inflation which determines the real return on money. When wage setters set the wage with the view of reaching an optimal trade-off between the real wage and employment, saving affects natural production through the real interest rate in the case of a closed economy and, in the open economy, through a terms-of-trade effect.

The finding that utility offered by securities causes monetary non-neutrality in a model based on full price and wage flexibility and rational expectations is new. Tobin (1969) explicitly rules out monetary non-neutrality in the long term.[1]

Section 6.2 discusses the rationale behind securities rendering the same services as money and thus being a substitute to money. *Section 6.3* sets out a basic macroeconomic model. Both a small open economy and a closed economy are analysed. *Section 6.4* derives natural production. *Section 6.5* considers policy implications. *Section 6.6* gives a summary and conclusion.

6.2   The substitution between money and securities

The precautionary demand for securities

A distinction is usually made between three motives for holding money: the transactions motive, the speculative motive, and the precautionary motive.[2] With respect to the first two motives, investors face the alternative of placing either in securities or in money. Depending on the transaction cost associated with changing between securities and money, the investor may thus find it optimal to economise on money balances when money is held for transactions planned over shorter time horizons and the interest rate is high. Money and securities are similarly viewed as alternative placements in the speculative motive because the investor's

---

[1]Tobin (1969) stresses monetary neutrality in the long term. Tobin writes: 'If the market rate on money, as well as the rates on all other financial assets, were flexible and endogenous, then they would all simply adjust to the marginal efficiency of capital...There would be no room for monetary policy to affect aggregate demand. The real economy would call the tune for the financial sector, with no feedback in the other direction...something like this happens in the long run, where the influence of monetary policy is not on aggregate demand but on the relative supplies of monetary and real assets, to which all rates of return must adjust' (p. 26).
[2]Recent discussions are found in Cuthbertson (1997) and Laidler (1997).

return from money, in terms of direct yield and risk characteristics, is different from that on a security.

With respect to the third motive for holding money, the precautionary motive, one may see money and securities holdings not as alternative placements but as substitutes. The precautionary demand for money arises because unexpected expenditure needs may arise, caused by either unexpected changes in prices or unexpected changes in the investor's income. It is, however, possible also through sales of securities to meet such unexpected payments needs. It is thus possible at a low cost through sales of securities to take advantage of unexpected offers and to implement consumption smoothing when there are unexpected shortfalls in income. The extent to which securities function as a substitute for money, depends on the costs associated with the sales of securities and the time horizon within which sales are possible, that is, the liquidity of the securities. The organisation of the market for securities determines to what extent securities can offer such liquidity services. The efforts which are made by authorities in all countries to increase the efficiency of securities markets, suggest that the utility derived from securities is considerable.

An increase in real securities holdings clearly reduces the need for money to meet the precautionary motive. An increase in real holdings of securities makes it possible to a larger extent to meet unexpected payment needs through sales of securities rather than drawing down on money holdings.

The basic idea that securities are characterised by a certain degree of liquidity and in this way function as a substitute for money is in line with the 'Divisia' approach, first proposed by Barnett and Spindt (1982), where liquidity-based weights are given to each financial asset, forming a broad measure of liquidity. In the Divisia approach, weights are given to each financial asset on the basis of the difference between the return on the asset in question and the return on an asset which is held solely for investment.[3] One may think of all assets as incorporating a certain degree of liquidity, causing a substitution between all assets and money.[4]

---

[3]For a recent discussion, see Barnett (1997).
[4]The same basic point is made by Cuthbertson (1997) who notes regarding the choice of benchmark asset in the Divisia approach: 'Given the imprecision of what is meant by "monetary services" the choice of the benchmark asset is extremely arbitrary. Surely, any asset with an active secondary market provides some transaction services (that is, provides an "American" call option on money)' (p. 1190).

Credit-based purchases

As a second reason why securities function as a substitute for money, we may point to the possibility that an increase in real holdings of securities enhances the efficiency of a credit-based payment system. Banks are more willing to establish credit lines for customers who have large securities holdings as the securities can function as collateral for the credit advanced to the customer. Holdings of securities are appropriate as collateral as the price of securities is easy to verify. This is notably the case when well-functioning secondary markets have been organised for such securities, that is, when securities have a high degree of liquidity. A rise in real securities holdings increases the security behind credit lines which are advanced to customers who want to make payments, thus making it possible to organise payments more efficiently.

6.3   Model specification

The firm's optimisation

The representative firm operates in goods and financial markets characterised by perfect competition, being unable to affect the price and the interest rate. It is furthermore unable to affect the nominal wage. Capital depreciates fully after use in the current time period. Assuming Cobb–Douglas technology, the firm's profit maximisation in each time period can be expressed as

$$\frac{v_t}{P_t} = Y_t - (1 + r_{t-1})K_t - \left(\frac{W_t}{P_t}\right)L_t, \tag{6.1}$$

$$Y_t = K_t^a L_t^{1-a}, \quad 0 < a < 1, \tag{6.2}$$

$$\log(1 + r_t) \equiv \log(1 + i_t) - (p_{t+1} - p_t), \tag{6.3}$$

where v is profit, P and p the producer price (respectively non-logarithmic and logarithmic values), K capital, W the nominal wage, L labour, r the real interest rate, and i the nominal interest rate.

Optimising (6.1) with respect to labour and capital, and using (6.2), gives the optimum conditions for the firm

$$(1 - a)\left(\frac{Y_t}{L_t}\right) = \left(\frac{W_t}{P_t}\right), \tag{6.4}$$

$$\frac{K_{t+1}}{Y_t} = \frac{I_t}{Y_t} = \left(\frac{a}{1 + r_t}\right)\left(\frac{Y_{t+1}}{Y_t}\right), \tag{6.5}$$

where I is (gross) investment.

The firm finances investment through issues of securities. This gives

$$K_{t+1} = \frac{S_t}{P_t},\tag{6.6}$$

where S is the supply of securities from firms.

The household

We consider a representative household h which supplies labour to the firm and holds money and securities as means to reach consumption smoothing and other liquidity services. The point of departure is the overlapping generations model with infinitely lived households set out in the appendix. Each household represents a generation which diverges only with respect to labour income. The household optimises utility over an infinite time horizon. In each time period, utility depends on consumption and the liquidity services provided by real money and securities. This gives the following optimisation problem at time t

$$\max_{C^h, M^h, S^h} \left\{ \sum_{T=t}^{\infty} \beta^{T-t} u_T^h \Big| \frac{\partial(W/P)}{\partial C^h} = 0, \ \frac{\partial(W/P)}{\partial(M^h/P)} = 0, \ \frac{\partial(W/P)}{\partial(S^h/P)} = 0 \right\},$$

$$0 < \beta < 1, \quad T = t, t+1, \ldots, \quad h = 1, 2, \ldots,\tag{6.7}$$

$$u_T^h = u_c^h(C_T^h) + u_\ell^h\left(\frac{M_T^h}{P_T(Y_T^W)^h}, \frac{S_T^h}{P_T(Y_T^W)^h} \right),$$

$$(Y_T^W)^h \equiv \Gamma_T^h W_T \left(\frac{L_T}{L_T''} \right),$$

$$\frac{\partial u_c^h}{\partial C^h} > 0, \quad \frac{\partial^2 u_c^h}{\partial(C^h)^2} < 0,$$

$$\frac{\partial u_\ell^h}{\partial(M^h/P)} > 0, \quad \frac{\partial^2 u_\ell^h}{\partial(M^h/P)^2} < 0, \quad \frac{\partial u_\ell^h}{\partial(S^h/P)} > 0, \quad \frac{\partial^2 u_\ell^h}{\partial(S^h/P)^2} < 0,$$

$$\tag{6.8}$$

$$\Gamma_T^h W_T \left(\frac{L_T}{L_T''} \right) + M_{T-1}^h + S_{T-1}^h(1 + i_{T-1}) + \tau_T^h$$

$$= P_T C_T^h + M_T^h + S_T^h,\tag{6.9}$$

$$L_T'' = L_{T-1}'' \equiv 1, \quad \tau_T^h = M_T^h - M_{T-1}^h, \quad T = t, t+1, \ldots,$$

$$\Gamma_T^h = \Gamma_0 \Gamma^{(h-1)+(T-t)}, \quad \sum_h \Gamma_T^h \equiv 1, \quad 0 < \Gamma < 1,\tag{6.10}$$

where u^h is the instantaneous utility derived by a representative household h, β the time discounting factor, C^h the household's consumption of physical goods, u_c^h the utility derived from the consumption of the physical good in a given period, u_ℓ^h the utility derived from money and securities in a given time period, M^h the household's money holdings, S^h the household's securities holdings, L'' full employment, and τ^h is a lump-sum net transfer, the size of which equals the increase in the household's money holdings. Γ^h shows the determination of labour income for household h as a function of unemployment L/L'' and the general wage level W. Γ reflects the development over time in a household's possibility of receiving a labour income. $(Y^W)^h$ is the labour income received by a household.

Relation (6.7) shows the household's optimisation of utility over an infinite time horizon. The household cannot affect the real wage, the household being unable to determine working hours and thus leisure. The household has full information regarding the variables which enter the utility function. (6.8) shows that utility in each time period is derived from the consumption of the physical good and from the liquidity services offered by money and securities. The marginal utilities are positive but declining. The utility is determined on the basis of real holdings of money and securities relative to the household's labour income.[5] (6.9) gives the household's budget restraint. At the household's disposal for consumption and saving is the labour income derived from working in the current time period T with the addition of financial wealth left over from the previous time period, consisting of financial assets in the form of money M_{T-1}^h and in the form of securities S_{T-1}^h with the addition of the interest income earned during the previous time period. In the current time period the household consumes C_T^h of the physical good and places S_T^h in securities. M_T^h is money at the household's disposal during time period T. The household receives at a given time a labour income corresponding to $\Gamma^h(L/L'')$. We assume that the government or the central bank hand back revenue from inflation tax/seigniorage to the household as a lump-sum net transfer τ^h. The effects of inflation tax/seigniorage on consumption can thus be ignored, making it possible to concentrate exclusively on the real effects which arise because inflation affects the real economy through liquidity services from securities. The labour force is constant in each time period, being normalised to one. (6.10)

---

[5]The assumption that the utility derived from securities and money is determined relative to production simplifies the analysis but has no impact on conclusions.

shows the development over time in a generation's possibility of receiving a labour income, labour income declining at the rate Γ.

The instantaneous utilities which can be derived respectively from consumption of the physical good, from real money, and from real securities holdings, are specified as follows

$$u_c^h(C_T^h) = \log(C_T^h),$$ (6.11)

$$u_\ell^h\left(\frac{M_T^h}{P_T(Y_T^W)^h}, \frac{S_T^h}{P_T(Y_T^W)^h}\right) = \xi\left(\frac{S_T^h}{P_T(Y_T^W)^h}\right)^\Phi \left(\frac{M_T^h}{P_T(Y_T^W)^h}\right)^{1-\Phi},$$
$$\xi > 0, \quad 0 < \Phi < 1.$$ (6.12)

Relation (6.11) shows the instantaneous utility derived from the consumption of physical goods. (6.12) expresses positive but diminishing marginal utilities from real money and real securities holdings relative to production. An increase in real money holdings diminishes the utility from real securities and vice versa.

Goods market equilibrium

We next turn to the specification of goods market equilibrium. Total demand in the economy is defined as the sum of total consumption and investment, that is

$$D_t \equiv C_t + I_t, \quad \sum_h C_t^h \equiv C_t,$$ (6.13)

where D is total domestic demand in the economy, and C consumption in the whole economy.

In a closed economy, total demand equals production while the households' total securities holdings equal securities issued by the firm. This gives

$$D_t = Y_t, \quad \sum_h S_t^h = S_t.$$ (6.14)

In a small open economy, goods market equilibrium in steady-state equilibrium is characterised as follows

$$0 = z(p_t^B + x_t - p_t) + \Omega_s, \quad \Omega_s \equiv \log(D_t/Y_t)_s, \quad z > 0,$$ (6.15)

$$p_t^B = \bar{p}_t^B, \quad r_t^B = \bar{r}_t^B,$$ (6.16)

$$r_t = r_t^B,$$ (6.17)

where Ω_s is domestic demand relative to production in steady-state equilibrium (logarithmic value), and x the nominal exchange rate (number of domestic currency units per foreign currency unit) (logarithmic value). y is the logarithmic value of production. The subscript s denotes the steady state.

Relations (6.15)–(6.17) specify goods market equilibrium in a small open economy A. The rest of the world is represented by a large economy B. All variables relate to country A unless otherwise specified. (6.15) gives demand for the domestic good as a function of the real exchange rate and of total domestic demand relative to production. Domestic demand relative to production lies at the steady-state level.[6] (6.16) shows the foreign price and the foreign real interest rate to be exogenously given in the small economy. (6.17) reflects perfect financial integration, the real interest rate in the domestic country being equal to the foreign real interest rate (see section A.10).

Wage setting
The wage setters determine the nominal wage at which there is an optimal trade-off between the real wage and employment as

$$
l_t - l_t'' = \left(\frac{\theta}{\gamma}\right)(w_t - q_t) - \left(\frac{1}{\gamma}\right)\epsilon,
$$

$$
\epsilon \equiv \log\left(\frac{\theta a}{f^u \gamma}\right), \quad \theta > 0, \quad \gamma > 0, \quad f^u > 0,
$$

(6.18)

$$
q_t \equiv p_t + \varphi(p_t^B + x_t - p_t), \quad 0 \le \varphi < 1. \tag{6.19}
$$

where q is the consumer price (logarithmic value), and l'' the labour force (logarithmic value). w, l, and l'' are the logarithmic values of respectively W, L, and L''.

Relation (6.18) specifies the wage setters' optimum. A decentralised wage setting is assumed. It is furthermore assumed that wage setters are unable to affect the capital stock within the wage contract period which is the wage setters' time horizon for optimisation. This may be explained by a long planning period for investments, implying that wage setters have no influence on the capital stock during the wage contract period. (6.19) defines the consumer price.

---

[6]For a derivation of (6.15), see section A.6 in the appendix.

Monetary regime
The authorities set the price increase through the control of money. The monetary regime is thus characterised as

$$v_{p,t} = \bar{v}_{p,t}, \quad v_{p,t} = v_{p,t-1} \equiv v_p, \quad v_{p,t} \equiv \frac{P_t - P_{t-1}}{P_{t-1}}, \tag{6.20}$$

where v_p is the price increase.

Relation (6.20) expresses that the authorities set the price increase at a constant level in each time period.

Steady-state equilibrium
The analysis considers a steady-state equilibrium characterised by a constant growth rate of output and constant levels of financial assets relative to nominal production, that is

$$y_t = y_{t-1} \equiv y, \quad \frac{S_t}{P_t Y_t} = \frac{S_{t-1}}{P_{t-1} Y_{t-1}} \equiv \frac{S}{PY},$$
$$\frac{M_t}{P_t Y_t} = \frac{M_{t-1}}{P_{t-1} Y_{t-1}} \equiv \frac{M}{PY}, \quad \sum_h M_t^h \equiv M_t, \tag{6.21}$$

where M is households' total holdings of money.

Relation (6.21) characterises a steady-state equilibrium. In the absence of technical progress, production lies at a constant level while money and securities holdings are constant relative to nominal production.

6.4   Determination of natural production

The closed economy
Optimising (6.7) with respect to consumption, money, and securities holdings, and using (6.7)–(6.9) and (6.11)–(6.12), gives the conditions for the household's optimum

$$\xi\Phi\left(\frac{M_t^h}{S_t^h}\right)^{1-\Phi}\left(\frac{1}{(Y_t^W)^h}\right) + \beta(1 + r_t)\left(\frac{1}{C_{t+1}^h}\right) = \left(\frac{1}{C_t^h}\right), \tag{6.22}$$

$$\xi(1 - \Phi)\left(\frac{M_t^h}{S_t^h}\right)^{-\Phi}\left(\frac{1}{(Y_t^W)^h}\right) + \beta\left(\frac{1}{1 + v_p}\right)\left(\frac{1}{C_{t+1}^h}\right) = \left(\frac{1}{C_t^h}\right). \tag{6.23}$$

Relation (6.22) shows that the marginal utility derived from the accumulation of securities, in the form of marginal utility from liquidity services in the current time period and from increased consumption of physical goods in the future time period, equals the marginal utility of foregoing consumption of physical goods in the current time period. Relation (6.23) gives the corresponding condition for the household's money holdings.

The household's consumption is restricted by the budget constraint. In equilibrium, the real interest rate is constant. Combining (6.4)–(6.6), (6.8)–(6.11), (6.13)–(6.14), and (6.21), we derive the following relationship from the household's budget constraint

$$\frac{C_t}{Y_t} = \left[1 - \left(\frac{1}{1+r}\right)\left(\frac{C_{t+1}^h}{C_t^h}\right)\right]N_1,$$

$$N_1 \equiv (1-a)\left(1 - \Gamma\frac{1}{1+r}\right)^{-1} + a > 0, \ 1 - \Gamma\frac{1}{1+r} > 0. \tag{6.24}$$

Combining (6.24) with (6.4), (6.8), (6.13), and (6.21)–(6.23) gives the following relationship (deleting time indications as all variables relate to steady-state equilibrium)

$$F\left(\frac{C}{Y}, r; v_p\right) \equiv c - y + \log(\xi) + \Phi\log(\Phi) + (1-\Phi)\log(1-\Phi)$$

$$- (1-\Phi)\log\left\{1 - \beta\left(\frac{1}{1+v_p}\right)\left(\frac{1}{1+r}\right)\left[1 - \left(\frac{C}{Y}\right)\left(\frac{1}{N_1}\right)\right]^{-1}\right\}$$

$$- \Phi\log\left\{1 - \beta\left[1 - \left(\frac{C}{Y}\right)\left(\frac{1}{N_1}\right)\right]^{-1}\right\} = 0,$$

$$F_C \equiv \frac{\partial F}{\partial\left(\frac{C}{Y}\right)} > 0, \quad F_r \equiv \frac{\partial F}{\partial r}, \quad F_{v_p} \equiv \frac{\partial F}{\partial v_p} < 0. \tag{6.25}$$

Relation (6.25) represents the combinations of consumption relative to production C/Y and the real interest rate r that are compatible with the households' optimisation over time. The impact of the real interest rate on the function F depends on the economic structure. If a higher real interest rate induces households to plan higher growth in consumption over time, that is, if $\partial(C_{t+1}^h/C_t^h)/\partial r > 0$, it follows that $F_r < 0$. Conversely, $F_r > 0$ when $\partial(C_{t+1}^h/C_t^h)/\partial r < 0$. It follows from (6.25) that inflation affects the relationship and thus the demand for goods when $1 > \Phi > 0$.

Combining (6.13)–(6.14) with (6.5) gives the following relationship which reflects goods market equilibrium

$$G\left(\frac{C}{Y}, r\right) \equiv \left(\frac{C}{Y}\right) + \left(\frac{a}{1+r}\right) - 1 = 0,$$

$$G_C \equiv \frac{\partial G}{\partial\left(\frac{C}{Y}\right)} = 1, \quad G_r \equiv \frac{\partial G}{\partial r} < 0. \tag{6.26}$$

Combining (6.2), (6.4), and (6.18)–(6.19) gives natural production in the closed economy as a function of the real interest rate

$$y = -\left(\frac{a}{1-a}\right)\left(1 + \frac{\theta}{\gamma}\right) \log(1+r) - \left(\frac{1}{\gamma}\right)\epsilon$$

$$+ \left(\frac{a}{1-a}\right)\left(1 + \frac{\theta}{\gamma}\right) \log(a) + \left(\frac{\theta}{\gamma}\right) \log(1-a). \tag{6.27}$$

Equations (6.25)–(6.27) give three relations which determine consumption relative to production C/Y, the real interest rate r, and natural production y. Inflation affects natural production through the real interest rate. We can find the following impact of inflation on natural production

$$\frac{\partial y}{\partial v_p} = -\left(\frac{a}{1-a}\right)\left(1 + \frac{\theta}{\gamma}\right)\left(\frac{1}{1+r}\right)\left(\frac{\partial r}{\partial v_p}\right)$$

$$= -\left(\frac{a}{1-a}\right)\left(1 + \frac{\theta}{\gamma}\right)\left(\frac{1}{1+r}\right)\left(\frac{-F_{v_p}}{F_r - F_C G_r}\right),$$

$$F_{v_p} < 0, \quad F_C > 0, \quad G_r < 0. \tag{6.28}$$

It follows from (6.28) that the impact of inflation on natural production cannot be determined unambiguously as the sign of F_r depends on the economic structure. In the case where F_r is positive it follows that higher inflation reduces the real interest rate and increases natural production due to the rise in capital accumulation which improves the combinations of employment and the real wage that can be reached by the wage setters.

The open economy

In the case of the open economy, the optimum conditions given by (6.22) and (6.23) still apply. The maintenance of a stable level of net claims on foreigners is only possible if the growth rate of production is higher than the real interest rate. In the present analysis with zero production increase, this implies a negative real interest rate, that is, $r < 0$. The relationship between consumption relative to production and the household's planned increase in consumption over time can be found from (6.4)–(6.6), (6.8)–(6.11), (6.13)–(6.17), and (6.21) as

$$\left(\frac{C_t}{Y_t}\right)\left(\frac{1}{N_2 + \left(\frac{1+r}{r}\right)\left(\frac{C_t}{Y_t}\right)}\right) = \left[1 - \left(\frac{1}{1+r}\right)\left(\frac{C_{t+1}^h}{C_t^h}\right)\right],$$

$$N_2 \equiv -\left(\frac{1+r}{r}\right) + (1-a)\left(1 - \Gamma\frac{1}{1+r}\right)^{-1} > 0. \tag{6.29}$$

Relation (6.29) gives the relationship between consumption relative to production C/Y and the household's planned growth in consumption C_{t+1}^h/C_t^h that is compatible with the household's optimisation over time.

In the small open economy with perfect financial integration, the real interest rate is exogenously determined as the foreign real interest rate, cf. (6.16). Combining (6.29) with (6.4), (6.8), (6.13), and (6.21)–(6.23) gives the following relationship between consumption relative to production, the real interest rate and inflation

$$H\left(\frac{C}{Y}; r, v_p\right) \equiv c - y + \log(\xi) + \Phi\log(\Phi) + (1 - \Phi)\log(1 - \Phi)$$

$$- (1 - \Phi)\log\left\{1 - \beta\left(\frac{1}{1+v_p}\right)\left(\frac{1}{1+r}\right)\left[1 - \left(\frac{C}{Y}\right)\left(\frac{1}{N_2 + \left(\frac{1+r}{r}\right)\left(\frac{C}{Y}\right)}\right)\right]^{-1}\right\}$$

$$- \Phi\log\left\{1 - \beta\left[1 - \left(\frac{C}{Y}\right)\left(\frac{1}{N_2 + \left(\frac{1+r}{r}\right)\left(\frac{C}{Y}\right)}\right)\right]^{-1}\right\} = 0,$$

$$H_C \equiv \frac{\partial H}{\partial\left(\frac{C}{Y}\right)} > 0, \quad H_r \equiv \frac{\partial H}{\partial r}, \quad H_{v_p} \equiv \frac{\partial H}{\partial v_p} < 0. \tag{6.30}$$

Combining (6.2), (6.4), (6.15), (6.19), and (6.21) gives natural production in the open economy

$$y = \left(\frac{\theta}{\gamma}\right)\left(\frac{\varphi}{z}\right)\Omega_s - \left(\frac{a}{1-a}\right)\left(1 + \frac{\theta}{\gamma}\right)\log(1+r) - \left(\frac{1}{\gamma}\right)\epsilon$$

$$+ \left(\frac{\theta}{\gamma}\right)\log(1-a) + \left(\frac{a}{1-a}\right)\left(1 + \frac{\theta}{\gamma}\right)\log(a). \tag{6.31}$$

Relation (6.31) gives the condition for the wage setters' optimum. In (6.31) the real interest rate is exogenously given. Inflation has an impact on natural production through the demand for goods relative to production, a rise in the demand for goods causing a real appreciation. Combining (6.30)–(6.31) gives the impact of inflation on natural production as

$$\frac{\partial y}{\partial v_p} = -\left(\frac{\theta}{\gamma}\right)\left(\frac{\varphi}{z}\right)\left(\frac{Y}{D}\right)\left(\frac{H_{v_p}}{H_C}\right) > 0,$$

$$H_{v_p} < 0, \quad H_C > 0. \tag{6.32}$$

Relation (6.32) shows that a rise in inflation has a positive impact on natural production in the small open economy. Inflation increases consumption relative to production and thus the demand for goods relative to production. This causes a real appreciation which improves the combinations of the real wage and employment that can be reached by the wage setters and thus natural production.

6.5   Policy implications

The optimal inflation

We have demonstrated that inflation has an impact on natural production in a model characterised by rational expectations and price and wage flexibility when securities offer liquidity services and thereby function as a substitute for money. This channel of monetary non-neutrality is additional to those known from the literature, that is, the impact of inflation on the investor's portfolio choice between money and capital, the distributional effects caused by inflation tax/seigniorage, and effects arising from the impact of inflation on the efficient utilisation of money (see chapter 2).

The impact of inflation on natural production makes it impossible to claim that the exclusive pursuit of a price stability goal is unambiguously desirable. The analysis thus questions whether it is advisable to implement reforms, for example, the establishment of an independent central bank, which aim at increasing the weight attached to lower inflation. In the open economy with perfect financial integration, higher inflation causes an increase in natural production. In the closed economy or in the open economy with imperfect financial integration, it depends on the economic structure whether a rise in inflation decreases or increases natural production.

The reasoning behind the impact of inflation on the real economy when there is substitution between money and securities can be explained as follows. When securities provide utility in the form of liquidity services, higher inflation and thus a rise in the opportunity cost of holding money, induces households to substitute securities for money to meet liquidity needs, thereby causing households to increase their securities holdings relative to money. In the open economy with perfect financial integration, at an exogenously given real interest rate, the stronger incentive for holding securities leads to more consumption smoothing, implying that the household's planned future increase in consumption becomes smaller, thus causing consumption to increase relative to production. This increase in consumption relative to production leads in the open economy to a real appreciation which improves the combinations of employment and the real wage that can be reached by the wage setters, thus increasing natural production. In the closed economy or in an open economy with imperfect financial integration, it depends on the households' preferences and the economic structure whether substitution from money to securities increases or decreases consumption relative to production. In the case where the decrease in real money holdings leads to lower consumption relative to production, higher inflation reduces the real interest rate, this effect working to increase capital accumulation and thus to increase natural production.

The monetary non-neutrality was demonstrated in a model setting where the utility from the consumption of physical goods and the utility from liquidity services enter as separable elements into the household's utility function. This assumption of separability corresponds to Sidrauski (1967) and Benassy (1995a) who demonstrate monetary neutrality when there is no substitution between money and securities with respect to payment services.

The conclusion from the closed economy of the real interest rate being affected by inflation is clearly in conformity with the empirical evidence which indicates an impact of inflation on the real interest rate (see section 2.5.3).

The finding from the closed economy that it depends on the economic structure how a rise in inflation affects the real interest rate, is counter to the standard neoclassical monetary growth model based on Mundell (1963) and Tobin (1965) where higher inflation leads to a reduction in the real interest rate. It is, however, in conformity with the empirical evidence which fails to come up with an unambiguously positive or negative relationship between inflation and the real interest rate, see, for example, Summers (1983), Evans and Lewis (1992), and Cowder and Hoffman (1996).

Fiscal policy

To simplify, we have taken no account of government securities in the analysis. An increase in the supply of government securities in a small open economy would have the effect of reducing natural production as the marginal utility from the total stock of securities is reduced, inducing households to decrease consumption relative to production and thus causing a real depreciation. In a closed economy, it depends on the economic structure whether a rise in the issues of government securities increases or decreases the real interest rate. Due to this difference in the production effect of government securities, fiscal discipline in a small open economy would seem to be tighter than in the closed economy.

Financial reform

The analysis can be extended to incorporate several kinds of securities, distinguished by different degrees of liquidity. The analysis thus highlights the importance of structural reforms in the financial markets as a means to reach a lower real interest. Financial reforms which increase the liquidity of securities, affect natural production. A crowding-out effect may arise from the government's issues of securities insofar as these securities are superior to private sector securities with respect to liquidity.

6.6   Summary and conclusion

The analysis has examined the macroeconomic implications when both money and securities are used to cover an agent's liquidity needs. The analysis demonstrates that inflation has an impact on natural unemployment when wage setters determine the nominal wage to reach an optimal trade-off between the real wage and employment. Inflation affects natural unemployment through a terms-of-trade effect in the small open economy and through the real interest rate in the closed economy. This means that substitution between money and securities provides a channel for monetary non-neutrality in a model setting characterised by full wage and price flexibility and by rational expectations. In the closed economy, it depends on the economic structure whether a rise in inflation raises or lowers the real interest rate and thus natural production. In the open economy with perfect financial integration, a rise in inflation increases natural production through an improvement in the terms of trade.

7 Hysteresis effects from monetary policy

7.1 Introduction

Hysteresis effects imply that real economic variables are affected by the levels of economic variables in prior periods. Among possible sources of hysteresis may be mentioned capital accumulation, effects in the labour market, for example labour skills which are depleted during terms of unemployment, and unexpected inflation which influences production in subsequent periods by changing the real value of financial wealth.

Hysteresis effects cause natural production, which represents the wage setters' optimisation between the real wage and employment, to follow a dynamic adjustment path.[1] Assuming such a dynamic adjustment, one may conceive monetary factors to affect the economy in four different ways: (i) through an impact on the adjustment path towards a steady-state equilibrium, (ii) by affecting the speed with which the economy moves towards a steady-state equilibrium, (iii) through an impact on the stability of the economy, determining whether production moves towards a steady-state equilibrium, and (iv) by affecting the properties of the steady-state equilibrium. Throughout the discussion below we will concentrate only on the last of these four implications, i.e. the impact of hysteresis on the steady-state equilibrium.

The chapter examines a model where hysteresis is caused by capital which is left over from previous periods. It is demonstrated that monetary policy which is unexpected by the wage setters in the initial period influences the properties of the steady-state equilibrium only when there is an output elasticity of capital at the macroeconomic level which is equal to one. A unit output elasticity of capital may be explained by external effects on labour productivity arising from capital accumulation. This would seem to represent a special case although it has played an important role in the economic discussion where it has been at the basis

[1]See Karanassou and Snower (1996, 1998).

of much of the literature on endogenous growth, cf. Romer (1986) and Barro (1990). The model which is examined in this chapter, corresponds basically to Pelloni (1997).

The chapter briefly surveys some other sources of hysteresis effects, arising from structural characteristics in the labour market, and from the effect of unexpected inflation on the household's saving decision through changes in net financial wealth.

Section 7.2 examines hysteresis effects arising from capital accumulation. A model is presented which analyses the possibility of unexpected monetary policy having an impact on long-term steady-state production. *Section 7.3* discusses hysteresis effects arising from other sources. *Section 7.4* gives a summary and conclusion.

7.2   Hysteresis arising from capital accumulation

Hysteresis effects may arise because capital accumulation is affected by unexpected price changes. McKinnon (1981) points to unexpected inflation as causing a higher profit when nominal wages adjust slowly, in turn giving rise to an increase in capital accumulation. Benassy (1995a) examines on the basis of nominal wage contracts how monetary shocks in a real business cycle model may affect production in subsequent time periods through the effect on capital accumulation. The model specified below is basically similar to Pelloni (1997) who finds that unexpected monetary shocks affect long-term growth in an endogenous growth model where the output elasticity of capital is one due to the external effects of capital accumulation on labour productivity. In difference to Pelloni (1997), the discussion below is based on an overlapping generations model, thus extending the basic findings found in Pelloni (1997) to this model framework.

7.2.1   Model specification

The firm's optimisation
    We consider a representative firm j which maximises the firm owners' consumption possibilities over an infinite time horizon. This gives the following specification of the firm's profit maximisation at a given time t

$$\max_{L^j, K^j} \left\{ \left(\frac{v_T^j}{P_T} \right) \mid \frac{\partial P}{\partial Y^j} = 0, \ \frac{\partial W}{\partial Y^j} = 0, \ \frac{\partial i}{\partial Y^j} = 0, \ \frac{\partial \Lambda}{\partial Y^j} = 0, \right\},$$

$$T = t, t+1, \ldots, \tag{7.1}$$

$$\frac{v_T^j}{P_T} = Y_T^j - L_T^j \frac{W_T}{P_T} - K_T^j r_{T-1} - K_T^j \kappa, \tag{7.2}$$

$$Y_T^j = \Lambda_T^j (K_T^j)^a (L_T^j)^{1-a}, \quad \Lambda_T^j > 0, \quad 0 < a < 1, \tag{7.3}$$

$$\Lambda_T = K_T^b, \quad b > 0, \tag{7.4}$$

where v_j is profit in firm j, Y^j production in firm j, i the nominal interest rate, W the nominal wage, P the producer price, K^j the capital stock in firm j, L^j employment in firm j, κ the depreciation of the capital stock, r the real interest rate, and i the nominal interest rate. Λ expresses a shift in the production function. a is the elasticity of production with respect to capital. p is the logarithmic value of the producer price.

Relation (7.1) specifies that the firm maximises the present value of real profit with respect to employment and capital. Optimisation takes place under the following assumptions: (i) the firm is unable to affect the producer price, that is, there is perfect competition in the goods markets, (ii) the firm is unable to affect the nominal wage which is prefixed through nominal wage contracts, (iii) the firm is unable to affect the nominal interest rate, that is, there is a perfect financial market, and (iv) the firm has perfect information regarding the variables which are relevant for profit maximisation. Relation (7.2) gives the definition of real profit, capital stock depreciating by κ. (7.3) expresses Cobb–Douglas production technology with a homogeneous production function of degree 1. The term Λ represents shifts in the production function, arising from the external effects of capital accumulation on labour productivity. (7.4) expresses that labour productivity is increased through larger capital accumulation, for example due to external effects associated with learning. No prior assumptions are made with respect to the value of b except that it is non-negative.

Optimising (7.2) with respect to employment and capital, and using (7.1) and (7.3), gives the firm's optimum conditions

$$\left(\frac{\partial Y^j}{\partial L^j} \right) = (1-a) \left(\frac{Y_T^j}{L_T^3} \right) = \frac{W_T}{P_T}, \tag{7.5}$$

$$\frac{\partial Y^j}{\partial K^j} = a \left(\frac{Y_t^j}{K_t^j} \right) = r_t + \kappa, \tag{7.6}$$

The consumption decision

The point of departure is taken in an overlapping generations model. Each generation is represented by a representative household h which optimises utility over an infinite time horizon, forming correct expectations concerning future income levels. Generations are similar, except that the probability of finding employment differs among generations.[2] The household's optimisation problem at time t can be shown as

$$\max_{C^h, M^h} \left\{ \sum_{s=0}^{\infty} \beta^s u_{T+s}^h \,\Big|\, \frac{\partial(W/P)}{\partial C^h} = 0, \frac{\partial(W/P)}{\partial M^h} = 0 \right\},$$

$$0 < \beta < 1, \quad T = t, t+1, \ldots, \quad h = 1, 2, \ldots, \tag{7.7}$$

$$u_T^h = \log(C_T^h) + \log\left(\frac{M_T^h}{P_T}\right), \quad h = 1, 2, \ldots, \tag{7.8}$$

$$M_{T-1}^h + S_{T-1}^h(1 + i_{T-1}) + \Gamma_T^h W_T^h\left(\frac{L_T}{L_T''}\right) + \tau_T^h = P_T C_T^h + S_T^h + M_T^h,$$

$$\tau_T^h = M_T^h - M_{T-1}^h, \quad h = 1, 2, \ldots, \tag{7.9}$$

$$\Gamma_T^h = \Gamma_0 \Gamma^{(h-1)+(T-t)}, \quad 0 < \Gamma < 1,$$

$$\sum_h \Gamma_T^h = 1, \quad h = 1, 2, \ldots, \tag{7.10}$$

where u_T^h is the utility derived by household h in a given time period T, C^h the household's consumption of the physical good, L'' full employment, M^h the household's holding of money, τ^h a lump-sum transfer, S^h the nominal value of securities held by domestic households (non-monetary wealth), Γ^h the household's probability of finding employment, and β expresses the time discounting factor.

Relation (7.7) shows that the household determines the consumption of physical goods and money holdings to optimise utility over an infinite time horizon. The household has perfect information regarding future and current variables which enter the utility function. The household is unable to affect the real wage, implying that the household is unable to determine working hours and thus leisure. (7.8) shows that utility in each time period is represented as a separable function of consumption of the physical good and of real money holdings. The utilities from the physical good and from real money holdings are expressed by the logarithmic utility functions. (7.9) gives the household's budgetary constraint. At

---

[2]The model is described in the appendix.

the household's disposal for consumption and saving is the disposable nominal wage derived from working in period T with the addition of financial wealth left over from the previous time period, consisting of financial assets in the form of money M_{T-1}^h and in the form of securities S_{T-1}^h with the addition of the interest income earned in the course of the previous time period $T-1$. The household faces the probability $\Gamma^h(L/L'')$ of receiving a labour income. In time period T the household consumes C_T^h of respectively the physical good and places S_T^h in securities and M_T^h in money. The household receives in each period a lump-sum transfer which equals the government's revenue from money creation. This last assumption makes it possible to ignore the effects of inflation tax/seigniorage in the further analysis. (7.10) shows that each generation's probability of finding employment decreases at a constant rate Γ over time.

Optimising (7.7)–(7.8) under the constraint of (7.9) gives the following optimum conditions

$$\frac{C_{T+1}^h}{C_T^h} = \beta(1 + r_T), \tag{7.11}$$

$$\frac{M_T^h}{P_T} = C_T^h \left(\frac{1 + i_T}{i_T} \right). \tag{7.12}$$

Relation (7.11) shows that the household's planned growth in consumption is affected positively by the household's subjective time discounting factor and by the real interest rate. It follows from (7.12) that real money demand is a positive function of consumption and a negative function of the nominal interest rate. As the household's utility function is separable with respect to consumption of real goods and the services rendered by real money and the revenue effect of inflation tax/seigniorage is neutralised through lump-sum transfers, money has no impact on the real economy (see the appendix).

Wage formation
The wage setters set the nominal wage through contracts. This means that the wage setters first fix the nominal wage contracts, forming correct expectations regarding the economic policy and the economic structure during the wage contract period. Firms subsequently determine capital stock and employment on the basis of the prefixed nominal wage. The wage setters set the nominal wage to reach a desired employment level, assumed to equal full employment.

We assume that there is a constant labour force in each period, that is

$$L_T'' = L'' \equiv 1. \tag{7.13}$$

Relation (7.13) shows that full employment lies at the same level in each period, normalised at one.

Goods market equilibrium

We next turn to the macroeconomic level. Production, capital, and employment correspond at the macroeconomic level to the levels in the representative firm. This gives

$$Y_T^j = Y_T, \quad K_T^j = K_T, \quad L_T^j = L_T, \quad \sum_h C_T^h = C_T,$$

$$\sum_h M_T^h = M_T, \sum_h S_T^h = S_T, \tag{7.14}$$

where K, L, C, S, and M are capital, labour, consumption, securities holdings, and money at the macroeconomic level.

Domestic demand is the sum of investment, consumption, and government expenditure on goods and services undertaken by domestic agents. To simplify, the role of the government is not considered. In a closed economy, domestic demand corresponds to production. This gives

$$Y_T = C_T + I_T, \tag{7.15}$$

where I is (gross) investment.

We next specify consumption. Using (7.5), (7.9)–(7.11), and (7.13)–(7.14), the household's inter-temporal budgetary constraint gives the following relationship between consumption and production

$$C_T^h + \frac{C_{T+1}^h}{1+r_T} + \frac{C_{T+2}^h}{(1+r_T)(1+r_{T+1})} + \ldots = C_T^h\left(\frac{1}{1-\beta}\right) =$$

$$\left(\frac{S_{T-1}^h}{P_{T-1}}\right)(1+r_{T-1}) + Y_T(1-a)\Gamma_T^h + \frac{Y_{T+1}}{1+r_T}(1-a)(\Gamma_T^h)\Gamma$$

$$+ \frac{Y_{T+2}}{(1+r_T)(1+r_{T+1})}(1-a)(\Gamma_T^h)\Gamma^2 + \ldots \tag{7.16}$$

Relation (7.16) expresses that the discounted value of consumption equals the sum of (i) the real value of securities in the previous period with the addition of the real interest income, and (ii) the discounted value of future income streams from labour income.

Using (7.10) and (7.14), consumption for each household specified by (7.16) can be summed to give the following relationship for total consumption and growth in the economy as a whole

$$C_T\left(\frac{1}{1-\beta}\right) = \left(\frac{S_{T-1}}{P_{T-1}}\right)(1+r_{T-1}) + Y_T(1-a)$$
$$+ \frac{Y_{T+1}}{1+r_T}(1-a)\Gamma + \frac{Y_{T+2}}{(1+r_T)(1+r_{T+1})}(1-a)\Gamma^2 + \dots$$

(7.17)

Firms finance investments through securities with a fixed nominal interest rate. The value of the securities issued by the firms is thus given as

$$\frac{S_T}{P_T} = K_{T+1}.$$

(7.18)

Gross investment corresponds to the optimal capital in the subsequent time period with the deduction of capital left over from the previous period, that is

$$I_T = K_T - (1-\kappa)K_{T-1}.$$

(7.19)

Combining (7.15) and (7.19), the condition for goods market equilibrium can be rewritten

$$\left(\frac{C_T}{Y_T}\right) + \left(\frac{K_{T+1}}{Y_T}\right) - (1-\kappa) = 1.$$

(7.20)

The condition for goods market equilibrium specified by relation (7.20) is generally holding for all time periods.

7.2.2 Steady-state with non-unit capital–production ratio

As wages are fixed through nominal wage contracts, unanticipated monetary policy affects production and capital formation during the wage contract period. In the following we will examine whether a change in production and capital caused by an increase in the money stock, which is unexpected by the wage setters, has an impact on subsequently realised production in steady-state equilibrium, implying that unanticipated monetary policy has permanent effects. We will make a distinction between two cases: (i) the case where $a+b \neq 1$, and (ii) the case where $a+b = 1$. The latter case corresponds to Romer (1986) and Barro (1990).

In the case where $a+b \neq 1$, (7.3) combined with (7.4) and (7.13) gives the relationship between production and capital as

$$Y_T = K_T^{a+b}, \quad a+b \neq 1.$$

(7.21)

In steady-state equilibrium, characterised by a constant growth rate in production, it follows from (7.17)–(7.18) and (7.20) that the capital–output ratio must be constant. This is only consistent with (7.21) when capital and output lie at the same level in each time period. This gives

$$v_y = v_k = 0, \tag{7.22}$$

where v_y and v_k are the growth rates of respectively production and capital in the steady state.

In the case of a constant capital–output ratio, it follows from (7.6) that the real interest rate lies at a constant level. Combining (7.17)–(7.21) gives the following condition for the determination of the real interest rate

$$\left(\frac{a}{T+\kappa}\right)[(1+r)(1-\beta)+\kappa]+(1-a)(1-\beta)\left(\frac{1}{N_1}\right)-1=0,$$

$$N_1 \equiv 1 - \Gamma\left(\frac{1}{1+r}\right), \tag{7.23}$$

where r is the real interest rate under steady-state equilibrium.

Having determined the real interest rate from (7.23), the production and capital levels are determined by (7.6) and (7.21). It follows that production and capital levels in steady-state equilibrium are determined unambiguously, that is, production and capital levels in steady-state equilibrium do not depend on production and capital levels in prior periods. This means that unanticipated monetary policy has no impact on the real economy in steady-state equilibrium. The real economy has a well-defined steady-state equilibrium characterised by specific levels of production, capital, and consumption. This steady-state equilibrium is unaffected by changes in the capital stock in a given period brought about by, for example, unanticipated changes in the money supply.

7.2.3   Steady state with unit capital–production ratio

Outline of analysis

We next examine the effect of an increase in the money supply which is unexpected by the wage setters when they set the nominal wage through contracts, making the assumption that the output elasticity of capital is one, that is, $a + b = 1$. The unexpected increase in the money supply takes place in time period t after the nominal wage has been fixed. The wage setters are able from the next period $t + 1$ and all subsequent time periods to foresee structural shifts and changes in economic policy, implying that full employment is realised in all time periods from period $t + 1$ and onwards. It is the aim to investigate whether the unanticipated money supply increase in period t has consequences for production in subsequent time periods.

The analysis is divided into two parts. We first examine the determination of production from time period $t+1$ and onwards, that is, when there are no unexpected changes in the money supply. Using this in the further analysis, we next show that a change in production in time period t, caused by unexpected monetary policy, affects production from time period $t+1$ and onwards, implying that unexpected one time shifts in the money supply have permanent affects on production.

Analysis of steady-state equilibrium

As there are no unexpected shifts in policy from time period $t+1$, it results that full employment is realised from time period $t+1$ onwards, that is

$$L_T = L'' \equiv 1, \quad T = t+1, t+2, \dots \tag{7.24}$$

Relation (7.24) expresses that the wage setters' desired employment – that is, full employment – is realised from time period $t+1$ – that is the time period following the monetary shock – as the wage setters form correct expectations about the economic structure and economic policy.

Using that full employment is realised from period $t+1$, that is, (7.24), and using (7.3)–(7.4), it follows in the case where $a+b=1$, that production equals capital from time period $t+1$, that is

$$Y_T = K_T, \quad T = t, t+2, \dots \tag{7.25}$$

Using (7.25) in (7.26) shows the real interest rate to lie at a constant level from time period $t+1$. The real interest rate is given as

$$r_T = a - \kappa \equiv r, \quad T = t, t+1, \dots \tag{7.26}$$

Using (7.18), (7.25) and (7.26) in the relationship for consumption relative to production, given by (7.17), and in the relationship for goods market equilibrium, shown by (7.20), gives the following relationship for consumption relative to production and goods market equilibrium in time periods from time period $t+1$ and onwards.

$$\left(\frac{C_T}{Y_T}\right) = (1+r)(1-\beta) + (1-a)(1-\beta)$$

$$+ \left(\frac{Y_{T+1}}{Y_T}\right)(1+r)^{-1}(1-a)\Gamma(1-\beta)$$

$$+ \left(\frac{Y_{T+2}}{Y_T}\right)(1+r)^{-2}(1-a)\Gamma^2(1-\beta) + \ldots ,$$

$$T = t+1, t+2, \ldots \tag{7.27}$$

$$\left(\frac{C_T}{Y_T}\right) = 2 - \kappa - \left(\frac{Y_{T-1}}{Y_T}\right), \quad T = t+1, t+2, \ldots \tag{7.28}$$

From (7.27) the following relationship results between consumption relative to production in two subsequent periods

$$\left(\frac{C_{T+1}}{Y_{T+1}}\right)\left(\frac{Y_{T+1}}{Y_T}\right)(1+r)^{-1}\Gamma(1-\beta)^{-1}$$

$$= \left(\frac{C_T}{Y_T}\right)(1-\beta)^{-1} - \left[1 - (1+r)^{-1}\Gamma\left(\frac{Y_{T+1}}{Y_T}\right)\right][(1+r)+(1-a)],$$

$$T = t+1, t+2, \ldots \tag{7.29}$$

Combining (7.28) and (7.29) and using (7.26) gives the following first-order difference equation with respect to production growth from time period $t+1$:

$$1 + v_{y,T+2} = -[1 + (2-\kappa)\beta](1+r)(1+v_{y,T+1})^{-1}$$

$$- (1+r)\frac{1}{\Gamma} + 1 + (2-\kappa)\beta, v_{y,T+2} \equiv \frac{Y_{T+2} - Y_{T+1}}{Y_{T+1}},$$

$$v_{y,T+1} \equiv \frac{Y_{T+1} - Y_T}{Y_T}, T = t+1, t+2, \ldots , \tag{7.30}$$

where $v_{y,T+2}$ is the growth rate of production between time periods $T+1$ and $T+2$ and $v_{y,T+1}$ is the growth rate of production between time periods T and $T+1$.

The difference equation (7.30) determines production after time period $t+1$. Having determined production in time period $t+1$, that is Y_{t+1}, it is possible from (7.30) to determine subsequent levels of production, that is $Y_{t+2}, Y_{t+3}, \ldots$. Below we turn to the determination of production in time period $t+1$, that is Y_{t+1}. If it can be established that Y_{t+1} is determined by Y_t, which in turn is affected by the unanticipated change in the money supply brought about in period t, it follows that there are hysteresis effects from unexpected changes in the money supply, implying that unexpected changes in the money supply affect subsequent levels of production.

Production impact of unanticipated monetary policy

We next examine the determination of production when the monetary authorities in time period t implement an unanticipated increase in the money supply and thus in the price level. The monetary authorities implement the unanticipated price increase after nominal wages have been fixed through contracts at the beginning of the time period. The unanticipated price increase affects production in period t.

The authorities control the price level directly through the money supply. Given the assumption of a prefixed nominal wage, the conditions for the firm's optimisation specified by (7.5)–(7.6) give the following relations for the determination of production, in time period t characterised by the unanticipated price increase

$$-\left(\frac{a}{1-a}\right)y_t + \left(\frac{1}{1-a}\right)k_t + \log(1-a) = w_t - p_t,$$
$$w_t = \bar{w}_t, \quad p_t = \bar{p}_t, \tag{7.31}$$

$$k_t = E_{t-1}\left(\frac{a}{r+K}\right), \tag{7.32}$$

where y, k, w, and p are the logarithmic values of respectively production, capital, nominal wage, and the price level.

Relation (7.31) expresses that production in time period t is determined by the price level in period t which is determined by the authorities through the money supply. (7.32) shows that capital in time period t is pre-fixed in the prior period, being determined by the production level which was expected in the prior time period.

It follows from (7.26) that the real interest rate in period t is determined as r. It further follows from (7.25) that the capital–output relationship is one from period $t+1$. Using this in relations (7.17) and (7.20) and further using (7.18) gives the conditions for goods market equilibrium in period t as

$$\left(\frac{C_t}{Y_t}\right) = (1 - \beta)(1 + r)K_t + (1 - a)(1 - \beta)$$

$$+ \left(\frac{Y_{t+1}}{Y_t}\right)\left(\frac{1}{1 + r_t}\right)(1 - a)\Gamma(1 - \beta)$$

$$+ \left(\frac{Y_{t+2}}{Y_t}\right)\left(\frac{1}{1 + r}\right)^2 (1 - a)\Gamma^2(1 - \beta) + \ldots,$$

$$r = a - \kappa, \tag{7.33}$$

$$\left(\frac{C_t}{Y_t}\right) + \left(\frac{Y_{t+1}}{Y_t}\right)\left(\frac{a}{r + \kappa}\right) - (1 - \kappa)K_t - 1 = 0. \tag{7.34}$$

Combining (7.33) and (7.34) gives the following relationship which expresses production in period $t + 1$ as a function of production in time period t and production levels in subsequent time periods, that is from time period $t + 2$ and onwards

$$(1 - a)(1 - \beta) - 1 + K_t[(1 - \beta)(1 + r) - (1 - \kappa)]$$

$$+ \left(\frac{Y_{t+1}}{Y_t}\right)\left(\frac{a}{r + \kappa}\right) + \left(\frac{Y_{t+1}}{Y_t}\right)\left(\frac{1}{1 + r}\right)(1 - a)\Gamma(1 - \beta)$$

$$+ \left(\frac{Y_{t+2}}{Y_t}\right)\left(\frac{1}{1 + r}\right)^2 (1 - a)\Gamma^2(1 - \beta) + \ldots \tag{7.35}$$

As production in period t is determined by (7.31) and the capital stock in period t is determined by (7.32), while production levels after period $t + 1$ are determined as a function of production in time period $t + 1$ by (7.30), relation (7.35) determines production in time period $t + 1$. It follows that production in time period $t + 1$ is a function of production in time period t. This means that unanticipated changes in the money supply cause a change in production which permanently changes the production level in all subsequent time periods.

7.2.4   Policy implications

In the model examined above, hysteresis arises from capital accumulation due to two effects: (i) the capital stock in the previous period determines the volume of investments which is necessary to bring about a desired capital stock in the next period, thus determining the pressure on the goods market and through this the real interest rate, and (ii) the capital stock in the previous period determines the resources which are available for consumption, a larger capital stock increasing the consumption possibilities and thus inducing households to increase consumption.

It has been demonstrated that unanticipated monetary policy has no effect on the steady-state equilibrium, unless the output elasticity of capital is one. An output elasticity of one corresponds to the case which has been examined extensively in the literature on endogenous growth, cf. Romer (1986) and Barro (1990).

The same conclusion applies to other variables which are determined endogenously in the model. As real holdings of financial assets are determined endogenously in the model, it follows that changes in real financial wealth due to unexpected inflation do not affect the long-term steady-state equilibrium except in the case of a capital–output elasticity of one. This is in contrast to shifts which change structural relationships, for example changes in the productivity of labour or shifts in the wage setters' preferences, which affect the steady-state equilibrium.

7.3 Other sources of hysteresis

7.3.1 Structural characteristics in the labour market

Hysteresis may arise due to a number of structural effects in the labour market: (i) job skills deteriorate under unemployment spells, (ii) unemployed workers become less inclined to look for jobs, causing an increase in structural unemployment, (iii) asymmetric information among employers make them reluctant to employ unemployed workers as firms first cut down on those workers with the lowest labour productivity, or (iv) a disproportionate influence of insiders on the decision making in trade unions makes it possible for insiders to exercise an upward pressure on the nominal wage which leads to a permanent increase in unemployment.[3]

Karanassou and Snower (1996) specify a model in which firms incur training costs by employing newly hired workers. Hysteresis effects arise because labour productivity in the firm as a whole becomes a function of the time workers have been employed.

Hysteresis effects arising from labour market characteristics imply that the unemployment rate in a given period becomes a function of unemployment in previous periods. It depends on the size of the coefficients for unemployment in preceding periods whether unemployment converges towards a steady-state equilibrium, follows a random walk, or explodes. To the extent that there is a permanent change in labour productivity, natural production in steady-state equilibrium is affected in models which

---

[3]Discussions are found in Bianchi and Zoega (1997), Layard, Nickell, and Jackman (1991), and Vinals and Jimeno (1996).

imply that wage setters undertake optimisation with respect to the real wage and employment.[4]

7.3.2   Real wealth effects from unexpected inflation

Unexpected inflation may affect natural production through two channels: (i) unexpected inflation influences wage setting by affecting the real financial wealth of the wage setters, and (ii) unexpected inflation influences the demand for goods by causing a transfer of real wealth from holders to issuers of financial assets which carry a fixed interest rate. The change in the demand for goods influences natural production through the channels discussed in chapter 2: in the open economy, with perfect financial integration, through a change in the real exchange rate; in the closed economy, or an economy with imperfect financial integration, through a change in the real interest rate.

The first of these two effects, that is, the effect on wage setting, depends on the net financial position of the wage setters. If wage setters have positive net financial wealth, unexpected inflation has the effect of reducing natural production. This is because a reduction in real financial wealth induces wage setters to attach a larger weight to reaching a high real wage, in turn causing them to opt for lower production, that is, natural production falls.

The effect on the demand for goods of real wealth transfers from holders to issuers of fixed interest rate financial assets cannot be determined unambiguously. Households have traditionally a positive net financial wealth while firms and the government are issuers of nominal financial debt. Unexpected inflation causes in this case a transfer of real wealth from households to firms and the government. Whether saving increases or decreases depends on how demand is affected for these three groups. A lower real financial debt induces firms to increase capital accumulation because a reduction in the firms' real financial liabilities reduces the bankruptcy risk. Whether a reduction in the real debt induces the government to increase expenditure depends on the weight which the government attaches to the net budgetary deficit as a guideline for government expenditure and revenue. If the government experiences an

---

[4]If the sum of coefficients for previous periods is smaller than one, unemployment converges towards an equilibrium, if it is larger than one, unemployment explodes, and, if it is equal to one, a random walk is followed. Empirical evidence suggests that unemployment moves towards an equilibrium although over long periods, see Bianchi and Zoega (1997) and Song and Wu (1997).

increasing marginal disutility from a larger real net budgetary deficit, the government reacts to a reduction in the real value of government debt by increasing expenditure or reducing taxes. The transfer from households with negative net financial positions to households with positive net financial positions causes an increase in the demand for goods insofar as the households with a negative net financial position are liquidity constrained.

A government may use unexpected inflation to bring about a reduction in the real value of government debt. The government's possibility of creating unexpected inflation is usually seen as socially undesirable as it creates uncertainty about future inflation.[5] Several economists stress, however, that the transfer of wealth which takes place through unexpected inflation from holders of government bonds to the government (and thus to the other taxpayers in the economy), may be desirable. Buiter (1995) and Wyplosz (1989) emphasise unexpected inflation as a means of reducing real government debt. De Grauwe (1997) stresses unexpected inflation, causing a reduction in real government debt, as an instrument to avoid tax increases when the economy is exposed to negative shocks. Grilli (1989) discusses that the government's incentive to undertake surprise inflation is determined by the share of domestic government debt which is held by foreigners, and by the duration of outstanding government bonds.

Bohn (1988) finds it optimal to issue government debt with a fixed interest rate as shocks that increase the need for government expenditure are positively correlated with inflation. As the real value of the government's fixed interest rate debt is reduced through unexpected inflation, the use of fixed interest government bonds makes it possible to stabilise the tax rate on labour income. This may increase the labour supply as it reduces the uncertainty with respect to labour supply decisions.

Unexpected inflation may further affect the demand for goods and thus production by changing the borrowing possibilities of firms and households. Unexpected inflation changes the nominal value of capital goods which are used as collateral in lending. This increases the possibility of obtaining credit when the firm or household has incurred debt carrying a fixed interest rate.[6]

---

[5]See, for example, Friedman and Schwartz (1986). The literature based on Kydland and Prescott (1977) and Barro and Gordon (1983a, 1983b) views the government's possibility of creating unexpected inflation as socially harmful as it increases inflation while leaving unemployment at the exogenously determined natural level.
[6]See Bernanke and Gertler (1989, 1990).

It follows from the model in section 7.2 that production and capital are unambiguously determined in steady-state equilibrium unless the output elasticity of capital is one. This means that unexpected inflation is able only to affect the steady-state equilibrium in the special case when there is a unit output elasticity of capital at the macroeconomic level.

7.3.3   Effects of goods demand on labour productivity

A number of hysteresis effects may arise from the impact of the pro-duction level on productivity.[7] A higher employment may lead to tech-nical innovations as a larger number of employees are involved in production ('learning by doing'). Research and development activities may be affected negatively during cyclical downturns due to a reduction in profit. Enterprises are in a better position during cyclical downturns to engage in projects which raise long-term productivity, for example, restructuring, introduction of new technologies, etc. Recessions may force the least-efficient producers out of the market. The discipline imposed on company managers by the financial markets is stronger under recessions due to an increased bankruptcy risk. Workers have a stronger incentive during recessions to look for jobs which offer high remuneration and where workers' skills are therefore best utilised. As these structural shifts cause permanent changes in the production function, they affect the wage setters' desired combinations of the real wage and employment and thus have an effect on long-term natural production.

7.4   Summary and conclusion

We have examined the impact of various hysteresis effects on production. Our discussion has centred on the question whether an unexpected change in the money supply in a single time period can affect steady-state equilibrium. In an analysis of capital accumulation, we reached the conclusion that unanticipated inflation only affects steady-state equi-librium when there are the external effects of capital accumulation on labour productivity which cause the output elasticity of capital to be one. This assumption has been used in a large part of the endogenous growth literature, see Romer (1986) and Barro (1990). Besides capital

---

[7]A survey is given in Saint-Paul (1997).

accumulation, the chapter has briefly surveyed other channels through which hysteresis effects can arise, notably through the labour market and through the impact of unexpected inflation on the real value of debt.

8 The impact of inflation on bank earnings

8.1 Introduction

The analysis is based on banks which operate under imperfect competition in the market for bank deposits. Due to imperfect competition, banks are able to derive above normal earnings. Real bank earnings have implications for the real economy in two areas: (i) as the bank earnings from deposits arise from imperfect competition, it constitutes a potential source of revenue for the government, and (ii) assuming asymmetric information between the suppliers of external finance to the bank, the level of real bank earnings affects the conditions under which banks can raise finance from non-deposit external sources and through this there is an impact on the real bank lending rate. We will argue that the level of real bank earnings is affected by inflation, constituting a channel through which money can influence the real economy. Due to the impact of inflation on real bank earnings, we will further argue that the banks' willingness to undertake lending is determined by fluctuations in the inflation rate which are effected by the monetary regime. An investigation of real bank earnings in Denmark shows real bank earnings to be influenced by inflation, a lower inflation causing a fall in real bank earnings.

Section 8.2 outlines the theoretical framework. *Section 8.3* discusses the implications of real bank earnings for the real economy. *Section 8.4* reports the findings from an investigation of real bank earnings in Denmark over the 1976–1996 period. *Section 8.5* brings a summary and conclusion.

8.2 The theoretical framework

The household's demand for bank deposits
We consider a representative household which optimises utility over an infinite time horizon. Utility depends in each time period on

160

consumption and on the liquidity services provided by bank deposits and legal tender. The household is able to place savings in (i) securities, (ii) bank deposits which carry an interest rate determined by the bank through profit maximisation, and (iii) legal tender which offers no nominal return. The household is unable to affect leisure. This gives the following optimisation problem at time t

$$\max_{C^h, S^h, B^h, \ell^h} \left\{ \sum_{T=t}^{\infty} \beta^{T-t} u_T^h \mid \frac{\partial (W/P)}{\partial C^h} = 0, \frac{\partial (W/P)}{\partial S^h} = 0, \frac{\partial (W/P)}{\partial B^h} \right.$$

$$\left. = 0, \frac{\partial (W/P)}{\partial \ell^h} = 0 \right\},$$

$$0 < \beta < 1, T = t, t+1, \ldots, \tag{8.1}$$

$$u_T^h = u_c^h(C_T^h) + u_m^h(B_T^h, \ell_T^h),$$

$$\frac{\partial u_c^h}{\partial C^h} > 0, \quad \frac{\partial^2 u_c^h}{\partial (C^h)^2} < 0, \quad \frac{\partial u_m^h}{\partial B^h} > 0, \quad \frac{\partial^2 u_m^h}{\partial (B^h)^2} < 0,$$

$$\frac{\partial u_m^h}{\partial \ell^h} > 0, \quad \frac{\partial^2 u_m^h}{\partial (\ell^h)^2} < 0, \tag{8.2}$$

$$\Gamma_T^h W_T \left(\frac{L_T}{L''} \right) + S_{T-1}^h (1 + i_{T-1}) + P_{T-1} B_{T-1}^h (1 + \rho_{T-1}) + P_{T-1} \ell_{T-1}^h$$

$$= P_T C_T^h + S_T^h + P_T B_T^h + P_T \ell_T^h, \tag{8.3}$$

where u^h is the utility derived by a representative household in a given time period, β the time discounting factor, C^h consumption of physical goods, u_c^h the utility derived from the consumption of the physical good in each time period, u_m^h the utility derived from holding bank deposits and legal tender in each time period, S^h securities, B^h real bank deposits, ℓ^h the real value of legal tender, ρ the nominal interest rate on bank deposits, i the nominal interest rate on securities, W the nominal wage, P the price level, L employment, and L'' full employment. Γ^h shows the probability of household h finding employment.

Relation (8.1) shows that the household optimises utility over an infinite time horizon, being unable to affect the real wage and thus determine working hours and leisure. (8.2) expresses that utility in each time period can be represented as a separable function where utility is derived from the consumption of physical goods, bank deposits, and legal tender. The utility function is well-behaved, the marginal utilities being positive but declining. (8.3) gives the household's budget constraint. At the household's disposal for consumption and saving is the nominal wage derived from working in period T with the addition of financial wealth left over from the previous time period, consisting of securities S_{T-1}^h with the addition of the interest accrued during the previous time period i_{T-1}, bank deposits B_{T-1}^h with the addition of interest accrued in the previous period ρ_{T-1}, and legal tender ℓ_{T-1}^h. In time period T the household consumes C_T^h of the physical good and places S_T^h in securities, B_T^h in bank deposits, and ℓ_T^h in legal tender.

We assume the following specifications of the instantaneous utilities from respectively consumption of the physical good, real money, and real bond holdings

$$u_c^h(C_T^h) = \log(C_T^h),\tag{8.4}$$

$$u_m^h(B_T^h, \ell_T^h) = \left[\ell_T^{\Phi_1} + \xi B_T^{\Phi_2}\right]^\delta,$$

$$\xi > 0, \quad 0 < \delta < 1, \quad 0 < \Phi_i < 1, \quad i = 1, 2.\tag{8.5}$$

By (8.4) it is assumed that the instantaneous utility derived from the consumption of physical goods is represented by the logarithmic function. (8.5) expresses the utility derived from real bank deposits and legal tender. There is positive but declining marginal utility from real bank deposits and real holdings of legal tender. It is further assumed from (8.5) that an increase in real bank deposits causes a reduction in the marginal utility derived from legal tender, that is, $\partial^2 u_m^h / \partial \ell^h \partial B^h < 0$. This is because a rise in real bank deposits decreases the need for legal tender.

Combining (8.1)–(8.5) gives the following condition for the household's optimum, representing the household's demand function for bank deposits

$$\Psi_t^h \equiv \left[N_1(B_t^h)^{N_2}\left(\frac{i_t - \rho_t}{i_t}\right)^{N_3} + \xi\right]^{\delta - 1} \delta\xi\Phi_2(B_t^h)^{N_4}$$

$$- \left(\frac{1}{C_t^h}\right)\left(\frac{i_t - \rho_t}{1 + i_t}\right) = 0, \quad i_t > \rho_t > 0,$$

$$N_1 \equiv \left(\frac{\Phi_1}{\Phi_2}\right)^{N_3}\xi^{-N_3} > 0, \quad N_2 \equiv \frac{\Phi_1 - \Phi_2}{1 - \Phi_1},$$

$$N_3 \equiv \frac{\Phi_1}{1 - \Phi_1} > 0, \quad N_4 \equiv \delta\Phi_2 - 1 < 0.\tag{8.6}$$

It follows from (8.6) that $\partial\Psi^h / \partial B^h < 0$ and $\partial\Psi^h / \partial\rho > 0$. This causes the household's demand for bank deposits to be a positive function of the interest rate on bank deposits ρ, that is, $\partial\rho / \partial B^h > 0$. It depends on the level of the nominal interest rate, whether there is an increase in the demand for bank deposits when the nominal interest rate on securities rises.

Monetary regime

The authorities determine the price increase through the money supply. The monetary regime is thus characterised as

$$v_{p,t} = v_{p,t-1} \equiv \bar{v}_p, \quad v_{p,t} \equiv \frac{P_t - P_{t-1}}{P_{t-1},} \tag{8.7}$$

where v_p is the price increase.

Relation (8.7) states that the monetary authorities set monetary policy to reach a specific price increase.

The bank's profit maximisation

A representative bank b maximises profits from receiving deposits. The bank is unable to affect macroeconomic variables. The bank is in a monopoly position with respect to receiving deposits and can, by changing the interest rate on deposits, affect the size of deposits. The bank's profit from deposits is thus given as

$$v_t^b = B_t^b P_t (i_t - \rho_t), \tag{8.8}$$

where v^b is profit for the representative bank b.

Relation (8.8) shows bank earnings from receiving deposits as the difference between the income from the alternative placement, that is a placement in the securities market, and the expenditure which a bank incurs on interest payments on bank deposits.

We may conceive of a small open economy where the interest rate on securities is determined exogenously through uncovered interest rate parity. Considering an equilibrium, the real interest rate on securities is exogenously determined and lies at the same level in each time period, that is

$$r_t = r_{t-1} = \bar{r}, \quad \log(1 + r_t) \equiv \log(1 + i_t) - (p_{t+1} - p_t), \tag{8.9}$$

where r is the real interest rate in the securities market.

Optimising bank earnings given by (8.8) with respect to the nominal interest rate on bank deposits and making use of (8.9), gives the conditions for the bank's profit maximisation as

$$i_t = \rho_t + \left(\frac{\partial \rho}{\partial b}\right)^b, \tag{8.10}$$

$$\left(\frac{\partial \rho}{\partial b}\right)^b + \left(\frac{\partial^2 \rho}{\partial b^2}\right)^b > 0, \tag{8.11}$$

where $(\partial \rho / \partial b)^b$ shows the increase in the deposit rate which is necessary to attract one unit of bank deposits. b is the logarithmic value of real bank deposits.

Throughout the following discussion we assume that (8.11) is met. It follows from (8.6) that $(\partial \rho / \partial b)^b = \partial \rho / \partial b > 0$ as the bank is unable to affect macroeconomic variables. It results from (8.9) that an increase in inflation causes a similar increase in the nominal interest rate. This means that the impact of inflation on real bank earnings corresponds to the impact of the nominal interest rate on real bank earnings. Optimising bank earnings from bank deposits specified by (8.8) with respect to the nominal interest rate gives

$$\frac{\partial (v^b / P)}{\partial i} = \frac{B_t}{P_t} \left[\frac{\partial b}{\partial i}(i_t - \rho_t) + 1 - \frac{\partial \rho}{\partial i} \right]. \tag{8.12}$$

Using (8.10) in (8.12) shows that $\partial (v^b / P)/\partial i > 0$ when the bank maximises profit. This means that bank earnings increase when inflation rises.

This finding can be explained as follows. The interest rate on bank deposits is set somewhere between 0 and the nominal interest rate on securities, that is, the returns on the two substitutes for bank deposits. If inflation falls, it becomes more attractive to place in legal tender which still provides the return 0 and real bank earnings are thus squeezed.

8.3   The impact of real bank earnings on the real economy

Bank earnings as a source of government revenue
One may argue that bank earnings constitute a source of revenue for the government which takes two different forms: (i) there is a revenue from the company tax on bank earnings, and (ii) bank earnings constitute an economic rent, implying that the government disposes of a potential revenue source, also when it chooses not to tax bank earnings. Even though the direct loss of company tax revenue due to lower bank earnings caused by lower inflation may be relatively small, for example, because the company tax rate is low or because banks may find ways to circumvent taxation, the potential loss of revenue for the government resulting from a reduction in inflation would seem to be large. This is because bank earnings arising from bank deposits constitute an economic rent which arises from the banks' monopoly position in the deposit market and which can be taxed by the government. In those countries where banks

are owned by the government, for example, France and Italy, the government suffers an additional direct loss of revenue corresponding to the total fall in banks' earnings.

One may further argue that the monopoly earnings derived by banks from bank deposits result from government intervention, as it is the government which, through regulation and due to the central bank's role as a lender of last resort, provides depositors with a safety net which makes it possible to place in bank deposits safely, providing banks with a monopoly position. In reality, it is thus the government which creates the monopoly earnings for banks, the government delegating its competence of issuing money to the banks. The government may further ensure a monopoly position for banks by facilitating payments through bank deposits, for example, by organising the technical facilities or laying down the legal foundations for inter-bank transfers.

It is not certain that an increase in the potential for bank earnings causes an actual increase in earnings. Being large organisations with usually small shareholder influence, banks may use the larger revenue potential arising from higher inflation to the benefit of employees, raising salaries or increasing the number of employees. In this case, an increase in real bank earnings can be viewed as socially undesirable, causing larger use of resources in the financial sector.

An increase in the banks' earnings potential due to higher inflation may further be used to set a lower real lending rate, the higher inflation being used to the advantage of the borrowers. The authorities may forego the possibility of taxing the banks because the banks use the bank earnings for purposes which are considered desirable by the authorities, for example, a reduction in the real bank lending rate or lending to projects considered socially beneficial.

Impact on financial intermediation

Assuming asymmetric information, smaller bank earnings cause a rise in a bank's marginal cost when raising finance from non-deposit sources, that is, through the inter-bank market or through the securities market. Lower real bank earnings increase the risk of a bank going bankrupt in the case where there is uncertainty regarding economic variables. The bank's higher marginal costs associated with external funding cause an increase in the bank's real lending rate or imply that the bank makes more use of credit rationing. In the case of asymmetric information among borrowers, a reduction in bank lending leads to a reduction in the demand for goods which in turn can affect natural production, for example because increased demand for goods causes a real appreciation which improves the wage setters' trade-off between the real wage and employment.

Impact of inflation uncertainty

It follows from the analysis that changes in inflation cause a fluctuation in real bank earnings. This represents a further channel through which money can affect the real economy. When a price stability rule is introduced, there will be less uncertainty concerning the determination of the nominal interest rate, banks thus facing smaller variations in the volume of deposits.

The lesser uncertainty concerning bank deposits in the case of a stable nominal interest rate may affect bank lending in two ways. First, assuming a positive relationship between bank deposits and bank lending, and assuming the bank exhibits risk aversion, less uncertainty concerning the volume of bank deposits causes an increase in bank lending. Second, less uncertainty concerning the funding of banks may induce banks to lengthen loan periods, to a larger extent placing in risky assets.

Choice of monetary regime

A number of economists have been sceptical about a monetary union with a price stability goal, due to the resulting loss of inflation tax/seigniorage (see section 2.3). In this analysis, we have pointed to a loss of a further potential revenue source, that is, the decrease in real bank earnings which follows from lower inflation. The estimate for the fall in bank earnings due to lower inflation which results from the empirical investigation in section 8.4 below, is larger than those which have been obtained concerning inflation tax/seigniorage and suggests that the implementation of a price stability rule may have important consequences even in traditional low-inflation countries.

The analysis casts doubt upon the claim, argued by Posen (1993, 1995), that low inflation and central bank independence is due to pressure from the financial sector.[1] It follows from the analysis that high inflation increases bank earnings due to a rise in the real interest rate on bank deposits.

8.4   Empirical evidence

The bank statistics in Denmark permit us to estimate the reduction in real bank earnings which arise from a fall in inflation. This is because the

---

[1]It is still possible that an inflation aversion in the financial sector can be explained by the negative effects for the financial sector arising from changes in inflation.

Danish statistics on bank deposit rates give average bank deposit rates as the total of the bank's interest expenditure relative to the average level of deposits for the quarter in question.

The impact of inflation on real bank earnings from bank deposits has been tested on the Danish data over the 1976–96 period (quarterly data). To evaluate the earnings arising exclusively from deposits it is assumed that banks place the deposits in ten-year bonds. The price increase is measured by the rise in the GDP deflator. The Danish banks' earnings from deposits has for most of the 1976–96 period ranged between 1 and 3 per cent of GDP. The maximum was reached in the second quarter of 1982 when bank earnings from deposits amounted to 3.5 per cent of GDP due to a very high nominal interest rate on Danish bonds. The lowest bank earnings were recorded during the currency crisis in 1992–3 when Danish banks were forced to increase the deposit rates, leading to very low earnings from deposits ranging between 0.13 and 0.59 per cent of GDP in the period from the fourth quarter of 1992 to the third quarter of 1993.

A reduction in Danish deposit rates has taken place from 1994. It is natural to see this shift in the setting of the deposit rate as resulting from a structural shift in competition. Competition in the Danish banking market has been reduced as a result of mergers between the largest Danish banks which have led to the formation of two large banks which cover approximately 65 per cent of the deposit market. Competition was further reduced due to a number of bank failures. To take account of reduced bank competition, in one estimation a dummy with the value of 1 has been included from 1994 onwards.

Table 8.1 reports the findings from the estimations. The results show that the price increase has a significant impact on bank earnings from deposits. It follows from the estimation which does not include a structural shift in Danish bank competition from 1994, that an increase in inflation of 1 percentage point causes an increase in bank earnings corresponding to 0.03 per cent of GDP in the current quarter rising to a long-term increase of 0.21 per cent of GDP. In the estimation, which includes a dummy to allow for the shift in Danish bank competition from 1994, a rise in inflation of 1 percentage point increases bank earnings from deposits by 0.06 per cent of GDP in the current quarter rising to 0.21 per cent of GDP in the long term.

8.5   Summary and conclusion

We have demonstrated that higher inflation increases real bank earnings when banks operate in a deposit market characterised by imperfect com-

Table 8.1. *OLS estimations for the impact of inflation on Danish bank earnings*

Test without inclusion of dummy for structural shift in 1994

$BANKEAR_t = 0.2214 + 0.8494\,BANKEAR_{t-1} + 0.0309\,INFL_t$
          (2.09)   (13.03)   (2.14)

$R_2 = 0.80,\quad F(2, 79) = 154.82,\, JB = 3.27$

Test with inclusion of dummy for structural shift in 1994

$BANKEAR_t = 0.1969 + 0.7218\,BANKEAR_{t-1} + 0.0587\,INFL_t + 0.3867\,STRUC_t$
          (1.96)   (11.17)   (3.65)   (3.23)

$R^2 = 0.82,\quad F(3, 78) = 119.06,\quad JB = 3.20$

Note: The table shows two OLS estimations of the impact on real bank earnings from deposits over the period 1976.3–1996.4 (quarterly basis). *BANKEAR*: bank earnings from deposits measured as bank deposits relative to GDP with a return calculated as the interest rate on 10-year bonds with the deduction of the average interest rate on bank deposits. *INFL*: the rise in the GDP deflator over the next four quarters. *STRUC*: a dummy with the value 0 from 1976.3 to 1993.4 and 1 from 1994.1 to 1996.4.

petition. It has further been argued that real bank earnings constitute a source of government revenue either directly through an increase in company taxation or due to state ownership of banks, or indirectly because the government can choose to tax the whole of the banks' monopoly earnings which constitute an economic rent. The loss of government revenue due to lower bank earnings appears to be more important than the loss of inflation tax/seigniorage which has traditionally constituted a main argument against a monetary union. The size of real bank earnings can affect the real economy through a number of other channels, for example by affecting the bank's marginal funding cost which in turn influences the real bank lending rate. It is possible that a bank, possibly due to political pressure, passes the larger earnings potential either on to the borrowers through a lower lending rate or to the bank employees in the form of wage increases or an expansion of staff. An empirical investigation of real bank earnings from deposits in Danish banks over the 1976–96 period shows considerable impact from inflation on real bank earnings.

Part III
The impact of monetary regimes

9 Centralised wage formation

9.1 Introduction

This chapter examines the determination of natural unemployment and inflation in a model setting corresponding to Kydland and Prescott (1977) and Barro and Gordon (1983a). The Kydland–Prescott and Barro–Gordon model is based on the assumption that the authorities have preferences which involve both inflation and employment goals while wage setters have preferences which involve only employment. Wage setters set the nominal wage in advance, forming correct expectations regarding the authorities' preferences and thus the authorities' subsequent policy reaction to a wage increase. It is a main conclusion in the traditional model that the authorities' preferences have no impact on natural production which results from the non-cooperative game between wage setters and authorities.[1]

In difference to the traditional Barro–Gordon model, we assume that (i) the wage setters have preferences which involve both employment and the real wage, and (ii) the demand for goods can be affected by inflation. A distinction is made between expected inflation which is fully incorporated in nominal interest rate financial contracts, and unexpected inflation which causes a real wealth transfer between holders and issuers of nominal financial contracts. The inclusion of expected inflation as a determinant of the demand for goods can be explained by the mechanisms which were analysed in previous chapters, for example imperfect international integration of securities markets or imperfect competition in the markets for bank deposits and bank lending. It is demonstrated

---

[1]This basic finding would not be changed if it is assumed that wage setters optimise preferences which include both employment and real wage goals if the real wage is a function only of employment. This case is analysed by Tabellini (1988), Horn and Persson (1988), and Artus (1991).

that the authorities' preferences affect natural unemployment both under a decentralised and a centralised wage setting when expected inflation can influence the demand for goods. It is further demonstrated that authorities' preferences affect natural unemployment under a centralised wage formation when the demand for goods is affected by unexpected inflation.

The finding that natural production is affected by authorities' preferences, means that the authorities, by abandoning monetary policy autonomy in a monetary union or by establishing an independent central bank with a price stability goal, lose a possibility of influencing production. This causes natural production to be affected by the choice of monetary regime.

Section 9.2 briefly discusses the impact of inflation on the demand for goods. *Section 9.3* specifies the economic model. *Section 9.4* analyses natural production. *Section 9.5* discusses policy implications. *Section 9.6* gives a summary and conclusion.

9.2   The impact of inflation on the demand for goods

The analysis is based on the assumption that domestic demand is affected by inflation. Throughout the discussion, we use the term expected inflation to denote a price increase which is expected by economic agents when both wage contracts and financial contracts are fixed. Unexpected inflation is used to denote inflation which is not incorporated in expectations when financial contracts are fixed. One may conceive of a time sequence in which investment and other decisions involving finance, for example, issues of government securities, are taken in advance, for example, due to a long planning period. These financial decisions are taken in anticipation of a certain price increase. The price level may subsequently be changed, giving rise to unexpected inflation. Nominal wage contracts and employment in firms are determined on the basis of the actual realised price level.

The inclusion of expected inflation as a determinant of the demand for goods can be justified by the mechanisms analysed in previous chapters, i.e., imperfect international integration of securities markets (chapter 4), imperfect competition in bank markets (chapter 5), and substitution between securities and money with respect to the provision of liquidity services (chapter 6). The inclusion of expected inflation as a determinant of the demand for goods can also be explained by inflation tax/seigniorage or by the changes in saving which take place because higher inflation decreases an investor's total investment possibilities due to the reduction in the real return on non-interest-bearing money (see chapter 2).

In the overlapping generations model which is at the basis of the analysis and which is examined in the appendix, unexpected inflation influences the demand for goods through two channels. One effect arises because a reduction in the real value of government debt lessens the budgetary constraint for the government, making it possible either to increase government purchases of goods and services or to reduce the tax rate on labour income. The resulting increase in the demand for goods has an expansive effect on natural production. Another effect arises because the lower real value of government debt diminishes the financial wealth of households, causing households to increase saving. This last negative effect on the demand for goods works to reduce natural production. It depends on the economic structure which of these two effects is the stronger and it is therefore uncertain how unexpected inflation affects the demand for goods and natural production.

The impact of unexpected inflation on the demand for goods can be analysed as follows. We take as the point of departure the specification of consumption shown by (A.19) in the appendix. It follows that the household's consumption is negatively affected by a reduction in the initial levels of real government debt and of real net claims on foreigners. It depends on the level of net claims on foreigners and on the households' time preference how a change in the initial level of real net financial wealth changes consumption.

The impact of unexpected inflation on the government is found from the government's budgetary balance which is specified as

$$P_t G_t = \tau_t (1 - a) P_t Y_t + S_t^g - S_{t-1}^g (1 + i_{t-1}) + M_t - M_{t-1}, \quad (9.1)$$

where P is the price level, G government purchases of goods and services, τ the tax rate on labour income, S^g the stock of government securities, Y production, i the nominal interest rate, and M the money supply. a is the output elasticity with respect to capital in the Cobb–Douglas production function.

We may further assume, as a simplification, that money holdings are proportional to nominal income, that is

$$M_t = b P_t Y_t, \quad b > 0. \quad (9.2)$$

Combining (9.1) with (9.2), the government's budgetary constraint can be written as

$$g_t - \tau_t (1 - a) - \left(\frac{S_t^g}{P_t Y_t} \right) = - \left(\frac{S_{t-1}^g}{P_{t-1} Y_{t-1}} \right) \left(\frac{P_{t-1} Y_{t-1}}{P_t Y_t} \right) (1 + i_{t-1}) + b$$

$$- b \left(\frac{P_{t-1} Y_{t-1}}{P_t Y_t} \right), \quad \left(\frac{M_t}{P_t Y_t} \right) = b, \quad 0 < a < 1, \quad b > 0, \quad (9.3)$$

where g is government purchases of goods and services relative to production.

Assuming that a rise in the price level causes a rise in production, it follows from (9.3) that an increase in the price level at the beginning of the period, represented as a rise in P_t, causes an increase in the right-hand side of (9.3). It must therefore give rise to either (i) an increase in government purchases of goods and services relative to production g, (ii) a reduction in the tax rate τ, and/or (iii) a reduction in the real value of outstanding government debt at the end of the period, expressed as S^g/PY. The total impact of unexpected inflation on the demand for goods depends on how the government reacts to a lessening of its budgetary constraint and households' reaction to this government policy. If, for example, the real value of government debt was kept unchanged at the initial level while government purchases of goods and services were increased, the demand for goods relative to production would increase. A negative impact on the demand for goods would arise if the government used its increased budgetary room to reduce the real value of government securities, inducing households to reduce consumption. It thus depends on the economic structure how unexpected inflation affects the demand for goods relative to production.

9.3   Model specification

The firm's optimisation

We consider a representative firm which produces with Cobb–Douglas technology. The firm's optimisation is represented as follows

$$y_t = ak_t + (l - a)l_t, \quad 0 < a < 1, \quad l_t \leq l'' \equiv 0, \tag{9.4}$$

$$y_t - k_t = \log(1 + r_{t-1}) - \log(a), \tag{9.5}$$

$$y_t - l_t = w_t - p_t - \log(1 - a), \tag{9.6}$$

where y represents production (logarithmic value), k the capital stock (logarithmic value), l employment (logarithmic value), l'' full employment (logarithmic value), w the nominal wage (logarithmic value), and p the producer price (logarithmic value).

Relation (9.4) shows Cobb–Douglas technology. (9.5) expresses the optimum condition for capital, capital depreciating in the course of one time period. (9.6) gives the condition for the firm's profit maximisation with respect to labour. It follows from (9.5) that investment relative to production can be shown as

$$\left(\frac{I_t}{Y_t}\right) = \left(\frac{a}{1+r_t}\right)\left(\frac{Y_{t+1}}{Y_t}\right), \tag{9.7}$$

where I is investment. Relation (9.7) shows investment relative to production, assuming that capital depreciates in the course of one time period.

Specification of goods demand

We examine a single time period. A small economy A is considered. The rest of the world is represented by a large economy B. All variables relate to country A unless otherwise specified. Based on the discussion above, we use the following specification of goods market equilibrium

$$y_t = z(p_t^B + x_t - p_t) + d_t, \quad z > 0, \tag{9.8}$$

$$\Omega_t = \Omega(y_t, r_t, v_{p,t}^*, v_{p,t}^u), \quad v_{p,t}^* \equiv E_t^f(p_t - p_{t-1}), \quad v_{p,t}^u \equiv v_{p,t} - v_{p,t}^*,$$

$$\Omega_y \equiv \frac{\partial \Omega_t}{\partial y_t} < 0, \quad \Omega_{pe} \equiv \frac{\partial \Omega_t}{\partial v_p^*}, \quad \Omega_{pu} \equiv \frac{\partial \Omega_t}{\partial v_p^u}, \quad \Omega_t \equiv d_t - y_t, \tag{9.9}$$

$$q_t \equiv p_t + \varphi(p_t^B + x_t - p_t), \quad 0 < \varphi < 1, \tag{9.10}$$

$$p_t^B = \bar{p}_t^B, \quad r_t = \bar{r}_t^B, \tag{9.11}$$

$$r_t = r(v_{p,t}^*), \quad \text{or}, \quad r_t = r_t^B, \tag{9.12}$$

where Ω is domestic demand relative to production (logarithmic value), v_p the price increase, v_p^* the price increase expected at the fixing of financial contracts, that is, expected inflation, v_p^u unexpected inflation, x the exchange rate (number of home country currency units per currency unit of the foreign country) (logarithmic value), and q the consumer price (logarithmic value). d is the logarithmic value of domestic demand. $E_t^f(\cdot)$ shows expectation concerning a variable when financial contracts are fixed.

Relation (9.8) shows goods market equilibrium, the demand for goods being a function of the real exchange rate and domestic demand. Relation (9.9) specifies that domestic demand at a given time t is a function of (i) production in the current time period y_t, (ii) the real interest rate r_t, (iii) expected inflation $v_{p,t}^*$, and (iv) inflation which is unexpected when financial contracts were fixed $v_{p,t}^u$. We assume that fiscal policy instruments are changed only due to changes in unexpected inflation, cf. section 9.2. No specific assumptions are made concerning the impact of expected and unexpected inflation on the demand for goods, cf. the discussion above. (9.10) gives the definition of the consumer price. (9.11) reflects the assumption of a small economy. (9.12) expresses that the real interest is determined either by expected inflation (this is the case when there is imperfect financial integration, cf. chapters 4 and 5), or is exogenously determined as the foreign real interest rate (in the case of perfect financial integration).

Wage setting

We make a distinction between a centralised or decentralised wage setting. In the case of a centralised wage setting, the wage is determined by a trade union which includes all employees in the economy. A decentralised wage setting is characterised by a trade union that includes all employees in a single firm. The nominal wage is set one period ahead, the wage setters forming correct expectations regarding the economic variables which are realised during the wage contract period. This corresponds to Kydland and Prescott (1977) and to Barro and Gordon (1983a). The wage setting is characterised as follows

$$\max_{w}\left\{U_t^u \mid \left(\frac{\partial(w-q)}{\partial w}\right)\Big/\left(\frac{\partial l}{\partial w}\right) = A_t^i\right\}, \quad i = DW, CW,$$

$$A^{DW} = \left\{\left(\frac{\partial(w-q)}{\partial w}\right)\Big/\left(\frac{\partial l}{\partial w}\right) \mid \frac{\partial p}{\partial w} = 0, \ \frac{\partial q}{\partial w} = 0, \ \frac{\partial k}{\partial w} = 0\right\} = -a,$$

$$A_t^{CW} = \left\{\left(\frac{\partial(w-q)}{\partial w}\right)\Big/\left(\frac{\partial l}{\partial w}\right) \mid \frac{\partial k}{\partial w} = 0\right\}, \tag{9.13}$$

$$U_t^u = -f^u\left(\frac{L_t}{L_t''}\right)^{-\gamma} - \left(\frac{W_t}{Q_t}\right)^{-\theta}, \quad f^u > 0, \quad \gamma > 0, \quad \theta > 0, \tag{9.14}$$

where U^u shows the wage setters' utility (a higher positive net value signifying an increase in utility). DW denotes a decentralised wage setting and CW a centralised wage setting. L, L'', W, and Q show the non-logarithmic values of respectively employment, full employment, the nominal wage, and the consumer price.

Relation (9.13) characterises the wage setting. Wages are fixed after firms have taken decisions on capital adjustment, implying that the nominal wage setting has no impact on capital. The term A^i reflects the wage setters' trade-off between the real wage and employment. Under a decentralised wage setting the trade union expects a change in the nominal wage to cause a similar change in the real wage while the impact of the nominal wage on employment given a fixed capital stock can be found from (9.4) and (9.6) as a. Under a centralised wage setting the trade union's trade-off between the real wage and production corresponds to the relationship at the macroeconomic level. Relation (9.14) specifies the wage setters' preferences. Positive but declining marginal utility is derived from higher employment relative to full employment and from a higher real wage.

Policy setting

The authorities set the price level to reach an optimal trade-off between production and inflation after the nominal wage has been fixed through contracts. The economic policy setting can be shown as

$$\max_{p} \left\{ U_t^g \mid \frac{\partial w}{\partial p} = 0, \quad \frac{\partial k}{\partial p} = 0 \right\}, \tag{9.15}$$

$$U_t^g = -f^g(y_t - y_t'')^2 - (q_t - q_{t-1})^2, \tag{9.16}$$

where U^g shows the authorities' utility (a higher positive net value signifying an increase in utility). y'' is the production level which corresponds to full employment.

Relation (9.15) states that the authorities set the price level to optimise their preferences. The authorities are unable to affect the nominal wage due to nominal wage contracts. The authorities' preferences, shown by (9.16), reflect that positive utility is derived from higher production and a lower consumer price increase.

9.4 Determination of natural production

General solution

Optimising (9.9) and using (9.4)–(9.11) gives the condition for the wage setters' optimum at each given time t as

$$y_t = \left(\frac{\theta}{\gamma}\right)\left(\frac{\varphi}{z}\right)\Omega_t - \left(\frac{1}{\gamma}\right)\log\left[\left(\frac{\theta}{f^u\gamma}\right)(-A_t^i)\right]$$

$$- \left(\frac{a}{1-a}\right)\left(1 + \frac{\theta}{\gamma}\right)\log(1 + r_{t-1}) + \left(\frac{\theta}{\gamma}\right)\log(1 - a)$$

$$+ \left(\frac{a}{1-a}\right)\left(1 + \frac{\theta}{\gamma}\right)\log(a). \tag{9.17}$$

Relation (9.17) shows the combinations of production and the real wage that are consistent with the wage setters' optimisation. The wage setters aim at full employment if they face a positive trade-off between the real wage and employment, implying that production lies at the full employment level if $-A_t^i \leq 0$. We assume throughout the following that $A_t^i < 0$, implying that there is unemployment.

Optimising (9.16) with respect to the price level and using (9.15) gives the condition for the authorities' optimum as

$$y_t - y'' = -\left(\frac{1}{f^g}\right)B_t(q_t - q_{t-1}), \quad B_t \equiv \left\{\left(\frac{\partial q}{\partial p}\right)\Big/\left(\frac{\partial y}{\partial p}\right) \mid \frac{\partial w}{\partial p} = 0, \frac{\partial k}{\partial p} = 0\right\}. \quad (9.18)$$

Relation (9.18) shows the combinations of production and consumer price increase that are compatible with the authorities' optimisation.

It follows immediately from (9.17) in combination with (9.18) that the authorities' preferences, represented by f^g, determine natural production, if expected inflation affects either the real interest rate or the demand for goods relative to production. This applies both to a decentralised and a centralised wage setting.

In the following we will demonstrate that the authorities' preferences influence natural production when there is centralised wage setting and when unexpected inflation affects domestic demand relative to production.

In the case of fixed nominal wage contracts, the change in the consumer price which follows from a change in employment, can be found from combining (9.4), (9.6), (9.8)–(9.11), and (9.15)

$$B_t = \left(\frac{a}{1-a}\right)\left[1 - \left(\frac{\varphi}{z}\right)\Omega_y\left(\frac{1-a}{a}\right) - \left(\frac{\varphi}{z}\right)(\Omega_{pe} + \Omega_{pu})\right]. \quad (9.19)$$

Under centralised wage setting, wage setters base wage setting on the authorities' policy reaction, represented by (9.18) and (9.19). Combining (9.4), (9.6), (9.8)–(9.13), and (9.18), the wage setters' trade-off between the real wage and production under centralised wage setting can be found as

$$A_t^{CW} = -a + \left(\frac{\varphi}{z}\right)\Omega_y(1-a)$$

$$- \left(\frac{\varphi}{z}\right)(1-a)(\Omega_{pe} + \Omega_{pu})\left[\left(\frac{f^g}{B_t}\right) - \left(\frac{\varphi}{z}\right)\Omega_y\right]\left(\frac{1}{N_1}\right),$$

$$N_1 \equiv 1 - \left(\frac{\varphi}{z}\right)(\Omega_{pe} + \Omega_{pu}). \quad (9.20)$$

It follows from (9.20) that the centralised wage setter's trade-off between the real wage and employment, represented by A^{CW}, is affected by the authorities' preferences, shown by f^g.

Steady-state equilibrium

In a steady-state equilibrium, unexpected inflation has no impact on the demand for goods relative to production. It further results that domestic demand relative to production is unaffected by current and prior production levels (see section A.6 in the appendix). Inflation lies at a constant level in each time period. The demand for goods relative to production can thus be expressed as

$$\Omega_s = \Omega_s(r, v_p^e),$$

$$(\Omega_y)_s = \left\{ \left(\frac{\partial \Omega_t}{\partial y_t} \right) \mid y_{t-1} = y_s, \Omega_{t-1} = \Omega_s \right\},$$

$$(\Omega_{pe})_s = \left\{ \left(\frac{\partial \Omega_t}{\partial v_{pe}} \right) \mid y_{t-1} = y_s, \Omega_{t-1} = \Omega_s \right\},$$

$$(\Omega_{pu})_s = \left\{ \left(\frac{\partial \Omega_t}{\partial v_{pe}} \right) \mid y_{t-1} = y_s, \Omega_{t-1} = \Omega_s \right\}, \tag{9.21}$$

where the subscript s shows a steady-state equilibrium.

Relation (9.21) shows that the demand for goods relative to production in steady-state equilibrium is a function only of expected inflation and of the real interest rate. (9.21) corresponds to (A.47) in the appendix which is derived on the basis of the overlapping generations model. The terms $(\Omega_y)_s$, $(\Omega_{pe})_s$, and $(\Omega_{pu})_s$ show the changes in domestic demand relative to production which arise in the steady-state equilibrium when there is respectively a change in production, a change in the expected rate of price increase, and a change in the price level which is unexpected at the fixing of financial contracts.

Relation (9.17) applies in all time periods. Combining (9.21) with (9.17) and (9.19)–(9.20) determines natural production in steady-state equilibrium as

$$y_s = \left(\frac{\theta}{\gamma} \right)\left(\frac{\varphi}{z} \right)\Omega_s - \left(\frac{1}{\gamma} \right)\log\left[\left(\frac{\theta}{f^u \gamma} \right)(-A^i)_s \right]$$

$$- \left(\frac{a}{1-a} \right)\left(1 + \frac{\theta}{\gamma} \right)\log(1+r) + \left(\frac{\theta}{\gamma} \right)\log(1-a)$$

$$+ \left(\frac{a}{1-a} \right)\left(1 + \frac{\theta}{\gamma} \right)\log(a), \tag{9.22}$$

$$B_s = \left(\frac{a}{1-a} \right)\left[1 - \left(\frac{\varphi}{z} \right)(\Omega_y)_s\left(\frac{1-a}{a} \right) - \left(\frac{\varphi}{z} \right)\left[(\Omega_{pe})_s + (\Omega_{pu})_s \right] \right], \tag{9.23}$$

$$(A^{DW})_s = -a,$$

$$(A^{CW})_s = -a + \left(\frac{\varphi}{z}\right)(\Omega_y)_s(1-a)$$

$$- \left(\frac{\varphi}{z}\right)(1-a)\left[(\Omega_{pe})_s + (\Omega_{pu})_s\right]\left[\frac{f^g}{B_s} - \left(\frac{\varphi}{z}\right)(\Omega_y)_s\right]\left(\frac{1}{N_1}\right),$$

$$N_1 \equiv 1 - \left(\frac{\varphi}{z}\right)\left[(\Omega_{pe})_s + (\Omega_{pu})_s\right]. \tag{9.24}$$

Relations (9.22)–(9.24) give the determination of production in steady-state equilibrium. (9.22)–(9.24) correspond to (9.17), (9.19), and (9.20) except that the demand for goods relative to production lies at the steady-state level.

It follows from (9.22) that expected inflation can have an impact on natural production in steady-state equilibrium through an impact on the real interest rate and/or on the demand for goods relative to production. This means that the authorities' preferences, shown by f^g, influence natural production in steady-state equilibrium when expected inflation has an impact on the real interest rate and/or on the demand for goods relative to production.

It follows from (9.24) that the term A^{CW} is affected by the authorities' preferences in steady-state equilibrium also. The term A^{CW} represents the change in the real wage which the wage setters can expect to reach at a given change in the nominal wage relative to the change in employment which can be reached through a change in the nominal wage, that is, the trade-off between the real wage and employment faced by the wage setters. As A^{CW} is affected by the authorities' preferences, it follows from (9.22)–(9.24) that the authorities' preferences have an impact on natural production in steady-state equilibrium under centralised wage formation when unexpected inflation has an influence on the demand for goods relative to production. The wage setters take the impact of unexpected inflation on the demand for goods into account in steady-state equilibrium when they form expectations regarding the authorities' policy reaction.

9.5   Policy implications

It follows from the determination of natural production in steady-state equilibrium, given by (9.22), that the authorities' preferences with respect to employment and inflation affect natural production in two cases.

First, the authorities' preferences affect natural production both under decentralised and centralised wage setting when fully expected inflation influences either the demand function for goods or the real interest rate. In an open economy with perfect financial integration, the real interest rate is exogenously given and expected inflation affects natural production through an impact on the demand for goods, a change in the demand for goods having an effect on the real exchange rate and thus on the wage setters' consumption possibilities. In the closed economy or in the case of imperfect financial integration, inflation can affect the real interest rate, cf. chapters 4, 5, and 6.

Second, it follows from the model that the authorities' preferences affect natural production in the case of centralised wage setting also when fully expected inflation has no impact on the demand for goods, implying that $(\Omega_{pe})_s = 0$ and r is exogenously determined, but when inflation that is not incorporated in financial contracts has an impact on the demand for goods, $(\Omega_{pu})_s \neq 0$. This is because the authorities' preferences affect centralised wage setters' trade-off between the real wage and production, represented by A^{CW}.

It follows from the discussion above that it cannot be determined unambiguously how unexpected inflation affects the demand for goods. In the case where $(\Omega_{pu})_s < 0$, that is, unexpected inflation causes a reduction in the demand for goods, it results from (9.22) that a stronger preference for employment among the authorities, that is, a larger value of f^g, increases natural production. In the case where $(\Omega_{pu})_s > 0$, that is, the demand for goods is increased by unexpected inflation, it depends on the economic structure whether a stronger preference for employment on the part of the authorities, that is, a larger value of f^g, increases or decreases natural production. If $N_1 > 0$, a stronger preference among the authorities for employment, i.e. a larger value of f^g, lowers natural production when $(\Omega_{pu})_s > 0$. If $N_1 < 0$, a stronger preference among the authorities for employment increases natural production when $(\Omega_{pu})_s > 0$.

The finding that the authorities' preferences with respect to employment affect natural production is important because it shows that there is an influence on natural unemployment if the authorities abandon using monetary policy for pursuing an employment goal, for example, through the establishment of an independent central bank. In contrast to the traditional analysis based on Kydland and Prescott (1977) and Barro and Gordon (1983a), it is thus impossible to argue that there are no employment consequences of an anti-inflation policy.

9.6 Summary and conclusion

It has been demonstrated that the authorities' preferences with respect to employment and inflation affect steady-state natural unemployment under a decentralised wage setting when the demand function for goods is affected by expected inflation, implying that inflation is fully reflected in financial contracts. In the case of a centralised wage setting, it is demonstrated that steady-state natural production is affected by the authorities' preferences with respect to employment and inflation not only in the case where expected inflation influences the demand for goods but also when the demand for goods is affected by unexpected inflation, i.e., when there is a change in saving due to real wealth transfers caused by unexpected price changes. It depends on the economic structure whether a stronger preference for employment among the authorities increases or lowers natural production.

It is an important policy implication that natural production is determined by the authorities' policy preferences. It cannot be claimed, as in the analysis based on Kydland and Prescott (1977) and Barro and Gordon (1983a), that the authorities' abandonment of a production target, for example, through the creation of an independent central bank with a price stability goal, is unambiguously desirable. If the authorities no longer pursue an employment goal, there is a change in natural production.

10 Fiscal policy

10.1 Introduction

This chapter examines natural unemployment and inflation in a model setting corresponding to Kydland and Prescott (1977) and Barro and Gordon (1983a) where the wage setters fix the nominal wage through contracts and form correct expectations regarding the authorities' subsequent policy setting. Contrary to the analysis in Kydland and Prescott and Barro and Gordon, it is assumed that the wage setters set the nominal wage to reach an optimal trade-off between the real wage and employment. The authorities have at their disposal not only monetary policy but also fiscal policy. Fiscal policy affects the combinations of the real wage and employment which can be reached by the wage setters, and thus the natural unemployment, through a terms-of-trade effect and – in the case of changes in taxation of labour income – through a direct impact on the real disposable wage.

The analysis demonstrates as a new finding that natural unemployment is determined by the monetary regime. This conclusion of natural unemployment being affected by the monetary regime has important policy implications. Based on a model with no stochastic shifts in economic structure, it is no longer possible to claim, as in the models based on Kydland and Prescott and Barro and Gordon, that it is unambiguously desirable to give up the possibility of using monetary policy, for example by establishing an independent central bank.[1] According to the analysis presented in this chapter, a change in the monetary regime, for example, the establishment of an independent central bank with a price stability goal, has an impact not only on

---

[1] As there are no stochastic shifts in structural relationships, we ignore throughout the analysis the possible trade-off which the authorities may face with respect to a reduction in inflation and a reduction in output variability.

inflation but causes at the same time a change in natural unemployment.

The reason for the impact of the monetary regime on natural production can be explained as follows. In a model where wage setters set the nominal wage to reach an optimal trade-off between the real wage and employment, natural production is determined by combinations of the real wage and employment which can be reached by the wage setters. As the relationship between the real wage and employment is affected by fiscal policy, natural unemployment will be affected by the authorities' inclination to pursue an expansive fiscal policy. The chapter analyses two reasons why the authorities' inclination to pursue an expansive fiscal policy depends on the monetary regime. First, the monetary regime influences the impact which fiscal policy has on employment and inflation because fiscal policy, in line with the traditional Kydland–Prescott and Barro-Gordon model setup, is determined after the nominal wage has been fixed through contracts. This means that the impact of fiscal policy on employment and inflation which determines the authorities' inclination to use fiscal policy, can be found from a model based on a fixed nominal wage. It is well-known from models of the open economy based on wage inflexibility, for example, a standard Mundell–Fleming model, that the impact of fiscal policy on employment and inflation is different under, for example, a floating exchange rate regime than when the authorities maintain a fixed exchange rate or price level. Second, the extent to which the authorities are inclined to use fiscal policy depends on to what extent the authorities can use an alternative policy instrument, in this case monetary policy, to reach the authorities' policy goals. This causes differences in the inclination to use fiscal policy under monetary regimes as monetary regimes differ with respect to the constraints which are imposed on monetary policy. The authorities are, for example, unable to use monetary policy under an irrevocably fixed exchange rate while monetary policy under a price stability regime is tied to the pursuit of the price stability goal. Under policy regimes with full policy discretion, the authorities can use both monetary and fiscal policies to reach employment and inflation goals.

Based on a standard model of a small open economy, the analysis considers four monetary regimes: (i) a floating exchange rate regime with policy discretion in which the authorities set the money supply and fiscal policy instruments to optimise their preferences, (ii) a fixed-but-adjustable exchange rate regime in which the authorities set the exchange rate and fiscal policy instruments to optimise preferences, (iii) a price stability rule in which monetary policy is used to bring about consumer price stability while fiscal policy is determined to opti-mise the authorities' preferences, and (iv) a monetary union where the common monetary authorities pursue a price stability goal while the national authorities set fiscal policy to optimise preferences. Assuming decentralised wage formation, we find natural unemployment to lie at the highest level under a fixed-but-adjustable exchange rate regime. Lower natural unemployment results under the floating exchange rate regime in which the authorities set the money supply and fiscal policy discretely to optimise preferences. A further reduction in natural unem-ployment can be reached in a regime in which monetary policy is used to bring about price stability. The lowest natural unemployment is found in a monetary union where the common monetary authorities pursue a price stability goal.

The analysis suggests that a reduction in the costs associated with using fiscal policy is welfare-improving, leading at the same time to a fall in inflation and a reduction in natural unemployment. The analysis thus questions whether it is appropriate, as in the European Monetary Union, to increase the costs associated with an expansive fiscal policy.

The analysis shows a positive relationship between natural unemploy-ment and inflation, a rise in unemployment causing higher inflation because the authorities are more inclined to pursue an expansive mone-tary policy at high unemployment. This finding raises doubt about the empirical investigations which, on the basis of a positive relationship between unemployment and inflation, conclude that inflation is harmful.

Section 10.2 discusses the literature. *Section 10.3* specifies the model. *Section 10.4* gives the determination of natural production and inflation. *Section 10.5* discusses policy implications. *Section 10.6* examines the rela-tionship between inflation and production. *Section 10.7* gives a summary and a conclusion.

10.2   The literature

The basic model framework with wage setters who optimise preferences with respect to the real wage and employment and authorities who have at their disposal both fiscal policy and monetary policy, corresponds to Jensen (1994) and Agell, Calmfors, and Jonsson (1996). In line with Jensen and Agell, Calmfors, and Jonsson, it is assumed that the autho-rities experience a cost when they use the fiscal policy instrument. Jensen argues that natural unemployment may be increased in a mone-tary union because the authorities have to increase the tax rate on labour income as they lose the revenue from inflation tax/seigniorage in a monetary union.[2] Agell, Calmfors, and Jonsson find a difference between the fiscal policy stance under a policy regime in which the authorities discretely use the exchange rate instrument to optimise preferences relative to a regime with an irrevocably fixed exchange rate. In contrast to the present analysis, Agell, Calmfors, and Jonsson assume wage setter preferences which cause natural unemployment to lie at an unchanged level. Two other differences between the present model and the model in Agell, Calmfors, and Jonsson are important. The finding of a different fiscal policy stance across monetary regimes in Agell, Calmfors, and Jonsson is caused by the possibility of using an additional instrument, that is, exchange rate adjustments, under a regime of policy discretion. In the present analysis, the difference in natural unemployment between monetary regimes is caused not only by the authorities' disposal of an additional policy instrument under some monetary regimes but also on the impact of fiscal policy on employment and inflation which differs across monetary regimes, assuming a fixed nominal wage. Moreover, the analysis below is based on an overlapping generations model, implying that the authorities can maintain a given budgetary deficit relative to production for an indefinite period, assuming the real interest rate is lower than the production growth rate.

10.3   Model specification

The firm's optimisation

A representative firm determines employment and capital to optimise profit. Assuming a Cobb–Douglas production function, the firm's optimisation is characterised as follows

$$y_t = ak_t + (1-a)l_t, \quad 0 < a < 1, \quad l_t \le l'' \equiv 0, \tag{10.1}$$

$$y_t - l_t + \log(1-a) = w_t - p_t, \tag{10.2}$$

$$y_t - k_t + \log(a) = \log(1 + r_{t-1}), \tag{10.3}$$

---

[2]This effect depends on the distribution of inflation tax/seigniorage in the monetary union. In addition, insofar as seigniorage/inflation tax is a tax on consumption because money is held prior to consumption expenditure, the wage setters' disposable income is unchanged if taxation is changed from inflation tax/seigniorage to a tax on labour income, causing natural unemployment to be unchanged in a monetary union relative to a monetary regime with autonomy to set an inflation rate different from 0. This last point is made in Obstfeld and Rogoff (1996).

where y is production (logarithmic value), k the capital stock (logarithmic value), l employment (logarithmic value), l'' the labour force (logarithmic value), w the nominal wage (logarithmic value), p the producer price (logarithmic value), and r the real interest rate.

Relation (10.1) specifies Cobb–Douglas production technology. (10.2) and (10.3) give the firm's optimum conditions with respect to employment and capital. The optimum condition shown by (10.3) is based on the assumption that the firm is unable to affect wage setting through its capital adjustment. This can be explained by wages which are set at an institutional level higher than the firm, for example, at the level of the industrial sector. (10.3) is further based on the assumption that capital depreciates fully in the course of one time period.

Goods market and money market equilibrium

We study a small open economy A. The rest of the world is represented by a large economy B. Equilibrium in goods and money markets is given as follows (all variables relating to economy A unless otherwise specified)

$$y_t = z(p_t^B + x_t - p_t) + d_t, \quad z > 0, \tag{10.4}$$

$$\Omega_t = \Omega(y_t, g_t, \tau_t, r_t, s_{t-1}), \quad \Omega_t \equiv d_t - y_t,$$

$$\Omega_y \equiv \frac{\partial \Omega_t}{\partial y_t} < 0, \quad \Omega_g \equiv \frac{\partial \Omega_t}{\partial g_t} > 0, \quad \Omega_\tau \equiv \frac{\partial \Omega_t}{\partial \tau_t} < 0,$$

$$0 < \tau_t < 1, \quad g_t \equiv \frac{G_t}{Y_t}, \quad s_{t-1} \equiv \frac{S_{t-1}^g}{P_{t-1}} + \frac{F_{t-1}^p}{P_{t-1}}, \tag{10.5}$$

$$m_t = p_t + b y_t, \quad b > 0 \tag{10.6}$$

$$g_t = \bar{g}_t, \quad \tau_t = \bar{\tau}_t, \tag{10.7}$$

$$\log(1 + r_t) = \log(1 + r_t^B), \tag{10.8}$$

$$p_t^B = \bar{p}_t^B \equiv 0, \quad r_t^B = \bar{r}_t^B, \quad r_t^B = r_{t-1}^B \equiv r^B, \tag{10.9}$$

where d is domestic demand (logarithmic value), x the exchange rate between the home country and the foreign country (number of domestic currency units per foreign currency unit) (logarithmic value), g government purchases of goods and services relative to production, Ω domestic demand relative to production (logarithmic value), τ the tax rate on labour income, G government purchases of goods and services, Y production (non-logarithmic value), m the money supply (logarithmic value), and s the real value of the private sector's net financial wealth, defined as the sum of private sector real holdings of securities issued by the government S^g and the net foreign position F^p.

Relation (10.4) gives the condition for goods market equilibrium, the demand for goods being a function of the real exchange rate and of domestic demand. (10.5) shows domestic demand relative to production as a function of production in the current time period y_t, government purchases of goods and services relative to production g_t, the tax rate on labour income τ_t, the real interest rate r_t, and the real value of the private sector's net financial wealth at the end of the previous period s_{t-1}. (10.5) corresponds to relation (A.58) in the appendix and is derived on the basis of an overlapping generations model with infinitely lived households. (10.6) shows money market equilibrium, money demand being a function of the production and price levels. (10.7) expresses that the authorities use government purchases of goods and services relative to production g and taxation on labour income τ as policy instruments. By (10.8) it is assumed that there is perfect financial integration, the domestic real interest rate being equal to the foreign real interest rate.[3] (10.9) expresses the assumption of the home country being a small economy, foreign variables being determined exogenously. It is further assumed that the foreign real interest rate in each time period lies at an unchanged level while the foreign price level is constant.

Wage setting

The wage setters determine the nominal wage through contracts which are concluded at the beginning of the time period with a duration of one period. Wage setting is specified as follows

$$\max_{w}\left\{ U_t^u \mid \frac{\partial q}{\partial w} = 0, \frac{\partial p}{\partial w} = 0, \frac{\partial k}{\partial w} = 0 \right\}, \tag{10.10}$$

$$U_t^u = -f^u\left(\frac{L_t}{L_t''}\right)^{-\gamma} - \left(\frac{W_t(1 - \tau_t)}{Q_t}\right)^{-\theta}, \quad f^u > 0, \quad \gamma > 0, \quad \theta > 0, \tag{10.11}$$

$$q_t \equiv p_t + \varphi(p_t^B + x_t - p_t), \quad 0 < \varphi < 1, \tag{10.12}$$

where U^u is the utility of wage setters (a larger positive net value indicates an increase in utility), q the consumer price (logarithmic value), and φ the share of imported goods in consumption. L, L'', Q, and W represent the

---

[3]A discussion is found in section A.10 in the appendix.

non-logarithmic values of respectively employment, full employment, the nominal wage, and the consumer price.

Relation (10.10) gives the conditions for the wage setters' optimisation. A decentralised wage setting is assumed, implying that wage setters are unable to affect the consumer and producer price levels. It is further assumed that wage setters are unable to affect capital accumulation. (10.12) defines the consumer price as a weighted average of the domestic producer price and the price on imported goods.

Monetary regimes and setting of policy instruments

A distinction is made between four monetary regimes: (i) a floating exchange rate regime with policy discretion where the authorities use changes in the money supply and fiscal policy instruments to optimise preferences, (ii) a fixed-but-adjustable exchange rate regime with policy discretion where the authorities set the nominal exchange rate and fiscal policy instruments to optimise preferences, (iii) a price stability rule where the authorities use monetary policy to pursue a goal of price stability while fiscal policy instruments are set to optimise the authorities' preferences, and (iv) a monetary union where a price stability goal is pursued in the union while the national authorities set fiscal policy to optimise their preferences. The four monetary regimes can be represented as follows

$$\max_{m,g,\tau}\{U_t^g \mid w_t = \overline{w}_t\}, \tag{10.13}$$

$$\max_{x,g,\tau}\{U_t^g \mid w_t = \overline{w}_t\}, \tag{10.14}$$

$$\max_{g,\tau}\{U_t^g \mid w_t = \overline{w}_t, \quad q_t = \overline{q}_t\}, \tag{10.15}$$

$$\max_{g,\tau}\{U_t^g \mid w_t = \overline{w}_t, \quad x_t = \overline{x}_t\}, \tag{10.16}$$

$$U_t^g = -f_1^g(y_t - y_t'')^2 - f_2^g(q_t - q_{t-1})^2 - f_3^g(g_t - g'')^2 - f_4^g(\tau_t)^2,$$
$$f_i^g > 0, \quad i = 1, 2, 3, 4, \tag{10.17}$$

where y'' is the production level which corresponds to full employment.

Relation (10.13) characterises the authorities' optimisation under a floating exchange rate with policy discretion. The authorities have at their disposal both changes in the money supply and the two fiscal policy instruments, that is, changes in government purchases of goods and services and changes in the tax rate on labour income. (10.14) gives optimisation under a fixed-but-adjustable exchange rate regime where changes in the fixed exchange rate and fiscal policy instruments are used to optimise preferences. (10.15) shows that the authorities under a price stability rule optimise their preferences using only fiscal policy instruments. The price stability rule implies that the consumer price lies at an unchanged level in each time period. (10.16) shows the authorities' optimisation in a monetary union. The nominal exchange rate is fixed while the authorities use fiscal policy instruments to optimise preferences. Under all monetary regimes, policy instruments are determined after the nominal wage has been fixed through contracts. This means that the authorities in their optimisation take the nominal wage as given. This corresponds to Kydland and Prescott (1977) and Barro and Gordon (1983a).

Relation (10.17) shows that the authorities' utility depends on (i) the deviation of production from the level which corresponds to full employment y'', (ii) the consumer price increase, shown by $q_t - q_{t-1}$, (iii) the deviation of government purchases of goods and services from a specific level g'' (in the following referred to as the 'efficient' level of government purchases of goods and services), and (iv) the tax rate τ. Negative utility results from higher unemployment, a higher consumer price increase, a deviation of government purchases from the efficient level, and a higher tax rate.

One may perceive the efficient level of government purchases of goods and services g'' to reflect the level of government consumption and investment when these items are designed exclusively from the perspective of reaching an efficient resource allocation, that is, when government expenditure and revenue are determined exclusively on the basis of marginal utilities and costs associated with the different forms of government consumption and investment. g'' therefore shows the effect on the demand for goods of government consumption and investment which would result if fiscal policy was not used to affect production and/or inflation. The third term in the preference function thus represents the cost associated with using government purchases of goods and services to pursue the other goals in the preference function, that is, a high production and a low consumer price increase. Agell, Calmfors, and Jonsson (1996) view the fiscal policy goal in the authorities' preferences as reflecting the political cost associated with a budget deficit and the government's concern about the inter-temporal redistribution of consumption which takes place due to budget deficits.

The cost associated with the tax rate on labour income, i.e. the fourth term in (10.17), can be viewed as reflecting the political cost associated with taxation. There may be a perception among voters that labour income 'belongs' to the wage earners and taxation may thus be seen as confiscation. The term may further reflect an increased cost associated with tax enforcement when there is a high tax rate.

10.4   Determination of natural production and inflation

We first examine the authorities' setting of government purchases of goods and services under the four monetary regimes. We next consider the authorities' setting of the tax rate on labour income. Assuming the authorities in the overlapping generations setup have no preferences with respect to the level of government debt (see below), the optimum conditions for government consumption and taxation can be derived separately. It is finally analysed how fiscal policy affects natural production.

10.4.1   The setting of government consumption

Floating exchange rate with policy discretion
    Under a floating exchange rate with policy discretion, the authorities have at their disposal both changes in the money supply and government purchases of goods and services. Economic policy is set after nominal wage contracts have been fixed, implying that the effects of economic policy can be found from the model specified by (10.1)–(10.9) and (10.12) assuming a fixed nominal wage. Optimising (10.17) with respect to production and government purchases of goods and services, using (10.13), and using from (10.2), (10.4)–(10.9), and (10.12) that $\partial q/\partial y = [a/(1-a)] - (\varphi/z)\Omega_y$ and $\partial q/\partial g = -(\varphi/z)\Omega_g$, we derive the following conditions for the authorities' setting of economic policy

$$q_t - q_{t-1} = -\left(\frac{f_1^g}{f_2^g}\right)\left[\left(\frac{a}{1-a}\right) - \left(\frac{\varphi}{z}\right)\Omega_y\right]^{-1}(y_t - y'')^{FE}, \qquad (10.18)$$

$$(g_t - g'')^{FE} = \Phi_t^{FE}(y_t - y'')^{FE},$$

$$\Phi_t^{FE} \equiv -\left(\frac{f_1^g}{f_3^g}\right)\Omega_g\left(\frac{\varphi}{z}\right)\left[\frac{a}{1-a} - \left(\frac{\varphi}{z}\right)\Omega_y\right]^{-1}, \qquad (10.19)$$

where Φ^{FE} shows the relationship between government purchases of goods and services and production which is compatible with the authorities' optimum under a floating exchange rate regime with policy discretion. *FE* denotes a floating exchange rate regime with policy discretion.
    Relations (10.18)–(10.19) give the combinations of inflation, production, and fiscal policy stance that are consistent with optimising the authorities' preferences under a floating exchange rate regime with policy

discretion. As $y - y'' \leq 0$ and $\Phi_t^{FE} < 0$, it follows that fiscal policy is set at a more expansive level than the efficient level. An increase in government purchases of goods and services causes a real appreciation and thus a lower consumer price increase which induces the authorities to pursue a more expansive monetary policy to reach higher production. A rise in the numerical value of Φ_t^{FE} implies that the authorities pursue a more expansive fiscal policy at a given production level. The authorities' inclination to pursue an expansive fiscal policy to reach low inflation and high production, represented by Φ_t^{FE}, depends on (i) the cost associated with production smaller than full employment production relative to the cost associated with using fiscal policy for stabilisation, expressed by f_1^g / f_3^g, and (ii) the extent to which it is possible through fiscal policy to increase production, expressed by $(\varphi/z)\Omega_g[(a/1 - a) - (\varphi/z)\Omega_y]^{-1}$ which corresponds to $(\partial q / \partial g) / (\partial q / \partial y)$ given a prefixed nominal wage. It follows from (10.5) that Ω_g and Ω_τ depend on the variables which determine Ω_t, that is, the production levels in the current period, the fiscal policy instruments, private sector net financial wealth in the previous period, and the real interest rate level.

It follows from (10.18) that there is positive inflation for all values of production except when production lies at the full employment level. The relationship is an 'inverse' Phillips curve where higher production corresponds to lower inflation. The reasoning behind this negative relationship between inflation and production is the authorities' desire to pursue a more expansive monetary policy at lower production, causing them to increase inflation.

Fixed-but-adjustable exchange rate

Under a fixed-but-adjustable exchange rate regime in which the exchange rate and government purchases of goods and services are set to optimise preferences, the optimum conditions for the authorities' policy setting can be found from (10.2), (10.4)–(10.5), (10.7)–(10.9), (10.12), (10.14), and (10.17) as

$$q_t - q_{t-1} = -\left(\frac{f_1^g}{f_2^g}\right)\left(\frac{1-a}{a}\right)\left(\frac{1}{1-\varphi}\right)(y_t - y'')^{FA}, \tag{10.20}$$

$$(g_t - g'')^{FA} = \Phi_t^{FA}(y_t - y'')^{FA}, \quad \Phi_t^{FA} \equiv 0, \tag{10.21}$$

where Φ^{FA} shows the relationship between government purchases of goods and services and production under a fixed-but-adjustable exchange rate regime. *FA* denotes a fixed-but-adjustable exchange rate regime in which the exchange rate is adjusted to optimise the authorities' preferences.

Relation (10.20) gives inflation under the fixed-but-adjustable exchange rate regime. (10.21) specifies that government purchases of goods and services are set at the efficient level regardless of production.

Price stability rule

Under the price stability rule, the authorities set government consumption on the basis of a prefixed nominal wage and on the basis of a prefixed consumer price. Optimising (10.17) with respect to g, and using from (10.2), (10.4)–(10.5), (10.7)–(10.9), and (10.12) that $(\partial y/\partial g) = [(1 - a)/a](\varphi/z)\Omega_g$, the optimum condition for the authorities' fiscal policy setting can be found as

$$(g_t - g'')^{PS} = \Phi_t^{PS}(y_t - y'')^{PS}, \quad \Phi_t^{PS} \equiv -\left(\frac{f_1^g}{f_3^g}\right)\Omega_g\left(\frac{\varphi}{z}\right)\left(\frac{1-a}{a}\right),$$
(10.22)

where Φ^{PS} shows the relationship between government purchases of goods and services and production under a price stability rule. *PS* denotes a monetary regime under which the authorities pursue a fixed consumer price.

Relation (10.22) reflects that there is a more expansive fiscal policy at a given production when (i) there is a lower cost associated with using government purchases of goods and services relative to production, shown by f_1^g/f_3^g, and (ii) there is a larger impact of a given change in fiscal policy on production, shown by $[(1 - a)/a](\varphi/z)\Omega_g$.

Monetary union

We assume that a monetary union is formed between the small country A and the large country B. A price stability goal is pursued in the monetary union. The authorities set government consumption to optimise their preferences given a prefixed nominal wage. Optimising (10.17) with respect to g, and using from (10.2), (10.4)–(10.5), (10.7)–(10.9), and (10.12) that $(\partial y/\partial g) = [(1 - a)/a](1/z)\Omega_g$, and $\partial q/\partial g = -(\varphi/z)\Omega_g$, the authorities' policy setting is determined through the following condition

$$f_1^g(y_t - y_{t-1})^{MU}\left(\frac{1-a}{a}\right)\left(\frac{1}{z}\right)\Omega_g =$$
$$f_2^g(q_t - q_{t-1})\left(\frac{\varphi}{z}\right)\Omega_g - f_3^g(g_t - g'')^{MU},$$
(10.23)

where *MU* denotes a monetary union.

Relation (10.23) specifies a dynamic path for the development of fiscal policy. This corresponds to Agell, Calmfors, and Jonsson (1996) who reach the conclusion that the budget deficit in a monetary union follows a dynamic path.

Throughout the following analysis, we consider the case where the national authorities in a monetary union do not pursue a price stability goal, implying that $f_2^g = 0$. One may find it likely that the authorities abstain from pursuing price stability in the monetary union, leaving this to the authorities in the union who are charged with price stability. Using $f_2^g = 0$, we derive from (10.23) the following relationship between fiscal policy and production

$$(g_t - g'')^{MU} = \Phi_t^{MU}(y_t - y'')^{MU}, \quad \Phi_t^{MU} \equiv -\left(\frac{f_1^g}{f_3^g}\right)\Omega_g\left(\frac{1}{z}\right)\left(\frac{1-a}{a}\right),$$

(10.24)

where Φ^{MU} shows the relationship between fiscal policy and production which follows from the authorities' optimisation of their preferences under a monetary union, assuming that national authorities do not pursue a price stability goal.

10.4.2   The setting of taxation

Optimising the preferences given by (10.17), the authorities' setting of the tax rate on labour income under the four monetary regimes can be determined in the same way as the setting of government purchases of goods and services. We derive the following optimum conditions

$$\tau_t^{FE} = \Psi_t^{FE}(y_t - y'')^{FE}, \quad \Psi_t^{FE} \equiv -\left(\frac{f_1^g}{f_4^g}\right)\Omega_\tau\left(\frac{\varphi}{z}\right)\left(\frac{a}{1-a} - \frac{\varphi}{z}\Omega_y\right)^{-1},$$

(10.25)

$$\tau_t^{FA} = \Psi_t^{FA}(y_t - y'')^{FA}, \quad \Psi_t^{FA} \equiv 0,$$

(10.26)

$$\tau_t^{PS} = \Psi_t^{PS}(y_t - y'')^{PS}, \quad \Psi_t^{PS} \equiv -\left(\frac{f_1^g}{f_4^g}\right)\Omega_\tau\left(\frac{\varphi}{z}\right)\left(\frac{1-a}{a}\right),$$

(10.27)

$$\tau_t^{MU} = \Psi_t^{MU}(y_s - y'')^{MU}, \quad \Psi_t^{MU} \equiv -\left(\frac{f_1^g}{f_4^g}\right)\Omega_\tau\left(\frac{1}{z}\right)\left(\frac{1-a}{a}\right),$$

(10.28)

where Ψ^{FE}, Ψ^{FA}, Ψ^{PS}, and Ψ^{MU} express the authorities' inclination to set a low tax rate on labour income under respectively a floating exchange rate regime with policy discretion, a fixed-but-adjustable exchange rate regime, a price stability rule, and in a monetary union.

10.4.3 The natural production

Optimising the wage setters' preferences (10.11) with respect to the nominal wage, and using (10.1)–(10.5), (10.8)–(10.10), and (10.12) gives the condition for the wage setters' optimum as

$$
y_t = \left(1 + \frac{\theta}{\gamma}\right)\left(\frac{a}{1-a}\right)\log(a) + \left(\frac{\theta}{\gamma}\right)\log(1-a)
$$
$$
- \left(1 + \frac{\theta}{\gamma}\right)\left(\frac{a}{1-a}\right)\log(1 + r_{t-1})
$$
$$
+ \left(\frac{\theta}{\gamma}\right)\left(\frac{\varphi}{z}\right)\Omega(y_t, g_t, \tau_t, r_t, s_{t-1}) + \left(\frac{\theta}{\gamma}\right)\log(1 - \tau_t) - \left(\frac{1}{\gamma}\right)\epsilon,
$$
$$
\epsilon \equiv \log\left(\frac{\theta a}{\gamma f^u}\right). \tag{10.29}
$$

Relation (10.29) shows the combinations of production and fiscal policy which are consistent with the wage setters' optimisation. Natural production is determined by (i) the wage setters' preferences with respect to production and the real wage, expressed by θ, f^u, and γ, (ii) government purchases of goods and services g, and (iii) the tax rate on labour income τ. Production and inflation are determined in a non-cooperative one-shot game between wage setters and authorities in which both parties optimise their preferences.

As $\Omega_g > 0$ and $\Omega_\tau < 0$, it follows from (10.29) that a higher level of government purchases of goods and services and a lower tax rate on labour income cause an increase in natural production. An increase in government purchases of goods and services has a positive effect on natural production because it causes an increase in domestic demand and through this a real appreciation which improves the combinations of the real wage and employment levels that can be reached by the wage setters. A reduction in the tax rate has a positive effect on natural production by improving the combinations of the real wage and employment which can be reached by the wage setters through two channels: (i) by raising domestic demand and thus causing a real appreciation, and (ii) by increasing the level of real disposable wage income which can be reached at each given employment level.

Using (10.19), (10.21)–(10.22), and (10.24)–(10.28), relation (10.29) for the determination of natural production can be rewritten as

$$
y_t = -\left(1 + \frac{\theta}{\gamma}\right)\left(\frac{a}{1-a}\right)\log(a) + \left(\frac{\theta}{\gamma}\right)\log(1-a)
$$

$$
- \left(1 + \frac{\theta}{\gamma}\right)\left(\frac{a}{1-a}\right)\log(1 + r_{t-1})
$$

$$
+ \left(\frac{\theta}{\gamma}\right)\left(\frac{\varphi}{z}\right)\Omega\left[y_t, \Phi_t^k(y_t - y''), \Psi_t^k(y_t - y''), r, s_{t-1}\right]
$$

$$
+ \left(\frac{\theta}{\gamma}\right)\log\left[1 - \Psi_t^k(y_t - y'')\right] - \left(\frac{1}{\gamma}\right)\epsilon,
$$

$$
k = FE, FA, PS, MU, \quad \Omega_y < 0, \quad \Omega_g > 0, \quad \Omega_r < 0,
$$

$$
\Phi^k \leq 0, \quad \Phi^k \geq 0. \tag{10.30}
$$

It follows from (10.30) that natural production depends on the authorities' inclination to set a high level of government purchases of goods and services, shown by Φ^k, and a low tax rate on labour income, shown by Ψ^k. A lower value of Φ^k and a higher value of Ψ^k cause an increase in natural production.

As the inclination to pursue an expansive fiscal policy differs among monetary regimes, it results that natural production depends on the monetary regime. From (10.19), (10.21)–(10.22), and (10.24)–(10.28) follows

$$
\Phi_t^{FA} > \Phi_t^{FE} > \Phi_t^{PS} > \Phi_t^{MU}, \tag{10.31}
$$

$$
\Psi_t^{FA} < \Psi_t^{FE} < \Psi_t^{PS} < \Psi_t^{MU}. \tag{10.32}
$$

Relation (10.31) shows that the inclination to set a high level of government purchases of goods and services at a given production level, is strongest in a monetary union, implying that the numerical value of Φ^k under this regime is higher than under the other regimes. The second strongest inclination to set a high level of government purchases of goods and services is found under price stability. The inclination to increase government purchases of goods and services is less strong under the two regimes with policy discretion, that is, the fixed-but-adjustable exchange rate regime and the floating exchange rate regime, with the weakest inclination found under a fixed-but-adjustable exchange rate. (10.32) shows correspondingly that the inclination to set a low tax rate on labour income is strongest in a monetary union, next strongest under a price stability rule, third strongest under a floating exchange rate regime with policy discretion, and weakest under a fixed-but-adjustable exchange rate regime with policy discretion.

Combining (10.30)–(10.32), it follows

$$y_t^{MU} > y_t^{PS} > y_t^{FE} > y_t^{FA}. \tag{10.33}$$

Relation (10.33) specifies that natural production is increased in a monetary union relative to price stability rule. The lowest levels of natural production are found under the floating exchange rate regime with policy discretion and the fixed-but-adjustable exchange rate regime, the fixed-but-adjustable exchange rate regime leading to the lowest natural production.

10.4.4   Steady-state equilibrium

The ranking of the four monetary regimes with respect to the level of natural production was derived without making any specific assumptions regarding the level of domestic demand relative to production. The conclusion thus applies to all levels of production and domestic demand. This means that it applies also to a steady-state equilibrium. In the case of steady-state equilibrium, demand relative to production and the impacts of production and fiscal policy instruments on demand relative to production can be specified as follows

$$\Omega_s = \Omega_s(r, g, \tau),$$

$$(\Omega_y)_s = \left\{ \frac{\partial \Omega_t}{\partial y_t} \mid y_{t-1} = y_s, s_{t-1} = \left(\frac{S^g}{PY}\right)_s + \left(\frac{F^p}{PY}\right)_s \right\},$$

$$(\Omega_g)_s = \left\{ \frac{\partial \Omega_t}{\partial g_t} \mid y_{t-1} = y_s, s_{t-1} = \left(\frac{S^g}{PY}\right)_s + \left(\frac{F^p}{PY}\right)_s \right\}, \tag{10.34}$$

$$(\Omega_\tau)_s = \left\{ \frac{\partial \Omega_t}{\partial \tau_t} \mid y_{t-1} = y_s, s_{t-1} = \left(\frac{S^g}{PY}\right)_s + \left(\frac{F^p}{PY}\right)_s \right\},$$

where y_s is the steady-state production level, Ω_s domestic demand relative to production in the steady state (logarithmic value), $(S^g/PY)_s$ the real level of government debt relative to production in the steady state, and $(F^p/PY)_s$ the net foreign production relative to production in the steady state.

In the overlapping generations model which forms the framework of the analysis, government purchases of goods and services and the tax rate on labour income can be set independently of each other even in a steady-state equilibrium, implying that there are no long-term budgetary constraints when the production growth rate is above the real interest rate. In this model setting there is an impact from the two fiscal policy instruments g and τ on domestic demand also in a steady-state equilibrium, implying that Ricardian equivalence does not hold. The government debt level which in a steady-state equilibrium is compatible with given levels of government consumption and tax rates is determined as

$$\left(\frac{S^g}{PY}\right)_s = -\left(\frac{1}{r}\right)(g - \tau(1 - a)), v_y > r. \qquad (10.35)$$

Relation (10.35) gives the combinations of government purchases of goods and services g, tax rate on labour income τ, and real government debt relative to production S^g/PY which are consistent with a steady-state equilibrium characterised by (i) a constant production increase, and (ii) constant real levels of government debt and foreign debt relative to production. Relation (10.35) corresponds to (A.37) in the appendix, setting the growth rate of production equal to 0.

10.5   Policy implications

Employment consequences of monetary regimes
It follows from the analysis that natural production lies at different levels under different monetary regimes. This adds a new dimension to the analysis of optimum monetary regimes. A monetary regime should be chosen not only on the basis of the consideration to stabilise production or the aim to reduce inflation. The impact of the monetary regime on long-term production is a further consideration which must be taken into account when choosing a monetary regime.

The monetary regime has an impact on natural production because fiscal policy affects the combinations of the real wage and employment which can be reached by the wage setters. A more expansive fiscal policy, causing an improvement in the combinations of the real wage and employment which can be reached by the wage setters, makes it possible for the wage setters to reach a higher real wage at a given employment, inducing the wage setters to opt for higher production. This means that natural production is increased if the wage setters expect the authorities to pursue a more expansive fiscal policy during the wage contract period. Assuming there are costs associated with the use of fiscal policy, the authorities' inclination to use fiscal policy depends on the authorities' preferences, on the effectiveness of fiscal policy with respect to reaching the goals which enter the authorities' preference function, and on the possibility of using other policy instruments for attaining the authorities' macroeconomic goals. Natural production thus comes to depend on the monetary regime, due to the differences between monetary regimes with respect to the impact of fiscal policy on production and inflation and due to the differences between monetary regimes with respect to using monetary and exchange rate policies besides fiscal policy. As the authorities determine fiscal policy after the nominal wage has been fixed through contracts, the impact of fiscal policy on production and inflation can be derived from a standard open economy model based on nominal wage inflexibility.

It follows from the analysis that fiscal policy lies at the efficient level under the fixed-but-adjustable exchange rate regime. This is because both the exchange rate and fiscal policy work through the same channel to affect production and inflation, both causing a change in the demand for goods which in turn affects production and inflation. As both policy instruments affect the economy in the same way, and we have assumed that there are costs associated with using fiscal policy in contrast to using exchange rate changes, it is optimal for the authorities to keep fiscal policy at the efficient level while using exchange rate changes to reach production and price stability goals.

In the case where it is impossible to use fiscal policy, i.e. the cost of using fiscal policy rises towards infinity, it follows from (10.19), (10.21)–(10.22), (10.24)–(10.28), and (10.30) that natural production lies at the same level under the four monetary regimes.

The analysis builds on the assumption that a more expansive fiscal policy affects natural unemployment by bringing about a real appreciation or a lower tax on labour income, in this way improving the combinations of the real wage and production which can be reached by wage setters. One may, however, conceive of other channels through which fiscal policy can affect the wage setters' possibilities of reaching high employment and a high real wage, for example when there is imperfect competition in the goods market.[4] The basic finding of the monetary regime affecting natural unemployment therefore does not depend on the terms-of-trade channel and the impact of the tax rate on the real disposable wage but can be derived also from other channels where fiscal policy affects the wage setters' trade-off between the real wage and employment.

---

[4]See Lindbeck and Snower (1994) and Lindbeck (1998).

Fiscal policy effectiveness

Under a floating exchange rate regime with policy discretion where the authorities can use both monetary and fiscal policy to optimise preferences, it follows from (10.18)–(10.19) that fiscal policy is able to affect both natural production and inflation. A reduction in the cost associated with using fiscal policy for pursuing employment or inflation goals, that is, a lower value of f_3^g, increases at the same time natural production and reduces inflation. An improvement in the possibility of using fiscal policy to pursue production and inflation goals can thus be seen as a 'first-best' solution while other arrangements, for example, an independent central bank, are 'second-best' solutions. If there are no costs associated with using fiscal policy, the authorities can reach full employment and price stability at the same time.

It similarly follows from (10.22) and (10.24) that a reduction in the costs associated with using fiscal policy increases natural production under a price stability rule and in a monetary union.

One may point to a more efficient system of taxation, for example, a larger number of tax sources and a more flexible procedure for fiscal policy decisions, as possible institutional changes which can reduce the costs associated with using fiscal policy for employment or inflation goals.

Based on the model outlined by Kydland and Prescott (1977) and by Barro and Gordon (1983a), it is usually regarded as appropriate to restrict a country's possibility of imposing inflation tax/seigniorage which is seen as creating an incentive for the authorities to increase inflation. This can be achieved for example through reforms which promote indexation, see, for example, Horn and Persson (1988) and van der Ploeg (1991). The policy conclusion which follows from the model above may be different. Limiting a government's possibility of financing expenditure by imposing constraints on the use of inflation tax/seigniorage has the effect of both increasing the disutility associated with higher inflation, that is, increasing f_2^g, and raising the cost associated with fiscal policy, that is, increasing f_3^g. While the first effect, that is, a rise in utility caused by lower inflation, has a beneficial effect in terms of reducing inflation while not affecting employment, cf. (10.18), the second effect in the form of an increase in the costs associated with fiscal policy causes an increase in both inflation and unemployment and may thus leave the authorities worse off. It depends on the economic structure and on preferences which of these two effects is the stronger. It is thus impossible on the basis of the model above to reach an unambiguous conclusion whether it is optimal to restrict the possibility of using inflation tax/seigniorage.

Rules vs. discretion in monetary policy

It follows from the analysis that natural unemployment lies at a higher level under the two policy regimes with policy discretion, that is, the fixed-but-adjustable exchange rate regime and the floating exchange rate regime, in which the authorities can use changes in the monetary policy to optimise preferences. Natural unemployment is lower under the two regimes where the authorities are unable to use monetary policy as an instrument to pursue an employment goal, that is, the price stability rule and the monetary union. This finding of natural unemployment lying at a higher level under a policy regime with policy discretion may seem surprising but can be explained as follows. In the present model, natural unemployment is affected only by the fiscal policy stance which has an effect through the real exchange rate or through a direct impact of the tax rate on the wage setters' disposable income. In this model, a more expansive fiscal policy stance lowers natural unemployment. It is clear that the authorities are less inclined to pursue an expansive fiscal policy when they have at their disposal also a monetary policy instrument in addition to fiscal policy than when only fiscal policy is available for increasing employment. This means that the authorities' inclination to use fiscal policy is stronger when there is a constraint on monetary policy than when there is policy discretion.

This constitutes a further argument in favour of rules for monetary policy. Such rules, by strengthening the incentive for the authorities to make use of fiscal policy, reduces natural unemployment.

10.6 The relationship between production and inflation

Relations (10.18) and (10.20) show that there is a positive relationship between natural unemployment and inflation. This is because the authorities' inclination to pursue an expansive monetary policy is stronger when unemployment is low. This conclusion casts doubt upon the studies, see, for example, Fischer (1993) and Gylfason and Herbertsson (1996), which on the basis of empirical evidence show a negative relationship between inflation and unemployment, concluding that high inflation is harmful. The present analysis indicates the reverse causation. Low production causes high inflation.

10.7 Summary and conclusion

In the macroeconomic literature, based on Kydland and Prescott (1977) and on Barro and Gordon (1983a), inflation is viewed as resulting from a non-cooperative game between wage setters and the authorities where the authorities pursue an unemployment goal and a goal of low inflation while the wage setters desire an exogenously given unemployment level. The wage setters form correct expectations concerning the authorities' preferences. In this model setting it is seen as desirable that the authorities pursue exclusively a price stability goal as this leads to price stability while production is unchanged. This provides a justification for establishing an independent central bank with a price stability goal.

In this chapter we have examined how natural production is determined in a Barro–Gordon model setting where the wage setters pursue both an employment goal and a real wage goal and the authorities have at their disposal fiscal policies to optimise preferences. The analysis demonstrates that natural unemployment depends on the monetary regime. Natural unemployment lies at the lowest level in a monetary union where the common monetary authorities pursue a price stability goal. The second-lowest natural unemployment level results under a price stability rule. The highest natural unemployment levels are found under monetary regimes where the authorities besides fiscal policy dispose of a monetary policy instrument, that is, a fixed-but-adjustable exchange rate regime and a floating exchange rate regime with policy discretion.

It follows from this analysis that natural production is increased and inflation lowered when the costs associated with using fiscal policy are reduced. This means that the establishment of an independent central bank with a price stability goal can be seen as a 'second-best' solution which should be used only insofar as it is impossible to reduce the costs associated with using fiscal policy.

The analysis suggests that there is a positive relationship between natural unemployment and inflation, higher natural unemployment leading to higher inflation. This last finding conforms with empirical investigations which show a positive relationship between unemployment and inflation. The analysis sees, however, high inflation as being caused by lower unemployment. This means that the empirical investigations which demonstrate a negative relationship between production and inflation cannot be used as evidence that inflation is harmful.

11 Price stability goal

11.1 Introduction

Monetary authorities have traditionally pursued a price stability goal. Economic theory recommends that the monetary authorities should pursue either a price stability goal or establish an inflation rate corresponding to full liquidity, that is, inflation equal to the negative of the marginal productivity of capital (Fischer and Modigliani, 1978; Friedman, 1969). A price stability goal can be explained by the consideration to minimise menu costs associated with price changes and costs associated with information collection. The full liquidity rule is explained by the consideration to increase the efficiency of money. Optimal inflation may be derived from a balance between these goals, see for example Turnovsky (1987b). The pursuit of a specific inflation rate makes it possible to avoid the wealth transfers between holders and issuers of fixed interest securities caused by unexpected inflation.

What is important for this analysis is that the authorities pursue a goal of a specific inflation rate. This implies that the authorities' preferences become asymmetric: for rates of inflation above the optimal rate, both employment and inflation goals are pursued while for inflation rates below the optimal rate a production goal exclusively is pursued. In the case where optimal inflation has been realised, the authorities are free to increase employment through monetary policy.

This chapter examines the macroeconomic implications when the authorities have such asymmetric preferences, where both production and inflation goals are pursued when inflation lies above the optimal rate while only a production goal is pursued when the authorities have realised optimal inflation. For reasons of presentation, we assume that the authorities pursue a price stability goal. The wage setters set the nominal wage through contracts to reach an optimal trade-off between production and the real wage. The wage setters are unable to foresee actual inflation during the wage contract period due to stochastic shifts in functional relationships and exogenous variables and thus attach probabilities to the authorities pursuing either both a production and an inflation goal or exclusively a production goal. In a standard model following Kydland and Prescott (1977) and Barro and Gordon (1983a), we will demonstrate that the asymmetry in the authorities' preference function implies that the authorities' preferences with respect to production and inflation affect natural unemployment.

This finding of the authorities' policy preferences having an impact on natural unemployment makes it impossible to argue, as in the traditional analysis based on Kydland and Prescott (1977) and Barro and Gordon (1983a), that the exclusive pursuit of a price stability goal in monetary policy brings only benefits in the form of lower inflation while natural unemployment is unchanged. The analysis shows that the authorities, by abandoning the use of monetary policy to reach a production goal, for example by establishing a central bank with a price stability goal, lose the possibility of influencing natural unemployment. If monetary policy is used exclusively to pursue a price stability goal, natural unemployment rises. The analysis thus questions the advisability of reforms, for example, the establishment of an independent central bank, which implies that a price stability goal exclusively is pursued by monetary policy.

Section 11.2 gives the model specification. *Section 11.3* examines the determination of natural production. *Section 11.4* discusses policy implications. *Section 11.5* gives a summary and conclusion.

11.2   Model specification

The economic structure

We consider the determination of natural production at a given point in time, assuming a fixed capital stock. The structure of the economy is given as

$$y_t = -s(w_t - p_t) + \alpha_t, \ s \equiv \frac{1-a}{a} > 0,$$

$$y_t \leq y_t'' = a\alpha_t, \ 0 < a < 1, \tag{11.1}$$

$$\alpha_t \sim N(\mu_t^\alpha, \sigma_\alpha^2), \tag{11.2}$$

$$\alpha_{t-1} \equiv 0, \quad w_{t-1} \equiv 0, \tag{11.3}$$

where y is production (logarithmic value), y'' the production which corresponds to full employment (logarithmic value), w the nominal wage (logarithmic value), p is the domestic producer price level (logarithmic value), and α a shift in the production function (supply shock).

Relation (11.1) gives the supply of goods as a function of the real wage and a stochastic element α. (11.1) is derived on the basis of the assumption that the firm produces with Cobb–Douglas technology and assuming a fixed capital stock. As the firm produces on the basis of a Cobb–Douglas production function, full employment in each time period is given as αa where a is the output elasticity of capital in the production function. (11.2) shows supply shocks to be normally distributed. By (11.3) supply shocks and the nominal wage in the previous period are standardised at zero, implying that $y_{t-1} \equiv 0$. w_t thus represents the wage increase in period t.

The policy setting

The authorities optimise a preference function which for positive inflation rates includes both production and inflation and for price stability includes only production. The policy setting is characterised as follows

$$\max_{p}\{U_t^g \mid w_t = \overline{w}_t\}, \tag{11.4}$$

$$p_t - p_{t-1} > 0: \quad U_t^g = -f_1^g(y_t - y_t'')^2 - f_2^g(p_t - p_{t-1})^2, \quad f_i^g > 0, \quad i = 1, 2,$$

$$p_t - p_{t-1} \leq 0: \quad U_t^g = -f_1^g(y_t - y_t'')^2, \tag{11.5}$$

where U^g is the authorities' utility (a larger positive net value expressing an increase in utility).

Relation (11.4) states that the authorities set the price level to optimise their preferences, assuming that the nominal wage is preset through wage contracts. Relation (11.5) specifies that the authorities react in two different ways depending on inflation. If the price increase is positive, the authorities aim at both lower inflation and a low level of unemployment. If there is non-positive inflation, the authorities aim exclusively at low unemployment. This implies that the authorities make no attempt to deflate the economy by reducing the price level.

The following time sequence is assumed. At the beginning of the time period, wage setters set the nominal wage through contracts, forming correct expectations regarding stochastic distributions of functional relationships and exogenous variables during the wage contract period but not knowing the actual levels of these variables. Subsequently, after the nominal wage has been determined, shifts in functional relationships and exogenous variables occur. The authorities have full information concerning these shifts when economic policy is determined and, knowing the economic structure, set monetary policy at such a level that preferences are optimised. Thus, while the wage setters are subjected to stochastic uncertainty, this is not the case for the authorities.

The wage setting

The wage setters desire a high real wage and high employment/ production when production lies below the full employment level while aiming exclusively at a high real wage when there is full employment. Wage setting is characterised as follows

$$\max_{w}\left\{E_t(U_t^u) \mid \left(\frac{\partial(w_t - p_t)}{\partial w_t}\right) = 1, \left(\frac{\partial y_t}{\partial w_t}\right) = -s\right\}, \tag{11.6}$$

$$U_t^u = -f_1^u(y_t - y_t'')^2 + f_2^u(w_t - p_t), \quad f_i^u > 0, \quad i = 1, 2, \quad \gamma > 0, \quad \theta > 0, \tag{11.7}$$

where U^u is the wage setters' preference function (a larger positive net value expresses an increase in utility), and $E_t(\cdot)$ shows the expected value at the beginning of the time period.

Relation (11.6) states that the wage setters optimise the expected value of their preference function. The wage setters form correct expectations concerning the stochastic distributions of variables which enter the preference function, that is, production and the real wage, and thus concerning the expected value of the preference function. A decentralised wage formation is assumed, implying that the wage setters expect a change in the nominal wage to cause a similar change in the real wage while the production change which results from a given wage change, corresponds to the change in production undertaken by a single firm in response to a higher wage, thus being determined as $-s$ on the basis of relation (11.1). (11.7) shows that the wage setters pursue both a production and a real wage goal. The preference function specified by (11.7) is characterised by positive but declining marginal utilities from production and the real wage. As production cannot rise above the full employment level, (11.7) implies that the wage setters pursue exclusively a real wage goal when there is full employment.

11.3   Determination of natural production

The wage setters are unable to foresee the actual levels of economic variables during the wage contract period. This means that the wage setters, when they form expectations concerning economic variables, do not know whether the price increase in the contract period is positive. They are thus unaware whether the authorities pursue both a production and an inflation goal (in the case of positive inflation) or exclusively a production goal (in the case of price stability). This implies that the wage setters attach probabilities to the economic policies pursued by the authorities.

On the basis of (11.7) the utility expected by the wage setters during the wage contract period can be shown as

$$E_t(U_t^u) = \lambda_t E_t\left[-f_1^u(y_t - y_t'')^2 + f_2^u(w_t - p_t)\right] + (1 - \lambda_t)E_t[f_2^u(w_t - p_t)],$$
$$\lambda_t \equiv \Pr(y_t < y_t''), \tag{11.8}$$

where λ is the probability that production lies below the full employment level during the wage contract period.

Optimising (11.8) with respect to the nominal wage, and using (11.1)–(11.3) and (11.6), the following condition follows from the wage setters' optimum

$$E(y_t - y_t'') = -\left(\frac{1}{s}\right)\left(\frac{1}{\lambda_t}\right)\left(\frac{f_2^u}{f_1^u}\right)\left(\frac{1}{2}\right). \tag{11.9}$$

Relation (11.9) shows that the wage setters aim at a production level which depends on (i) the probability that there is less than full employment λ, and (ii) the wage setters' preferences, reflected by f_1^u and f_2^u.

Natural production depends on the probability of less than full employment λ because this probability determines the weight with which the employment goal enters the wage setters' preferences. In the case where full employment is brought about with a large probability, the wage setters place more weight on the real wage goal and therefore opt for lower expected natural production.

Whether full employment is realised in the wage contract period, depends on the monetary policy pursued by the authorities after the nominal wage has been set. It follows from the authorities' preference function specified by (11.5) that full employment is brought about when there is price stability. This means that the probability of less than full employment in the wage contract period corresponds to the probability that there is positive inflation, that is

$$\lambda_t = \Pr(p_t - p_{t-1} > 0). \tag{11.10}$$

The price increase during the wage contract period depends on the wage increase decided by the wage setters and on the stochastic shocks which occur in the course of the wage contract period. λ thus becomes a function of the nominal wage increase.

Optimising (11.5) with respect to price level and using (11.1)–(11.4) gives the condition for the authorities' optimum as

$$y_t - y_t'' = -\left(\frac{f_2^g}{f_1^g}\right)\left(\frac{1}{N_1}\right)(w_t + \Psi_t), \quad N_1 \equiv 1 + \left(\frac{f_2^g}{f_1^g}\right)\left(\frac{1}{s}\right),$$

$$\Psi_t \equiv -a\alpha_t, \quad \Psi_t \sim N(\mu_t^\Psi, \sigma_\Psi^2),$$

$$\mu_t^\Psi \equiv -a\mu_t^\alpha, \quad \sigma_\Psi^2 \equiv a^2\sigma_\alpha^2. \tag{11.11}$$

Inflation is positive when production lies below the full employment level, that is, $y_t < y_t''$. The condition for production to lie below the full employment level, given by $a\alpha$, can be found from (11.11) as

$$\lambda_t = \Pr(w_t > -\Psi_t). \tag{11.12}$$

Relation (11.12) shows that a higher wage increase implies a reduction in the probability of full employment being realised. When there is a high wage increase, it is less likely that the stochastic variables which determine inflation, take values such that price stability is realised, causing the authorities to pursue a policy which brings about full employment.

As Ψ follows a normal distribution, cf. (11.11), it follows that

$$\lambda_t = \lambda(w_t, \mu_t^\Psi, \sigma_\Psi^2),$$

$$\frac{\partial \lambda}{\partial w} \equiv \lambda_w = (2\pi\sigma_\Psi^2)^{-\frac{1}{2}} \exp\left(-\frac{(w_t - \mu_t^\Psi)^2}{2\sigma_\Psi^2}\right) > 0,$$

$$\frac{\partial \lambda}{\partial \mu^\Psi} \equiv \lambda_\mu > 0, \quad \frac{\partial \lambda}{\partial \sigma_\Psi^2} \equiv \lambda_\sigma > 0. \tag{11.13}$$

Relation (11.13) shows that the probability of less than full employment is a positive function of (i) the wage increase w, (ii) the expected change in the variable Ψ, shown by μ^Ψ, and (iii) the variance in the variable, shown by σ_Ψ^2.

The wage setters set the nominal wage, forming correct expectations regarding the authorities' policy setting. The wage setters thus base wage setting on the expected value of (11.11). This gives the following condition for the wage setting

$$E(y_t - y_t'') = -\left(\frac{f_2^g}{f_1^g}\right)\left(\frac{1}{N_1}\right)(w_t + \mu_t^\Psi). \tag{11.14}$$

Combining (11.9) and (11.14) gives the condition which determines the wage increase

$$w_t = -\mu_t^\Psi + N_2\left(\frac{1}{\lambda_t}\right), \quad N_2 \equiv \frac{1}{2}\left(\frac{1}{s}\right)\left(\frac{f_2^u}{f_1^u}\right)\left[\left(\frac{f_1^g}{f_2^g}\right) + \left(\frac{1}{s}\right)\right]. \tag{11.15}$$

Expected natural production can be found by combining relations (11.13)–(11.15) which determine the three endogenous variables: (i) the expected value of natural production, shown by $E(y_t - y_t'')$, (ii) the wage increase w, and (iii) the probability that production lies below the full employment level λ. As the authorities' preferences with respect to employment and inflation, given by f_1^g/f_2^g, enters (11.15), it follows that the authorities' preferences have an impact on natural production. A stronger preference for employment among the authorities, i.e. a larger value of f_1^g/f_2^g, increases natural production.

Combining (11.13)–(11.15), the impact of functional shifts on expected natural production can be found as

$$\frac{\partial E(y_t - y_t'')}{\partial \mu^\Psi} = \left(\frac{1}{s}\right)\left(\frac{f_2^u}{f_1^u}\right)\left(\frac{1}{2}\right)\left(\frac{1}{N_2}\right)\left(\frac{\lambda_t^2 + N_2\lambda_\mu}{\lambda_t^2 + N_2\lambda_w}\right) > 0, \qquad (11.16)$$

$$\frac{\partial E(y_t - y_t'')}{\partial \sigma_\Psi^2} = \left(\frac{1}{s}\right)\left(\frac{f_2^u}{f_1^u}\right)\left(\frac{1}{2}\right)\left(\frac{\lambda_t^2\lambda_\sigma}{\lambda_t^2 + N_2\lambda_w}\right) > 0. \qquad (11.17)$$

It results from (11.16) that a positive shift in the production function increases natural production. (11.17) shows that larger fluctuations in the production function lead to an increase in natural production.

11.4   Policy implications

Based on Kydland and Prescott (1977) and Barro and Gordon (1983a), it is traditionally argued that the authorities' preferences with respect to production and inflation have no impact on natural production. This means that institutional changes aimed at increasing the weight attached to low inflation by the authorities, for example, the establishment of an independent central bank, are unambiguously beneficial as they lead to lower inflation while having no impact on natural unemployment.

The findings derived in this analysis are different. It has been demonstrated that the authorities' preferences have an impact on natural production. It is therefore impossible to argue that institutional changes which strengthen the authorities' preferences for price stability, are unambiguously desirable. The reason for this shift in conclusions can be explained as follows. In the Kydland–Prescott and Barro–Gordon model framework, the wage setters' preferences concern exclusively production while the authorities have preferences both with respect to production and monetary variables, that is, inflation. The authorities' preference with respect to inflation means that the wage setters can reach their desired production by setting the nominal wage increase at such a level that the authorities optimise their preferences at the production level which corresponds to the wage setters' desired production.

The model examined above takes account of the asymmetry in the authorities' preference function which follows from the authorities taking an interest only in price stability, thus pursuing both an inflation and a production goal when inflation is positive, while pursuing only a production goal when there is price stability. This asymmetry in the authorities' preferences means that the authorities use monetary policy to reach full employment when there is price stability. Wage setters' optimisation thus comes to depend on the probability that full employment is established, the wage setters attaching probabilities to the authorities pursuing either both production and inflation goals or, in the case of price stability, only an employment goal. A rise in the probability of full employment during the wage contract period implies that the wage setters place greater emphasis on the real wage, opting for a higher wage increase and thus lower natural production. The probability that price stability is realised depends, however, on the nominal wage increase. This implies that the wage setters' preferences will come to include not only production but also the wage increase. This means that a purely monetary element, that is, the wage increase, enters the wage setters' preference function. This breaks the monetary neutrality in the wage setters' preference function which is found in Kydland and Prescott (1977) and Barro and Gordon (1983a). Both the wage setters' and the authorities' preferences become functions of production and of the wage increase. This means that natural production and the wage increase are determined jointly by the wage setters' and the authorities' preferences. It follows that the authorities' preferences with respect to production and inflation affect natural production, a stronger preference for employment relative to inflation causing an increase in natural production.

11.5   Summary and conclusion

The chapter examined, in a standard model framework based on Kydland and Prescott (1977) and Barro and Gordon (1983a), the implications of the asymmetry in the authorities' preferences which follows from the authorities' desire to bring about a specific inflation rate, assumed to be price stability. In the case where price stability is realised, the authorities use monetary policy to bring about full employment. It is demonstrated that the wage setters' preferences become a function of the wage increase as the wage increase determines the probability that price stability is brought about, the authorities pursuing in this case only a full employment goal. The presence of the wage increase in the wage setters' preference function means that natural production and the wage increase are determined jointly through both the wage setters' and the authorities' optimisation, causing the authorities' preferences to have an impact on natural production. This implies that the authorities lose the possibility of affecting natural production if the autonomy with respect to monetary policy is abandoned. If the authorities pursue only a price stability goal, there is a rise in natural unemployment.

12 Uncertainty concerning policy formation

12.1 Introduction

This chapter analyses the determination of inflation and natural unemployment in a Barro–Gordon model setting, assuming that the authorities' policy reaction to a given nominal wage increase is not known with certainty by the wage setters and assuming that natural production is determined endogenously through the wage setters' optimisation with respect to employment and the real wage. It is further assumed that the uncertainty faced by the wage setters regarding the authorities' policy response depends on the rate of inflation, higher inflation causing a rise in uncertainty. This last assumption can be justified both on empirical grounds, the empirical evidence showing greater uncertainty with respect to inflation at higher levels, and on theoretical grounds, for example, due to stronger pressure on policy makers when inflation is high.

The analysis demonstrates that the authorities' policy preferences have an impact on the combinations of the real wage and employment which can be reached by the wage setters, and thus on natural production. This makes it impossible to argue, as in the analysis based on Kydland and Prescott (1977) and Barro and Gordon (1983a), that institutional reforms aimed at bringing about price stability, for example, the establishment of an independent central bank, reduce inflation at no cost in terms of higher unemployment. The analysis shows that the authorities, by abandoning the use of monetary policy to reach a production goal, lose the possibility of influencing natural unemployment.

Section 12.2 explains why uncertainty regarding the economic policy setting is affected by the inflation rate. *Section 12.3* sets out a model for the impact of policy uncertainty on the natural production. *Section 12.4* gives the determination of natural production and inflation. *Section 12.5* discusses policy implications. *Section 12.6* gives a summary and conclusion.

12.2   Policy uncertainty affected by inflation

The analysis is based on the assumption that variation in monetary policy is affected by the level of inflation. This can be justified both through the design of the policy-making process and on empirical grounds.

One may conceive of monetary policy as being determined by a political process in which different interest groups and actors interact. Some interest groups/actors place great weight on reducing unemployment, for example, trade unions and left-wing political parties. Other participants in the monetary policy process take a greater interest in reducing inflation, for example, agents in the financial markets and right-wing political parties. One may also conceive that differences with respect to the assessment of the economy cause decision makers, for example, the members of the governing body in a central bank, to form different evaluations of the policy which should be pursued in a given economic situation.

As a result of such divisions in the decision-making process and assuming a certain degree of nominal wage rigidity, for example due to the presence of nominal wage contracts, the authorities set monetary policy at a level which represents a trade-off between inflation and production. While the institutional setup for monetary policy and other formal rules that govern decision making provide a framework within which decisions are taken, it is plausible that there is uncertainty about the actual outcome of the decision-making. The capability of different actors to affect the decision-making process cannot be known with certainty.

Assuming such a framework for the decision-making process with respect to monetary policy, the level of inflation affects the uncertainty regarding the policy setting for three main reasons.

First, high inflation increases the need to respond with a substantial change in monetary policy, that is, to implement a change in monetary policy which can bring about a considerable reduction in inflation. Assuming the economic structure is known with greater certainty when variables lie close to current levels, there is more uncertainty regarding the effect of the large changes in monetary policy which are required at high inflation than when only small adjustments are required.

Second, the pressure to take immediate policy action is stronger when there is high inflation. There is likely to be more uncertainty concerning policy decisions taken under stress than policy actions which are taken under less political pressure. The view that political pressure has an impact on decision making is stressed by, for example, Fischer and Modigliani (1978) who suggest that the authorities at high inflation are more inclined to take policy measures which reduce economic policy efficiency, for example, price controls.

As a final reason why policy uncertainty is affected by inflation, one may see policy makers as being concerned with inflation rates only above zero (cf. chapter 11). This means that the range of inflation rates which are advocated by the various interest groups/actors with an influence on monetary policy is wider at high inflation, causing greater uncertainty regarding the outcome of the monetary decision-making process. An example may illustrate this point. Let us assume production to be determined by the real wage through a log-linear function. If initially production lies at 90 per cent of the full employment level while the wage increase lies at 10 per cent, policy makers who desire full employment, advocate inflation of 20 per cent while policy makers who are concerned only with price stability, advocate a restrictive monetary policy which brings inflation to 0 per cent. In the case of a wage increase of 10 per cent, one may thus expect views on the setting of monetary policy which vary between zero inflation and inflation of 20 per cent. If the wage increase is set at 0 per cent, the inflation rates advocated by the various interest groups/actors vary between 0 per cent and 10 per cent. As it is uncertain which view prevails in political decision making, the variation in actual inflation is larger when a wide range of inflation rates is advocated, explaining why the uncertainty about monetary policy is smaller when the wage increase is low.

The empirical evidence supports the view that monetary policy uncertainty is affected by the rate of inflation. A number of investigations, see section 2.3.1, show a reduction in the fluctuations of inflation when the rate of inflation lies at a lower level. Ball (1992) explains the larger fluctuations in inflation at a high inflation rate with uncertainty concerning monetary policy.

12.3   Model specification

Economic policy setting

The wage setters conclude nominal wage contracts with a duration of one period at the beginning of time t. The authorities' policy response to a given wage increase is characterised as

$$y_t = y_t^* + v_t, \quad v_t \sim N(0, \sigma_t^2), \tag{12.1}$$

$$y_t^* = \arg \max E(U_t^g), \tag{12.2}$$

$$U_t^g = -f_1^g(y_t - y_t'')^2 - f_2^g(p_t - p_{t-1})^2 - f_3^g[(p_t - p_{t-1})$$
$$- (p_{t-1} - p_{t-2})]^2,$$
$$f_i^g > 0, \quad i = 1, 2, 3, \qquad y_t \leq y_t'', \qquad (12.3)$$

$$\sigma_t^2 = bv_{w,t} + \mu, \quad b > 0, \quad \mu > 0, \quad v_{w,t} \equiv w_t - w_{t-1}, \qquad (12.4)$$

where y is production (logarithmic value), y'' the production which corresponds to full employment (logarithmic value), w the nominal wage (logarithmic value), p the price level (logarithmic value), v_w the nominal wage increase, and U^g the authorities' preference function (a higher positive value denoting an increase in utility). v is a normally distributed stochastic disturbance with mean zero and variance σ_t^2 which reflects the stochastic element in the economic policy setting. y^* shows the expected value of production. μ represents exogenously determined uncertainty about monetary policy.

Relation (12.1) reflects that production in each time period is normally distributed with mean y^* and variance σ^2. v reflects the stochastic element in the economic policy setting. Relation (12.2) states that the production which results from the authorities' setting of monetary policy, corresponds on average to the production level which optimises the expected value of the authorities' preference function. In line with Kydland and Prescott (1977) and Barro and Gordon (1983a), we assume the nominal wage to be preset through contracts. (12.3) shows the authorities' preferences. An increase in utility results from higher production and lower price increases. It is further assumed that there are costs associated with changes in inflation. Such costs may be explained by, for example, resistance from economic agents who lose from a change in inflation, for example, agents who have incurred long-term fixed interest debt, the real value of which increases when inflation is reduced.

Relation (12.4) reflects that the uncertainty surrounding the setting of production depends on the wage increase, a higher wage increase leading to a larger variation in the monetary policy determined by the authorities and thus to larger fluctuations in production. The exogenously determined policy uncertainty μ is affected by, for example, the institutional setup and rules regarding the monetary decision-making procedure.

The wage setting
The wage setters have full information regarding the monetary decision-making process, the authorities' preferences, and the correct economic structure during the wage contract period. Due to the stochastic element in the monetary decision-making process, wage setters are

unable to foresee the actual production and price levels but know the stochastic distributions. A distinction is made between two kinds of wage setting: (i) decentralised wage formation where the wage setters consider macroeconomic variables as exogenously given, and (ii) centralised wage formation where the wage setters can affect the macroeconomic variables. Wage setting is characterised as follows

$$\max_{w} E_t(U_t^u) \mid E_t\left(\frac{\partial(w-p)}{\partial w}\right) = A_1^i, \quad E_t\left(\frac{\partial y}{\partial w}\right) = A_2^i, \quad i = CW, DW,$$

$$A_1^{CW} = E\left(\frac{\partial(w-p)}{\partial w}\right), \quad A_2^{CW} = E\left(\frac{\partial y}{\partial w}\right), \quad A_1^{DW} = 1, \quad A_2^{DW} = -s,$$

$$\tag{12.5}$$

$$U_t^u = -f^u \exp\{-(y_t - y'')\} + (w_t - p_t), \quad f^u > 0, \tag{12.6}$$

where U^u is the wage setters' preference function (a larger positive net value expresses an increase in utility).

Relation (12.5) states that the wage setters form correct expectations concerning the stochastic distributions of variables which enter the preference function, that is, production and the real wage. Under decentralised wage formation, the wage setters expect a change in the nominal wage to cause a similar change in the real wage while the production change which results from a given wage change, corresponds to the change in production undertaken by a single firm in response to a higher wage, cf. relation (12.7) below.

The preferences specified by (12.6) imply that the wage setters increase their utility through higher production, lower variation in production, and a higher real wage. We have chosen the specification of the preference function given by (12.6) because it simplifies calculations. The findings do not depend on this specification of preferences but would follow from all preference functions which are asymmetric with respect to production, causing the wage setters' optimum to depend on fluctuations in economic variables and thus on the stochastic element in economic policy.

The economic structure

The model covers a closed economy. We consider the determination of production at a given point in time, assuming a fixed capital stock. Production is determined as

$$y_t = -s(w_t - p_t), \quad s > 0. \tag{12.7}$$

Relation (12.7) gives the condition for the firm's optimum with respect to employment, the firm using Cobb–Douglas production technology. A fixed capital stock is assumed. Production is a negative function of the real wage.

12.4 Determination of natural production

Decentralised wage setting

Combining (12.2)–(12.3) and (12.7) gives the condition for the authorities' setting of monetary policy in reaction to a nominal wage increase

$$(y_t^* - y_{t-1}^*) + \left(\frac{f_3^g}{f_2^g}\right)(v_{w,t} - v_{w,t-1}) = -\left(\frac{f_1^g}{f_2^g}\right)sy_t^* - v_{w,t}. \tag{12.8}$$

Relation (12.8) shows the combinations of wage increase and production for which the authorities optimise their preferences.

The expected value of the wage setters' preference function can be found from (12.6) as

$$E(U_t^u) = -f^u \exp\left\{-(y_t^* - y'') + \frac{\sigma_t^2}{2}\right\} + (w_t - p_t^*), \tag{12.9}$$

where p^* shows the expected value of the price level.

Optimising (12.9) with respect to the nominal wage, using the conditions for a decentralised wage setting specified by (12.5), that is, $\partial y/\partial w = -s$ and $\partial(w - p)/\partial w = 1$, and using (12.4), gives the condition for the wage setters' optimum as

$$(y_t^*)^{DW} - y'' = \frac{1}{2}(bv_{w,t} + \mu) + \log(f^u s). \tag{12.10}$$

Relation (12.10) shows the combinations of wage increase and production which are consistent with the wage setters' optimum.

Production can be found by combining (12.8) with (12.10). As production follows a first-order autoregressive process, the first-order inhomogeneous difference equation which determines expected production is

$$(y_t^* - y_{t-1}^*)^{DW} = -\left(\frac{N_1}{N_2}\right)(y_t^*)^{DW} + \left(\frac{1}{N_2}\right)\left[N_1 y'' + \left(\frac{2}{b}\right)\log(f^u s) + \left(\frac{1}{b}\right)\mu\right],$$

$$N_1 \equiv \left(\frac{f_1^g}{f_2^g}\right)s + \left(\frac{2}{b}\right), \quad N_2 \equiv 1 + \left(\frac{f_3^g}{f_2^g}\right)\left(\frac{2}{b}\right). \tag{12.11}$$

The first-order difference equation given by (12.11) is stable. The steady-state solution is given as

$$(y_s^*)^{DW} - y'' = \left(\frac{1}{N_1}\right)\left(\frac{2}{b}\right)\left[\log(f^u s) + \frac{\mu}{2}\right], \quad \log(f^u s) + \frac{\mu}{2} \le 0,$$

$$(12.12)$$

where y_s^* is the steady-state solution for expected production.

It results from (12.12) that the equilibrium natural production level is affected by (i) the wage setters' preference for employment relative to the real wage f^u, a stronger preference for employment increasing natural production, (ii) the authorities' preferences with respect to production and inflation, shown by f_1^g and f_2^g, a stronger preference for employment relative to inflation causing higher natural production, and (iii) the uncertainty regarding economic policy setting, reflected by the terms b and μ. (12.12) shows that natural production is increased both if there is a larger exogenously determined uncertainty about monetary policy, shown by μ, and if there is a rise in uncertainty about the design of monetary policy at a given inflation level, reflected by b. Besides the factors mentioned above, it follows from (12.11) that the dynamic adjustment path is affected by the authorities' preferences with respect to changes in inflation shown by f_3^g. Inflation in steady-state equilibrium can be found from the wage setters' optimum specified by (12.10) combined with (12.12).

Centralised wage setting

Under a centralised wage setting, the expected changes in production and the real wage which follow from a change in the nominal wage, correspond to the changes which can be found from the macroeconomic model, implying that the nominal wage is determined by a trade union which includes all employees. Optimising the expected value of the wage setters' preference function given by (12.9) with respect to the nominal wage, and using (12.5) and (12.7), gives the condition for the wage setters' optimum as

$$\frac{\partial E(U^u)}{\partial w} = -f^u\left[-\left(\frac{\partial y^*}{\partial w}\right) + \frac{1}{2}\left(\frac{\partial \sigma^2}{\partial w}\right)\right]\exp\left\{-(y_t^* - y'') + \frac{\sigma_t^2}{2}\right\}$$

$$-\left(\frac{1}{s}\right)\left(\frac{\partial y^*}{\partial w}\right) = 0.$$

$$(12.13)$$

As the wage setters know the authorities' preferences and thus the authorities' reaction function given by (12.8), $\partial y^*/\partial w$ can be found as

$$A_1^{CW} \equiv \frac{\partial y^*}{\partial w} = -\left(1 + \frac{f_3^g}{f_2^g}\right)\left[1 + \left(\frac{f_1^g}{f_2^g}\right)s\right]^{-1}.$$

$$(12.14)$$

Combining (12.13)–(12.14), and using (12.4), gives the condition for the wage setters' optimisation of their preference function

$$(y_t^*)^{CW} - y'' = \left(\frac{bv_{w,t} + \mu_t}{2}\right) + \log(s) + \log(f^u) - \Psi,$$

$$\Psi \equiv \log\left(\frac{-A_1^{CW}}{-A_1^{CW} + b/2}\right). \tag{12.15}$$

Relation (12.15) shows the combinations of wage increase and production which are consistent with the wage setters' optimum. Combining (12.15) with (12.8) gives the steady-state solution for natural production as

$$(y_s^*)^{CW} - y'' = \left(\frac{1}{N_1}\right)\left(\frac{2}{b}\right)\left[\frac{\mu}{2} + \log(s) + \log(f^u) - \Psi\right]. \tag{12.16}$$

It follows from (12.16) that equilibrium natural production is affected by the wage setters' preferences regarding production and the real wage f^u, by the authorities' preferences reflected by f_1^g and f_2^g, and by the uncertainty surrounding the economic policy setting expressed by b and μ. It depends on the economic structure and on preferences whether uncertainty increases or decreases natural production. In addition, natural production is affected by f_3^g which reflects the costs associated with a change in inflation.

12.5   Policy implications

Natural production affected by the authorities' employment preferences
It follows from (12.11)–(12.12) and (12.16) that natural production is affected by the authorities' preferences with respect to production and inflation both under a decentralised and a centralised wage setting. An increase in f_1^g relative to f_2^g implies that the authorities place greater weight on production in their preferences. This leads to an increase in N_1, causing a rise in natural production relative to full employment production. Under centralised wage formation, an increase in the weight on employment f_1^g has an additional effect as a higher f_1^g leads to a decrease in A_1^{CW} which has a positive impact on natural production.

The finding that the authorities' preferences have an effect on natural production is important because it is impossible to claim, as in the traditional analysis based on Kydland and Prescott (1977) and Barro and Gordon (1983a), that the authorities' pursuit of a price stability rule and thus the abandonment of monetary policy for stabilisation have exclusively positive effects in the form of lower inflation while natural unemployment stays at an unchanged level. The establishment of an independent central bank with the exclusive goal of price stability leads to an increase in unemployment.

The impact of the authorities' preferences on natural production is caused by the impact of inflation on policy uncertainty. The relationship between policy uncertainty and inflation means that the wage setters' trade-off between production and the real wage becomes a function of the wage increase, thus creating a monetary channel through which production is affected.

Uncertainty regarding the policy setting as a policy instrument

It follows from (12.11)–(12.12) and (12.16) that natural production is affected by the uncertainty surrounding the policy setting, expressed by the parameters b and μ. This opens the possibility that policy uncertainty can be used deliberately to affect natural production. One may conceive of the authorities withholding information from the public to increase the uncertainty regarding the policy response.

It is generally accepted in the literature that a monetary policy based on rules is advantageous seen from the perspective of reducing inflation. Policy makers who want to reduce inflation must make this objective clear to the public to affect inflation expectations. Various possibilities, see, for example, Fischer (1990), have been discussed how the credibility of an anti-inflationary policy can be increased. Bernanke and Mishkin (1992) suggest that transparency with respect to the monetary decision-making process, and thus concerning the authorities' inflationary resolve, can help the authorities to reach lower inflation and possibly at the same time to counter shocks.

Several analyses suggest that it is advantageous for policy makers to hide their true preferences seen from the perspective of reaching high employment. Backus and Driffill (1985) demonstrate that it is advantageous for authorities who desire to increase employment in a given time period, to pretend that they want to bring down inflation in order to maximise the employment impact of an expansive policy. Cukierman (1992) stresses that monetary authorities have an interest in creating uncertainty concerning their policy intentions as it is only unexpected monetary policy which has a real effect. Alesina and Cukierman (1990) show that the authorities, by hiding their true preferences, are able to pursue their true policy objectives in terms of a desired employment/inflation trade-off.

The present analysis which is based on the specification of the wage setters' preferences shown by (12.6), gives a different conclusion. It follows from (12.12) and (12.16) that an increase both in b which reflects the uncertainty surrounding the authorities' policy response to inflation and in μ which reflects the basic, not inflation-related, component in policy uncertainty, causes an increase in natural production. This means that larger policy uncertainty can increase natural production. On the basis of the present analysis, one would thus reach the conclusion, contrary to traditional thinking, that an increase in policy uncertainty may be beneficial seen from the perspective of achieving an increase in natural production. While Backus and Driffill (1985) and others stress the possibility of reaching a higher production level in the short term by increasing uncertainty, it follows from this analysis that a policy based on uncertainty can lead to a permanent employment increase.

The conclusion of policy uncertainty causing an increase in natural production depends on the specification of the wage setter preference function given by (12.6) which shows wage setters to place a relatively large weight on maintaining high employment, thus inducing wage setters to aim at a higher mean production level to avoid low levels of employment when the economy is subjected to fluctuations. The opposite conclusion would follow if it was alternatively assumed that the wage setters place large weight on avoiding low levels of the real wage, the wage setters in this case opting for low production when there is policy uncertainty (see chapter 14). The basic finding of natural production being affected by the authorities' preferences still remains.

Costs associated with inflation changes

A high value of f_3^g reflects a high degree of policy inertia, implying that the authorities are unwilling to change inflation from the level in the previous period. Under centralised wage formation the size of f_3^g affects natural production through the term A_1^{CW}, cf. (12.14). It follows from (12.16) that a higher degree of policy inertia reduces natural production. The authorities may thus use policy inertia as a deliberate policy instrument. If the economic structure is designed in such a way that there are few costs associated with a change in inflation, for example, if there is widespread indexation, the political cost associated with a change in inflation, reflected by f_3^g, is small. This implies that natural production lies at a higher level. The use of indexation can therefore increase natural production.

Need for labour market reforms

A comparison between (12.12) and (12.16) shows that natural production is higher under decentralised than under centralised wage setting when the following condition is met

$$1 + \left(\frac{f_3^g}{f_2^g}\right) > \left(1 + \frac{b}{2}\right) + \left(\frac{b}{2}\right)\left(\frac{f_1^g}{f_2^g}\right)s. \tag{12.17}$$

From (12.17) it follows that it depends on the economic structure and on the authorities' preferences whether decentralised wage setting leads to higher or lower natural production. This means that it cannot be determined unambiguously whether reforms which aim at decentralised wage setting are in fact desirable. This conclusion is counter to Calmfors and Driffill (1988) who suggest that centralised wage setting reduces natural unemployment relative to wage setting based on sector negotiations, corresponding to the decentralised wage setting used in this analysis.

Uncertainty affected by the monetary regime

The monetary regime may have an indirect effect on natural production by influencing the uncertainty regarding the policy setting. It is, however, difficult to draw firm conclusions as to whether the uncertainty concerning monetary policy is increased under a floating exchange rate regime relative to a fixed exchange rate regime.

One difference between a floating and a fixed exchange rate regime likely to affect expectations formation arises because information is more easily available with a floating exchange rate regime than with a fixed exchange rate, cf. Kimbrough (1984) and Lächler (1985). It is likely that economic agents are able to observe price variables better than other variables. A fixed exchange rate regime thus causes a loss of information as agents are no longer able to use the information reflected in the exchange rate. Lächler (1985) stresses, however, that the lack of information may at the same time make it more difficult to control the money supply in a floating exchange rate regime, this effect working to increase the uncertainty in a floating exchange rate regime relative to a fixed exchange rate regime.

A second factor which affects the uncertainty under different monetary regimes, relates to the decision-making process. An independent central bank, and notably an independent central bank in a monetary union, is more likely to follow rules than when monetary policy is pursued by elected policy makers, as elected policy makers are less able to commit to a long-term policy. Thygesen (1991) emphasises that a common central bank in a monetary union, to a larger extent than a national central bank, has to follow prefixed rules because the national authorities are only willing to renounce competence with respect to monetary policy if the central bank is bound to follow fixed rules. In addition, it is more difficult to change rules which are based on an international understanding.

One may further perceive policy makers as being inclined to hide preferences when they want to avoid the failures which result from not being
able to reach policy objectives. A common central bank in a monetary
union may for this reason be less inclined to hide its policy preferences
because a common central bank's competence is more clearly defined
than the competence of national central banks which often find themselves in a struggle for influence with national governments, notably with
national finance ministries. A common central bank in a monetary union
might therefore be less concerned about the loss of prestige which results
when it is unable to reach stated policy objectives, thus being more
inclined to opt for transparency with respect to monetary policy.

The conclusion that decisions in a common central bank can be foreseen with greater certainty is not, however, unambiguous. Thus, countries
may appoint members of the governing board on the basis of their preferences relative to the perceived preferences of the other members of the
governing board who are appointed by the other countries. The aim of a
country would be to 'land' at a trade-off between production and inflation in the common monetary policy of a monetary union which corresponds to the country's own policy preferences. Thus, if a country places
greater emphasis on low unemployment relative to other members of a
monetary union, and it suspects that other countries will appoint members of the governing board who will attach greater weight to price
stability than desired by the country in question, it would be most advantageous to appoint a person who is known to care excessively about
unemployment. Such considerations open up for a game between countries in the appointment of members to the governing board which may
increase uncertainty with respect to policy setting.[1]

12.6   Summary and conclusion

The chapter has examined uncertainty concerning the authorities' policy
response to a given wage increase in a traditional Barro–Gordon model,
assuming that natural production is determined endogenously on the

[1]Alesina and Grilli (1991) analyse a situation where the preferences of the common central
bank do not reflect the true preferences of the populations in the EU because members of the
governing board are elected in electoral districts, being appointed by the governments in the
individual countries. Alesina and Grilli (1994) analyse countries' appointment of members
of the governing board of a common central bank viewed from the perspective of a country
wanting to reduce inflation and output variability. It is argued that a country is more likely
to choose a conservative member of the governing board; the smaller is the variation in the
country's output, the smaller is the correlation between output in the country and output in
other member countries of the union.

basis of the wage setters' weighing between the real wage and employment. It is further assumed that uncertainty depends on the rate of the
wage increase. Several important conclusions follow from this analysis.
First, in difference to Kydland and Prescott (1977) and Barro and
Gordon (1983a), we find that the authorities' preferences affect natural
production. Second, natural production is affected by the uncertainty
regarding monetary policy, making policy uncertainty a possible channel
through which it is possible to affect production and wage increases. The
analysis shows larger uncertainty to cause an increase in natural production. Finally, it is demonstrated that the authorities' inclination to set an
inflation level that is different from the inflation level in the previous
period, affects natural production under centralised wage formation. A
larger degree of policy inertia reduces natural production. As policy
inertia is influenced by the use of indexation, it results that structural
reforms aimed at expanding indexation can increase natural production.

13 Policy uncertainty in a fixed-but-adjustable exchange rate regime

13.1 Introduction

This chapter examines natural production in a fixed-but-adjustable exchange rate system in which there is uncertainty regarding the authorities' decision on exchange rate adjustments. Based on Obstfeld (1991, 1994, 1996), the point of departure is taken in the hypothesis that exchange rate adjustments are determined by the authorities' preferences with respect to unemployment. Depending on the costs associated with devaluation, the authorities are tempted to devalue when there is a large difference between actual unemployment and desired unemployment. Wage setters set the nominal wage in advance through contracts, corresponding to Kydland and Prescott (1977) and Barro and Gordon (1983a).

It is assumed that wage setters are unable to foresee the authorities' exchange rate decision with certainty even though they have correct knowledge about the economic structure and thus also about the shocks and the unemployment level which will be realised in the course of the wage contract period. We assume that exchange rate adjustment results from a political decision-making process which cannot be foreseen with certainty. At each given point in time, the probability of an exchange rate adjustment depends on the unemployment level and on the authorities' preferences. The wage setters attach correct probabilities to the authorities either maintaining an unchanged exchange rate or undertaking an exchange rate adjustment in the course of the wage contract period.

It is a main conclusion from the analysis that the authorities' preferences affect production when there is a decentralised wage formation. The authorities' preferences affect natural production through the probability of an exchange rate adjustment. The wage setters attach a certain probability to the exchange rate being either changed or maintained and aim at a production level which is a weighted average of the two situations. Natural production is thus determined on the basis of both the wage setters' preferences and the probability of an exchange rate adjustment. As the last factor depends on the authorities' preferences and on the unemployment situation prior to an exchange rate adjustment, it results that the authorities' preferences affect production.

The authorities' preferences only affect natural production under decentralised wage setting. If the wage setting was centralised, the wage setters would be able to affect the probability of an exchange rate adjustment. In this case, the wage setters would incorporate the probability of the exchange rate adjustment in their optimisation and they would therefore be able to bring about a production level, the expected value of which would correspond to the wage setters' desired level. In this case, natural production would be determined only by the wage setters' preferences and there would be no room for an impact from the authorities' preferences.

The conclusion of the authorities' preferences affecting production is important because it means that the authorities can use a fixed-but-adjustable exchange rate system to influence the real economy even when there is full wage and price flexibility. This implies that the authorities lose the possibility to affect production by giving up autonomy with respect to exchange rate policy, for example, by establishing an independent central bank with a price stability goal or by joining a monetary union. This is at variance with traditional theory, based on Barro and Gordon (1983a), which suggests that the authorities' use of monetary policy to affect production is harmful.

Other interesting findings result from the analysis. It is demonstrated that a rise in the political costs associated with a devaluation may reduce natural production. This casts doubt upon the discipline hypothesis, see Giavazzi and Pagano (1988) and Giavazzi and Giovannini (1989), which emphasises the gains from increasing the political costs associated with a devaluation as this reduces inflation while leaving natural unemployment unaffected.

The uncertainty in the model examined below is related to the political decision-making process as such. At each level of unemployment, there is a certain probability that the authorities devalue and a certain probability that the authorities maintain an unchanged exchange rate. This modelling of the uncertainty which surrounds the exchange rate decision is different from previous analyses which examine exchange rate adjustments under uncertainty. In the Obstfeld model, there is uncertainty about shifts in the economic structure during the wage contract period, implying that the wage setters would be able to foresee the authorities' exchange rate adjustment with certainty if they had knowledge about the economic shocks. In the Obstfeld model framework, the uncertainty relates to the shocks which hit the economy while the political decision-making process as such, given a specific unemployment level, leaves no uncertainty. In other models, based on Backus and Driffill (1985), there is uncertainty about the authorities' preferences but this uncertainty only affects production over a period until economic agents have learnt about the authorities' preferences.[1]

Section 13.2 discusses the underlying assumption of uncertainty regarding the authorities' exchange rate policy. *Section 13.3* gives the model specification. *Section 13.4* derives production. *Section 13.5* specifies the dynamic adjustment path when wage setters adjust wages slowly. *Section 13.6* discusses policy implications. *Section 13.7* gives a summary and conclusion.

13.2   Uncertainty regarding exchange rate adjustments

The analysis is based on the assumption that there is uncertainty with respect to exchange rate adjustments in a fixed-but-adjustable exchange rate system. The wage setters and other agents in the economy are therefore unable to foresee the actual future exchange rate even when they have perfect foresight regarding the economic situation during the wage contract period. The wage setters attach probabilities to the exchange rate being either adjusted or maintained at an unchanged level.

One may point to a number of reasons which could make it difficult, notably in a fixed-but-adjustable exchange rate regime, to foresee the outcome of the political decision-making process on exchange rate determination. Most importantly, the outcome depends on many factors which would seem impossible to foresee with certainty, for example, the capacity of single individuals to influence decisions. One may point to the experience of the European Monetary System where exchange rate adjustments have been decided only after lengthy negotiations and where the size of the actual adjustment in many cases has come as a surprise. Attempts by a single country to have a currency adjustment approved by the other participants in the EMS have in several instances met with failure, showing the importance of purely political circumstances.

As a further factor behind uncertainty about exchange rate decisions in a fixed-but-adjustable exchange rate regime, one may point to the authorities' interest in hiding their true preferences to prevent currency crises, emphasising in public that exchange rate parity will be maintained. It also

---

[1]See also Andersen and Risager (1991) for a discussion.

causes uncertainty that no mechanism exists in a fixed-but-adjustable exchange rate system through which the authorities can credibly signal changes in preferences with respect to exchange rate policy. This is different from a floating exchange rate regime where changes in monetary policy are signalled continuously through indicators which are easily observed, for example, the interest rate and the money supply.

It finally causes uncertainty about exchange rate determination in a fixed-but-adjustable exchange rate system that policy decisions are required only when there is pressure for an exchange rate adjustment, for example during a currency crisis or when there is political pressure to increase employment. It is possible that the authorities only embark on discussions on exchange rate policy, and form an opinion on possible changes in the exchange rate parity, when they are under pressure to do so, for example during a currency crisis. Experience from the exchange rate adjustments which have taken place in West European countries in the post-Bretton Woods period, demonstrate that exchange rate adjustments with few exceptions have taken place after currency crises.

13.3   Model specification

Economic policy setting

The analysis considers a small home country A which fixes its exchange rate to a large foreign country B. All variables relate to the home country unless otherwise specified. To simplify, only devaluations in the home country are considered. We assume that the authorities' preferences are given as

$$U_t^g = -f^g(y_t - y'')^2, \quad f^g > 0, \quad y'' \equiv 0, \tag{13.1}$$

where U^g represents the authorities' preferences (a larger positive net value indicating an increase in utility), y production (logarithmic value), and y'' the production corresponding to full employment (normalised at zero) (logarithmic value).

Relation (13.1) shows that the authorities derive negative utility when production diverges from the full employment production level. f^g indicates the weight attached by the authorities to reaching the full employment goal. No change in the basic working of the model would occur if other goals were included in the authorities' preference function, for example, an inflation goal or a goal of an unchanged exchange rate. Neither would there be any change in the basic working if a one-time cost associated with exchange rate changes was assumed. To keep the model simple, we have chosen the specification given by (13.1).

We take as the point of departure a situation in which the exchange rate decision of the authorities cannot be foreseen by the wage setters even when they have perfect knowledge of the economic structure during the wage contract period. The exchange rate decision therefore follows a stochastic process. This can be explained by the exchange rate decision being determined through a political process, the outcome of which is random, cf. the discussion in section 13.2.

We assume that the probability of a devaluation is determined by the unemployment level. The devaluation probability depends in each time period on the increase in utility which the authorities can reach through a devaluation and on the costs associated with a devaluation. We further assume that the authorities in the case of a devaluation set the nominal exchange rate so the preference function (13.1) is optimised. These assumptions can be expressed as follows

$$\frac{\pi_t}{1 - \pi_t} = \left(\frac{1}{c}\right)[f^g(y_t^\circ - y^*)^2], \quad c > 0, y_t^* = y'', \tag{13.2}$$

$$y_t^\circ \equiv \{y_t \mid x_t = x^\circ\}, \tag{13.3}$$

where π is the probability of the exchange rate being changed from x° to x^* ($x^* > x^\circ$) (x is the logarithmic value of domestic currency units per foreign currency unit), c the political cost associated with an exchange rate adjustment, y° shows the production which is realised if the exchange rate is maintained unchanged (logarithmic value), and y^* the production which results from an exchange rate adjustment (logarithmic value).

Relation (13.2) specifies that the probability of a devaluation is determined by the increase in utility which the authorities can reach through a devaluation. In addition, the devaluation risk depends on the political cost of changing the exchange rate. It follows from (13.2) that the probability of a devaluation approaches one when production falls relative to the full employment production level while the devaluation probability is zero when production equals the full employment production level. (13.3) shows that the authorities set the nominal exchange rate to optimise their preferences when a devaluation takes place, implying that full employment is realised as a result of a devaluation.

Throughout the following analysis we analyse the production level in the period between exchange rate adjustments. We use t to denote the time since the last exchange rate adjustment. It follows from (13.3) that the production level at time 0 equals full employment production, that is

$$y_0 = y'' \equiv 0. \tag{13.4}$$

We set the exchange rate at the last exchange rate adjustment equal to zero, that is, $x^\circ \equiv 0$.

The wage setting

The wage setters set the nominal wage through contracts to optimise preferences which include production. We consider a decentralised wage formation where the wage is set by a trade union which includes the employees of a representative firm j and where the trade union is unable to affect macroeconomic variables. The wage formation is characterised as follows

$$\max_{w}\left\{E_t(U_t^u) \mid \left(\frac{\partial p}{\partial w^j}\right) = 0, \left(\frac{\partial \pi}{\partial w^j}\right) = 0\right\}, \tag{13.5}$$

$$U_t^u = -f^u\left[y_t^j - (y'y^j\right]^2, \quad f^u > 0, \quad (y'y^j < (y''y^j, \tag{13.6}$$

where U^u is the wage setters' preference function, p the price level (logarithmic value), w^j the wage level set by a decentralised union covering firm j (logarithmic value), and $(y'y^j$ the production which optimises the wage setters' preferences (logarithmic value).

Relation (13.5) shows that the wage setters optimise the expected value of their preference function. The wage setters form correct expectations regarding production levels which result from alternative exchange rate policies, and the probability of a devaluation in the wage contract period. Under a decentralised wage formation, the wage setters are unable to affect the macroeconomic variables, that is, the price level and the probability of an exchange rate adjustment. The change in production levels which the wage setters expect from a given change in the nominal wage, can thus be found from (13.7) below as $-s$.

Relation (13.6) specifies that the wage setters desire a specific production level which is lower than full employment production. The assumption that the wage setters' preferences depend exclusively on production and do not include the real wage, is different from analyses in most of the book. This can be seen as a simplification. It also means that the effects in this analysis do not depend on a trade-off on the part of the wage setters between the real wage and employment.

The firm's optimisation

The condition for the profit maximisation of the representative firm j with respect to employment is given as follows

$$y_t^j = -s(w_t^j - p_t), \quad s > 0, \tag{13.7}$$

where p is the producer price (logarithmic value) and y^j the production level of the representative firm j (logarithmic value).

Relation (13.7) shows the condition for the firm's profit maximisation, assuming that the firm produces on the basis of a Cobb–Douglas production function which is homogeneous of degree one and assuming a fixed capital stock.

Goods market equilibrium

We consider a small open economy A. The rest of the world is represented by a large economy B. Goods market equilibrium can be represented as follows (all variables relating to the small periphery country A unless otherwise indicated)

$$y_t = z(p_t^B + x_t - p_t) + d_t, \quad z > 0, \tag{13.8}$$

$$p_t^B = \bar{p}_t^B, \quad d_t = \bar{d}_t, \tag{13.9}$$

where d is domestic demand.

Relation (13.8) represents goods market equilibrium, the demand for goods being a function of the real exchange rate and total domestic demand d. (13.9) reflects the assumption of the home country being a small economy. In addition, we assume that domestic demand is exogenously determined, for example, by fiscal policy.

Macroeconomic level

The transition from the microeconomic to the macroeconomic level is given as follows

$$(y_t^j)^\circ = (y_t)^\circ, \quad (y'')^j = y'', \quad (y')^j \equiv y', \quad w_t^j = w_t, \quad (y^*)^j = y^*, \tag{13.10}$$

where $(y^j)^\circ$ is the production level which will be realised in the representative firm j when there is an unchanged exchange rate (logarithmic value), y' represents the wage setters' desired production level at the macroeconomic level (logarithmic value), w is the wage level at the macroeconomic level (logarithmic value), and $(y^*)^j$ is the production level which will be realised in the representative firm j if the authorities undertake a devaluation.

13.4   Determination of equilibrium production

The wage setters face uncertainty due to the risk of a devaluation during the wage contract period. The wage setters' expected utility is given as

$$E_t(U_t^u) = \pi_t U^u[(y^*)^j - (y')^j] + (1 - \pi_t)U^u[(y_t^\diamond)^j - (y')^j]. \quad (13.11)$$

Optimising (13.11) with respect to the nominal wage, and using (13.3) and (13.5)–(13.6), gives the condition for the wage setters' optimum

$$\frac{\pi_t}{1 - \pi_t} = -\left(\frac{\partial U^u[(y_t^\diamond)^j - (y')^j]}{\partial w^j}\right) / \left(\frac{\partial U^u[(y^*)^j - (y')^j]}{\partial w^j}\right). \quad (13.12)$$

From (13.12) it follows that the nominal wage is determined by (i) the probability of an exchange rate adjustment and (ii) the marginal utilities which are derived by the wage setters in the event of an unchanged exchange rate and an exchange rate adjustment.

It follows from (13.6) that $\partial U^u/\partial w^j$ is positive for production levels which lie below the wage setters' optimal production level while $\partial U^u/\partial w^j$ is negative for production levels which lie above the optimal production level. It therefore results from (13.12) that the wage setters aim at a production level which lies between the levels which are realised in the events of respectively an unchanged exchange rate and a devaluation, that is, between $(y^*)^j$ and $(y^\diamond)^j$. The wage setters' optimal production level between these two levels is determined by the marginal utilities and by the probability of an adjustment. If the probability of an exchange rate adjustment increases, it follows from (13.12) that the wage setters aim at a lower production level. This can be explained as follows. When the likelihood of a devaluation increases, high production $(y^*)^j$, that is, the production level which results in firm j after a devaluation, enters with an increased weight in the wage setters' expected utility. This induces the wage setters to react with a higher wage increase, as the wage setters want to bring the production level towards the wage setters' optimal level which is lower than $(y^*)^j$.

Combining (13.2)–(13.3), (13.6), (13.10), and (13.12) gives the condition for the production level under decentralised wage formation as

$$(y_t^\diamond)^2 - \left(\frac{c}{f^g}\right)\left(\frac{1}{y'}\right)y_t^\diamond + \left(\frac{c}{f^g}\right) = 0, \quad y_t^\diamond \leq y'' \equiv 0. \quad (13.13)$$

Solving (13.13) gives the following solutions for the production level in the period between two exchange rate adjustments

$$y^{\circ}_{r_1} = \frac{1}{2}\left(\frac{c}{f^g}\right)\left(\frac{1}{y'}\right) + \frac{1}{2}\sqrt{\left(\frac{c}{f^g y'}\right)^2 - 4\left(\frac{c}{f^g}\right)},$$

$$y^{\circ}_{r_2} = \frac{1}{2}\left(\frac{c}{f^g}\right)\left(\frac{1}{y'}\right) - \frac{1}{2}\sqrt{\left(\frac{c}{f^g y'}\right)^2 - 4\left(\frac{c}{f^g}\right)},$$

$$c > 4(y')^2 f^g, \quad y' < 0, \tag{13.14}$$

where $y^{\circ}_{r_1}$ and $y^{\circ}_{r_2}$ are the equilibrium solutions for the production level between exchange rate adjustments.

Relation (13.14) specifies that two equilibrium solutions exist for the production level between exchange rate adjustments, assuming $c > 4(y')^2 f^g$. The conditions for both the wage setters' and the authorities' optimum are met in equilibrium. It cannot be determined on the basis of the present model specification which of these two solutions will be realised. In section 13.5 below we will specify a dynamic adjustment path, characterised by a slow wage adjustment, which makes it possible to map out a dynamic adjustment for the production level between two exchange rate adjustments.

Combining (13.7)–(13.10), gives a relationship between the wage increase and production level. Given natural production determined by (13.14), this relationship determines the wage level between exchange rate adjustments

$$y^{\circ}_{r_i} = \left(\frac{zs}{z+s}\right)(B_t - w_t), \quad y^{\circ}_{r_i} \leq 0, i = 1, 2,$$

$$B_t \equiv p^B_t + \left(\frac{1}{z}\right)d_t. \tag{13.15}$$

Relation (13.15) shows that the wage level is increased corresponding to changes in the term B, the wage level being determined by the foreign price level p^B and by domestic demand.

During the wage contract period a devaluation takes place with the probability π which can be found from (13.2) as

$$\pi_t = \frac{(y^{\circ}_{r_i})^2}{(y^{\circ}_{r_i})^2 + (c/f^g)}, \quad i = 1, 2. \tag{13.16}$$

Combining (13.16) with (13.3) and (13.14) gives the mean production which is realised in the fixed-but-adjustable exchange rate system

$$E(Y) = \left[\frac{(y_{r_i}^\diamond)^2}{(y_{r_i}^\diamond)^2 + (c/f^g)} \right] Y'' + \left[\frac{c/f^g}{(y_{r_i}^\diamond)^2 + (c/f^g)} \right] Y_{r_i}^\diamond, \quad i = 1, 2.$$

(13.17)

Differentiating (13.17) with respect to $y_{r_i}^\diamond$ gives the following expression for the impact of $y_{r_i}^\diamond$ on average production

$$\frac{\partial E(Y)}{\partial y_{r_i}^\diamond} = \frac{2(y_{r_i}^\diamond) + (c/f^g) Y_{r_i}^\diamond}{[(y_{r_i}^\diamond)^2 + (c/f^g)]} - 2y_{r_i}^\diamond \frac{(y_{r_i}^\diamond)^2 + (c/f^g) Y_{r_i}^\diamond}{[(y_{r_i}^\diamond)^2 + (c/f^g)]^2} > 0. \quad (13.18)$$

It follows from (13.18) that a higher value of $y_{r_i}^\diamond$, that is, a higher value of the equilibrium production level between exchange rate adjustments, leads to a higher average level of production in a fixed-but-adjustable exchange rate system.

It results from the sequential game between authorities and wage setters that the wage setters immediately after a devaluation set the nominal wage so production is brought to one of the two equilibrium solutions, expressed by $y_{r_1}^\diamond$ and $y_{r_2}^\diamond$. At these production levels, there is in each time period a constant probability of a devaluation, determined by (13.16). The wage increase which after a devaluation brings production to one of the equilibrium levels, can be found from (13.15). The mean inflation in the fixed-but-adjustable exchange rate system can thus be determined as

$$E(v_p) = \pi w_t = \frac{(y_{r_i}^\diamond)^2}{(y_{r_i}^\diamond)^2 + (c/f^g)} \left(\frac{z+s}{zs} \right) y_{r_i}^\diamond, \quad i = 1, 2,$$

$$v_p \equiv p_t - p_{t-1}, \quad y_{r_i}^\diamond < 0,$$

(13.19)

where v_p gives the growth rate the price level.

It follows from (13.19) that a lower equilibrium production level between exchange rate adjustments causes higher inflation. Inflation lies at a higher level when equilibrium production between exchange rate adjustments lies at a lower level, first because the wage setters have to set a higher nominal wage after an exchange rate adjustment to bring production to the lower level, and second because lower production increases the probability of a devaluation which causes the process to be repeated, the wage setters again bringing about a wage increase to reduce production below the full employment level.

13.5   The dynamic adjustment

Based on Kydland and Prescott (1977) and Barro and Gordon (1983a), the analysis in section 13.4 is held in terms of a sequential game between the authorities and the wage setters. This analysis is based on full wage and price flexibility. It cannot be determined in this model setting which equilibrium production is realised and it is likewise indeterminate what happens if no equilibrium production exists.

We now abandon the assumption of full wage flexibility. We assume that the wage setters in their wage setting derive utility not only from production but also desire to avoid too large a change in the nominal wage relative to the previous period. The wage setters' preference function is thus specified as

$$U_t^u = -f_1^u\left[(y_t)^j - (y'^y)^j\right]^2 - f_2^u(w_t^j - w_{t-1}^j)^2, \quad f_i^u > 0, \quad i = 1, 2.$$
(13.20)

Optimising the expected value of (13.20) and using (13.3), (13.5)–(13.6), (13.10), and (13.15), gives a first-order difference equation for the determination of production between exchange rate adjustments

$$y_t^\diamond - y_{t-1}^\diamond = -[(y_t^\diamond - y_{r_1}^\diamond)(y_t^\diamond - y_{r_2}^\diamond)] \, N_1,$$

$$N \equiv (-y')\left(\frac{zs}{z+s}\right)s\left(\frac{f_1^u}{f_2^u}\right)[(y_t^\diamond)^2 + (c/f^g)]^{-1} < 0, \quad c > 4(y')^2 f^g. \quad (13.21)$$

Relation (13.21) specifies the dynamic adjustment path between exchange rate adjustments. If the condition $c > 4(y')^2 f^g$ is met, that is, two equilibrium solutions for production exist at which both the authorities' and the wage setters' preferences are optimised, it results from (13.21) that the higher equilibrium production $y_{r_1}^\diamond$ is a stable solution while $y_{r_2}^\diamond$ is the unstable solution. When production lies between the full employment production level y'' and $y_{r_2}^\diamond$, production is thus moved towards the stable solution through the wage setting. If production through an unexpected change in exogenous variables is reduced to a lower level than the unstable equilibrium, that is, $y^\diamond < y_{r_2}^\diamond$, a continuous fall in production takes place, moving production away from full employment and causing a steady increase in the probability of an exchange rate adjustment.

13.6   Policy implications

Production affected by the authorities' preferences

The model set out above takes the point of departure in a fully rational wage setting where the wage setters derive utility exclusively from the production level and where the wage setters form rational expectations. No nominal rigidities are assumed except that the nominal wage is preset through nominal wage contracts. It is traditionally argued in such a model setting, based on Kydland and Prescott (1977) and Barro and Gordon (1983a), that the authorities' preferences have no influence on the production level which is determined entirely by the wage setters' preferences. It is further suggested that the authorities, to bring down inflation, must place infinite weight on the reduction of inflation, for example by appointing a conservative central banker, cf. Rogoff (1985b). A greater weight on inflation in the authorities' preference function has no impact on production while inflation is reduced.

The findings from the analysis of a fixed-but-adjustable exchange rate regime above are different. It follows from (13.14) and (13.17) that the authorities' preferences have an impact on the production level. A larger weight placed on employment, that is, a larger f^g, increases $y_{r_1}^\diamond$ while it depends on the economic structure how a larger value of f^g affects the lower equilibrium solution $y_{r_2}^\diamond$, that is, the equilibrium solution which is unstable when there is a slow wage adjustment. This means that there is a cost in the form of higher unemployment associated with a policy which places a smaller weight on production at least in the case of the stable equilibrium solution.

The impact of the authorities' preferences on production can be explained as follows. The model shows that the wage setters in a fixed-but-adjustable exchange rate regime aim at a production level which is determined as a weighted average of the production level which results when the exchange rate is maintained unchanged and the production level which is set by the authorities when there is a devaluation. The wage setters can affect the production level which is realised between exchange rate adjustments through the nominal wage. The weights attached by the wage setters to the two production levels are determined by the wage setters' preferences, represented by the marginal utilities derived from the two production levels, and by the probability of an exchange rate adjustment, cf. relation (13.12). It thus follows that the wage setters in a fixed-but-adjustable exchange rate regime face a trade-off in their wage setting between the production levels which result from alternative exchange rate policies, this trade-off being determined by the probability of an exchange rate adjustment. The authorities' preferences have an impact on this trade-off faced by the wage setters because the probability of a devaluation is determined by the authorities' preferences. The authorities' preferences are thus no longer neutral with respect to the determination of production, implying that the authorities' preferences have an impact on production.

The disciplinary effect of an exchange rate commitment
According to the 'discipline hypothesis', see Giavazzi and
Pagano (1988) and Giavazzi and Giovannini (1989), a fixed-but-adjustable exchange rate regime can increase the weight placed by the authorities
on the reduction of inflation, the authorities in countries with a low anti-
inflation credibility being subjected to the monetary discipline in countries with strong anti-inflation preferences. According to the discipline
hypothesis, lower inflation results when the political cost associated with
a devaluation *vis-à-vis* the low inflation country is increased.

The conclusions from the analysis above regarding the impact of the
political cost associated with devaluations are less clear cut. The political
cost associated with a devaluation is shown as c. The impact of c on the
stable steady-state solution for production $y_{r_1}^\diamond$ can be found from (13.14)
as

$$\frac{\partial y_{r_1}}{\partial c} = \left(\frac{1}{f^g y'}\right) + \frac{1}{2}\left[c\left(\frac{c}{f^g y'}\right)^2 - 4\left(\frac{c}{f^g}\right)\right]^{-\frac{1}{2}}\left[c\left(\frac{1}{f^g y'}\right) - \left(\frac{2}{f^g}\right)\right] < 0.$$

$$(13.22)$$

From (13.22) it follows that an increase in the political cost associated
with a devaluation has a negative impact on the stable equilibrium production level between exchange rate adjustments. This means that a
higher political cost associated with a devaluation involves a cost in the
form of a lower production level. The average wage increase under a
fixed-but-adjustable exchange rate system is found from (13.19). It follows that a higher political cost associated with a devaluation reduces
average inflation at a given production level, corresponding to the
'discipline hypothesis'. As inflation is increased by lower production, it
cannot, however, be determined unambiguously whether inflation is lowered or increased by a higher political cost associated with a devaluation
in a fixed-but-adjustable exchange rate system.

The authorities thus face a situation where a higher political cost associated with devaluations, depending on the economic structure, could
lead to both a reduction in production and a rise in inflation.

Currency crises
In the dynamic adjustment process specified by (13.21) a continuous fall in the production level occurs if production falls below the
unstable equilibrium value for production, that is, if $y^\diamond < y_{r_2}^\diamond$. Two different situations may thus arise in a fixed-but-adjustable exchange rate
system. Production may move either towards the stable equilibrium,
characterised by a constant devaluation probability, or there may be a

situation with a continuous fall in the production level, characterised by a continuous increase in the devaluation probability. The model thus shows that the fixed-but-adjustable exchange rate system may move to a state where the devaluation risk is rising, leading to a continuous increase in wage demands. This last state implies that the economy is facing a currency crisis.

Production between exchange rate adjustments and after wage contracts have been fixed, is determined by (13.15), that is, by the exogenous variables shown by B. It is possible that there is an unexpected change in the exogenous variables between two exchange rate adjustments and during the wage contract period, which may cause production to move to a lower level than the unstable production equilibrium level $y_{r_2}^\diamond$, leading to a currency crisis. The outbreak of a currency crisis can thus be explained in the same way as in Obstfeld (1991, 1994, 1996), being caused by changes in exogenous variables.

The political cost associated with a devaluation, shown by c, has two effects on the probability of a currency crisis. First, if the political cost is low, the condition $c > 4(y')^2 f^g$ may not be met. In this case no equilibrium production level exists and it follows that there is a steady fall in production. Second, it follows from (13.14) that a higher value of c could cause a lower value of the unstable equilibrium production level $y_{r_2}^\diamond$, implying that the likelihood of production falling under $y_{r_2}^\diamond$ for a given change in exogenous variables which enter B, becomes smaller.

For both of these two reasons it follows that an increase in the political cost associated with a devaluation may make it less likely that a currency crisis breaks out. The authorities may for this reason see it as advantageous to increase the political cost associated with devaluations to bring about stability and to prevent the outbreak of a currency crisis.

The authorities may thus face a dilemma with respect to determining the political cost associated with a devaluation. On the one side, a higher devaluation cost may cause a lower production level, cf. above. On the other side, a higher political cost associated with a devaluation reduces the risk of currency crises.

13.7   Summary and conclusion

The working of a fixed-but-adjustable exchange rate system has been examined in a model context where it cannot be foreseen whether a given level of unemployment causes a devaluation. At each unemployment level there is a certain probability of a devaluation. The wage setters set the nominal wage through contracts to optimise a preference function, forming correct expectations concerning the levels of economic variables in the wage contract period and the authorities' preferences, including the probability of a devaluation.

It is demonstrated that the production level is affected by the authorities' preferences. The authorities' preferences affect unemployment through the devaluation risk. This implies that there is a cost in the form of a loss of production if the authorities renounce the possibility of using exchange rate policy, for example, by joining a monetary union. A fixed-but-adjustable exchange rate system thus provides a channel through which the authorities' preferences can affect production when the wage setters form rational expectations and aim at a specific production level.

It further results that an increase in the political cost associated with a devaluation, depending on the economic structure and preferences, may cause a reduction in production and possibly also an increase in inflation. This finding raises doubt whether it is appropriate to increase the political cost associated with a devaluation as suggested in the 'discipline hypothesis'.

The analysis shows that several equilibrium solutions may exist, characterised by both the authorities and the wage setters optimising their preferences. With the model specification used in the present analysis two such equilibria exist. In the case where the wage setters adjust the nominal wage slowly to reach an optimal production, it is demonstrated that one of these equilibrium solutions is stable while the other is unstable. If production falls below the unstable equilibrium solution due to shocks during the wage contract period, there is a continuous fall in production and a continuous rise in the probability of a devaluation. These features characterise a currency crisis. A higher political cost may reduce the probability of a currency crisis.

14 The impact of uncertainty on wage setting

14.1 Introduction

It is demonstrated in this chapter that the monetary regime can influence natural production, determined by the wage setters' preferences with respect to production/employment and the real wage, by affecting the fluctuation in functional relationships. The stochastic fluctuations affect natural production in situations where the wage setters through contracts fix the nominal wage at a certain level in a future time period.

The analysis shows that it depends on the economic structure and preferences whether natural production is increased or lowered when there is a rise in the fluctuation of functional relationships. This can be explained as follows. The point of departure is wage setters who optimise preferences with respect to the real wage and employment that are asymmetric with respect to production. When the nominal wage is set in advance through contracts, the wage setters are subjected to the fluctuations in production and the real wage which take place during the wage contract period. We assume that fluctuations in economic relationships are normally distributed. When wage setters attach relatively large importance to reaching a high real wage relative to high production, they will aim at a low mean level of production because this improves the prospect of maintaining a high real wage when the economy experiences shocks. The increased certainty for a high real wage is thus reached at the cost of a higher mean level of natural unemployment. The reverse happens when the wage setters attach relatively large importance to maintaining high employment relative to a high real wage. The wage setters aim in this case at higher production to prevent low values of production when there are fluctuations in functional relationships.

The analysis has clear implications for the choice of optimum monetary regime. According to the traditional analysis, based on Mundell (1961), a monetary regime should be chosen from the viewpoint of stabilising production at the natural level. Seen from the viewpoint of realising high production, one may reach the opposite conclusion on the basis of the present analysis. It is demonstrated below that production fluctuations can increase the natural production level and may in this respect be seen as welfare improving. This conclusion depends, however, on the wage setters' preferences and on the economic structure and, in contrast to the traditional theory of optimum monetary regimes, the present analysis therefore does not suggest clear conclusions with respect to the optimum regime.

The finding in the present chapter of natural production being affected by fluctuations in employment and the real wage, is not new. Sørensen (1992) likewise reaches the conclusion that the natural production is affected by fluctuations in structural relationships. While Sørensen (1992) considers the wage setting of a monopoly union which maximises the total utility of employed and unemployed members, the analysis below makes no prior assumptions regarding the wage setters' preferences except that positive marginal utility is derived from higher production and a higher real wage. In difference to Sørensen (1992), the general specification of the wage setters' preference function used below means that no unambiguous conclusion can be reached whether an increase in fluctuations causes a rise or a reduction in natural production.

Section 14.2 gives the model specification. We will distinguish between two alternative preference functions for the wage setters: (i) preferences where the wage setters attach relatively large weight to avoiding unemployment, and (ii) preferences where the wage setters attach relatively large weight to avoding a low real wage. *Section 14.3* derives natural production both in the case where relatively large weight is attached to avoiding unemployment and in the case where the wage setters attach relatively large weight to avoiding a low real wage. *Section 14.4* discusses policy implications. *Section 14.5* gives a summary and conclusion.

14.2   Model specification

Economic structure

A small economy A is considered. The rest of the world is represented by a large economy B. We consider the short term, the capital stock being fixed. All variables refer to country A unless otherwise indicated. The structure of the economy is given as

$$y_t = -s(w_t - p_t) + \alpha_t, \quad y_t \leq y_t'' = a\alpha_t, \quad 0 < a < 1,$$

$$s \equiv \frac{1-a}{a} > 0, \quad \alpha_t \sim N(0, \sigma_\alpha^2), \tag{14.1}$$

$$y_t = z(p_t^B + x_t - p_t) + d_t, \quad z > 0, \quad d_t - y_t = \Omega_t,$$
$$\Omega_t \sim N(\mu_\Omega, \sigma_\Omega^2), \tag{14.2}$$

$$m_t = p_t + by_t + \delta_t, \quad b > 0, \quad \delta_t \sim N(0, \sigma_\delta^2), \tag{14.3}$$

$$q_t \equiv p_t + \varphi(p_t^B + x_t - p_t), \quad 0 < \varphi < 1, \tag{14.4}$$

$$COV(\alpha_t, \Omega_t) \neq 0, \quad COV(\alpha_t, \delta_t) = 0, \quad COV(\Omega_t, \delta_t) = 0, \tag{14.5}$$

$$p_t^B = \bar{p}^B, \tag{14.6}$$

where w is the nominal wage (logarithmic value), y production (logarithmic value), q the consumer price (logarithmic value), p the producer price (logarithmic value), x the nominal exchange rate between the home country A and the foreign country B (number of domestic currency units per foreign currency unit) (logarithmic value), m the nominal money supply (logarithmic value), α a supply shock, and δ a monetary shock.

Relation (14.1) gives the supply function for goods derived from a Cobb–Douglas production function and assuming a fixed capital stock. Full employment production is given as $a\alpha$ where a is the output elasticity with respect to capital. The production function is subjected to stochastic fluctuations with mean zero and variance σ_α^2. (14.2) expresses equilibrium in the goods market, the demand for goods depending on the real exchange rate and on domestic demand. Domestic demand relative to production is subjected to stochastic disturbances, for example caused by fluctuations in fiscal policy or by shifts in time preferences. (14.3) shows the money market equilibrium, the demand for money being subjected to stochastic fluctuations with mean zero and variance σ_δ^2. (14.4) gives the definition of the consumer price. (14.5) expresses that monetary shocks are uncorrelated with real shocks. (14.6) gives the assumption of exogenously given foreign variables which are non-stochastic.

The wage setting

Wage setters form correct expectations concerning the stochastic processes in economic relationships and with respect to economic policy when they set the nominal wage through contracts at the beginning of the time period. The wage setters optimise preferences that include production and the real wage and which are asymmetric with respect to production.

In order to demonstrate the point that fluctuations in production can both increase and reduce mean natural production, we will distinguish between two alternative preference functions. Both preference functions are characterised by positive but declining marginal utility from higher production and a higher real wage, that is, the properties which usually characterise preferences. In the case where wage setters attach a relatively large weight to avoiding low unemployment, the preference function is specified as

$$U_t^u = -f^u \exp[-(y_t - y_t'')] + (w_t - q_t), \quad f^u > 0, \tag{14.7}$$

where U^u is the wage setters' utility (a larger positive net value expresses an increase in utility).

Illustrating the case where the wage setters attach a relatively large weight to avoiding a low real wage, we use the following specification of the preference function

$$U_t^u = -\exp[-(w_t - q_t)] + f^u(y_t - y_t''), \quad f^u > 0. \tag{14.8}$$

Corresponding to (14.7), relation (14.8) reflects that the wage setters set the nominal wage to reach an optimal trade-off between the real wage and production. Both preference functions (14.7) and (14.8) are characterised by wage setters who derive positive but declining marginal utilities from increases in production and the real wage. It will be demonstrated below that the two preference functions give different conclusions with respect to the impact of stochastic fluctuations on natural production.

The basic finding that the fluctuation in relationships has an impact on natural production, pre-supposes that the variances with respect to functional relationships appear in the condition for the wage setters' optimum. This property follows from all preference functions which can be represented as asymmetric functions of production.

The monetary regime

Three monetary regimes are analysed: (i) a floating exchange rate regime characterised by a fixed nominal money supply, (ii) a monetary union characterised by a fixed exchange rate, and (iii) a price stability rule where the authorities maintain a fixed consumer price. The three monetary regimes are characterised as follows

$$m_t = \overline{m}_t, \tag{14.9}$$

$$x_t = \overline{x}_t, \tag{14.10}$$

$$q_t = \overline{q}_t. \tag{14.11}$$

In the case where there is uncertainty regarding the setting of the money supply under a floating exchange rate regime, the variance of money demand can also be used to show the uncertainty regarding the setting of the money supply and thus the uncertainty with respect to monetary policy.

14.3 Determination of natural production

Weight on avoiding low unemployment
As stochastic fluctuations follow a normal distribution, the wage setters' expected utility can be derived from (14.7) as

$$E(U_t^u) = -f^u \exp\left\{-[E(y_t) - y_t''] + \frac{1}{2}(\sigma_{y-y''}^2)^k\right\} + w_t - E(q_t),$$

$$k = FE, MU, PS, \tag{14.12}$$

where *FE* shows a floating exchange rate regime with a fixed money supply target, *MU* a monetary union, and *PS* a price stability rule.

Optimising (14.12) with respect to the nominal wage, and using (14.1)–(14.2) and (14.4), gives the condition for the wage setters' optimum as

$$E(y_t - y_t'') = \frac{1}{2}(\sigma_{y-y''}^2)^k + \log(sf^u), \quad k = FE, MU, PS. \tag{14.13}$$

From (14.13) it follows that the expected value of natural production depends on the variance of production. It results that natural production increases when there are increased fluctuations in economic relationships. This can be explained as follows. Assuming the preference function specified by (14.7), the wage setters place a relatively large weight on avoiding a reduction in production relative to a reduction in the real wage. In the case of greater fluctuations in production, this induces the wage setters to set natural production at a higher level to avoid the disutility associated with low production levels.

Combining (14.1)–(14.6) and (14.7)–(14.10) gives the variances of production which are expected by the wage setters under the different monetary regimes

$$(\sigma_{y-y''}^2)^{FE} = (1-a)^2 \left(\frac{1-b}{bs+1}\right)^2 \sigma_\alpha^2 + \left(\frac{s}{1+bs}\right)^2 \sigma_\delta^2, \tag{14.14}$$

$$(\sigma_{y-y''}^2)^{MU} = (1-a)^2\sigma_\alpha^2 + \left(\frac{s}{z}\right)^2\sigma_\Omega^2 + 2\left(\frac{1}{az}\right)COV(\alpha_t, \Omega_t),$$

$$(14.15)$$

$$(\sigma_{y-y''}^2)^{PS} = (1-a)^2\sigma_\alpha^2 + \left(\frac{\varphi s}{z}\right)^2\sigma_\Omega^2 + 2\left(\frac{\varphi}{az}\right)COV(\alpha_t, \Omega_t), \quad (14.16)$$

where $\sigma_{y-y''}^2$ expresses the variance of production.

The variances of production given by (14.14)–(14.16) can be combined with the condition for natural production, expressed by (14.13). It results that natural production lies at different levels under the three regimes due to the different variations in production levels. From (14.13) it follows that the highest natural production level is reached when variation in production is greatest.

A comparison between (14.14)–(14.16) shows that it depends on the economic structure under which of the three regimes variation in production is greatest. The variance in production relative to full employment production depends under all monetary regimes on supply shocks. Supply shocks cause greater fluctuations in production under price stability and in a monetary union than under a floating exchange rate regime. If the income elasticity of money demand b is close to 1, supply shocks have little impact on production under a floating exchange rate regime. Shifts in domestic demand affect the variance of production relative to full employment production in a monetary union and under a price stability rule but not under a floating exchange rate regime. Assuming that a greater variation in the production function increases fluctuation in domestic demand relative to production, that is, $COV(\alpha_t, \Omega_t) > 0$, it results from a comparison between (14.15) and (14.16) that shifts in domestic demand have the greatest impact on production under a monetary union, causing highest natural production under a monetary union. Monetary shocks only affect production under a floating exchange rate regime where they have the effect of increasing production.

Relative weight on avoiding low real wage

The preceding analysis was based on the assumption that the wage setters optimise the preference function specified by (14.7). Optimising the alternative preference function given by (14.8), gives the condition for the wage setters' optimum as

$$E(y_t - y_t'') = -\frac{1}{2}s(\sigma_{w-q}^2)^k + \left(\frac{\varphi s}{z}\right)\mu_\Omega + s\log(f^u s),$$

$$k = FE, MU, PS,$$

$$(14.17)$$

From (14.17) it follows that greater fluctuations in the real wage cause natural production to fall. This is opposite to the analysis of the wage setter preference function specified by (14.7) where greater fluctuations in economic relationships and in economic policy cause an increase in natural production. This reversal of conclusions can be explained as follows. In the analysis based on the preferences specified by (14.7), it is assumed that the wage setters attach large disutility to low production relative to a low real wage. This means that the wage setters set a high production level when there are large production fluctuations to avoid the risk of production falling to a low level. With the specification of the preference function given by (14.8), it is assumed that the wage setters place large weight on upholding the real wage, implying that the wage setters place large weight on avoiding the real wage falling to a low level. This specification of the wage setters' preferences means that the wage setters, to avoid large falls in the real wage, set production at a lower level and thus the real wage at a higher level when there are large fluctuations in production and real wage levels.

The variance in the real wage expected by the wage setters at the fixing of nominal wage contracts can under the three policy regimes be found from (14.1)–(14.6) and (14.8)–(14.10) as

$$(\sigma^2_{w-q})^{FE} = \left(\frac{1}{1+bs}\right)^2 \sigma^2_\alpha + \left(\frac{\varphi}{z}\right)^2 \sigma^2_\Omega + \left(\frac{s}{1+bs}\right)^2 \sigma^2_\delta$$
$$+ 2\left(\frac{1}{1+bs}\right)\left(\frac{\varphi}{z}\right) COV(\alpha_t, \Omega_t), \tag{14.18}$$

$$(\sigma^2_{w-q})^{MU} = \left(\frac{1-\varphi}{z}\right)^2 \sigma^2_\Omega, \tag{14.19}$$

$$(\sigma^2_{w-q})^{PS} = 0. \tag{14.20}$$

It again follows from (14.18)–(14.20) that it depends on the kind of shocks under which monetary regime production is stabilised the most. The lowest variance in the real wage is found under the price stability rule where there is no uncertainty regarding the real wage when the wage setters set the nominal wage. The highest natural production level is thus realised under a price stability rule. It depends on the shocks whether natural production is higher under a floating exchange rate regime relative to a monetary union. A monetary union offers protection against supply shocks but increases the fluctuations due to shifts in domestic demand.

14.4   Policy implications

Monetary regime affects natural production

The analysis shows that variation in the real wage and production affects natural production. As fluctuations in the real wage and production are affected by the monetary regime, it follows that the monetary regime influences natural production. This can form the basis for the choice of monetary regime. One may conceive that there is a societal interest in increasing natural production, for example due to the impact of unemployment benefit schemes, which cause wage setters to set production at a socially too low level. This means that the optimum monetary regime should be chosen on the grounds that it leads to a rise in natural production.

Such a criterion for increasing natural production is different from the traditional analysis based on Mundell (1961) which assumes that the optimum monetary regime must be chosen with the view of stabilising production. As discussed above, greater variation in production may increase natural production depending on the wage setters' preferences.

Sources of production instability

In the analysis above, the monetary regime has a direct impact on natural production through the economic structure. One may conceive of two further channels through which the monetary regime affects variations in production and real wage levels and thus natural production. These channels work in addition to the impact of the monetary regime on the structural characteristics of the economy.

First, the monetary regime may affect a country's possibility of counteracting production and/or price fluctuations through a state-contingent economic policy. In the analysis above it is assumed that economic policy is set independently of shocks, that is, there is no state-contingent economic policy. One may, however, conceive of the authorities being able to use economic policy to counteract shocks and thus bring about different variation in the real wage and production which in turn affects natural production. There may be differences in the effectiveness with which economic policy can be used for stabilisation under different monetary regimes. Assuming a preset nominal wage and economic structure given by (14.1)–(14.6), the authorities dispose of monetary policy and fiscal policy under a floating exchange rate regime while the authorities dispose only of fiscal policy in a monetary union and under a price stability rule. One may further perceive differences with respect to the political constraints on the use of these two policy instruments, facilitating the use of state-contingent economic policy under one monetary regime relative to another. Assuming costs associated with the use of policy instruments, the possibility of using two policy instruments for stabilisation under a floating rate regime suggests that this regime may be superior to the other two regimes with respect to the possibility of using state-contingent economic policy.

Second, the monetary regime may have an impact on the decision-making process in economic policy, thus affecting the uncertainty which surrounds the outcomes of economic-policy processes under different monetary regimes. Chapter 12 discussed whether the uncertainty concerning the decision-making process is greater when monetary policy is pursued by an independent central bank in a monetary union than when it is pursued by national monetary authorities. The impact on natural production of uncertainty regarding economic policy opens up the possibility that uncertainty may be used as a deliberate policy instrument to influence production.

The impact of structural policies in the labour market

It is a widespread view among policy makers and economists that reforms in the labour market to promote real wage flexibility are desirable because such reforms increase production. Reduction in unemployment benefits is traditionally seen as one kind of reform which can increase real wage flexibility, unemployment benefit forming a floor under the real wage.

One may question whether reforms aimed at increasing real wage flexibility are in fact desirable. Depending on the wage setters' preferences, it follows from the analysis above that greater uncertainty regarding the real wage may increase natural unemployment, corresponding to the analysis in section 14.3. The reduction in unemployment benefits may thus have the opposite effect of that intended, increasing natural unemployment. The same reasoning applies to, for example, profit sharing and other wage reform schemes which have the effect of increasing variations in the real wage.

14.5 Summary and conclusion

We have examined the determination of natural production when the wage setters face fluctuations in functional relationships and in economic policy during the wage contract period. It has been demonstrated that the monetary regime affects natural production because the monetary regime affects fluctuations in functional relationships and possibly also in economic policy. It cannot, however, be determined without knowledge of the economic structure and of the wage setters' preferences under which monetary regime natural production is highest. Depending on the wage setters' preferences, it may be optimal to choose the monetary regime which causes the greatest fluctuations in functional relationships and in exogenously determined variables. Policy makers may use uncertainty concerning economic policy as a means to affect natural production. It is possible that labour market reforms which increase fluctuations in the real wage, for example, a reduction in unemployment benefits, causes higher natural unemployment.

Part IV
Policy implications

15 Policy implications of monetary non-neutrality

15.1 Introduction

This book has addressed an important question in economics, that is, the role of monetary policy and of monetary regimes in determining the levels of production and employment.

For a long time, the economics profession has inclined to the 'new classical' view according to which demand policies have no impact on production beyond the shorter term, the length of which is determined by informational deficiencies or the duration of nominal wage contracts. It has been the aim of this book to reassess the role of money and monetary regimes as instruments which can affect natural unemployment also in the long term. Throughout the previous chapters we have set out different mechanisms which show either inflation, the monetary regime, or specific monetary instruments (open market operations, capital and lending restrictions, etc.) to have an impact on natural unemployment, defined as the unemployment level at which wage setters optimise their preferences. These effects work in a model setting characterised by (i) full price and wage flexibility, (ii) rational expectations, and (iii) only real variables enter the wage setters' preferences. The analyses have considered a steady-state equilibrium, characterised by a constant production growth rate and levels of financial variables which lie at constant levels relative to nominal production. This view of monetary effectiveness is clearly contrary to the traditional view held by economists of long-term monetary neutrality.

This chapter discusses some of the policy implications which follow from this view of long-term monetary non-neutrality. The discussion will address several topics which have been central in recent policy discussions. Through which channels does monetary policy affect real activity? What is the optimal rate of inflation? What is the optimal monetary regime? What are the implications of fixing exchange rates, for example within a monetary union? Is it desirable to delegate monetary authority to an independent central bank?

15.2   Money affects real activity

The most important policy message from this book is that inflation, other monetary policy instruments and the choice of monetary regime affect the real activity also in the long term when characterised by wage and price flexibility.

We have demonstrated that inflation, determined through the growth rate of the money supply, can affect natural unemployment in a number of situations, i.e. when there is (i) imperfect international integration of securities markets, (ii) imperfect competition and asymmetric information in bank markets, and (iii) substitution between money and securities in the provision of liquidity services. One-time changes in the money supply may affect equilibrium natural unemployment through hysteresis effects caused by capital accumulation when the output elasticity of capital at the macroeconomic level is one. In the case of imperfect integration of international securities markets, sterilised intervention and capital restrictions further affect natural unemployment. In the case where bank lending plays a role for real activity, natural unemployment is further affected by the central bank's reserve policy, by lending restrictions and by restrictions on capital movements.

If the wage setters take account of the authorities' policy formation in their wage setting, the authorities' preferences with respect to employment and inflation play a role for natural unemployment when the channels mentioned above are effective. In addition to these channels, the authorities' preferences with respect to employment and inflation affect natural unemployment when (i) there is a centralised wage setting and inflation has an impact on the demand for goods, (ii) the authorities pursue a price stability goal while no attempt is made to deflate the economy by reducing the price level, and (iii) uncertainty about the authorities' policy reaction is influenced by the inflation rate. The authorities' inflation–employment preferences furthermore affect natural unemployment in a fixed-but-adjustable exchange rate regime in which unemployment determines the probability of a devaluation. When the authorities besides monetary policy dispose of fiscal policy, the monetary regime has an impact on natural unemployment due to differences between monetary regimes with respect to the effectiveness of fiscal policy which in turn affects the authorities' inclination to use fiscal policy. The monetary regime finally influences natural unemployment by determining fluctuation in economic relationships when the wage setters have preferences with respect to the real wage and employment which are asymmetric with respect to production.

The possibility of affecting natural unemployment through monetary policy instruments or through the choice of monetary regime is an important message for policy makers because the policy discussion for the last two decades has centred almost exclusively on the possibility of using monetary policy for reducing inflation. Building an anti-inflation credibility for the central bank to affect inflation expectations has been a major discussion item. Most prominently, the consideration to reduce inflation has been a major motive behind the establishment of a European Central Bank with the exclusive goal of price stability. This view of monetary policy has also led to reforms in several countries, most recently the United Kingdom, where independence for the central bank and transparency regarding the decision process are seen as means to reduce inflation. Throughout the 1980s and the beginning of the 1990s, the objective of reducing inflation was seen as a main motive behind the fixing of exchange rates within the ERM.

The message that money affects real activity implies that monetary policy should no longer be directed exclusively at the reduction of inflation. The reduction in unemployment also has to be taken into account. This last consideration implies that policy makers incur a cost if they give up the possibility of using monetary policy to affect unemployment. Reforms, which are aimed at reducing inflation, for example the establishment of an independent central bank or the formation of the European Monetary Union, may not only bring advantages in the form of lower inflation but also costs in the form of higher unemployment.

Is this view of monetary policy having an impact on unemployment also in the longer term when characterised by wage and price flexibility realistic?

With the possible exception of a unit output elasticity of capital which would seem to be a coincidence, none of the assumptions underlying a monetary impact on production outlined above would seem to be overly restrictive. There is mounting empirical evidence which suggests that monetary variables do in fact affect the real economy also in the longer term. A number of studies show the real interest rate and the real stock return to be determined by inflation and most empirical studies indicate that production is affected by changes in the short-term interest rate which is controlled by the monetary authorities. With the exception of very long time horizons, the real exchange rate is closely correlated with the nominal exchange rate. There is also evidence of inflation having an impact on production and of real effects from changes in monetary aggregates. This empirical evidence indicates that monetary policy might in fact be effective in affecting the real economy. Several studies, see, for example, Friedman and Kuttner (1993) and Hubbard (1998), suggest the presence of credit constraints for borrowers.

Most of the channels for a monetary impact on the real economy outlined above rest on the assumption that wage setters desire to reach at the same time a high real wage and high employment. This view of the wage setting process is clearly realistic in the case where the wage setters are trade unions. The recent literature has, however, extended this view of the wage setting process to cover also the case when a single individual negotiates with an employer, cf. Blanchard and Katz (1997). Moreover, money would affect the real economy through the same channels in the case also where the wage is set by a firm which incurs costs associated with the turnover of workers, cf. Phelps (1994).

The monetary transmission mechanisms suggested in this book have been derived making the assumptions of wage and price flexibility, rational expectations and wage setter preferences based on real variables. No attempt has been made to pass judgement on these assumptions on which most recent literature on monetary policy has been based. Monetary policy is clearly effective if these assumptions are abandoned.

15.3   The optimal inflation rate

While policy makers have traditionally attached major importance to inflation as a policy goal, economic theory has in general found it difficult to derive factors which can justify this emphasis on inflation as a policy goal.[1] The analyses throughout this book demonstrate that inflation could in fact have real consequences. The analysis can thus be seen as a justification for policy makers who focus on the importance of inflation.

It follows from the preceding discussion that the impact of inflation on natural production should be considered when assessing the optimal inflation. Unfortunately, no unambiguous conclusion can be reached as to what should be the optimal inflation rate seen from the perspective of increasing production. The discussions analysing the impact of money on the real economy give conflicting answers. In the case of imperfect financial integration of securities markets, the authorities can increase natural production by raising the inflation rate, thus reducing the need to issue government securities. The analysis of banks in chapter 5 suggests that

---

[1]See, for example, Fischer and Modigliani (1978).

the authorities can increase natural production by holding an inflation rate which increases real bank deposits. It depends on the economic structure whether inflation increases or lowers real bank deposits. The impact of inflation on natural production depends on the economic structure when both securities and money are used to meet liquidity needs. An increase in the weight attached to inflation in the authorities' preferences lowers natural production when wage setting is based on expectations about the authorities' policy setting.

The dependence of optimal inflation on the economic structure and on the channels through which money influences production, suggests that the optimal inflation rate differs between countries. Furthermore, optimal inflation may vary over time. Both these findings suggest that monetary policy autonomy should be maintained. Attempts to lock monetary policy through rules which can only be changed at considerable costs, lower welfare. This casts doubt upon the monetary policies pursued by industrialised countries since the 1970s where a main tendency has been to lock monetary policy through rules.

15.4   Should exchange rates be fixed?

According to the traditional analyses, a monetary regime should be chosen from the viewpoint of reducing inflation or, based on Mundell (1961), stabilising production at the natural level.[2] The discussion in this book suggests that the choice of monetary regime affects natural production. This impact of the monetary regime on natural unemployment is an additional factor which should be taken into account when a country chooses a monetary regime. This consideration is additional to the factors which have traditionally been seen as determining a country's choice of monetary regime. Depending on preferences and on the economic structure, it has even been demonstrated that when considering increasing natural production it may be optimal not to stabilise production, that is, we derive conclusions which question the traditional view of output stabilisation first suggested by Mundell (1961).[3]

Our examination of the case where the demand for goods can be affected by fiscal policy (but not by monetary factors), suggests that a small country can lower its natural unemployment by joining a monetary union with a price stability goal. This conclusion depends, however, on

---

[2]Recent discussions are found in Feldstein (1997), Isard (1995), and Wyplosz (1997).
[3]The goal of output stabilisation may still be defended on the ground that it reduces costs associated with output fluctuations.

the economic model and might be changed with other model specifications.

Our analysis has cast doubt on the wisdom of joining a fixed-but-adjustable exchange rate regime in which a country incurs a cost when it devalues *vis-à-vis* a low inflation country. It has been demonstrated that such a cost could increase natural unemployment. A country may even end up in a situation where not only production is lowered but where inflation at the same time lies at a higher level. This again counters the conventional wisdom which throughout the 1980s saw the discipline imposed on countries in a fixed-but-adjustable exchange rate regime as a way to lower inflation while no costs in the form of higher unemployment would result.

As the employment consequences of monetary regimes depend on structural characteristics in the economy, they are likely to change over time. This casts doubt upon the stability of fixed exchange rate regimes. Structural changes may increase the costs incurred by a country of staying in a fixed exchange rate system and may thus induce a country to withdraw from the system. Financial markets may precipitate such withdrawals through speculative attacks, frequently testing the stability of fixed exchange rate systems.

15.5   Does an independent central bank increase welfare?

The independence of central banks has been strengthened through institutional reforms in many industrialised countries throughout the 1980s and the 1990s. One example is the recent reform in the United Kingdom. Another example is the status of the European Central Bank.

The motive behind this strengthening of central bank independence has been the reduction of inflation. As discussed above, our analysis questions the exclusive pursuit of a price stability goal. It has been argued that a change in inflation affects natural unemployment.

The independence of central banks has been attacked due to the resulting 'democratic deficit'. Proponents of independent central banks have argued that a democratic decision-making process is unnecessary as a restrictive monetary policy has only advantageous effects by lowering inflation.[4] According to our analysis policy makers are able to affect both inflation and natural unemployment through monetary policy. The optimal trade-off between inflation and unemployment should therefore reflect the general preferences of the public. This choice would seem

[4]See Thygesen (1991).

to be the responsibility of elected policy makers. Policy changes which leave the optimal inflation–unemployment combination to other parties, for example, an independent central bank, or which try to distort the decision-making process, for example, through the appointment of a conservative banker as central bank governor, may be seen as socially inefficient.

Two arguments may still justify an independent central bank. First, monetary policy decisions may require a degree of confidentiality and speedy decision making which are inconsistent with 'normal' democratic decision making. Second, elected policy makers can be seen as exercising an undesirable influence on monetary policy, for example by pursuing short-term goals such as re-election or neglecting politically troublesome long-term reforms. Our analysis would in fact seem to strengthen the latter consideration. In a world where natural unemployment is determined by technology and structural characteristics, economic policy only has effects over a shorter time horizon and the harm which can be caused by a wrong monetary policy, is therefore limited. In a world where economic policies have permanent effects on natural unemployment, the quality of the political decision-making process takes on a much larger significance.

Appendix

Microeconomic foundations

A.1 Introduction

Below we will set out some of the most important assumptions regarding the economic structure which are used throughout the book. We take as the point of departure that production is determined by the interaction of decisions made by (i) representative firms which determine the capital stock and employment to maximise profit, (ii) households who determine consumption to optimise inter-temporal utility, (iii) authorities who have at their disposal monetary and/or fiscal policy, and (iv) wage setters who set the nominal wage with the view to reaching an optimal trade-off between the real wage and employment. The analysis considers a steady-state equilibrium, characterised by a constant output growth rate and constant levels of financial assets relative to nominal production. The model setting is an overlapping generations model with infinitely lived households. Most analyses concern an open economy.

The appendix is organised as follows. *Section A.2* examines the firm's production decision, and *section A.3* household optimisation with respect to the consumption of domestic and foreign goods and with respect to money holdings. *Section A.4* considers the government, and *section A.5* the foreign position. *Section A.6* discusses the determination of domestic demand. *Section A.7* examines goods market equilibrium. *Section A.8* briefly surveys the short-term dynamics of the model. *Section A.9* analyses the case where households are able to hold bank deposits which carry an interest rate. *Section A.10* considers the securities market. *Section A.11* gives a summary and conclusion.

A.2   The firm's profit optimisation

We consider a representative firm j which maximises the firm owners' consumption possibilities over an infinite time horizon. The firm is able to change employment instantaneously while it depends on the specific assumptions to what extent capital can be adjusted. This gives the following specification of the firm's profit maximisation at a given time t

$$\max_{L^j, K^j} \left\{ \sum_{T=t}^{\infty} \left(\frac{\upsilon_T^j}{P_T} \right) \prod_{n=t}^{T-1} (1 + r_n)^{-1} \mid \frac{\partial P}{\partial Y^j} = 0, \; \frac{\partial W}{\partial Y^j} = 0, \; \frac{\partial i}{\partial Y^j} = 0 \right\},$$

$$T = t, t+1, \ldots, \tag{A.1}$$

$$\left(\frac{\upsilon_T^j}{P_T} \right) = Y_T^j - L_T^j \left(\frac{W_T}{P_T} \right) - K_T^j r_{T-1} - K_T^j \kappa^j, \tag{A.2}$$

$$Y_T^j = (K_T^j)^a (L_T^j)^{1-a}, \quad 0 < a < 1, \tag{A.3}$$

$$\log(1 + r_{T-1}) \equiv \log(1 + i_{T-1}) - (p_T - p_{T-1}), \tag{A.4}$$

where υ^j is profit in the representative firm j, P and p the producer price (respectively non-logarithmic and logarithmic values), r the real interest rate, Y^j production in firm j, W the nominal wage, K^j the capital stock in firm j, L^j employment in firm j, κ^j the depreciation of capital, and i the nominal interest rate. a is the elasticity of production with respect to capital. p is the logarithmic value of the producer price.

Relation (A.1) shows the firm to maximise the present value of real profit with respect to employment and capital. Optimisation takes place under the following assumptions: (i) the firm is unable to affect the producer price, that is, there is perfect competition in the goods markets, (ii) the firm is unable to affect the nominal wage, (iii) the firm is unable to affect the nominal interest rate, that is, there is a perfect financial market, and (iv) the firm has full information regarding the variables which are relevant for profit maximisation. Relation (A.2) specifies real profit, the capital stock depreciating by κ^j. (A.3) expresses Cobb–Douglas production technology with a homogeneous production function of degree 1. The use of money as a possible production factor is not considered in the specification of the firm's production function given by (A.3). (A.4) gives the definition of the real interest rate expressed by the nominal interest i_T adjusted for the price increase between periods $T - 1$ and T, that is, P_T / P_{T-1}.

It is assumed by (A.1) that the firm is unable to affect the nominal wage. This assumption requires either (i) that wage setting takes place at a higher sectoral level than the firm, for example, at the level of the industrial sector or through centralised wage negotiations for the economy as a whole, or (ii) that the nominal wage is set through contracts which are negotiated prior to the firm's decisions on capital and employment.

Optimising (A.2) with respect to employment and capital, and using (A.1) and (A.3), gives the optimum conditions

$$(1-a)\left(\frac{Y_t}{L_t}\right) = \left(\frac{W_t}{P_t}\right), \tag{A.5}$$

$$a\left(\frac{Y_t}{K_t}\right) = \kappa^j + r_{t-1}. \tag{A.6}$$

In the case where capital depreciates fully during the current time period, that is, $\kappa^j = 1$, the optimum condition (A.6) is given as

$$\frac{\partial Y^j}{\partial K^j} = a\left(\frac{Y_t^j}{K_t^j}\right) = 1 + r_{t-1}. \tag{A.7}$$

In the case where the firm is able to affect the nominal wage through its decision on capital adjustment, that is, the case when a decision on capital adjustment is made prior to wage setting and wage setting takes place at the level of the firm (see chapter 3 for a discussion), the optimum condition for capital can be found as (using the optimum condition for employment given by (A.5))

$$a\left(\frac{Y_t^j}{K_t^j}\right) = -(\kappa^j + r_{t-1})\left[\frac{1}{\left(\frac{\partial(w-p)}{\partial l}\right)^u}\right], \tag{A.8}$$

where $[\partial(w-p)/\partial l]^u$ shows the impact of employment on the wage setters' real wage demand. l and w are the logarithmic values of respectively employment and nominal wage.

Combining (A.2), (A.6), and (A.7) gives the real wage expressed by the producer price as a function of the real interest rate

$$w_t - p_t = \left(\frac{a}{1-a}\right)\log(a) - \left(\frac{a}{1-a}\right)\log(1 + r_{t-1}) + \log(1 - a). \tag{A.9}$$

It follows from (A.9) that the real wage expressed by the producer price is determined only by the real interest rate.

Firms finance investments through securities with a fixed nominal interest rate. The value of the securities issued by the representative firm is thus given as

$$\left(\frac{S_t^j}{P_t}\right) = K_{t+1}, \tag{A.10}$$

where S_t^j represents securities issued by the representative firm.

No distinction is made between shares and fixed interest rate securities. As the analysis is based on certainty, and there is no tax discrimination between shares and fixed interest rate securities, shares and fixed interest rate securities can be treated as similar.

A.3   The household's optimisation

Conditions for optimum

The analysis is based on an overlapping generations model with infinitely lived households, cf. Weil (1989).[1] Each generation is represented by a household h ($h = 1, 2, \ldots$) which optimises utility over an infinite time horizon. Generations are uniform, except that the probability of being employed at a given time differs between generations.

Household consumption consists of goods produced in the home country, represented by C_A^h, and goods produced in the foreign country, represented by C_B^h. Household optimisation at time t can be shown as

$$\max_{C_A^h, C_B^h, M^h} \left\{ \sum_{T=t}^{\infty} \beta^{T-t} u_T^h \mid \frac{\partial (W/P)}{\partial C_A^h} = 0,\ \frac{\partial (W/P)}{\partial C_B^h} = 0,\ \frac{\partial (W/P)}{\partial M^h} = 0 \right\},$$

$$0 < \beta < 1, \quad T = t, t+1, \ldots, \quad h = 1, 2, \ldots, \tag{A.11}$$

[1] One may find the assumption of an infinitely lived household artificial, even in the presence of a bequest motive. A more plausible interpretation would be to view the time-discounting factor as an approximation of a declining probability of being alive in a given time period. This view is taken by Friedman (1969) who argues that a discounting factor smaller than one can be justified by the probability of not being alive in a future time period.

$$u_T^h = u_c^h(C_{A,T}^h, C_{B,T}^h) + u_m^h\left(\frac{M_T^h}{P_T}\right),$$

$$u_{A,T}^{'} \equiv \frac{\partial u_T^h}{\partial C_{A,T}^h} > 0, \quad u_{A,T}^{''} \equiv \frac{\partial^2 u_T^h}{\partial (C_{A,T}^h)^2} < 0,$$

$$u_{B,T}^{'} \equiv \frac{\partial u_T^h}{\partial C_{B,T}^h} > 0, \quad u_{B,T}^{''} \equiv \frac{\partial^2 u_T^h}{\partial (C_{B,T}^h)^2} < 0,$$

$$u_m^{'} \equiv \frac{\partial u_T^h}{\partial (M_T^h/P_T)} > 0, \quad u_{m,T}^{''} \equiv \frac{\partial^2 u_T^h}{\partial (M_T^h/P_T)^2} < 0, \quad \text{(A.12)}$$

$$M_{T-1}^h + S_{T-1}^h(1 + i_{T-1}) + W_T(1 - \tau_T)\Gamma_T^h\left(\frac{L_T}{L_T^{''}}\right) = P_T C_T^h + S_T^h + M_T^h,$$

$$C_T^h \equiv C_{A,T}^h + \mathcal{E}_T C_{B,T}^h, \quad \mathcal{E}_T \equiv \frac{P_T^B X_T}{P_T}, \quad L_T^{''} = L_{T-1} \equiv 1,$$

$$\text{(A.13)}$$

$$\Gamma_T^h = \Gamma_0 \Gamma^{(T-t)+(h-1)}, \quad 0 < \Gamma < 1, \quad \sum_h \Gamma_T^h = \Gamma_0\left(\frac{1}{1-\Gamma}\right) = 1, \quad \text{(A.14)}$$

where u^h is the utility derived by a household in a given time period, u_c^h the utility derived from the consumption of goods, u_m^h the utility provided by the services offered by real money, C_A^h household consumption of the good produced in the home country A, C_B^h household consumption of the good produced in the foreign country B, S^h the nominal value of securities held by the domestic household (non-monetary financial wealth), M^h household holding of money, β the time-discounting factor, C^h the domestic household's total consumption, defined as $C_A^h + \mathcal{E}C_B^h$, τ the tax rate on labour income, X the nominal exchange rate (number of domestic currency units per foreign currency unit), $\mathcal{E}$ the real exchange rate between countries B and A (defined as the producer price in the foreign country B expressed in the home currency relative to the producer price in the home country A), Γ^h the probability of finding employment for household h, and $L^{''}$ full employment. All variables refer to the home country A unless otherwise specified.

Relation (A.11) shows that the household determines the consumption of domestic and foreign goods and money holdings to optimise utility over an infinite time horizon. The household has full information regarding future and current variables which enter the utility function. The household is unable to affect the real wage, implying that it is unable to determine working hours and thus leisure. It is further assumed (not written) that the household is unable to affect variables which are determined at the macroeconomic level, that is, the exchange rate, the interest rate, and the price level.

Relation (A.12) shows utility in each time period as a separable function of consumption of goods and of real money holdings. The household derives positive but declining marginal utility from consumption of the two goods and from real money.

Relation (A.13) gives the household budgetary constraint. At the household's disposal for consumption and saving is the after-tax nominal wage derived from working in period T with the addition of financial wealth. Financial wealth consists of money M_{T-1}^h and securities S_{T-1}^h with the addition of the interest income earned on securities which were bought in time period $T - 1$. In time period T the household consumes $C_{A,T}^h$ and $C_{B,T}^h$ of respectively the domestic and the foreign good and places S_T^h in securities and M_T^h in money. Due to the assumption of a homogeneous production function of degree one, all revenue in the firm is distributed between labour and capital and there are thus no dividend payments to households.

Relation (A.13) shows the household in each time period to receive a labour income determined as $\Gamma_T^h(L_T/L^{''})W$. The term $\Gamma_T^h(L_T/L^{''})$ represents the probability of finding employment.[2] The probability of being employed depends on the percentage of the total labour force which is in employment, shown by $L/L^{''}$, multiplied by a factor which reflects the generation-specific likelihood of finding employment, specified by Γ^h. Full employment $L^{''}$ is normalised at one.

Relation (A.14) specifies the probability for generation h of finding employment. Each generation experiences over time a decreasing likelihood of being employed, implying a gradual decline in working capabilities. The likelihood decreases by a constant factor Γ. The likelihood of finding employment in the first working period of a generation equals Γ_0.

Optimising (A.11)–(A.12) under the constraint of (A.13) gives the optimum conditions for the consumption of the two goods and the household's money holding

$$\frac{u_{A,t+1}'}{u_{A,t}'} = \frac{1}{\beta}\left(\frac{1}{1+r_t}\right), \tag{A.15}$$

[2]This is clearly a simplification. A more plausible modelling would imply a further differentiation of households, for example, through a distinction between workers in employment and unemployment with different probabilities of finding employment.

$$u'_{B,t} = Æ_t u'_{A,t},$$ (A.16)

$$u'_{m,t} = u'_{A,t}\left(\frac{i_t}{1 + i_t}\right).$$ (A.17)

Relation (A.15) specifies that saving is undertaken to the point where the marginal utility from consumption of the domestic good in the current time period equals the marginal utility from consumption of the domestic good in the subsequent time period with the addition of real interest and discounted to the current time period. (A.16) shows that the ratio between the marginal utilities derived from the consumption of respectively the foreign and the domestic good equals the real exchange rate, that is, the price ratio between the foreign and the domestic good expressed in the same currency. (A.17) finally determines money holdings as a function of the nominal interest rate.

We assume that production in the representative firm j corresponds to production in the economy as a whole, that is

$$Y^j_t = Y_t,$$ (A.18)

where Y shows production in the economy as a whole.

Combining the budgetary constraint (A.13) with (A.5), (A.14), and (A.18), and assuming $\lim(1 + r_{t+n})^{-n}\left(S^h_{t+n}\right) \to 0$ for $n \to \infty$, we derive the relationship

$$\sum_{T=t}^{\infty}\left\{C^h_T \prod_{n=t}^{T-1}(1 + r_n)^{-1}\right\} = (1 - a)\Gamma^h_t \sum_{T=t}^{\infty}\left\{Y_T(1 - \tau_T)\Gamma^{T-t}\prod_{n=t}^{T-1}(1 + r_n)^{-1}\right\}$$
$$+ \left(\frac{S^h_{t-1}}{P_{t-1}}\right)(1 + r_{t-1}) - \sum_{T=t}^{\infty}\left\{\left(\frac{M^h_T - M^h_{T-1}}{P_T}\right)\prod_{n=t}^{T-1}(1 + r_n)^{-1}\right\}.$$
(A.19)

Relation (A.19) shows that the discounted value of consumption corresponds to (i) the discounted value of real disposable labour income, (ii) the real value of securities holdings in the preceding period with the addition of the real interest rate, and (iii) the discounted value of the loss of purchasing power experienced by the household due to the household's holdings of money, that is, the household's loss from inflation tax/seigniorage.

Demand for domestic and foreign goods

We assume that the period utility derived from consumption of the domestic and the foreign good can be expressed as follows

$$u^h(C_{A,t}^h, C_{B,t}^h) = [(1 - \varphi)^{\frac{1}{\eta}}(C_{A,t}^h)^{\frac{\eta-1}{\eta}} + (\varphi)^{\frac{1}{\eta}}(C_{B,t}^h)^{\frac{\eta-1}{\eta}}]^{\delta},$$
$$0 < \varphi < 1, \quad \eta > 1, \quad 0 < \delta \le 1, \tag{A.20}$$

where φ reflects the utility derived from foreign goods relative to domestic goods.

Combining (A.20) with (A.15)–(A.16), and using the definition of the household's total consumption specified in (A.13), gives the following conditions for the consumption of the two goods

$$\frac{C_{T+1}^h}{C_T^h} = \left\{\frac{1 + \left(\frac{\varphi}{1-\varphi}\right)(\mathcal{E}_{T+1})^{1-\eta}}{1 + \left(\frac{\varphi}{1-\varphi}\right)(\mathcal{E}_T)^{1-\eta}}\right\}^{\frac{\delta\Upsilon}{\eta}} \beta^{\Upsilon}(1 + r_{T-1})^{\Upsilon}, \quad C_T^h \equiv C_{A,T}^h + \mathcal{E}_T C_{B,T}^h,$$
$$\Upsilon \equiv \frac{\eta}{1 + (\eta - 1)(1 - \delta)}, \quad 0 < \Upsilon < 1, \quad T = t, t+1, ..., \tag{A.21}$$

$$(C_{A,T}^h) = \left[\frac{(1 - \varphi)}{(1 - \varphi) + \varphi\mathcal{E}_T^{1-\eta}}\right]C_T^h, \tag{A.22}$$

$$(C_{B,T}^h) = \left[\frac{\mathcal{E}_T^{-\eta}\varphi}{(1 - \varphi) + \varphi\mathcal{E}_T^{1-\eta}}\right]C_T^h. \tag{A.23}$$

Relation (A.21) shows the growth in a generation's consumption over time, determined by (i) the expected change in the real exchange rate, that is, $\mathcal{E}_{T+1}$ relative to $\mathcal{E}_T$, (ii) the time discount factor β, and (iii) the real interest rate r. It follows from (A.21) that a real depreciation from time period T to time period $T + 1$, shown as a rise in the real exchange rate $\mathcal{E}$, induces households to place consumption earlier. It depends on Υ how the growth of consumption over time for a generation is affected by the real interest rate and by the time discount rate. As generations are uniform except for the employment rate, consumption growth is the same for all generations.

Relations (A.22) and (A.23) express the demand for respectively the domestic good and the foreign good as functions of (i) the real exchange rate $\mathcal{E}_T$, and (ii) the household's total consumption, defined as $C_T^h \equiv C_{A,T}^h + \mathcal{E}_T C_{B,T}^h$. At a given level of the household's total consumption, it follows from (A.20) that a rise in the real exchange rate $\mathcal{E}$, causing foreign goods to become more expensive relative to domestic goods, increases the share of domestic goods C_A^h in the household's total consumption C^h.

Steady-state equilibrium

We consider a steady-state equilibrium characterised by a constant growth rate of production. In addition, the real interest rate and the real exchange rate lie at unchanged levels in each time period. This gives

$$Y_{T+1} = Y_T(1 + v_y), \quad \text{Æ}_{T+1} = \text{Æ}_T \equiv \text{Æ}, \quad r_{T+1} = r_T \equiv r,$$

$$v_y \equiv \frac{Y_{T+1} - Y_T}{Y_T}, \quad T = t, t+1, \ldots, \tag{A.24}$$

$$\tau_{T+1} = \tau_T \equiv \tau, \quad g_{T+1} = g_T \equiv g, \tag{A.25}$$

where v_y is the growth rate in production, and g shows government purchases of goods and services relative to production. Variables without time indications show steady-state levels.

Relation (A.24) shows production to increase at a constant rate v_y in the steady state, while the real exchange rate and the real interest rate lie at unchanged levels. (A.25) specifies that the authorities set the tax rate on labour income and government purchases of goods and services relative to production at unchanged levels.

We further assume that the authorities increase the price level at a constant rate in each time period. This can be specified as

$$\frac{P_t - P_{t-1}}{P_{t-1}} = \bar{v}_p, \tag{A.26}$$

where v_p is the price increase. Relation (A.26) gives the assumption of a monetary policy characterised by a constant growth rate in the price level.

Total consumption relative to production

It follows from (A.21) and (A.24) that a generation's consumption over time in the steady state increases at a constant rate determined as

$$\frac{C_{t+1}^h}{C_t^h} = (1 + r)^\Upsilon \beta^\Upsilon. \tag{A.27}$$

Combining (A.15), (A.17), and (A.24)–(A.27), the discounted value of the household's real loss from seigniorage/inflation tax is found as

$$\sum_{T=t}^{\infty} \left(\frac{M_T^h - M_{T-1}^h}{P_T} \right) \left(\frac{1}{1+r} \right)^{T-t} = \left(\frac{M_{t-1}^h}{P_{t-1}} \right) \left(\frac{N_2}{N_1} \right)$$

$$N_1 \equiv 1 - (1+r)^{\Upsilon-1}\beta^{\Upsilon}, \quad 0 < (1+r)^{\Upsilon-1}\beta^{\Upsilon} < 1,$$

$$N_2 \equiv \beta^{\Upsilon}(1+r)^{\Upsilon} - \left[\frac{1}{1+v_p} \right] \left[\frac{N_1}{1 - N_1(1+v_p)} \right],$$

$$1 > N_1(1+v_p). \tag{A.28}$$

Combining (A.19) with (A.24)–(A.28) gives household total consumption in the steady state at a given time t as

$$C_t^h = (1-a)\Gamma_t^h N_1 Y_t (1-\tau) \left(\frac{1}{1 - \Gamma(1+r)^{-1}(1+v_y)} \right)$$

$$+ \left(\frac{S_{t-1}^h}{P_{t-1}} \right) N_1(1+r) - \left(\frac{M_{t-1}^h}{P_{t-1}} \right) N_2,$$

$$N_1 \equiv 1 - (1+r)^{\Upsilon-1}\beta^{\Upsilon}, \quad 0 < N_1 < 1,$$

$$N_2 \equiv \beta^{\Upsilon}(1+r)^{\Upsilon} - \left[\frac{1}{1+v_p} \right] \left[\frac{N_1}{1 - N_1(1+v_p)} \right], \quad 1 > N_1(1+v_p).$$

$$\tag{A.29}$$

Relation (A.29) shows the household's total consumption C^h in the steady state to be determined by (i) production in the current time period Y_t, (ii) the real interest rate r, (iii) the time discount rate β, (iv) the rate of withdrawal from the labour market Γ, (v) the growth rate of production v_y, and (vi) the household's real financial wealth brought over from the preceding period, expressed by S_{t-1}^h/P_{t-1} and M_{t-1}^h/P_{t-1}. The household's total consumption is positively affected by (i) a higher growth rate in production v_y, (ii) a rise in the withdrawal rate from the labour market Γ, and (iii) a reduction in the time discount rate β, causing households to value future consumption less. It depends on the economic structure how a rise in the real interest rate affects household consumption. A higher real interest rate reduces at the same time the real value of future labour income and increases the real return on securities. It follows from (A.29) that consumption is affected by monetary factors. The monetary impact arises because the household's purchasing power is reduced due to the holding of real money, that is, an effect caused by inflation tax/seigniorage.

Consumer price
The consumer price is defined as the minimum expenditure necessary to buy one unit of utility. In the case of the utility function

specified by (A.20), the consumer price can be found from (A.20) and (A.22)–(A.23) as

$$Q_t \equiv P_t \Big[(1 - \varphi) + \varphi \mathcal{E}_t^{1-\eta} \Big]^{\frac{1}{1-\eta}}, \tag{A.30}$$

where Q is the consumer price.

The money demand

We next turn to money demand. Relation (A.12) specifies that real money enters the household's utility function as a separable factor. We assume that the utility derived from the use of money can be expressed by the logarithmic utility function, that is

$$u_m \left(\frac{M_t^h}{P_t} \right) = \log \left(\frac{M_t^h}{P_t} \right). \tag{A.31}$$

Relation (A.31) specifies the utility of real money. Combining (A.17) and (A.31) gives

$$M_t^h = P_t \left(\frac{1}{u'_{A,t}} \right) \left(\frac{1 + i_t}{i_t} \right). \tag{A.32}$$

It follows from (A.32) that money demand depends on the price level, on the marginal utility of consumption for the home country good, and on the nominal interest rate. Money demand is increased by a higher price, a lower nominal interest rate, and by higher consumption (given $u''_{A,t} < 0$).

In the case where the utility from goods is specified by the utility function shown as (A.20), relation (A.32) changes into

$$\frac{M_t^h}{P_t} = \left(\frac{1}{\delta} \right) (C_t^h)^{\frac{1}{\Upsilon}} \left(\frac{Q_t}{P_t} \right)^{1-\frac{\delta}{\eta}} \left(\frac{\eta}{\eta - 1} \right) \left(\frac{1 + i_t}{i_t} \right). \tag{A.33}$$

Relation (A.33) shows household real holding of money as a function of (i) the household's consumption, (ii) the consumer price relative to the producer price, and (iii) the nominal interest rate. As $0 < \Upsilon < 1$, $\eta > 1$, and $0 < \delta \leq 1$, real money holdings are increased by a rise in consumption and a rise in the consumer price relative to the producer price. In addition, there is an increase in real money holdings when there is a reduction in the nominal interest rate.

A.4 The government

The government finances purchases of domestic and foreign goods through taxes, through money creation, and through the issue of government securities. Taxes are imposed only on labour income, the total tax revenue thus equalling $\tau_t W_t L_t = \tau_t(1 - a) Y_t P_t$. In each time period the government budgetary constraint is given as

$$P_t G_t = \tau_t(1 - a) Y_t P_t + S_t^g - S_{t-1}^g(1 + i_{t-1}) + M_t - M_{t-1}, \quad M_t \equiv \sum_h M_t^h,$$

(A.34)

where G is the government's purchase of goods and services, S^g securities issued by the government, and M money holdings in the economy as a whole.

Relation (A.34) shows that government expenditure for purchases of goods and services G equals revenue derived from (i) taxes on labour income, (ii) the net increase in government securities with the deduction of interest payments, and (iii) the increase in the money supply.

The government controls purchases of goods and services and the tax rate, causing G/Y and τ to be exogenously given. This gives

$$\frac{G_t}{Y_t} \equiv g_t = \bar{g}_t, \quad \tau_t = \bar{\tau}_t.$$

(A.35)

In the steady state net government debt and nominal money holdings lie at unchanged levels relative to nominal production in each time period. Combining (A.24)–(A.26) with (A.34)–(A.35) gives the condition for the government budgetary constraint in steady-state equilibrium as

$$g = \tau(1 - a) + \left(\frac{S^g}{PY}\right)\left(\frac{v_y - r}{1 + v_y}\right) + \left(\frac{M}{PY}\right)\left(1 - \frac{1}{(1 + v_y)(1 + v_p)}\right), \quad v_y > r.$$

(A.36)

Relation (A.36) shows the relationship between (i) the government's purchases of goods and services g, (ii) the tax rate on labour income τ, (iii) non-monetary government debt relative to nominal production S^g/PY, and (iv) money balances relative to nominal production M/PY, which are compatible with steady-state equilibrium, defined as a state characterised by (A.24), that is, a constant growth rate in production.

The impact of real money holdings on the government budgetary constraint is due to inflation tax/seigniorage. In the case where revenue from inflation tax/seigniorage is transferred back to households through lump-sum transfers, (A.36) can be rewritten as

$$\left(\frac{S^g}{PY}\right) = [g - \tau(1 - a)]\left(\frac{1 + v_y}{v_y - r}\right), \quad v_y > r.$$

(A.37)

Relation (A.37) shows the combinations of (i) government debt levels S^g /PY, (ii) government purchases of goods and services relative to production g, and (iii) tax rates on labour income τ, which are compatible with a steady-state equilibrium characterised by a constant output growth rate v_y and a constant real interest rate r.

It is only possible to maintain a permanent budgetary deficit with a stable level of government debt when output growth exceeds the real interest rate, imposing the condition that (A.36) only holds when $v_y >$ r. It follows from (A.36) that only in this case is it possible to combine a positive level of S^g/PY, implying a government debt, with a budgetary deficit, implying that $g- \tau(1 - a) > 0$. In the case where $v_y < r$, a permanent level of government debt is incompatible with the steady state and in this case the government has to maintain budgetary balance in the steady state.

For $v_y > r$, relation (A.37) shows that it is possible for the government to maintain a permanent deficit, implying $g- \tau(1 - a) > 0$, and at the same time maintain a stable level of government debt relative to production. This means that the government is not required to maintain budgetary balance over an infinite time horizon, implying that the principle of Ricardian equivalence does not apply. This feature is characteristic of the overlapping generations model which forms the basis of the analysis.

A.5   Foreign position

The net claim of domestic households on foreign households, referred to as the households' net foreign position, is determined as the trade balance net surplus in a given time period with the addition of the net claim in the previous period increased with interest payments. This gives

$$F_t^p = P_t(Y_t - D_t) + F_{t-1}^p(1 + i_{t-1}), \qquad (A.38)$$

where D is domestic demand and F^p is household net foreign position.

Relation (A.38) shows the determination of the net foreign position. The trade balance net surplus corresponds to production with the deduction of domestic demand. It is assumed from (A.38) that claims between domestic and foreign agents are settled in securities denominated in the home currency.[3]

In the steady state the level of net claims on foreigners lies at an unchanged level relative to nominal production in each time period. Using this in (A.38) gives the steady-state level of net foreign claims as

---

[3]This implies that households do not hold money in a foreign currency.

$$\left(\frac{F^p}{PY}\right) = \left[1 - \left(\frac{D}{Y}\right)\right]\left(\frac{1 + v_y}{v_y - r}\right), \quad v_y > r. \tag{A.39}$$

Relation (A.39) shows the steady-state net foreign position. The net foreign position is positively affected by an increase in the net trade balance surplus, shown by the term $1 - (D/Y)$, and by a higher real interest rate. A trade balance which is permanently different from 0 is only possible when the output growth rate v_y lies above the real interest rate r.

A.6   Domestic demand

Capital and employment correspond at the macroeconomic level to the levels in the representative firm. Holdings of securities and money at a given time are found from the summation of holdings for each generation. This gives

$$K_t^j = K_t, \quad L_t^j = L_t, \quad S_t^j = S_t^p, \quad S_t \equiv \sum_h S_t^h, \tag{A.40}$$

where K and L are capital and employment levels in the total economy, S household total holdings of securities, and S^p is the total issue of securities from firms.

Domestic demand is the sum of investment, consumption, and government expenditure on goods and services, that is

$$D_t \equiv C_t + I_t + G_t, \quad C_t \equiv \sum_h C_t^h, \tag{A.41}$$

where I is gross investment, and C total consumption in the economy as a whole.

Investment can be found from the condition for the firm's optimum with respect to capital and thus depends on capital adjustment. Consumption depends on the household's utility function.

Assuming that capital depreciates in the course of one time period, the optimum condition for the firm's capital adjustment is given as (A.7). This means that investment can be found as

$$I_t = K_{t+1}^j. \tag{A.42}$$

Assuming that the utility of household consumption is specified by the utility function (A.20), household consumption is given as (A.29). Combining (A.29) with (A.14), (A.24)–(A.26), (A.34), and (A.40)–(A.41), gives total consumption in the economy as

$$\left(\frac{C}{Y}\right) = (1 - a)N_1(1 - \tau)\left(\frac{1}{1 - \Gamma(1 + r)^{-1}(1 + v_y)}\right)$$

$$+ \left(\frac{S}{PY}\right)N_1\left(\frac{1 + r}{1 + v_y}\right) - \left(\frac{M}{PY}\right)\left(\frac{N_2}{1 + v_y}\right),$$

$$N_1 \equiv 1 - (1 + r)^{\Upsilon - 1}\beta^{\Upsilon}, \quad 0 < N_1 < 1,$$

$$N_2 \equiv \beta^{\Upsilon}(1 + r)^{\Upsilon} - \left[\frac{1}{1 + v_p}\right]\left[\frac{N_1}{1 - N_1(1 + v_p)}\right], \quad 1 > N_1(1 + v_p).$$

$$\text{(A.43)}$$

Household non-monetary financial wealth is composed of securities issued by domestic firms, by the domestic government, and by foreign residents. This gives

$$\frac{S_t}{P_t} \equiv \frac{S_t^p}{P_t} + \frac{S_t^g}{P_t} + \frac{F_t^p}{P_t}.$$

$$\text{(A.44)}$$

The first term on the right-hand side in (A.44) is determined by (A.10) in combination with (A.7) and (A.40) (assuming that capital depreciates fully in the course of one time period). The second term on the right-hand side of (A.44) can be found from the government budgetary constraint shown by (A.36). The last term, that is, the net foreign position, is found from the balance-of-payments position of the home country, expressed by (A.39).

Combining (A.7), (A.10), (A.24)–(A.26), (A.36), (A.39)–(A.41), and (A.44), gives domestic demand in the steady state as

$$\left(\frac{D}{Y}\right) = g - \tau(1 - a)\left(\frac{N_1}{N_3}\right)\left[\left(\frac{1}{1 - \Gamma(1 + r)^{-1}(1 + v_y)}\right) + \left(\frac{1 + r}{v_y - r}\right)\right]$$

$$+ a\left(\frac{1 + v_y}{1 + r}\right) + \left(\frac{N_1}{N_3}\right)\left[\left(\frac{1 + r}{1 + v_y}\right) + \left(\frac{(1 - a)}{1 - \Gamma(1 + r)^{-1}(1 + v_y)}\right)\right],$$

$$+ \left(\frac{M}{PY}\right)\left[\left(\frac{1}{v_y - r}\right)\left(1 + v_y - \frac{1}{1 + v_p}\right) - \left(\frac{N_2}{1 + v_y}\right)\right]$$

$$N_1 \equiv 1 - (1 + r)^{\Upsilon - 1}\beta^{\Upsilon} > 0,$$

$$N_2 \equiv \beta^{\Upsilon}(1 + r)^{\Upsilon} - \left(\frac{1}{1 + v_p}\right)\left(\frac{N_1}{1 - N_1(1 + v_p)}\right) > 0,$$

$$N_3 \equiv 1 + N_1\left(\frac{1 + r}{v_y - r}\right) > 0, \quad v_y > r.$$

$$\text{(A.45)}$$

Relation (A.45) shows total domestic demand relative to production in the steady state as a function of (i) government purchases of goods and services relative to production g, (ii) the tax rate on labour income τ, (iii) the real interest rate r, (iv) the output growth rate v_y, (v) the time discount factor β, and (vi) the withdrawal rate from the labour market Γ. In addition, total domestic demand relative to production depends on the households' money holdings. It follows from (A.45) that domestic demand relative to production is positively affected by a rise in government purchases in goods and services g, by a reduction in taxation τ, by a lower time discount factor β, and by a slower withdrawal from the labour market, shown by a higher Γ. The impact of the other variables, including the real interest rate, depends on the economic structure.

Two points are important seen from a policy perspective. First, it results from (A.45) that fiscal policy is effective in affecting the demand for goods in steady-state equilibrium characterised by a constant output growth rate and constant levels of financial assets relative to nominal production. The government can affect domestic demand relative to production both through changes in government purchases of goods and services relative to production g and through changes in the tax rate on labour income τ. Second, (A.45) shows that the real money supply affects total domestic demand through inflation tax/seigniorage. It depends on the economic structure whether inflation v_p increases or lowers total domestic demand relative to production.

For convenience, demand relative to production in steady-state equilibrium expressed by relation (A.45) can be rewritten as

$$\Omega_s = \Omega_s(r, g, \tau, v_y, v_p), \quad \Omega_s \equiv \log\left(\frac{D}{Y}\right),$$

$$\Omega_{sr} \equiv \frac{\partial \Omega_s}{\partial r} < 0, \quad \Omega_{sg} \equiv \frac{\partial \Omega_s}{\partial g} > 0,$$

$$\Omega_{s\tau} \equiv \frac{\partial \Omega_s}{\partial \tau} < 0, \quad \Omega_{sv} \equiv \frac{\partial \Omega_s}{\partial v_y} > 0, \quad \text{(A.46)}$$

where Ω_s shows the logarithmic value of total domestic demand relative to production in the steady state.

Relation (A.46) is the basic relation used to characterise goods market equilibrium throughout most analyses in the book. By (A.46) we have assumed that the real interest rate has a negative impact on domestic demand relative to production while a rise in the output growth rate raises domestic demand relative to production. We use these assumptions throughout the analyses in the book.

Assuming that revenue from inflation tax/seigniorage is transferred back to the households through lump-sum transfers, there is no impact of inflation on domestic demand. In this case relation (A.46) can be rewritten as

$$\Omega_s = \Omega_s(r, g, \tau, v_y),$$
$$\Omega_{sr} < 0, \quad \Omega_{sg} > 0, \quad \Omega_{s\tau} < 0, \quad \Omega_{sv} > 0. \qquad \text{(A.47)}$$

Relation (A.47) shows total domestic demand relative to production in the steady state when there is no impact of inflation tax/seigniorage.

The analysis above was based on the assumption that output growth is higher than the real interest rate, implying that $v_y > r$. This assumption makes it possible in the steady state to permanently maintain a net deficit on the government budget and on foreign trade. In the case where output growth is lower than the real interest rate, that is, $v_y < r$, steady-state equilibrium is only compatible with equilibrium on the government budget and on the balance of payments. The basic findings of the analysis above remain, however, unchanged. Thus, it results from (A.45) that fiscal policy is effective in influencing domestic demand also when government purchases of goods and services are equal to the tax revenue, implying that $g = (1 - a)\tau$. The real exchange rate will be determined to bring about equilibrium of the trade balance and will still be affected by the demand for goods in the home country.

A.7   Goods market equilibrium

Imperfect substitution between domestic and foreign goods is assumed. This means that the real exchange rate, expressed as the price of foreign goods relative to the price of domestic goods expressed in the same currency, can diverge from unity. We further assume that households have preferences corresponding to (A.20), implying that households' demand for domestic and foreign goods are represented by (A.22) and (A.23) respectively. We finally assume that investment demand and government purchases of goods and services are distributed between domestic and foreign goods in the same way as consumption. This gives the following relationship for the demand for domestic goods from home country residents

$$D_{A,t} = (1 - \varphi)\Big[(1 - \varphi) + \varphi \mathcal{E}_t^{1-\eta}\Big]^{-1} D_t, \qquad \text{(A.48)}$$

where D_A is the demand for domestic goods from domestic agents.

Making the assumption that a corresponding relationship exists for the foreign country, it follows from (A.23) that the demand for domestic goods from foreign agents is determined as

$$D_{A,t}^B = \varphi^B \cancel{E}_t^{\eta^B} \left[(1 - \varphi^B) + \varphi^B \cancel{E}_t^{\eta^B - 1} \right] D_t^B, \qquad (A.49)$$

where D_A^B is foreign demand for domestic goods measured in the home currency. D^B is total domestic demand in the foreign country.

Combining (A.48)–(A.49) gives the condition for domestic goods market equilibrium as

$$Y_t = (1 - \varphi) \left[(1 - \varphi) + \varphi \cancel{E}_t^{1-\eta} \right]^{-1} D_t + \varphi^B \cancel{E}_t^{\eta^B} \left[(1 - \varphi^B) + \varphi^B \cancel{E}_t^{\eta^B - 1} \right]^{-1} D_t^B.$$
$$(A.50)$$

Relation (A.50) shows demand for domestic goods as a function of (i) domestic demand in the two countries D and D^B, and (ii) the real exchange rate Æ. Domestic demand in the two countries is determined as a function of production, fiscal policy, the real interest rate, and the output growth rate, cf. (A.47). It follows from (A.50) that a rise in Æ, that is, a real depreciation, leads to a rise in the demand for home country goods from domestic residents, while it depends on the economic structure whether there is an increase in demand from foreign residents.

In the analyses which involve a small economy, to simplify we assume that the logarithmic value of domestic demand in the foreign country is normalised at zero. Undertaking a log-linear approximation of $[(1 - \varphi) + \varphi \cancel{E}_t^{1-\eta}]$, setting the initial level of Æ equal to 1, implies that $\log[(1 - \varphi) + \varphi \cancel{E}_t^{1-\eta}] \simeq (1 - \eta)\varphi \log(\cancel{E}_t)$ and $\log[(1 - \varphi^B) + \varphi^B \cancel{E}_t^{\eta^B - 1}]$ $\simeq (\eta^B - 1)\varphi^B \log(\cancel{E}_t)$. It follows in this case from (A.50) that goods market equilibrium and the consumer price can be specified as follows

$$y_t = ze_t + d_t + \log(1 - \varphi) + \log(\varphi^B),$$
$$z \equiv \varphi(\eta - 1) + \eta^B + (1 - \eta^B)\varphi^B, \qquad (A.51)$$

$$q_t = p_t + \varphi e_t, \qquad (A.52)$$

where e is the logarithmic value of the real exchange rate, that is, $e \equiv \log(\cancel{E})$.

Relation (A.51) shows goods market equilibrium. The demand for goods depends on (i) the real exchange rate e, and (ii) domestic demand d. To simplify, we assume throughout the book that the real exchange rate has a positive impact on the demand for domestic goods, that is, $z > 0$. (A.52) gives the consumer price level.

A.8   Short-term dynamics

As our concern is to demonstrate the real impact of inflation on the monetary regime in steady-state equilibrium, the short-term dynamics of the overlapping generations model specified in the preceding sections will be considered only briefly. It follows from (A.19) that consumption relative to production in a given time period is a function of production levels in the current and future time periods, consumption in future periods, the level of real financial wealth, and of the real interest rate. Combining (A.19) with (i) the definition of domestic demand specified by (A.41), (ii) the level of government expenditure determined by (A.35), and (iii) the level of investment determined by (A.7), (A.10), and (A.41), and assuming an exogenous real interest rate, for example, determined as the foreign real interest rate due to perfect international financial integration, gives the following relationship

$$\Omega_t = \Omega\big(y_t, y_{t+1,\dots}; \Omega_{t+1}\Omega_{t+2}, \dots; r, g, \tau, \varsigma_{t-1}\big),$$

$$\varsigma_{t-1} \equiv \frac{S_{t-1}^g}{P_{t-1}} + \frac{F_{t-1}^p}{P_{t-1}}, \tag{A.53}$$

where ς is the level of real financial net wealth relative to production.

Relation (A.53) shows the levels of production and domestic demand relative to production in current and future time periods which bring about goods market equilibrium.

It follows from (A.51) that the real exchange rate is determined by domestic demand relative to production. According to (A.50) the real exchange rate is determined as $\mathcal{E}_t = (D_t/Y_t)^{-(1/z)}N_4$, where $N_4 \equiv (1-\varphi)^{-(1/2)}(\varphi^B) - (1/2)$. Substituting domestic demand for consumption, and using from (A.51) that the real exchange rate is determined by domestic demand relative to production, relation (A.21) determines future levels of domestic demand relative to production as a function of the current domestic demand relative to production and current and future production levels. Combining (A.7), (A.10), (A.21), (A.35), (A.41), and (A.51) thus gives the following difference equation for the determination of domestic demand relative to production

$$\left(\frac{Y_{t+1}}{Y_t}\right) =$$

$$\beta^{\Upsilon}(1+r_t)^{\Upsilon}\left\{\frac{\left(\frac{D_t}{Y_t}\right) - \left(\frac{a}{1+r}\right)\left(\frac{Y_{t+1}}{Y_t}\right) - g}{\left(\frac{D_{t+1}}{Y_{t+1}}\right) - \left(\frac{a}{1+r}\right)\left(\frac{Y_{t+2}}{Y_{t+1}}\right) - g}\right\}$$

$$\left\{\frac{1 + \left(\frac{\varphi}{1-\varphi}\right)\left(N_4\right)^{1-z}\left(\frac{D_{t+1}}{Y_{t+1}}\right)^{-(1-\eta)(1/z)}}{1 + \left(\frac{\varphi}{1-\varphi}\right)(N_4)^{1-z}\left(\frac{D_t}{Y_t}\right)^{-(1-\eta)(1/z)}}\right\}^{\frac{\delta}{\eta}\Upsilon}. \qquad (A.54)$$

Relation (A.54) determines future levels of domestic demand relative to production as a function of (i) the level of domestic demand relative to production in the current time period, and (ii) production levels in the current and future time periods. Using (A.54), the relationship shown by (A.53) can be specified as

$$\Omega_t = \Omega\left(y_t, y_{t+1}, \ldots; r, g, \tau, \varsigma_{t-1}\right). \qquad (A.55)$$

Relation (A.55) shows that domestic demand relative to production depends on current and future levels of production, on the exogenously given real interest rate, on fiscal policy, and on the level of real net financial wealth at the beginning of the current time period.

In most analyses, we specify a wage setting which implies that wage setters desire a trade-off between, on one side, the real wage, expressed by the consumer price, and, on the other side, employment which is a function of production. Wage setting thus gives a relationship between domestic demand relative to production Ω, which determines the real exchange rate, and production y. Expressing this relationship which follows from wage setting as $\Omega_t = R(y_t)$, production in a given time period can be found as

$$R(y_t) = \Omega\left(y_t, y_{t+1}, \ldots; r, g, \tau, \varsigma_{t-1}\right). \qquad (A.56)$$

Relation (A.56) gives the relationship for the determination of production at a given time, assuming that wage setters optimise their preferences. (A.56) specifies the adjustment path of production over time.

In the case of nominal wage contracts, the authorities can determine production in the current time period through monetary policy, an increase in the price level brought about by an expansive monetary policy leading to a rise in production. The production level in subsequent time periods is determined by the wage setters who are viewed as optimising preferences which include the real wage and employment, causing for future time periods a relationship between production and domestic demand relative to production. This implies that the relationship between domestic demand relative to production and production is determined as $\Omega_t = R(y_t)$ in subsequent time periods. Thus, if the authorities increase production in the current time period through monetary policy, production in the next time period y_{t+1} will be determined by a relationship corresponding to (A.56). The expansive monetary policy conducted in the current time period has, however, an impact on production in future time periods because the expansive monetary policy affects the real net financial wealth which is brought over to the next time period, that is, ς_t. This means that an expansive monetary policy which determines production in the current time period, has the following impact on production in subsequent time periods where wage setters optimise their preferences

$$R(y_{t+1}) = \Omega(y_{t+1}, y_{t+2}, \ldots; r, g, \tau, \varsigma_t),$$

$$\varsigma_t = \varsigma(y_t, \varsigma_{t-1}), \quad y_t = \bar{y}_t. \tag{A.57}$$

Relation (A.57) shows the determination of production when the authorities in the current time period t change production through monetary policy, assuming nominal wage contracts, and the wage setters in subsequent time periods set the nominal wage to optimise their preferences. It results that an expansive monetary policy in the current time period affects production in future time periods because production in the current time period affects the household saving and thus the accumulation of financial wealth in the form of claims on foreigners and claims on the government.

Throughout the following analysis, we assume that changes in production and exogenous variables in the current time period have the following impact on domestic demand relative to production in the current time period

$$\Omega_t = \Omega(y_t, r, g_t, \tau_t, \varsigma_{t-1}),$$

$$0 > \Omega_y > -1, \quad \Omega_y \equiv \frac{\partial \Omega_t}{\partial y_t}, \quad \Omega_g \equiv \frac{\partial \Omega_t}{\partial g_t} > 0,$$

$$\Omega_\tau \equiv \frac{\partial \Omega_t}{\partial \tau_t} < 0, \quad \Omega_r \equiv \frac{\partial \Omega_t}{\partial r_t} < 0, \quad \Omega_\varsigma \equiv \frac{\partial \Omega_t}{\partial \varsigma_{t-1}} > 0, \tag{A.58}$$

where Ω_y, Ω_g, Ω_τ, Ω_r, and Ω_ς show the impact on domestic demand relative to production in the current time period of changes in production in the current time period, in government purchases of goods and services relative to production in the current time period, in the tax rate on labour income in the current time period, in the real interest rate in the current time period, and in the real level of financial assets relative to production in the preceding time period.

The assumptions specified by (A.58) imply that a rise in current production, brought about, for example, by an expansive monetary policy after nominal wage contracts have been fixed, raises domestic demand in the current time period. The increase in domestic demand is smaller than the production increase in the current time period. Correspondingly, a rise in government purchases of goods and services, a reduction in taxation, a lowering of the real interest rate, and a rise in the households' real financial wealth increase domestic demand relative to production in the current time period.

A.9   Bank deposits

Chapter 5 examines monopolistic competition in bank markets. Bank deposits with a fixed nominal interest are introduced as a separate asset alongside with securities and legal tender. The specification of inter-temporal optimisation given by (A.11) is unchanged. The period utility function and the budgetary constraint can be specified as

$$u_T^h = u_c^h(C_{A,T}^h, C_{B,T}^h) + u_m^h\left(\ell_T^h, B_T^h\right), \quad T = t, t, \ldots, \quad h = 1, 2, \ldots,$$

$$\frac{\partial u_T^h}{\partial B_T^h} > 0, \quad \frac{\partial^2 u_T^h}{\partial (B_T^h)^2} < 0, \quad \frac{\partial u_T^h}{\partial(\ell_T^h)} > 0, \quad \frac{\partial^2 u_T^h}{\partial(\ell_T^h)^2} < 0, \tag{A.59}$$

$$\ell_{T-1}^h P_{T-1} + S_{T-1}^h(1 + i_{T-1}) + B_{T-1}^h P_{T-1}(1 + \rho_{T-1}) + W_T(1 - \tau_T)\Gamma_T^h\left(\frac{L_T}{L_T''}\right)$$

$$= P_T C_T^h + S_T^h + B_T^h P_T + \ell_T^h P_T + \tau + \Theta_T^h,$$

$$\tau = \ell^h P_{t-1} - \ell_T^h P_T,$$

$$\Theta_T^h \equiv B_{T-1}^h P_{T-1}(1 + \rho_{T-1}) - B_T^h P_T$$

$$+ \Gamma_T^h\left[v_T^b - B_{T-1}P_{T-1}(1 + \rho_{T-1}) + B_T P_T\right], \tag{A.60}$$

where B is real bank deposits, ℓ the real value of legal tender, ρ the nominal interest rate on bank deposits, and Θ^h dividend payments from banks to households.

Relation (A.59) shows that positive but declining marginal utility is derived from real bank deposits and real legal tender. (A.60) gives the household budgetary constraint. We assume that households receive transfers from the government and the banks which correspond to the government and the bank earnings from issuing money. This means that inflation tax/seigniorage has no impact on the household budgetary constraint. In addition, households receive dividend payments from the banks corresponding to bank profit (with the deduction of the transfers which neutralise the household losses from bank revenue from inflation). Dividend payments and transfers from banks and the government are paid as lump sums.

Optimising (A.11) and (A.59) with respect to real bank deposits and real legal tender and using (A.60) gives

$$\frac{\partial u_t}{\partial B_t^h} = u'_{A,t}\left(\frac{r_t - \varpi_t}{1 + r_t}\right), \quad 1 + \varpi_t \equiv (1 + \rho_t)\frac{P_{t+1}}{P_t}, \tag{A.61}$$

$$\frac{\partial u_t}{\partial \ell_t^h} = P_t u'_{A,t}\left(\frac{i_t}{1 + i_t}\right), \tag{A.62}$$

where ϖ shows the real interest rate on bank deposits.

Relations (A.61) and (A.62) show the conditions for equilibrium in respectively the market for bank deposits and the market for legal tender.

We assume that the household derives declining marginal utility from larger holdings of legal tender and bank deposits. Assuming a Cobb–Douglas function with respect to utility from bank deposits and legal tender, we obtain

$$u_{m,t} = (\ell_t)^{\sigma_1}(B_t)^{\sigma_2}, \quad 1 > \sigma_i > 0, \quad \sigma_1 + \sigma_2 < 1, \quad i = 1, 2. \tag{A.63}$$

Using (A.63) in (A.61) and (A.62), gives the following specification of optimum conditions

$$b_t = b_1\left(\frac{1}{u'_{A,t}}\right) - b_2 \log\left(\frac{r_t - \varpi_t}{1 + r_t}\right) - b_3 \log\left(\frac{i_t}{1 + i_t}\right) + \mu_t,$$

$$\mu \equiv \left(\frac{\sigma_1}{1 - \sigma_1 - \sigma_2}\right)\log(\sigma_1) + \left(\frac{1 - \sigma_1}{1 - \sigma_1 - \sigma_2}\right)\log(\sigma_2),$$

$$b_1 = \frac{1}{1 - \sigma_1 - \sigma_2} > 1, \quad b_2 \equiv \left(\frac{1 - \sigma_1}{1 - \sigma_1 - \sigma_2}\right) > 1,$$

$$b_3 = \left(\frac{\sigma_1}{1 - \sigma_1 - \sigma_2}\right) > 1, \tag{A.64}$$

$$\ell_t = \ell_1\left(\frac{1}{u'_{A,t}}\right) + \ell_2\log(1 + \varpi_t) - \ell_2\log(1 + r_t) - \ell_3\log\left(\frac{i_t}{1 + i_t}\right) + \Xi_t,$$

$$\Xi_t \equiv -\left(\frac{1 - \sigma_2}{1 - \sigma_1 - \sigma_2}\right)\log(\sigma_1) + \left(\frac{\sigma_2}{1 - \sigma_1 - \sigma_2}\right)\log(\sigma_2),$$

$$\ell_1 = \frac{1}{1 - \sigma_1 - \sigma_2}, \quad \ell_2 = \frac{\sigma_2}{1 - \sigma_1 - \sigma_2}, \quad \ell_3 = \frac{1 - \sigma_2}{1 - \sigma_1 - \sigma_2}. \tag{A.65}$$

Relations (A.64)–(A.65) specify the demands for respectively bank deposits and legal tender. These relations correspond to the demand functions used in chapter 5 except that the marginal utility of consumption of domestic goods, that is, $u'_{A,t}$, has been replaced by the inverse of production, that is, $1/Y$.

A.10 The securities markets

It is assumed in most analyses that fixed interest rate securities denominated in the domestic and foreign currency are perfect substitutes. This means that the uncovered interest rate parity holds, implying that the return on foreign currency securities corresponds to the return which can be obtained on a security denominated in the domestic currency adjusted for the expected exchange rate change. This gives

$$\log(1 + i_t) = \log(1 + i_t^B) + E_t(x_{t+1} - x_t), \tag{A.66}$$

where $E_t(\cdot)$ shows the expectation at time t concerning a variable.

Using the definitions of the real interest rate and of the real exchange rate given by (A.4) and (A.13), the uncovered interest rate parity specified by (A.68) can be rewritten as

$$\log(1 + r_t) = \log(1 + r_t^B) + E_t(e_{t+1} - e_t), \tag{A.67}$$

where e is the logarithmic value of the real exchange rate.

In the case where (i) the actual shifts in functional relationships occur unexpectedly to all agents, (ii) shifts in functional relationships and in exogenous variables determining the real exchange rate are expected to be permanent, that is, they lie at unchanged levels in each time period, and (iii) the economic structure is such that variables are adjusted instantaneously to the new equilibrium, that is, there are no lags, the real exchange rate expected in a future time period equals the real exchange rate in the current time period, that is

$$E_t(e_{t+1}) = e_t. \tag{A.68}$$

In this case, combining (A.67) and (A.68) shows that the real interest rate is permanent and uniform in all countries and lies at the same level in each time period, that is

$$r_{t+1} = r_t = r^B. \tag{A.69}$$

The assumptions of perfect international financial integration and permanent and unexpected shifts in the exogenous variables and functional relationships that determine the real exchange rate, thus imply a real interest rate which is uniform in all countries.

A.11   Summary and conclusion

The appendix has discussed the most important assumptions which are generally used in models throughout the book. These assumptions are: (i) perfect competition in the goods market, (ii) imperfect substitution among domestic and foreign goods, (iii) that households determine saving to optimise inter-temporal utility, (iv) that financial markets are perfect, the interest rate being exogenous to the firm, (v) that expectations are formed rationally, and (vi) that there is perfect substitution among domestic and foreign securities. The basis of the analysis is an overlapping generations model. We examine a steady-state equilibrium, which is characterised by (i) a constant growth rate in production and (ii) financial variables which lie in each time period at constant levels relative to nominal production. In the overlapping generations framework, fiscal policy is effective in affecting the demand for goods in a steady-state equilibrium when production growth exceeds the real interest rate.

Bibliography

Abraham, K. and Haltiwanger, J. C. (1995). Real Wages and the Business Cycle. *Journal of Economic Literature*, 33, 1215–1264.

Abuaf, N. and Jorion, P. (1990). Purchasing Power Parity in the Long Run. *The Journal of Finance*, 45, 157–174.

Adler, M. and Dumas, B. (1983). International Portfolio Choice and Corporation Finance: A Synthesis. *The Journal of Finance*, 38, 925–984.

Agell, J., Calmfors, L., and Jonsson, G. (1996). Fiscal Policy when Monetary Policy is Tied to the Past. *European Economic Review*, 40, 1413–1440.

Akerlof, G. A., Dickens, W. T. and Perry, G. L. (1996). The Macroeconomics of Low Inflation. *Brooking Papers on Economic Activity*, no. 1, 1–76.

Akerlof, G. A. and Yellen, J. L. (1985). A Near-Rational Model of the Business Cycle, with Wage and Price Inertia. *Quarterly Journal of Economics*, 100 Supplement, 823–838.

Alesina, A. and Cukierman, A. (1990). The Politics of Ambiguity. *The Quarterly Journal of Economics*, 105, 829–850.

Alesina, A. and Grilli, V. (1991). The European Central Bank: Reshaping Monetary Politics in Europe. National Bureau of Economic Research, working paper no. 3860.

(1994). The European Central Bank: Reshaping Monetary Policies in Europe. In T. Persson and G. Tabellini (eds.), *Monetary and Fiscal Policy – Volume I: Credibility*. The MIT Press, 247–277.

Alogoskoufis, G. S. (1989a). Monetary, Nominal Income and Exchange Rate Targets in a Small Open Economy. *European Economic Review*, 33, 687–705.

(1989b). Stabilization Policy, Fixed Exchange Rates and Target Zones. In M. Miller, B. Eichengreen, and R. Portes (eds.), *Blueprints for Exchange-Rate Management*. Academic Press, 75–94.

(1994). On Inflation, Unemployment, and the Optimum Exchange Rate Regime. In F. van der Ploeg (ed.), *The Handbook of International Macroeconomics*. Blackwell, 192–223.

Alogoskoufis, G. S. and Smith, R. (1991). The Phillips Curve, the Persistence of Inflation and the Lucas Critique: Evidence from Exchange-Rate Regimes. *American Economic Review*, 81, 1254–1275.

Andersen, P. S. (1989). Inflation and Output: A Review of the Wage-Price Mechanism. *Bank for International Settlements Economic Papers* 24.

Andersen, T. M. and Risager, O. (1991). The Role of Credibility for the Effects of a Change in the Exchange-Rate Policy. *Oxford Economic Papers*, 43, 85–98.

Andrés, J., Doménech, R., and Molinas, C. (1996). Macroeconomic Performance and Convergence in OECD Countries. *European Economic Review*, 40, 1683–1704.

Andrés, J., and Hernando, I. (1997). Does Inflation Harm Economic Growth? Evidence for the OECD. National Bureau of Economic Research, working paper no. 6062.

Andrés, J., Hernando, I., and Kruger, M. (1996). Growth, Inflation and the Exchange Rate Regime. *Economics Letters*, 53, 61–65.

Argy V., McKibbin, W., and Siegloff, E. (1989). Exchange-Rate Regimes for a Small Economy in a Multi-Country World. *Princeton Studies of International Finance*, 67.

Artis, M. J. and Taylor, M. P. (1988). Exchange Rates, Interest Rates, Capital Controls and the European Monetary System: Assessing the Track Record. In F. Giavazzi, S. Micossi, and M. Miller (eds.), *The European Monetary System*. Cambridge University Press, 185–206.

(1994). The Stabilizing Effect of the ERM on Exchange Rates and Interest Rates. *IMF Staff Papers*, 41, 123–148.

Artus, P. (1991). The European Monetary System, Exchange Rate Expectations and the Reputation of the Authorities. In C. Carraro, D. Laussel, M. Salmon, and A. Soubeyran (eds.), *International Economic Policy Co-ordination*. Basil Blackwell, 9–34.

Backus, D. K. and Driffill, J. (1985). Inflation and Reputation. *American Economic Review*, 75, 530–538.

Backus, D. K. and Kehoe, P. J. (1992). International Evidence on the Historical Properties of Business Cycles. *American Economic Review*, 82, 864–888.

Backus, D. K. and Smith, G. W. (1993). Consumption and Real Exchange Rates in Dynamic Economies with Non-Traded Goods. *Journal of International Economics*, 35, 297–316.

Baillie, R. T. and Osterberg, W. P. (1997). Why do Central Banks Intervene? *Journal of International Money and Finance*, 16, 909–919.

Balduzzi, P. (1995). Stock Returns, Inflation, and the 'Proxy Hypothesis': A New Look at the Data. *Economics Letters*, 48, 47–53.

Ball, L. (1992). Why Does High Inflation Raise Inflation Uncertainty? *Journal of Monetary Economics*, 29, 371–388.

Baltensperger, E. (1980). Alternative Approaches to the Theory of the Banking Firm. *Journal of Monetary Economics*, 6, 1–37.

Barnett, W. A. (1997). Which Road Leads to Stable Money Demand? *The Economic Journal*, 107, 1171–1185.

Barnett, W. A. and Spindt, P. A. (1982). Divisia Monetary Aggregates: Their Compilation, Data and Historical Behaviour. Federal Reserve Board Staff Study, 116.

Barro, R. J. (1990). Government Spending in a Single Model of Endogenous Growth. *Journal of Political Economy*, 98, S103–S125.

(1995). Inflation and Economic Growth. *Bank of England Quarterly Bulletin*, May, 166–176.

Barro, R. J. and Gordon, D. B. (1983a). A Positive Theory of Monetary Policy in a Natural Rate Model. *Journal of Political Economy*, 91, 589–610.

(1983b). Rules, Discretion and Reputation in a Model of Monetary Policy. *Journal of Monetary Economics*, 12, 101–121.

Bayoumi, T. (1994). A Formal Model of Optimum Currency Areas. Centre for Economic Policy Research, discussion paper no. 968.

Bayoumi, T. and Gagnon, J. (1996). Taxation and Inflation: A New Explanation for Capital Flows. *Journal of Monetary Economics*, 38, 303–330.

Baxter, M. and Jerkmann, U. J. (1997). The International Diversification Puzzle is Worse than You Think. *American Economic Review*, 87, 170–180.

Baxter, M. and Stockman, A. C. (1989). Business Cycles and the Exchange-Rate Regime: Some International Evidence. *Journal of Monetary Economics*, 23, 377–400.

Bean, C. (1992). Economic and Monetary Union in Europe. *Journal of Economic Perspectives*, 6, 31–52.

Benassy, J.-P. (1995a). Money and Wage Contracts in an Optimizing Model of the Business Cycle. *Journal of Monetary Economics*, 35, 303–315.

(1995b). Nominal Rigidities in Wage Setting by Rational Trade Unions. *The Economic Journal*, 105, 635–643.

Bernanke, B. S. (1983). Nonmonetary Effects of the Financial Collapse in the Propagation of the Great Depression. *American Economic Review*, 73, 257–276.

Bernanke, B. S. and Blinder, A. S. (1988). Credit, Money, and Aggregate Demand. *American Economic Review*, 78, 435–439.

(1992). The Federal Funds Rate and the Channels of Monetary Transmission. *American Economic Review*, 82, 901–921.

Bernanke, B. S. and Gertler, M. (1989). Agency Costs, Net Worth and Business Fluctuations. *American Economic Review*, 79, 14–31.

(1990). Financial Fragility and Economic Performance. *Quarterly Journal of Economics*, 105, 87–114.

(1995). Inside the Black Box: The Credit Channel of Monetary Policy Transmission. National Bureau of Economic Research, working paper no. 5146.

Bernanke, B. S., Gertler, M., and Watson, M. (1997). Systematic Monetary Policy and the Effects of Oil Price Shocks. *Brookings Papers on Economic Activity*, no. 1, 91–157.

Bernanke, B. S. and Mishkin, F. (1992). Central Bank Behavior and the Strategy of Monetary Policy: Observations from Six Industrialised Countries. National Bureau of Economic Research, working paper no. 4082.

Bhandari, J. S. (1985). World Trade Patterns, Economic Disturbances and Exchange-Rate Management. *Journal of International Money and Finance*, 4, 331–360.

Bianchi, M. and Zoega, G. (1997). Challenges Facing Natural Rate Theory. *European Economic Review*, 41, 535–547.

Blanchard, O. J. (1990). Why Does Money Affect Output? A Survey. In B. M. Friedman and F. H. Hahn (eds.), *Handbook of Monetary Economics, vol. II*. North-Holland, 779–835.

Blanchard, O. J. and Katz, L. F. (1997). What We Know and Do Not Know About the Natural Rate of Unemployment? *Journal of Economic Perspectives*, 11, 51–72.

Bofinger, P. (1994). Is Europe An Optimum Currency Area? Centre for Economic Policy Research, discussion paper no. 915.

Bohn, H. (1991). Time Consistency of Monetary Policy in the Open Economy. *Journal of International Economics*, 30, 249–266.

Booth, A. L. (1995). *The Economics of the Trade Union*. Cambridge University Press.

Bordo, M. D., Choudhri, E. U., and Schwartz, A. J. (1995). Could Stable Money Have Averted the Great Contraction? *Economic Inquiry*, 33, 484–505.

Boschen, J. F. and Mills, L. O. (1994). Tests of Long-Run Neutrality Using Permanent Monetary and Real Shocks. *Journal of Monetary Economics*, 35, 25–44.

Bottazzi, L. and Manasse, P. (1998). Bankers' versus Workers' Europe (I): Adverse Selection in EMU. Centre for Economic Policy Research, discussion paper no. 1846.

Bottazzi, L., Pesenti, P., and van Wincoop, E. (1996). Wages, Profits and the International Portfolio Puzzle. *European Economic Review*, 40, 219–254.

Boughton, J. M. (1984). Exchange Rate Movements and Adjustment in Financial Markets: Quarterly Estimates for Major Currencies. *IMF Staff Papers*, 31, 445–468.

Branson, W. H. (1990). Financial Market Integration and Macro-economic Policy in 1992. Working paper at the conference on 'Financial regulation and monetary arrangements after 1992', Marstrand, May 1990.

Branson, W. H. and Henderson, D. W. (1985). The Specification and Influence of Asset Markets. In R. W. Jones and P. B. Kenen (eds.), *Handbook of International Economics, vol. II*. Elsevier Science Publishers, 745–805.

Brennan, M. J. and Cao, H. H. (1997). International Portfolio Investment Flows. *The Journal of Finance*, 52, 1851–1880.

Brock, W. (1974). Money and Growth: The Use of Long Run Perfect Foresight. *International Economic Review*, 15, 750–777.

Brunner, K. (1971). A Survey of Selected Issues in Monetary Theory. *Schweizerische Zeitschrift für Volkswirtschaft und Statistik*, 9–135.

Bruno, M. (1991). High Inflation and the Nominal Anchor in an Open Economy. *Princeton Essays in International Finance*, 183.

(1995). Inflation and Growth in an Integrated Approach. *Understanding Interdependence: The Macroeconomics of the Open Economy*. Princeton University Press, 313–367.

Bruno, M. and Easterly, W. (1998). Inflation Crises and Long-Run Growth. *Journal of Monetary Economics*, 41, 3–26.

Buiter, W. (1995). Macroeconomic Policy during a Transition to Monetary Union. Centre for Economic Policy Research, discussion paper no. 1222.

Bullard, J. and Keating, J. W. (1995). The Long-Run Relationship between Inflation and Output in Postwar Economies. *Journal of Monetary Economics*, 36, 477–496.

Calmfors, L. and Driffill, J. (1988). Centralization of Wage Bargaining. *Economic Policy*, 8, 13–61.

Caporale, G. M., Kalyvitis, S., and Pittis, N. (1994). Persistence in Real Variables under Alternative Exchange Rate Regimes: Some Multi-Country Evidence. *Economics Letters*, 45, 93–102.

Caporale, G. M. and Pittis, N. (1995). Nominal Exchange Rate Regimes and the Stochastic Behavior of Real Variables. *Journal of International Money and Finance*, 14, 395–415.

Chari, V. V., Christiano, J., and Kehoe, P. J. (1996). Optimality of the Friedman Rule in Economies with Distorting Taxes. *Journal of Monetary Economics*, 37, 203–223.

Chinn, M. and Frankel, J. (1994). Patterns in Exchange Rate Forecasts for Twenty-Five Currencies. *Journal of Money, Credit, and Banking*, 26, 759–767.

Christiano, L. J. and Ljungqvist, L. (1988). Money Does Not Granger-Cause Output in the Bivariate Output-Money Relation. *Journal of Monetary Economics*, 22, 217–235.

Clarida, R., Gali, J., and Gertler, M. (1997). Monetary Policy Rules in Practice: Some International Evidence. Centre for Economic Policy Research, discussion paper no. 1750.

Clark, T. E. (1997). Cross-Country Evidence on Long-Run Growth and Inflation. *Economic Inquiry*, 35, 70–81.

Clower, R.W. (1967). A Reconsideration of the Microfoundations of Monetary Theory. *Western Economic Journal*, 6, 1–9. [Reprinted in R. W. Clower (ed.), *Monetary Theory*, Penguin, 1969, 202–211.]

Cochrane, J. H. (1998). What do the VARs Mean? Measuring the Output Effects of Monetary Policy. *Journal of Monetary Economics*, 41, 277–300.

Cohen, D. (1985). Inflation, Wealth and Interest Rates in an Intertemporal Optimizing Model. *Journal of Monetary Economics*, 1, 73–85.

Cohen, D. and Wyplosz, C. (1989). The European Monetary System: An Agnostic Evaluation. In R. C. Bryant, D. A. Currie, J. A. Frenkel, P. R. Masson, and R. Portes (eds.), *Macroeconomic Policies in an Interdependent World*. The Brookings Institution, Centre for Economic Policy Research, International Monetary Fund, 311–337.

Coleman, W. J. (1996). Money and Output: A Test of Reverse Causation. *American Economic Review*, 86, 90–111.

Committee for the Study of Economic and Monetary Union (1989). *Report on Economic and Monetary Union in the European Community* (Delors report).

Committee on the Working of the Monetary System (1959). Radcliffe Report, Cmnd. 827, HMSO.

Cooley, T. F. and Hansen, G. D. (1989). The Inflation Tax in a Real Business Cycle Model. *American Economic Review*, 79, 733–748.

Cooper, I. A. and Kaplanis, B. (1994). Home Bias in Equity Portfolios, Inflation Hedging, and International Capital Market Equilibrium Investment. *Review of Financial Studies*, 7, 45–60.

Correia, I. and Teles, P. (1996). Is the Friedman Rule Optimal When Money is an Intermediate Good. *Journal of Monetary Economics*, 38, 223–244.

Cowder, W. J. and Hoffman, D. L. (1996). The Long-Run Relationship between Nominal Interest Rates and Inflation: The Fisher Equation Revisited. *Journal of Money, Credit, and Banking*, 28, 102–118.

Cukierman, A. (1982). Relative Price Variability, Inflation and the Allocative Efficiency of the Price System. *Journal of Monetary Economics*, 9, 131–162.

   (1992). *Central Bank Strategy, Credibility, and Independence: Theory and Evidence*. MIT Press.

Cukierman, A. and Meltzer, A. H. (1986). A Theory of Ambiguity, Credibility, and Inflation under Discretion and Asymmetric Information. *Econometrica*, 54, 1099–1228.

Currie, D. (1992). European Monetary Union: Institutional Structure and Economic Performance. *The Economic Journal*, 102, 248–264.

Cushman, D. A. and Zha, T. (1997). Identifying Monetary Policy in a Small Open Economy under Flexible Exchange Rates. *Journal of Monetary Economics*, 39, 433–448.

Cuthbertson, K. (1997). Microfoundations and the Demand for Money. *The Economic Journal*, 107, 1186–1201.

Danthine, J.-P. and Hunt, J. (1994). Wage Bargaining Structure, Employment and Economic Integration. *The Economic Journal*, 104, 528–541.

Daveri, F. and Tabellini, G. (1997). Unemployment, Growth and Taxation in Industrial Countries. Centre for Economic Policy Research, discussion paper no. 1681.

Davis, G. and Kanago, B. (1996). On Measuring the Effect of Inflation Uncertainty on Real GDP Growth. *Oxford Economic Papers*, 48, 163–175.

Davis, M. S. and Tanner, J. E. (1997). Money and Economic Activity Revisited. *Journal of International Money and Finance*, 16, 955–968.

De Grauwe, P. (1997). Exchange Rate Arrangements between the Ins and the Outs. Centre for European Policy Research, discussion paper no. 1640.

De Gregorio, J. (1993). Inflation, Taxation and Long-Run Growth. *Journal of Monetary Economics*, 31, 271–298.

De Gregorio, J., Giovannini, A., and Wolf, H. C. (1994). Terms of Trade, Productivity, and the Real Exchange Rate. National Bureau of Economic Research, working paper no. 4807.

Devereux, M. (1989). A Positive Theory of Inflation and Inflation Variance. *Economic Inquiry*, 27, 105–116.

De Vries, C. G. (1994). Stylized Facts of Nominal Exchange Rate Returns. In F. van der Ploeg (ed.), *The Handbook of International Macroeconomics*. Blackwell, 348–389.

Diamond, D. W. (1984). Financial Intermediation and Delegated Monitoring. *Review of Economic Studies*, 51, 393–414.

Diba, B. T. and Martin, P. (1995). Causality Implications of the Public-Finance Approach to Inflation and Seigniorage. Centre for Economic Policy Research, discussion paper no. 1121.

Diebold, F. X. and Pauly, P. (1988). Endogenous Risk in a Portfolio-Balance Rational-Expectations Model of the Deutschemark–Dollar Rate. *European Economic Review*, 32, 27–53.

Dixon, H. (1995). Of Coconuts, Decomposition, and a Jackass: The Genealogy of the Natural Rate. In R. Cross (ed.), *The Natural Rate of Unemployment: Reflections on 25 Years of the Hypothesis*. Cambridge University Press, 57–74.

Domberger, S. (1987). Relative Price Variability and Inflation: A Disaggregated Analysis. *Journal of Political Economy*, 95, 547–566.

Dominguez, K. and Frankel, J. (1993a). *Does Foreign Exchange Intervention Work?* Institute for International Economics.

(1993b). Does Foreign Exchange Intervention Matter? The Portfolio Effect. *American Economic Review*, 83, 1356–1369.

Dooley, M. (1996). A Survey of Literature on Controls over International Capital Transactions. *IMF Staff Papers*, 43, 639–687.

Dornbusch, R. (1989). Discussion. In M. Cecco and A. Giovannini (eds.), *A European Central Bank? Perspectives on Monetary Unification after Ten Years of EMS*. Cambridge University Press, 79–84.

Dornbusch, R., Favero, C. and Giavazzi, F. (1998a). Immediate Challenges for the ECB. *Economic Policy*, 26, 17–64.

(1998b). A Red Letter Day? Centre for Economic Policy Research, discussion paper no. 1804.

Dornbusch, R. and Giovannini, A. (1990). Monetary Policy in the Open Economy. In B. M. Friedman and F. H. Hahn (eds.), *Handbook of Monetary Economics, vol. II*. North-Holland, 1231–1303.

Drazen, A. (1981). Inflation and Capital Accumulation under a Finite Horizon. *Journal of Monetary Economics*, 8, 247–260.

(1989). Monetary Policy, Capital Controls and Seigniorage in an Open Economy. In M. Cecco and A. Giovannini (eds.), *A European Central Bank? Perspectives on Monetary Unification after Ten Years of EMS*. Cambridge University Press, 13–32.

Drazen, A. and Hamermesh, D. S. (1986). Inflation and Wage Dispersion. National Bureau of Economic Research, working paper no. 1811.

Duca, J. V. (1987). The Spillover Effects of Nominal Wage Rigidity in a Multisector Economy. *Journal of Money, Credit, and Banking*, 19, 117–121.

Dumas, B. (1994). Partial Equilibrium Versus General Equilibrium Models of the International Capital Markets. In F. van der Ploeg (ed.), *The Handbook of International Macroeconomics*. Blackwell, 301–347.

Dutkowsky, D. H. and Dunsky, R. M. (1996). Intertemporal Substitution, Money, and Aggregate Labor Supply. *Journal of Money, Credit, and Banking*, 28, 216–232.

EC Commission (Commission for the European Communities) (1990a). Economic and Monetary Union: The Economic Rationale and Design of the System.

(1990b). One market, one money: An evaluation of the potential benefits and costs of forming an economic and monetary union. *European Economy*, no. 44.

Edey, M. (1994). Costs and Benefits of Moving from Low Inflation to Price Stability. *OECD Economic Studies*, 23, 109–130.

Edison, H. J. and Pauls, B. D. (1992). A Re-Assessment of the Relationship Between Real Exchange Rates and Real Interest Rates: 1974–1990. *Journal of Monetary Economics*, 31, 165–187.

Eichengreen, B. (1990). One Money for Europe? Lessons from the US Currency Union. *Economic Policy*, 10, 118–187.

(1993). European Monetary Unification. *Journal of Economic Literature*, 31, 1321–1357.

Eichengreen, B., Tobin, J., and Wyplosz, C. (1995). Two Cases for Sand in the Wheels of International Finance. *The Economic Journal*, 105, 162–172.

Evans, M. (1991). Discovering the Link between Inflation Rates and Inflation Uncertainty. *Journal of Money, Credit, and Banking*, 23, 169–184.

(1998). Real Rates, Expected Inflation, and Inflation Risk Premia. *The Journal of Finance*, 53, 187–220.

Evans, M. and Lewis, K. K. (1995). Do Expected Shifts in Inflation Policy Affect Estimates of the Long-Run Fisher Relation? *The Journal of Finance*, 50, 225–253.

Evans, M. and Lothian, J. R. (1993). The Response of Exchange Rates to Permanent and Transitory Shocks under Floating Exchange Rates. *Journal of International Money and Finance*, 11, 563–586.

Evans, M. and Wachtel, P. (1993). Inflation Regimes and the Sources of Inflation Uncertainty. *Journal of Money, Credit, and Banking*, 25, 475–518.

Fama, E. F. (1981). Stock Returns, Real Activity, Inflation, and Money. *American Economic Review*, 71, 545–546.

Fama, E. F. and Gibbons, M. R. (1982). Inflation, Real Returns and Capital Investments. *Journal of Monetary Economics*, 9, 297–323.

Farber, H. S. (1986). The Analysis of Union Behavior. In O. Ashenfelter and R. Layard (eds.), *Handbook in Labor Economics*. Elsevier Science Publishers, 1039–1089.

Faruqee, H. (1995). Long-Run Determinants of the Real Exchange Rate: A Stock-Flow Perspective. *IMF Staff Papers*, 42, 80–107.

Feldstein, M. (1997). The Political Economy of the European Economic and Monetary Union: Political Sources of an Economic Liability. *Journal of Economic Perspectives*, 11, 23–42.

Fischer, S. (1977). Long Term Contracts, Rational Expectations and the Optimal Money Supply Rule. *Journal of Political Economy*, 85, 191–205.

(1979). Capital Accumulation on the Transition Path in a Monetary Optimizing Model. *Econometrica*, 47, 1433–1439.

(1988). Recent Developments in Macroeconomics. *Economic Journal*, 98, 294–339.

(1990). Rules versus Discretion in Monetary Policy. In B. M. Friedman and F. Hahn (eds.), *Handbook of Monetary Economics, vol. II.* North-Holland, 1156–1184.

(1993). The Role of Macroeconomic Factors in Growth. *Journal of Monetary Economics*, 32, 485–512.

(1995). Modern Approaches to Central Banking. National Bureau of Economic Research, working paper no. 5064.

Fischer, S. and Modigliani, F. (1978). Towards an Understanding of the Real Effects and Costs of Inflation. *Weltwirtschaftliches Archiv*, 114, 810–833.

Fisher, M. E. and Seater, J. J. (1993). Long-Run Neutrality and Superneutrality in an ARIMA Framework. *American Economic Review*, 83, 402–415.

Flood, R. P. and Isard, P. (1989). Monetary Policy Strategies. *IMF Staff Papers*, 36, 612–632.

Flood, R. P. and Rose, A. K. (1993). Fixing Exchange Rates: A Virtual Quest for Fundamentals. Centre for Economic Policy Research, discussion paper no. 838.

French, K. R. and Poterba, J. M. (1991). Investor Diversification and International Equity Markets. *American Economic Review*, 81, 222–226.

Friedman, B. M. (1995). Does Monetary Policy Affect Real Economic Activity? Why Do We Still Ask this Question? National Bureau of Economic Research, working paper no. 5212.

(1997). Comment. *Brookings Papers on Economic Activity*, no. 1, 148–153.

Friedman, B. M. and Kuttner, K. N. (1993). Economic Activity in the Short-Term Credit Markets: An Analysis of Prices and Quantities. *Brookings Papers on Economic Activity*, no. 2, 193–266.

Friedman, M. (1968). The Role of Monetary Policy. *American Economic Review*, 58, 1–17.

(1969). *The Optimum Quantity of Money*. Chicago University Press.

Friedman, M. and Schwartz, A. J. (1963). *A Monetary History of the United States, 1867–1960*. Princeton University Press.

(1986). Has Government Any Role in Money? *Journal of Monetary Economics*, 17, 37–62.

Fuerst, T. S. (1992). Liquidity, Loanable Funds and Real Activity. *Journal of Monetary Economics*, 29, 3–24.

Fukao, M. (1987). A Risk Premium Model of the Yen-Dollar and DM-Dollar Exchange Rates. *OECD Economic Studies*, 9, 79–104.

Fukao, M. and Hanazaki, M. (1986). Internationalization of Financial Markets: Some Implications for Macroeconomic Policy and for the Allocation of Capital. OECD working paper, no. 37.

Garber, P. and Taylor, M. P. (1995). Sand in the Wheels of Foreign Exchange Markets: A Sceptical Note. *The Economic Journal*, 105, 173–180.

Giavazzi, F. (1989). The Exchange Rate Question in Europe. In R. C. Bryant, D. C. Currie, J. A. Frenkel, P. R. Masson and R. Portes (eds.), *Macroeconomic Policies in an Interdependent World*. The Brookings Institution, Centre for Economic Policy Research, International Monetary Fund, 283–304.

(1990). The EMS: Lessons from Europe and Perspectives in Europe. In P. Ferri (ed.), *Prospects for the European Monetary System*. Macmillan, 36–55.

Giavazzi, F. and Giovannini, A. (1989). *Limiting Exchange Rate Flexibility: The European Monetary System*. MIT Press.

Giavazzi, F. and Pagano, M. (1988). The Advantage of Tying One's Hands. *European Economic Review*, 32, 1055–1082.

Gillman, M. (1993). The Welfare Cost of Inflation in a Cash-in-Advance Economy With Costly Credit. *Journal of Monetary Economics*, 31, 97–115.

Giovannini, A. (1990a). Currency Substitution and Monetary Policy. Working paper from the conference 'Financial regulation and monetary arrangements after 1992', Marstrand, 20–24 May 1990.

(1990b). European Monetary Reform: Progress and Prospects. *Brookings Papers on Economic Activity*, 2, 217–291.

Giovannini, A. and Turtelboom, B. (1994). Currency Substitution. In F. van der Ploeg (ed.), *The Handbook of International Macroeconomics*. Blackwell, 390–436.

Golub, S. S. (1989). Foreign-Currency Government Debt, Asset Markets, and the Balance of Payments. *Journal of International Money and Finance*, 8, 285–294.

Gomme, P. (1993). Money and Growth Revisited – Measuring the Costs of Inflation in an Endogenous Growth Model. *Journal of Monetary Economics*, 32, 51–77.

Gordon, R. J. (1995). Is There a Trade-Off between Unemployment and Productivity Growth? Centre for Economic Policy Research, discussion paper no. 1159.

(1996). Macroeconomic Policy in the Presence of Structural Maladjustment. *Centre for Economic Policy Research*, discussion paper no. 1493.

(1997). The Time-Varying NAIRU and its Implications for Economic Policy. *Journal of Economic Perspectives*, 11, 11–32.

Greenwald, B. C. and Stiglitz, J. E. (1993). Financial Market Imperfections and Business Cycles. *Quarterly Journal of Economics*, 108, 77–114.

Grilli, V. (1989). Financial Markets. *Economic Policy*, 9, 388–411.

Grilli, V. and Milesi-Ferretti, G. M. (1995). Economic Effects and Structural Determinants of Capital Controls. *IMF Staff Papers*, 42, 517–551.

Gros, D. (1989). Seigniorage in the EC: The Implications of the EMS and Financial Market Integration. IMF Working Paper, no. 89/7.

Gurley, J. G. and Shaw, E. S. (1960). *Money in a Theory of Finance*. The Brookings Institution.

Gylfason, T. and Herbertsson, T. T. (1996). Does Inflation Matter for Growth? Centre for Economic Policy Research, discussion paper no. 1503.

Hansen, L. P. and Hodrick, R. J. (1983). Risk Averse Speculations in the Forward Exchange Market: An Econometric Analysis of Linear Models. In J. A. Frenkel (ed.), *Exchange Rates and International Macroeconomics*. University of Chicago Press.

Hasan, S. and Wallace, M. (1996). Real Exchange Rate Volatility and Exchange Rate Regimes: Evidence from Long-Term Data. *Economics Letters*, 52, 67–73.

Haug, A. A. and Lucas, R. F. (1997). Long-Run Neutrality and Superneutrality in an ARIMA Framework: Comment. *American Economic Review*, 87, 756–759.

Hayek, F. A. (1978). *Denationalization of Money: The Argument Refined*. The Institute of Economic Affairs.

Heckman, J. J. (1993). What has been Learned about Labour Supply in the Past Twenty Years? *American Economic Review*, 83, 116–121.

Helpman, E. (1981). An Exploration in the Theory of Exchange-Rate Regimes. *Journal of Political Economy*, 89, 865–890.

Holland, A. S. (1993). Uncertain Effects of Money and the Link between the Inflation Rate and Inflation Uncertainty. *Economic Inquiry*, 31, 39–51.

(1995). Inflation and Uncertainty: Tests for Temporal Ordering. *Journal of Money, Credit and Banking*, 27, 827–837.

Hoon, H. T. and Phelps, E. S. (1992). Macroeconomic Shocks in a Dynamized Model of the Natural Rate of Unemployment. *American Economic Review*, 82, 889–900.

(1997). Growth, Wealth and the Natural Rate: Is Europe's Jobs Crisis a Growth Crisis? *European Economic Review*, 41, 549–557.

Hoover, K. D. and Perez, S. J. (1994a). Post Hoc Ergo Propter Once More – An Evaluation of 'Does Monetary Policy Matter?' in the Spirit of James Tobin. *Journal of Monetary Economics*, 34, 47–73.

(1994b). Money May Matter, But How Could You Know? *Journal of Monetary Economics*, 34, 84–99.

Horn, H. and Persson, T. (1988). Exchange Rate Policy, Wage Formation and Credibility. *European Economic Review*, 32, 1621–1636.

House of Lords (1989). *The Delors Committee Report*. Select Committee on the European Communities, Session 1989–1990.

Hubbard, R. G. (1998). Capital-Market Imperfections and Investment. *Journal of Economic Literature*, 36, 193–225.

Huh, C. G. (1993). Causality and Correlations of Output and Nominal Variables in a Real Business Cycle Model. *Journal of Monetary Economics*, 32, 147–168.

Huizinga, J. (1987). An Empirical Investigation of the Long-Run Behavior of Real Exchange Rates. *Carnegie-Rochester Conference Series on Public Policy*, 27, 149–214.

(1993). Inflation Uncertainty, Relative Price Uncertainty, and Investment in U.S. Manufacturing. *Journal of Money, Credit, and Banking*, 25, 521–549.

Ingram, J. C. (1973). The Case for European Monetary Integration. *Princeton Essays in International Finance*, 98.

Ireland, J. (1994). Money and Growth: An Alternative Approach. *American Economic Review*, 84, 47–65.

Isard, P. (1995). *Exchange Rate Economics*. Cambridge University Press.

Ishiyama, Y. (1975). The Theory of Optimum Currency Areas: A Survey. *IMF Staff Papers*, 22, 344–383.

Jefferson, P. N. (1997). On the Neutrality of Inside and Outside Money. *Economica*, 64, 567–586.

Jensen, H. (1994). Loss of Monetary Discretion in a Simple Dynamic Policy Game. *Journal of Economic Dynamics and Control*, 18, 763–779.

Johnson, H. G. (1968). Theoretical Problems of the International Monetary System. *Journal of Economic Studies*, 2, 3–35.

(1969a). The Case for Flexible Exchange Rates, 1969. *The Federal Reserve Bank of St. Louis Review*, 51, 12–24.

(1969b). Inside Money, Outside Money, Income, Wealth and Welfare in Monetary Theory. *Journal of Money, Credit, and Banking*, 1, 30–45.

(1972). The Keynesian Revolution and the Monetarist Counter-Revolution. In H. G. Johnson (ed.), *Further Essays in Monetary Economics*. George Allen & Unwin, 1972, 50–69.

Jorion, P. and Sweeney, R. J. (1996). Mean Reversion in Real Exchange Rates: Evidence and Implications for Forecasting. *Journal of International Money and Finance*, 15, 535–550.

Kandel, S., Ofer, A. R. and Sarig, O. (1996). Real Interest Rates and Inflation: An Ex-Ante Empirical Analysis. *The Journal of Finance*, 51, 205–225.

Karanassou, M. and Snower, D. J. (1996). Is The Natural Rate a Reference Point? Centre for Economic Policy Research, discussion paper no. 1507.

(1998). How Labour Market Flexibility Affects Unemployment: Long-Term Implications of the Chain Reaction Theory. *The Economic Journal*, 108, 832–849.

Kashyap, A. K. and Stein, J. C. (1994). Monetary Policy and Bank Lending. In N. G. Mankiw (ed.), *Monetary Policy*. University of Chicago Press, 221–256.

Kenen, P. B. (1969). The Theory of Optimum Currency Areas: An Eclectic View? In R. A. Mundell and A. K. Swoboda (eds.), *Monetary Problems of the International Economy*. University of Chicago Press, 41–60.

(1989). *Exchange Rates and Policy Coordination*. Manchester University Press.

(1995). Capital Controls, the EMS and EMU. *The Economic Journal*, 105, 181–192.

(1997). Preferences, Domains, and Sustainability. *American Economic Review*, 87, 211–213.

Keynes, J. M. (1936). *The General Theory of Employment, Interest and Money*. Macmillan, Cambridge University Press.

Kimbrough, K. P. (1984). Aggregate Information and the Role of Monetary Policy in an Open Economy. *Journal of Political Economy*, 92, 268–285.

King, R. G. and Plosser, C. I. (1984). Money, Credit, and Prices in a Real Business Cycle. *American Economic Review*, 74, 363–380.

King, R. G. and Watson, M. W. (1994). The Post-War U.S. Phillips Curve – A Revisionist Econometric History. *Carnegie-Rochester Conference Series on Public Policy*, 41, 157–219.

Krugman, P. (1995). What Do We Need to Know about the International Monetary System? In P. Kenen (ed.), *Understanding Interdependence: The Macroeconomics of the Open Economy*. Princeton University Press, 509–529.

Kuo, B.-S. and Mikkola, A. (1997). The Behaviour of the Real Exchange Rate: A Re-Examination Using Finite Sample Approach. Centre for Economic Policy Research, discussion paper no. 1716.

Kydland, F. E. and Prescott, E. C. (1977). Rules Rather than Discretion: The Inconsistency of Optimal Plans. *Journal of Political Economy*, 85, 473–493.

Lächler, U. (1985). Fixed versus Flexible Exchange Rates in an Equilibrium Business Cycle Model. *Journal of Monetary Economics*, 16, 95–107.

Laidler, D. (1997). Notes on the Microfoundations of Monetary Economics. *The Economic Journal*, 107, 1213–1223.

Layard, R. and Nickell, S. (1986). Unemployment in Britain. *Economica*, 53, 121–169.

Layard, R., Nickell, S., and Jackman, R. (1991). *Unemployment: Macroeconomic Performance and the Labour Market*. Oxford University Press.

Leeper, E. M. (1997). Narrative and VAR Approaches to Monetary Policy: Common Identification Problems. *Journal of Monetary Economics*, 40, 641–657.

Leeper, E. M., Sims, C. A. and Zha, T. (1996). What Does Monetary Policy Do? *Brookings Papers on Economic Activity*, No. 2, 1–78.

Levhari, D. and Patinkin, D. (1968). The Role of Money in a Simple Growth Model. *American Economic Review*, 58, 713–753.

Lewis, K. K. (1990). The Behavior of Eurocurrency Returns Across Different Holding Periods and Monetary Regimes. *The Journal of Finance*, 45, 1211–1236.

Lindbeck, A. (1998). New Keynesianism and Aggregate Economic Activity. *The Economic Journal*, 108, 167–180.

Lindbeck, A. and Snower, D. J. (1994). How Are Product Demand Changes Transmitted to the Labour Market? *The Economic Journal*, 104, 386–398.

Lothian, J. R. and Taylor, M. P. (1997). Real Exchange Rate Behavior. *Journal of International Money and Finance*, 16, 945–954.

Lucas, R. E. (1972). Expectations and the Neutrality of Money. *Journal of Economic Theory*, 4, 103–124.

(1978a). Asset Prices in an Exchange Economy. *Econometrica*.

(1978b). Unemployment Policy. *American Economic Review*, 68, 353–357.

(1981). Tobin and Monetarism: A Review Article. *Journal of Economic Literature*, 19, 558–567.

(1982). Interest Rates and Currency Prices in a Two-Country World. *Journal of Monetary Economics*, 10, 335–360.

(1986). Principles of Fiscal and Monetary Policy. *Journal of Monetary Economics*, 17, 117–134.

MacDonald, R. (1995). Long-Run Exchange Rate Modeling: A Survey of the Recent Evidence. *IMF Staff Papers*, 42, 437–489.

MacDonald, R. and Taylor, M. P. (1992). Exchange Rate Economics. *IMF Staff Papers*, 34, 1–57.

Madsen, J. B. (1998). General Equilibrium Macroeconomic Models of Unemployment: Can They Explain the Unemployment Path in the OECD? *The Economic Journal*, 108, 850–867.

Mankiw, N. G. (1985). Small Menu Costs and Large Business Cycles: A Macroeconomic Model of Monopoly. *Quarterly Journal of Economics*, 100, 529–539.

(1987). The Optimal Collection of Seigniorage: Theory and Evidence. *Journal of Monetary Economics*, 20, 327–341.

Mankiw, N. G. and Romer, D. (1991). Introduction. In N. G. Mankiw and D. Romer (eds.), *New Keynesian Economics, vol. I*. The MIT Press, 1–26.

Manzini, P. and Snower, D. J. (1996). On the Foundations of Wage Bargaining. Centre for Economic Policy Research, discussion paper no. 1514.

Mark, N. C. (1985a). On Time Varying Risk Premia in the Foreign Exchange Market. *Journal of Monetary Economics*, 16, 3–18.

(1985b). Some Evidence on the International Inequality of Real Interest Rates. *Journal of International Money and Finance*, 4, 189–208.

(1995). Exchange Rates and Fundamental Evidence on Long-Horizon Predictability. *American Economic Review*, 85, 201–218.

Marston, R. C. (1985). Stabilization Policies in Open Economies. In R. W. Jones and P. B. Kenen (eds.), *Handbook of International Economics, vol. II*. Elsevier Science Publishers, 859–916.

Marty, A. L. (1969). Notes on Money and Economic Growth. *Journal of Money, Credit, and Banking*, 1, 252–266.

Masson, P. R., Kremers, J., and Horne, J. (1994). Net Foreign Assets and International Adjustment: The United States, Japan and Germany. *Journal of International Money and Finance*, 13, 27–40.

McKinnon, R. I. (1963). Optimum Currency Areas. *American Economic Review*, 53, 717–725.

(1973). *Money and Capital in Economic Development*. Brookings Institution.

(1981). The Exchange Rate and Macroeconomic Policy: Changing Postwar Perceptions. *Journal of Economic Literature*, 19, 531–537.

Mishkin, F. (1992). Is the Fisher Effect for Real? *Journal of Monetary Economics*, 30, 195–215.

Moroney, J. R. (1972). The Current State of Money and Production Theory. *American Economic Review*, 62, 335–343.

Mundell, R. A. (1961). A Theory of Optimum Currency Areas. *American Economic Review*, 51, 657–665.

(1963). Inflation and Real Interest. *Journal of Political Economy*, 71, 280–283.

Mussa, M. (1986). Nominal Exchange Rate Regimes and the Behavior of Real Exchange Rates: Evidence and Implications Currency. *Carnegie-Rochester Series on Public Policy*, 25, 117–214.

(1997). Political and Institutional Commitment to a Common Currency. *American Economic Review*, 87, 217–220.

Neumann, M. J. M. (1991). Central Bank Independence as a Prerequisite of Price Stability. *European Economy*, special edition no. 1, 79–92.

Neumeyer, P. A. (1998). Currencies and the Allocation of Risk: The Welfare Effects of a Monetary Union. *American Economic Review*, 88, 246–259.

Obstfeld, M. (1991). Destabilizing Effects of Exchange-Rate Escape Clauses. Centre for Economic Policy Research, discussion paper no. 518.

(1994). The Logic of Currency Crises. National Bureau of Economic Research, working paper no. 4640.

(1995). International Capital Mobility in the 1990s. In P. B. Kenen (ed.), *Understanding Interdependence: The Macroeconomics of the Open Economy*. Princeton University Press, 201–261.

(1996). Models of Currency Crises with Self-Fulfilling Features. *European Economic Review*, 40, 1037–1047.

Obstfeld, M. and Rogoff, K. (1995). Exchange Rate Dynamics Redux. *Journal of Political Economy*, 103, 624–660.

(1996). *Foundations of International Macroeconomics*. MIT Press, Cambridge (Mass.).

Oswald, A. J. (1985). The Economic Theory of Trade Unions: An Introductory Survey. *Scandinavian Journal of Economics*, 87, 160–193.

Ott, M. (1996). Post Bretton Woods Deviations from Purchasing Power Parity in G7 Exchange Rates: An Empirical Exploration. *Journal of International Money and Finance*, 15, 899–924.

Oxelheim, L. (1990). *International Financial Integration*. Springer-Verlag.

Padoa-Schioppa, T. (1983). Europäische Kapitalmärkte zwischen Liberalisierung und Restriktion. *Integration*, 1, 10–23.

Padoa-Schioppa, T. (1985). Policy Cooperation and the EMS Experience. In W. H. Buiter and R. C. Marston (eds.), *International Economic Policy Cooperation*. Cambridge University Press, 331–355.

Palokangas, T. (1997). Inflation and Growth in an Open Economy. *Economica*. 64, 509–518.

Patelis, A. D. (1997). Stock Return Predictability and the Role of Monetary Policy. *The Journal of Finance*, 52, 1951–1972.

Pelloni, A. D. (1997). Nominal Shocks, Endogenous Growth and the Business Cycle. *The Economic Journal*, 107, 467–474.

Phelps, E. S. (1968). Money-Wage Dynamics and Labor Market Equilibrium. *Journal of Political Economy*, 76, 678–711.

(1972). *Inflation Policy and Unemployment Theory*. Macmillan.

(1994). *Structural Slumps: The Modern Equilibrium Theory of Unemployment, Interest, and Assets*. Harvard University Press.

Phelps, E. S. and Zoega, G. (1998). Natural-Rate Theory and OECD Unemployment. *The Economic Journal*, 108, 782–801.

Posen, A. S. (1993). Why Central Bank Independence Does Not Cause Low Inflation: There is No Institutional Fix for Politics. In R. O'Brian (ed.), *Finance and the International Economy*. Oxford University Press, 41–65.

(1995). Declarations Are Not Enough: Financial Sector Sources of Central Bank Independence. *NBER Macroeconomics Annual*, 10, 253–274.

Rankin, N. (1994). Quantity-constrained Models of Open Economies. In F. van der Ploeg (ed.), *The Handbook of International Macroeconomics*. Blackwell, 3–30.

(1998). Nominal Rigidity and Monetary Uncertainty. *European Economic Review*, 42, 185–199.

Razin, A. and Yuen, C. (1995). Can Capital Controls Alter the Inflation-Unemployment Trade-Off? Centre for Economic Policy Research, discussion paper no. 1252.

Rogoff, K. (1984). On the Effects of Sterilized Intervention: An Analysis of Weekly Data. *Journal of Monetary Economics*, 14, 133–150.

(1985a). Can International Monetary Policy Cooperation be Counterproductive? *Journal of International Economics*, 18, 199–217.

(1985b). The Optimal Degree of Commitment to an Intermediate Monetary Target. *Quarterly Journal of Economics*, 100, 1169–1189.

(1996). The Purchasing Power Parity Puzzle. *Journal of Economic Literature*, 34, 647–668.

Romer, C. D. and Romer, D. H. (1989). Does Monetary Policy Matter? A New Test in the Spirit of Friedman and Schwartz. *NBER Macroeconomics Annual*, 121–170.

(1990). New Evidence on the Monetary Transmission Mechanism. *Brookings Papers on Economic Activity*, No. 1, 149–214.

(1994). Monetary Policy Matters. *Journal of Monetary Economics*, 34, 75–88.

Romer, P. M. (1986). Increasing Returns and Long Run Growth. *Journal of Political Economy*, 94, 1002–1038.

Roubini, N. and Sachs, J. D. (1989). Political and Economic Determinants of Budget Deficits in the Industrial Countries. *European Economic Review*, 33, 903–938.

Rowthorn, R. (1995). Capital Formation and Unemployment. *Oxford Review of Economic Policy*, 11, 26–39.

Saint-Paul, G. (1997). Business Cycles and Long-Run Growth. Centre for Economic Policy Research, discussion paper no. 1642.

Santomero, A. M. (1984). Modeling the Banking Firm. *Journal of Money, Credit, and Banking*, 16, 576–602.

Santoni, G. J. and Moehring, H. B. (1994). Asset Returns and Measured Inflation. *Journal of Money, Credit, and Banking*, 26, 232–248.

Sarel, M. (1996). Nonlinear Effects of Inflation on Economic Growth. *IMF Staff Papers*, 43, 199–215.

Serletis, A. and Koustas, Z. (1998). International Evidence on the Neutrality of Money. *Journal of Money, Credit and Banking*, 30, 1–25.

Serletis, A. and Krause, D. (1996). Empirical Evidence on the Long-Run Neutrality Hypothesis Using Low-Frequency International Data. *Economics Letters*, 50, 323–327.

Shapiro, M. D. (1994). Federal Reserve Policy: Cause and Effect. In N. G. Mankiw (ed.), *Monetary Policy*. The University of Chicago Press, 307–334.

Sibert, A. and Sutherland, A. (1997). Monetary Regimes and Labour Market Reforms. Centre for Economic Policy Research, discussion paper no. 1731.

Sidrauski, M. (1967). Rational Choice and Patterns of Growth in a Monetary Economy. *American Economic Review*, 57, 534–539.

Sims, C. A. (1992). Interpreting the Macroeconomic Time Series Facts – The Effects of Monetary Policy. *European Economic Review*, 36, 975–1011.

Song, F. M. and Wu, Y. (1997). Hysteresis Effects in Unemployment: Evidence from 48 U.S. States. *Economic Inquiry*, 35, 235–243.

Sørensen, J. R. (1992). Uncertainty and Monetary Policy in a Wage Bargaining Model. *Scandinavian Journal of Economics*, 94, 443–455.

Stiglitz, J. and Weiss, A. M. (1981). Credit Rationing in Markets with Imperfect Information. *American Economic Review*, 71, 393–410.

(1983). Incentive Effects of Termination: Applications to the Credit and Labor Markets. *American Economic Review*, 73, 912–927.

(1992). Asymmetric Information in Credit Markets and Its Implications for Macro-Economics. *Oxford Economic Papers*, 44, 694–724.

Stockman, A. C. (1981). Anticipated Inflation and the Capital Stock in a Cash-in-Advance Economy. *Journal of Monetary Economics*, 8, 387–393.

(1983). Real Exchange Rates under Alternative Nominal Exchange Rate Systems. *Journal of International Money and Finance*, 2, 147–166.

Stockman, A. C. and Dellas, H. (1989). International Portfolio Nondiversification and Exchange Rate Variability. *Journal of International Economics*, 26, 271–289.

Summers, L. (1983). The Non-Adjustment of Nominal Interest Rates: A Study of the Fischer Effect. In J. Tobin (ed.), *Macroeconomics, Prices and Quantities*. Brookings Institution.

Svensson, L. E. O. (1985). Currency Prices, Terms of Trade, and Interest Rates. *Journal of International Economics*, 18, 17–41.

(1997). Optimal Inflation Targets, "Conservative" Central Banks, and Linear Inflation Contracts. *American Economic Review*, 87, 98–114.

Tabellini, G. (1988). Centralized Wage Setting and Monetary Policy in a Reputational Equilibrium. *Journal of Money, Credit, and Banking*, 20, 102–118.

Tavlas, G. S. (1993). The 'New' Theory of Optimum Currency Areas. *World Economy*, 16, 663–685.

Taylor, J. B. (1979). Staggered Price Setting in a Macro Model. *American Economic Review*, 69, 108–113.

(1980). Aggregate Dynamics and Staggered Contracts. *Journal of Political Economy*, 88, 1–23.

(1997). A Core of Practical Macroeconomics. *American Economic Review*, Papers and Proceedings, 233–235.

Taylor, M. P. (1995). Exchange-Rate Behavior Under Alternative Exchange-Rate Agreements. In P. B. Kenen (ed.), *Understanding Interdependence: The Macroeconomics of the Open Economy*. Princeton University Press, 34–83.

Tesar, L. L. (1993). International Risk-Sharing and Non-Traded Goods. *Journal of International Economics*, 35, 69–89.

Tesar, L. L. and Werner, I. M. (1992). Home Bias and the Globalization of Securities Markets. National Bureau of Economic Research, working paper no. 4218.

(1995). Home Bias and High Turnover. *Journal of International Money and Finance*, 14, 467–492.

Thoma, M. A. (1994). The Effects of Money Growth on Inflation and Interest Rates Across Spectral Frequency Bands. *Journal of Money, Credit, and Banking*, 26, 218–231.

Thomas, S. H. and Wickens, M. R. (1989). International CAPM: Why has it Failed? Centre for Economic Policy Research, discussion paper no. 354.

Thorbecke, W. (1997). On Stock Market Returns and Monetary Policy. *The Journal of Finance*, 52, 635–654.

Thygesen, N. (1991). Monetary Management in a Monetary Union. *European Economic Review*, 35, 474–483.

Tobin, J. (1955). A Dynamic Aggregative Model. *Journal of Political Economy*, 63, 103–115.

(1961). Money, Capital and Other Stores of Value. *American Economic Review*, 51, 26–37.

(1965). Money and Economic Growth. *Econometrica*, 33, 671–684.

(1969). A General Equilibrium Approach to Monetary Theory. *Journal of Money, Credit, and Banking*, 1, 322–338.

Tower, E. and Willett, T. D. (1976). The Theory of Optimum Currency Areas and Exchange-Rate Flexibility. Princeton University, Special Papers in International Finance, no. 11.

Turnovsky, S. J. (1978). Macroeconomic Dynamics and Growth in a Monetary Economy. *Journal of Money, Credit, and Banking*, 10, 1–26.

(1987a). Optimal Monetary Policy and Wage Indexation under Alternative Disturbances and Information Structures. *Journal of Money, Credit, and Banking*, 19, 157–180.

(1987b). Optimal Monetary Growth with Accommodating Fiscal Policy in a Small Open Economy. *Journal of International Money and Finance*, 6, 179–193.

(1993). Macroeconomic Policies, Growth, and Welfare in a Stochastic Economy. *International Economic Review*, 34, 953–981.

Ungar, M. and Zilberfarb, B. (1993). Inflation and Its Unpredictability: Theory and Empirical Evidence. *Journal of Money, Credit, and Banking*, 25, 709–720.

Van der Ploeg, F. (1991). Unanticipated Inflation and Government Finance: A Case for a Common Central Bank. *Centre for Economic Policy Research,* discussion paper no. 562.

Van der Ploeg, F. and Alogoskoufis, G. S. (1994). Money and Endogenous Growth. *Journal of Money, Credit, and Banking,* 26, 771–795.

Vinals, J. and Jimeno, J. F. (1996). Monetary Union and European Unemployment. *Centre for Economic Policy Research,* discussion paper no. 1485.

Von Hagen, J. and Fratianni, M. (1993). The Transition to European Monetary Union and the European Monetary Institute. *Economics and Politics,* 5, 167–185.

Walsh, C. E. (1995). Optimal Contracts for Central Bankers. *American Economic Review,* 85, 150–167.

Weber, A. A. (1994). Testing Long-Run Neutrality: Empirical Evidence with Special Emphasis on Germany. *Carnegie-Rochester Conference Series on Public Policy,* 41, 67–117.

Weil, P. (1989). Overlapping Families of Infinitely Lived Agents. *Journal of Public Economics,* 38, 183–198.

Wihlborg, C. (1994). EMU: Economic Substance or Political Symbolism? *World Economy,* 17, 651–661.

Wren-Lewis, S. (1995). The Natural Rate in Empirical Macroeconomic Models. In R. Cross (ed.), *The Natural Rate of Unemployment: Reflections on 25 Years of the Hypothesis.* Cambridge University Press, 299–311.

Wyplosz, C. (1989). Discussion. In M. de Cecco and A. Giovannini (eds.), *A European Central Bank? Perspectives on Monetary Unification after Ten Years of EMS.* Cambridge University Press, 212–216.

(1997). EMU: Why and How It Might Happen. *Journal of Economic Perspectives,* 11, 3–22.

Index